S0-AYA-414

ON BRANCH

GRAPHIC NOVEL

Descendants of Darkness™

Yami no Matsuei

0 1197 0605428 3

Story & Art by Yoko Matsushita

8

Descendants of Darkness
Yami no Matsuei
Vol. 8
Shôjo Edition

Story & Art by
Yoko Matsushita

English Adaptation/Lance Caselman
Translation/David Ury
Touch-Up & Lettering/Gia Cam Luc
Graphics & Cover Design/Courtney Utt
Editors/Pancha Diaz & Nancy Thistlethwaite

Managing Editor/Annette Roman
Director of Production/Noboru Watanabe
Vice President of Publishing/Alvin Lu
Sr. Director of Acquisitions/Rika Inouye
VP of Sales & Marketing/Liza Coppola
Publisher/Hyoe Narita

Yami no Matsuei by Yoko Matsushita © Yoko Matsushita 1999. All rights reserved. First published in Japan in 1999 by HAKUSENSHA, Inc., Tokyo. English language translation rights in America and Canada arranged with HAKUSENSHA, Inc., Tokyo. New and adapted artwork and text © 2005 VIZ Media, LLC. The DESCENDANTS OF DARKNESS logo is a trademark of VIZ Media, LLC. The stories, characters and incidents mentioned in this publication are entirely fictional.

No portion of this book may be reproduced or transmitted in any form or by any means without written permission from the copyright holders.

Printed in the U.S.A.

Published by VIZ Media, LLC
P.O. Box 77064
San Francisco, CA 94107

Shôjo Edition
10 9 8 7 6 5 4 3 2 1
First printing, October 2005

For advertising rates or media kit, e-mail advertising@viz.com

www.viz.com

store.viz.com

PARENTAL ADVISORY
DESCENDANTS OF DARKNESS, Yami no Matsuei, is rated T+ for Older Teen and is recommended for ages 16 and up. This volume contains violence and mature situations.

Table of Contents

Roanoke County Public Library
Vinton Branch Library
800 East Washington Ave.
Vinton, VA 24719

闇の末裔

<ruby>闇<rt>やみ</rt></ruby>の<ruby>末裔<rt>まつえい</rt></ruby>

DESCENDANTS OF DARKNESS
YAMI NO MATSUEI

CHAPTER 24

COME
...

COME
TO ME
...

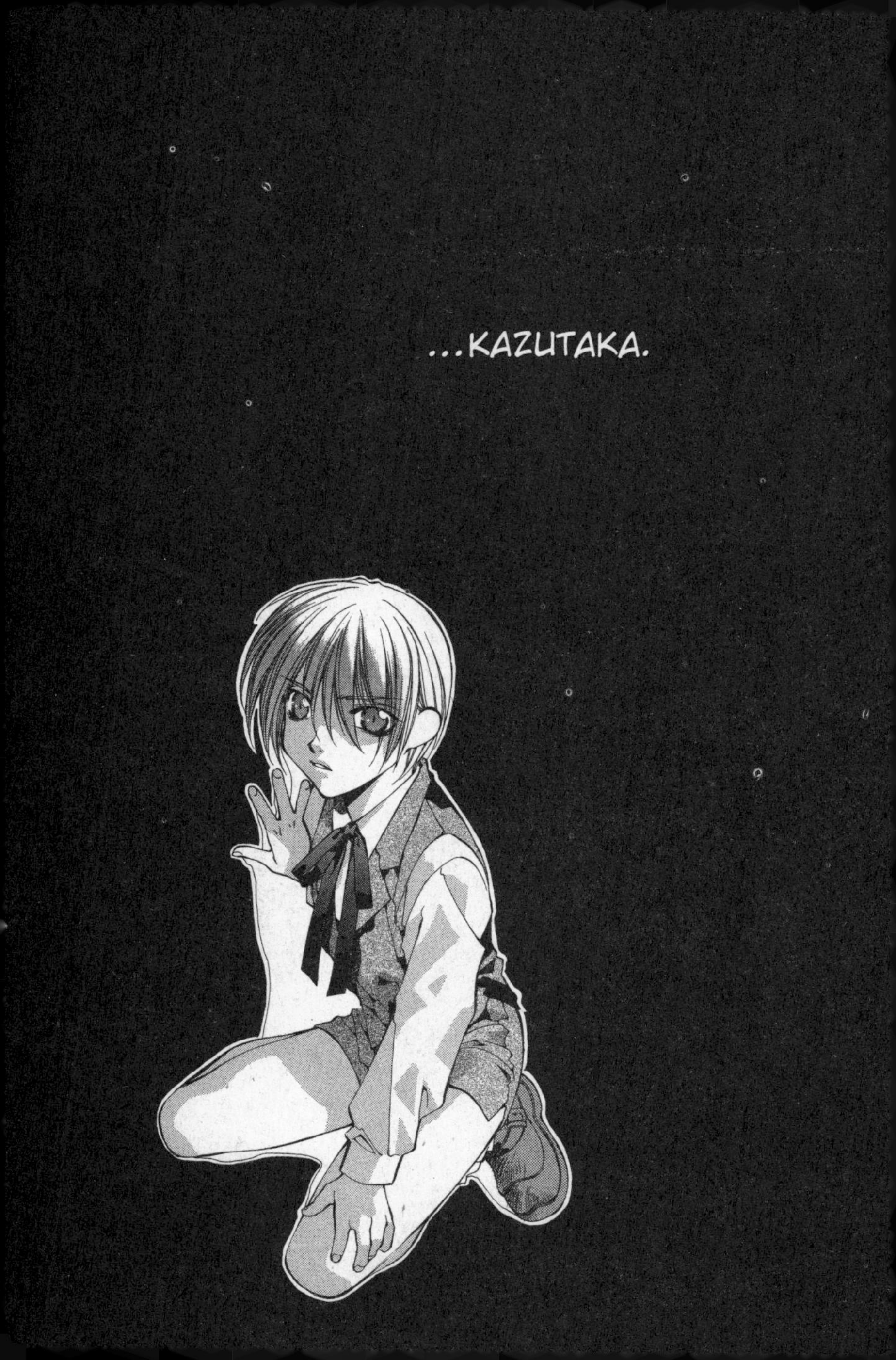
...KAZUTAKA.

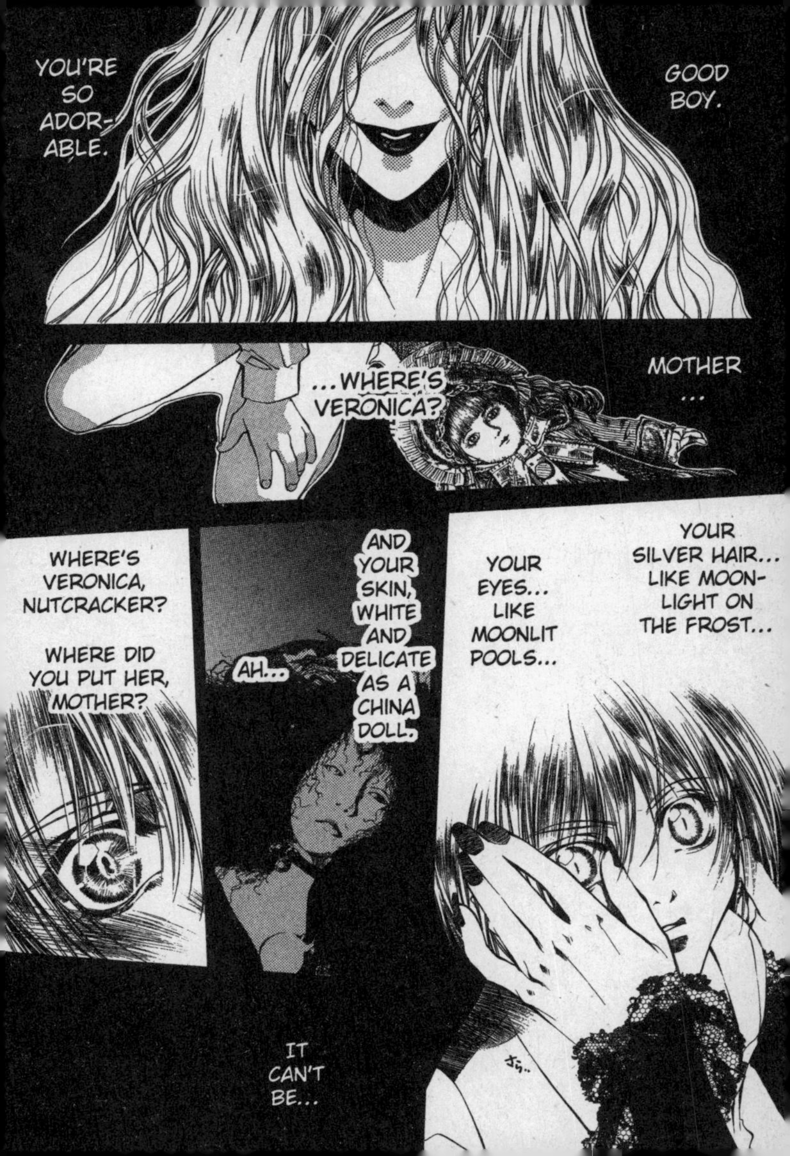
GOOD BOY.
YOU'RE SO ADORABLE.
MOTHER ...
...WHERE'S VERONICA?
YOUR SILVER HAIR... LIKE MOONLIGHT ON THE FROST...
YOUR EYES... LIKE MOONLIT POOLS...
AND YOUR SKIN, WHITE AND DELICATE AS A CHINA DOLL.
AH...
WHERE'S VERONICA, NUTCRACKER?
WHERE DID YOU PUT HER, MOTHER?
IT CAN'T BE...

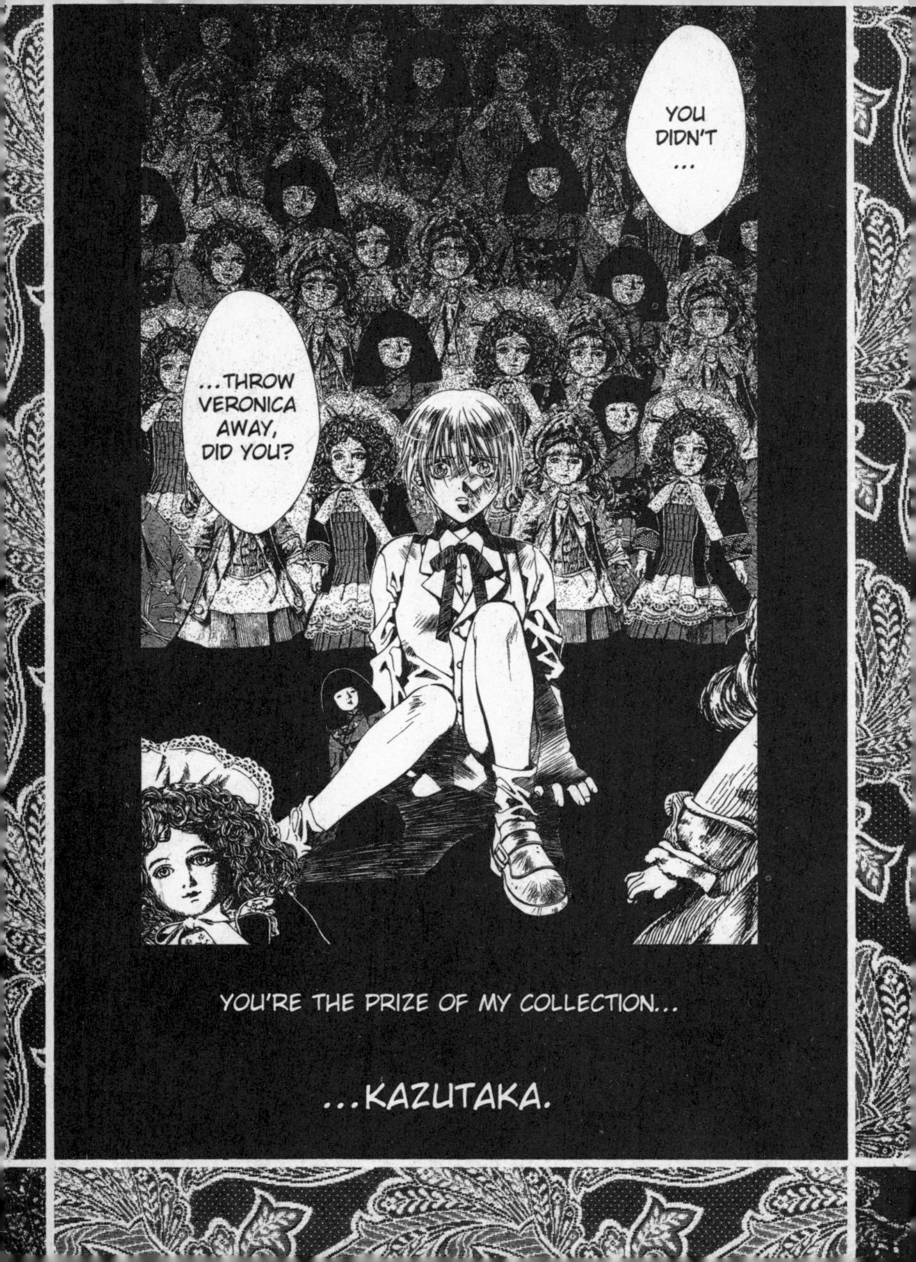
YOU DIDN'T ...
...THROW VERONICA AWAY, DID YOU?
YOU'RE THE PRIZE OF MY COLLECTION...
...KAZUTAKA.

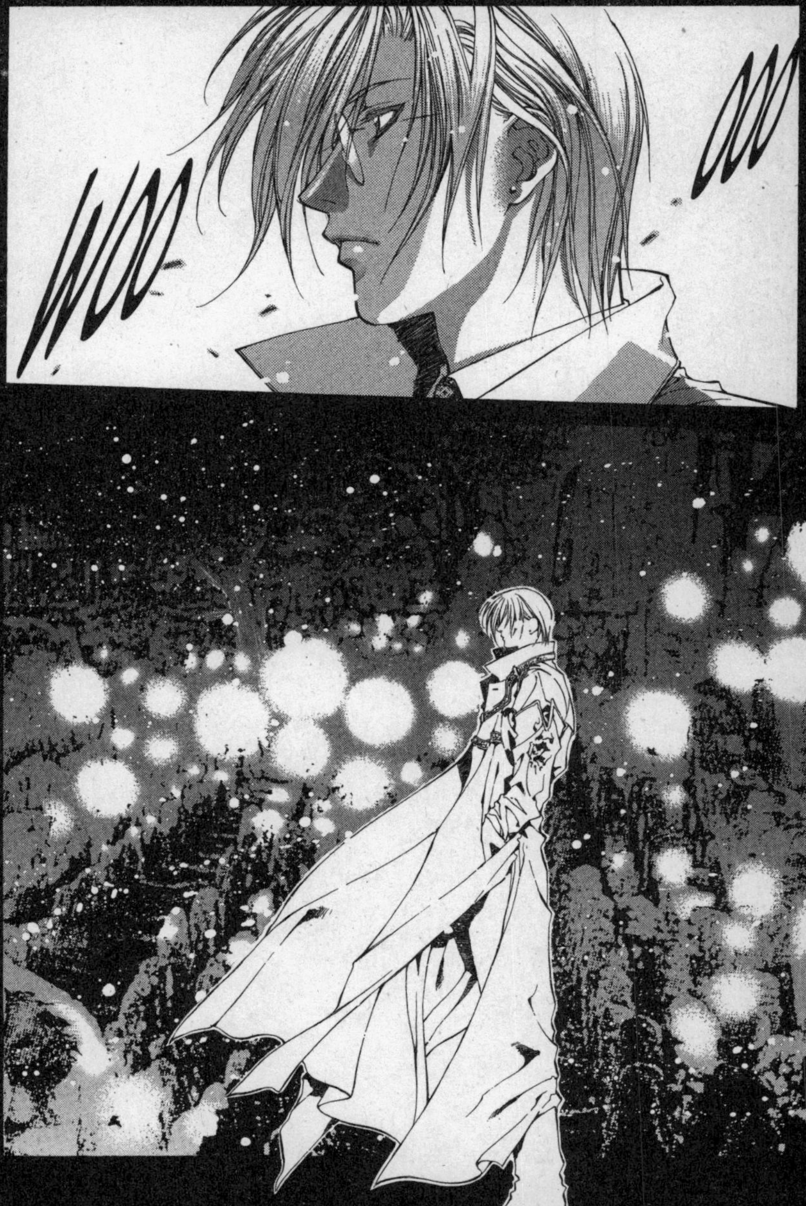
WOO
OOO

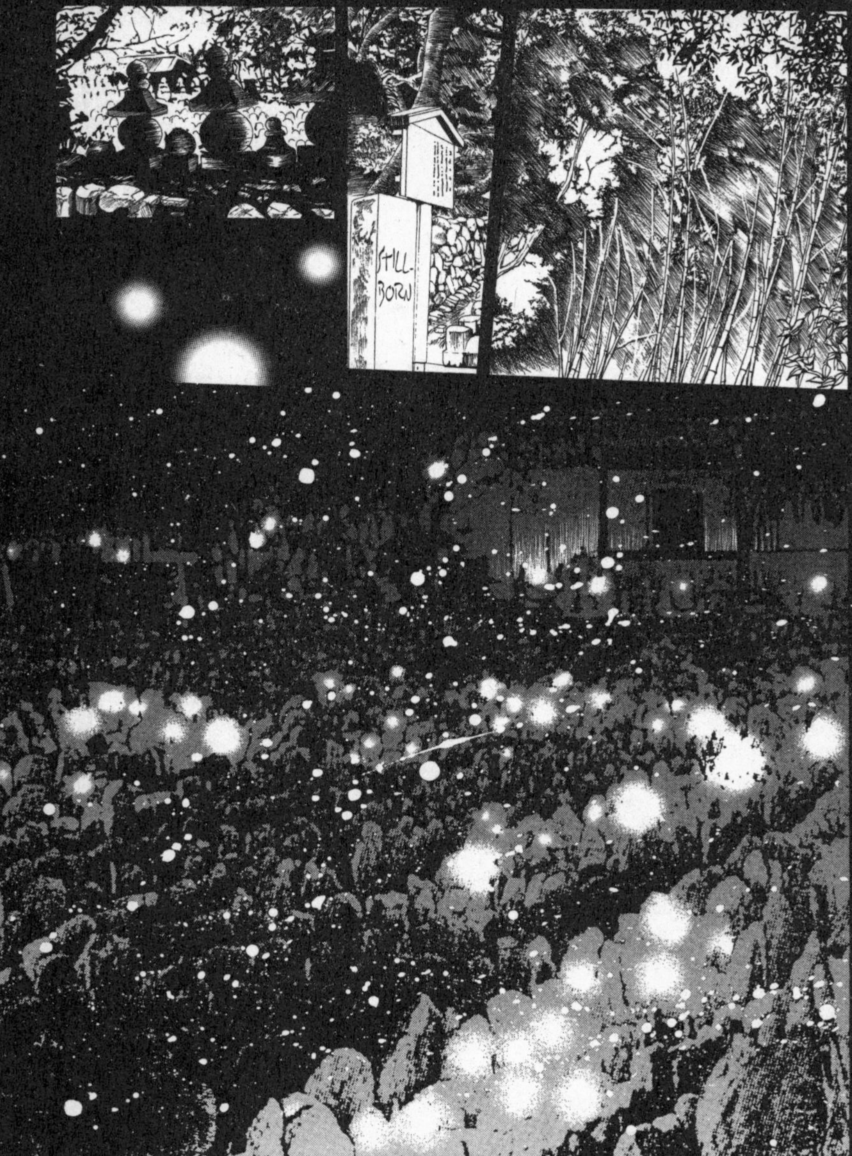
STILL-BORN

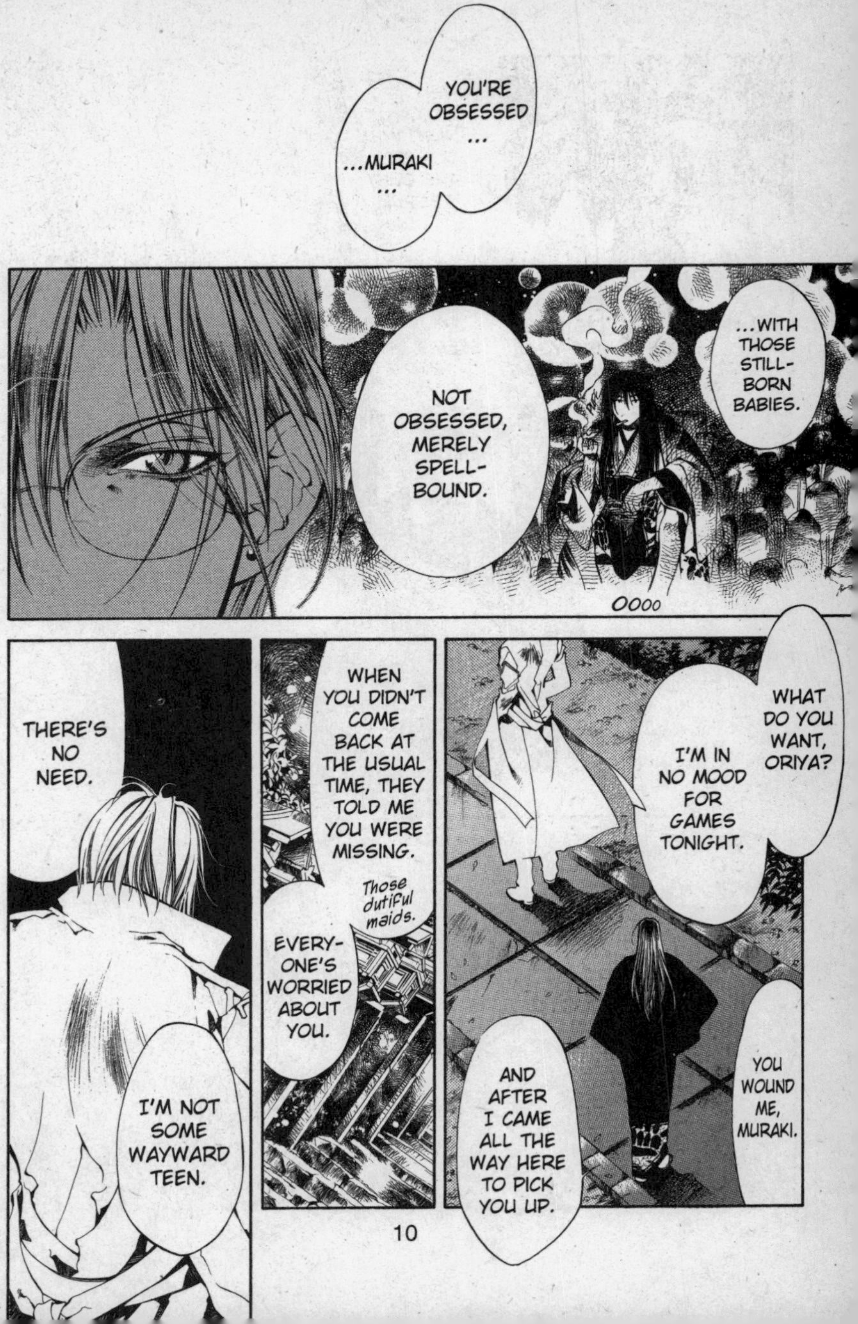
YOU'RE OBSESSED ...
...MURAKI ...
...WITH THOSE STILL-BORN BABIES.
NOT OBSESSED, MERELY SPELL-BOUND.
OOOO
WHAT DO YOU WANT, ORIYA?
I'M IN NO MOOD FOR GAMES TONIGHT.
YOU WOUND ME, MURAKI.
AND AFTER I CAME ALL THE WAY HERE TO PICK YOU UP.
WHEN YOU DIDN'T COME BACK AT THE USUAL TIME, THEY TOLD ME YOU WERE MISSING.
Those dutiful maids.
EVERY-ONE'S WORRIED ABOUT YOU.
THERE'S NO NEED.
I'M NOT SOME WAYWARD TEEN.

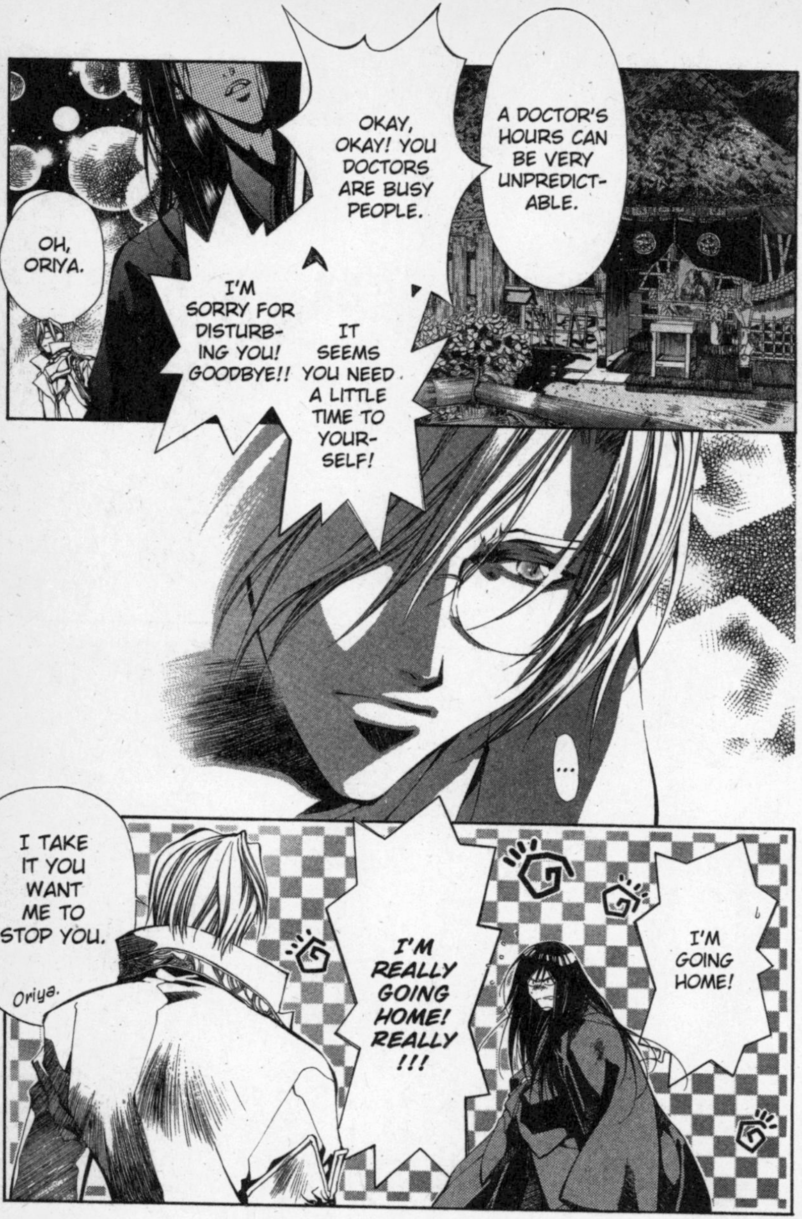
A DOCTOR'S HOURS CAN BE VERY UNPREDICT-ABLE.
OKAY, OKAY! YOU DOCTORS ARE BUSY PEOPLE.
OH, ORIYA.
IT SEEMS YOU NEED A LITTLE TIME TO YOUR-SELF!
I'M SORRY FOR DISTURB-ING YOU! GOODBYE!!
...
I'M GOING HOME!
I'M REALLY GOING HOME! REALLY !!!
I TAKE IT YOU WANT ME TO STOP YOU.
Oriya.

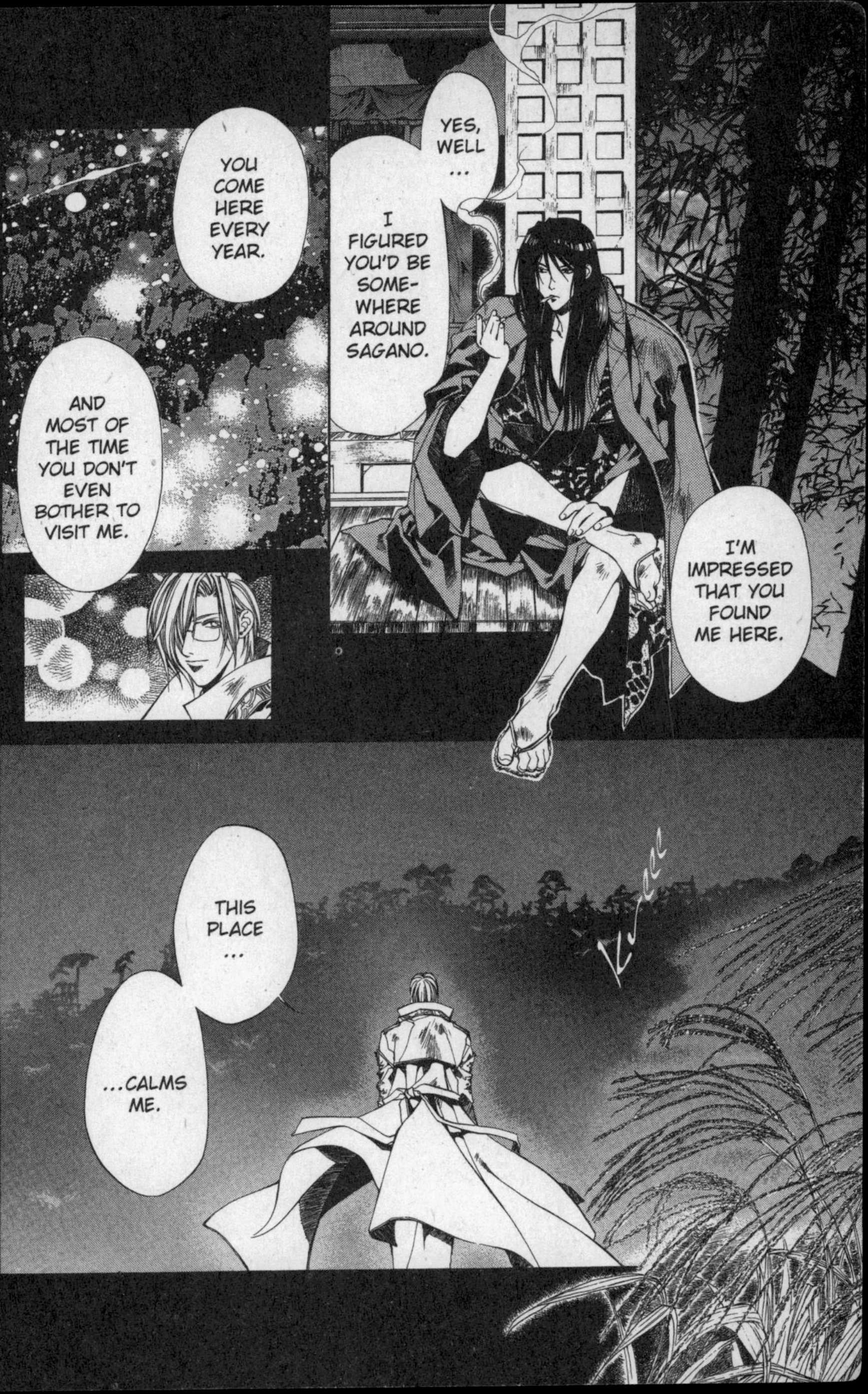
I'M IMPRESSED THAT YOU FOUND ME HERE.
YES, WELL ...
I FIGURED YOU'D BE SOME-WHERE AROUND SAGANO.
YOU COME HERE EVERY YEAR.
AND MOST OF THE TIME YOU DON'T EVEN BOTHER TO VISIT ME.
THIS PLACE ...
...CALMS ME.

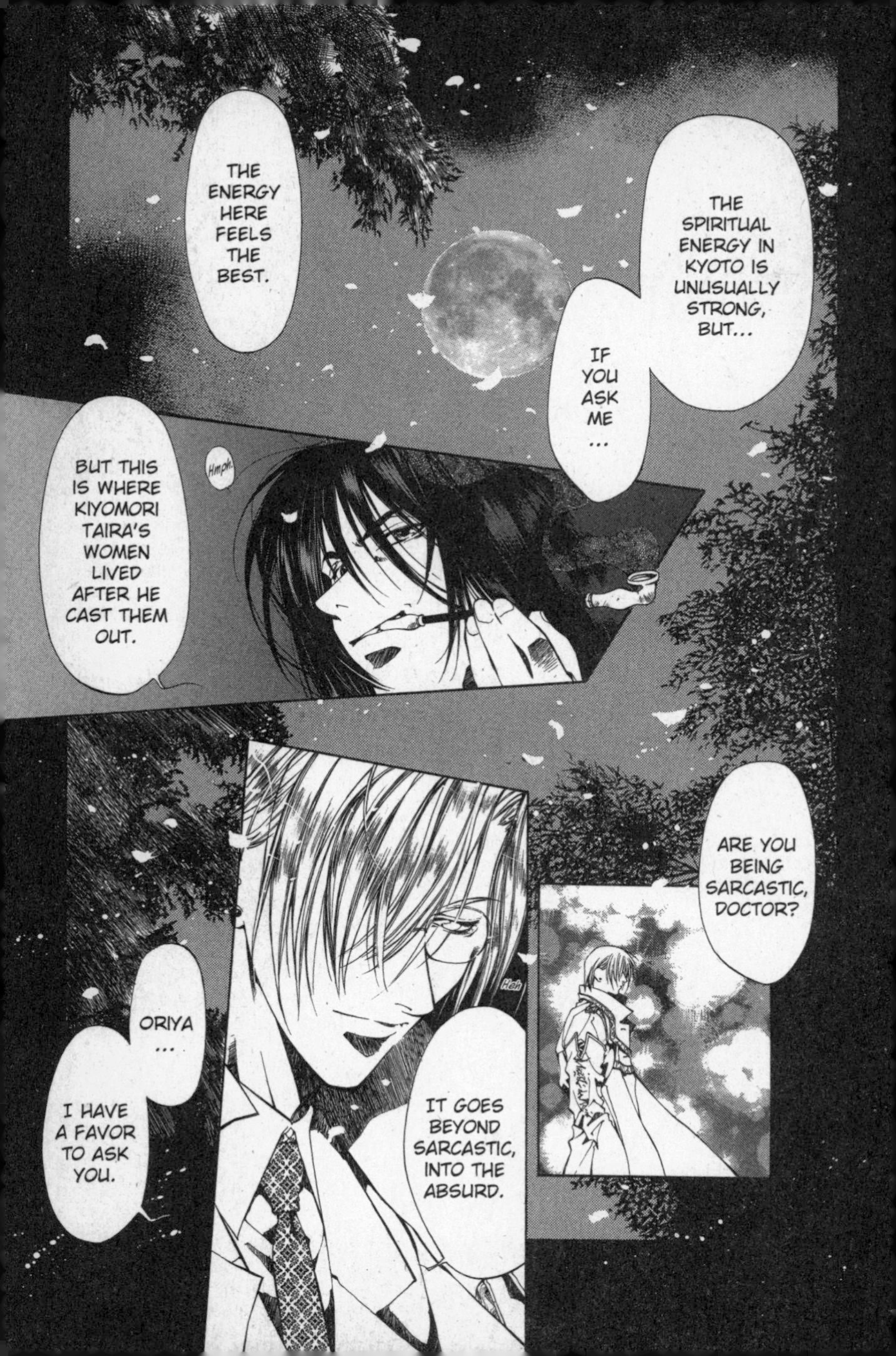
THE SPIRITUAL ENERGY IN KYOTO IS UNUSUALLY STRONG, BUT...
IF YOU ASK ME ...
THE ENERGY HERE FEELS THE BEST.
Hmph.
BUT THIS IS WHERE KIYOMORI TAIRA'S WOMEN LIVED AFTER HE CAST THEM OUT.
ARE YOU BEING SARCASTIC, DOCTOR?
Heh
IT GOES BEYOND SARCASTIC, INTO THE ABSURD.
ORIYA ...
I HAVE A FAVOR TO ASK YOU.

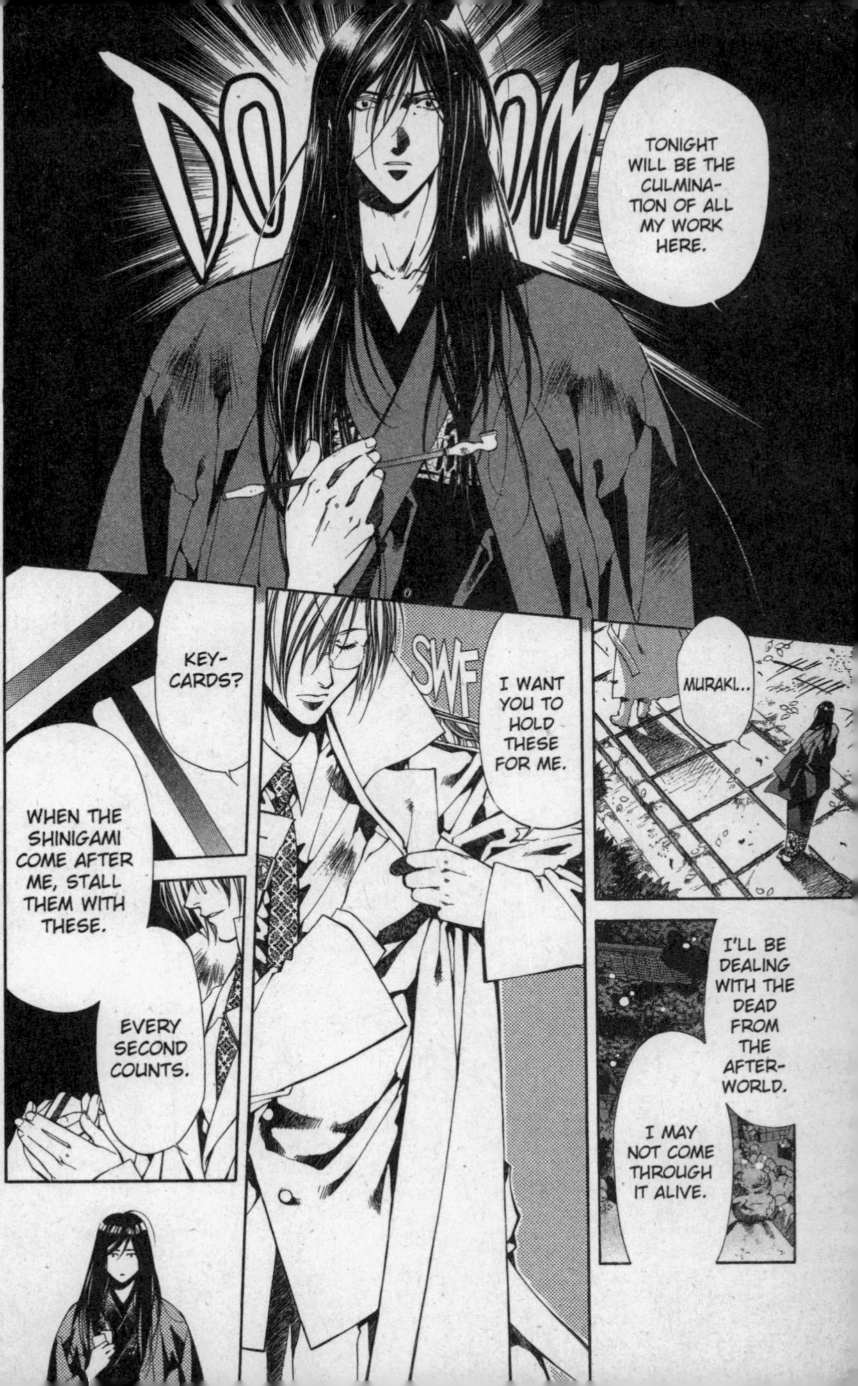
DOOM
TONIGHT WILL BE THE CULMINATION OF ALL MY WORK HERE.
MURAKI...
I'LL BE DEALING WITH THE DEAD FROM THE AFTER-WORLD.
I MAY NOT COME THROUGH IT ALIVE.
SWF
I WANT YOU TO HOLD THESE FOR ME.
KEY-CARDS?
WHEN THE SHINIGAMI COME AFTER ME, STALL THEM WITH THESE.
EVERY SECOND COUNTS.

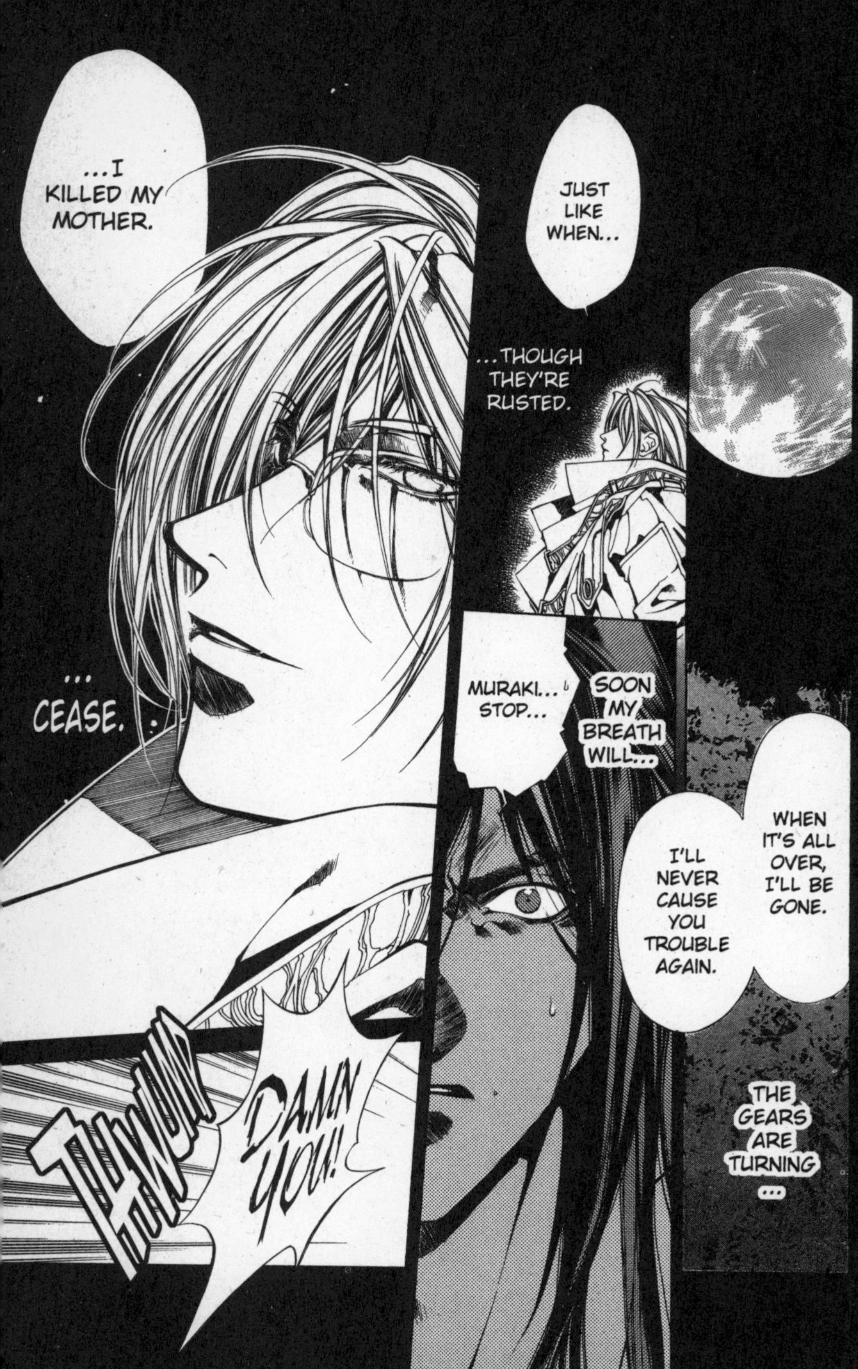
JUST LIKE WHEN...
...THOUGH THEY'RE RUSTED.
...I KILLED MY MOTHER.
WHEN IT'S ALL OVER, I'LL BE GONE.
I'LL NEVER CAUSE YOU TROUBLE AGAIN.
SOON MY BREATH WILL...
MURAKI... STOP...
... CEASE.
THE GEARS ARE TURNING ...
DAMN YOU!
THWUMP

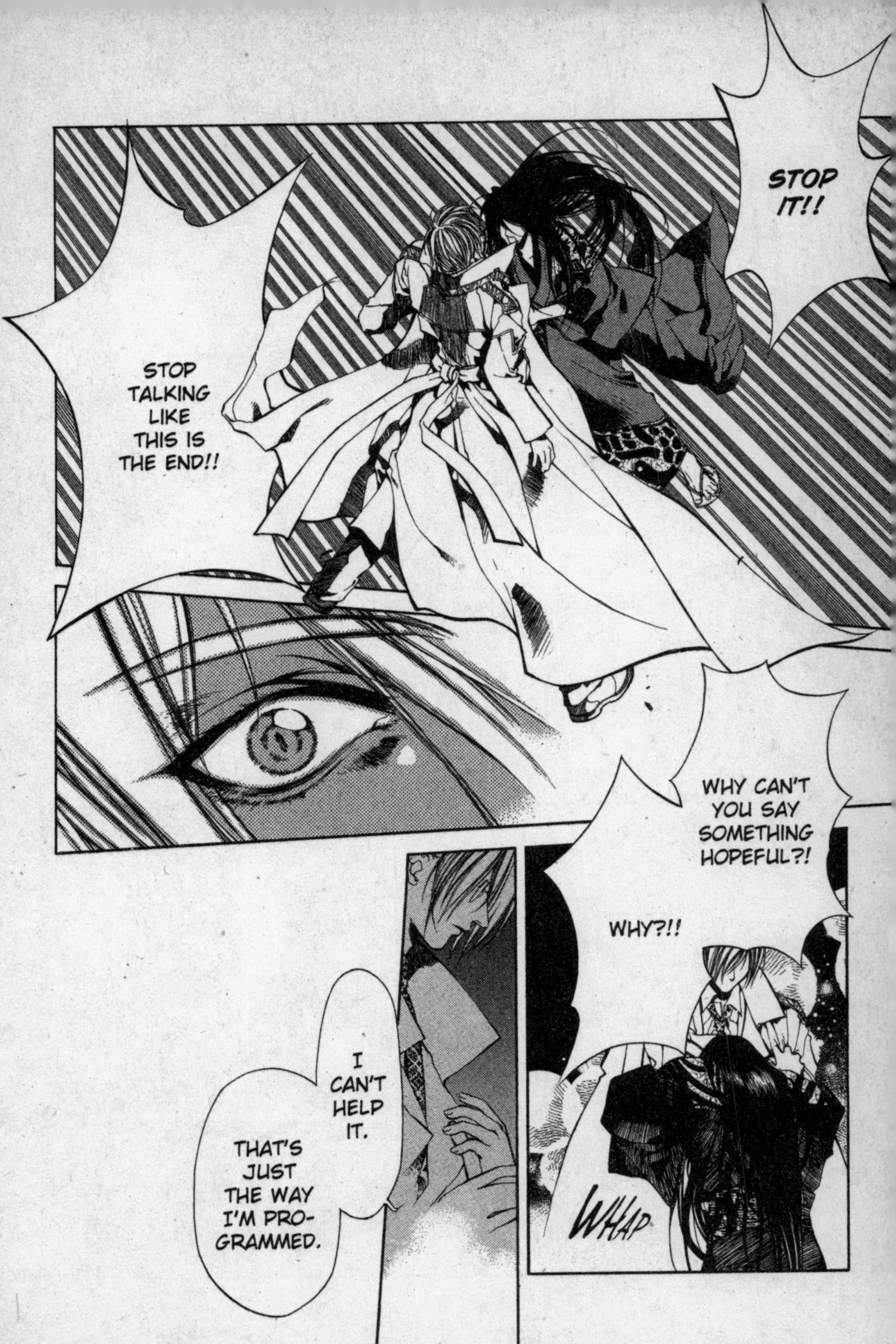
STOP IT!!
STOP TALKING LIKE THIS IS THE END!!
WHY CAN'T YOU SAY SOMETHING HOPEFUL?!
WHY?!!
WHAP
I CAN'T HELP IT.
THAT'S JUST THE WAY I'M PRO-GRAMMED.

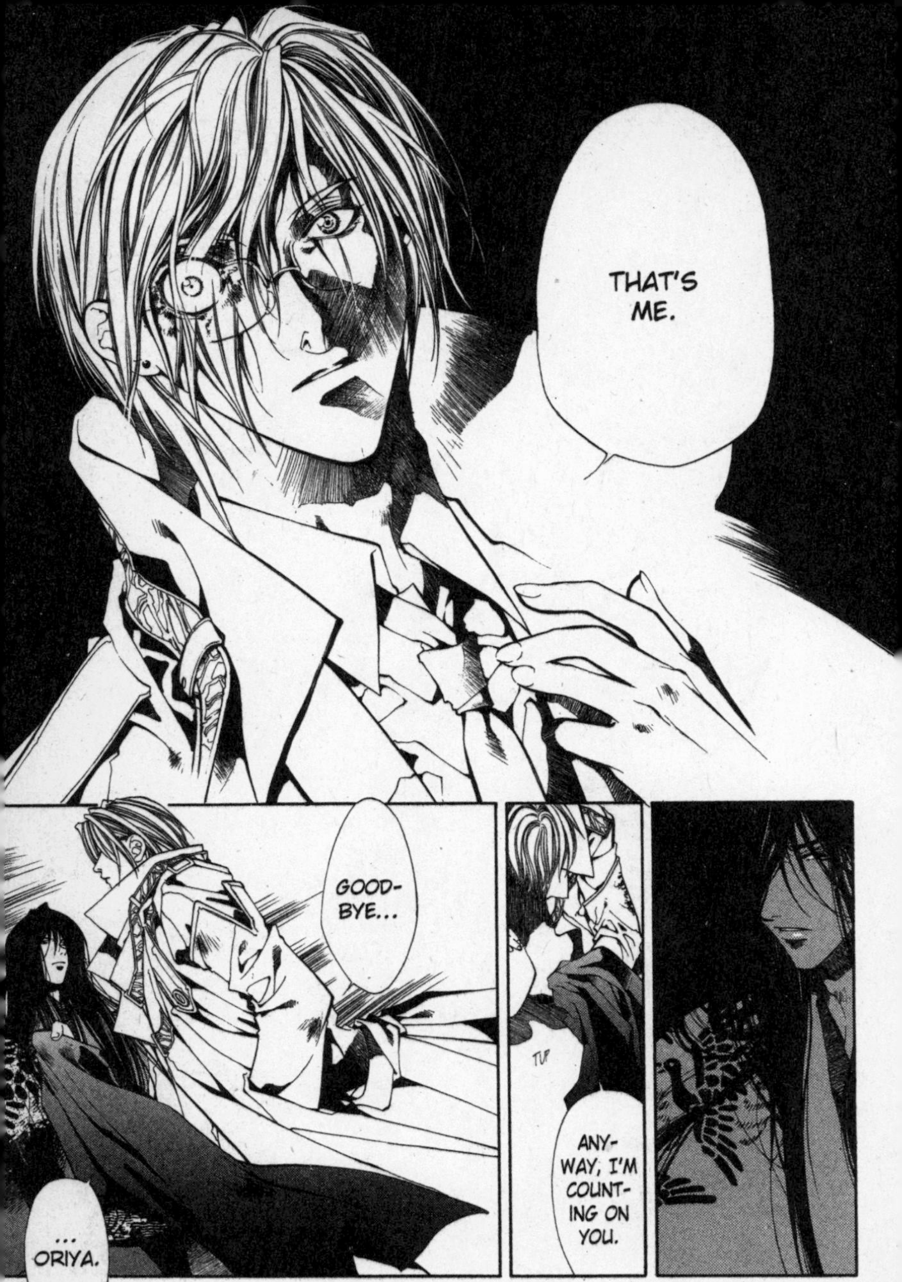
THAT'S ME.
TUP
ANYWAY, I'M COUNTING ON YOU.
GOODBYE...
...ORIYA.

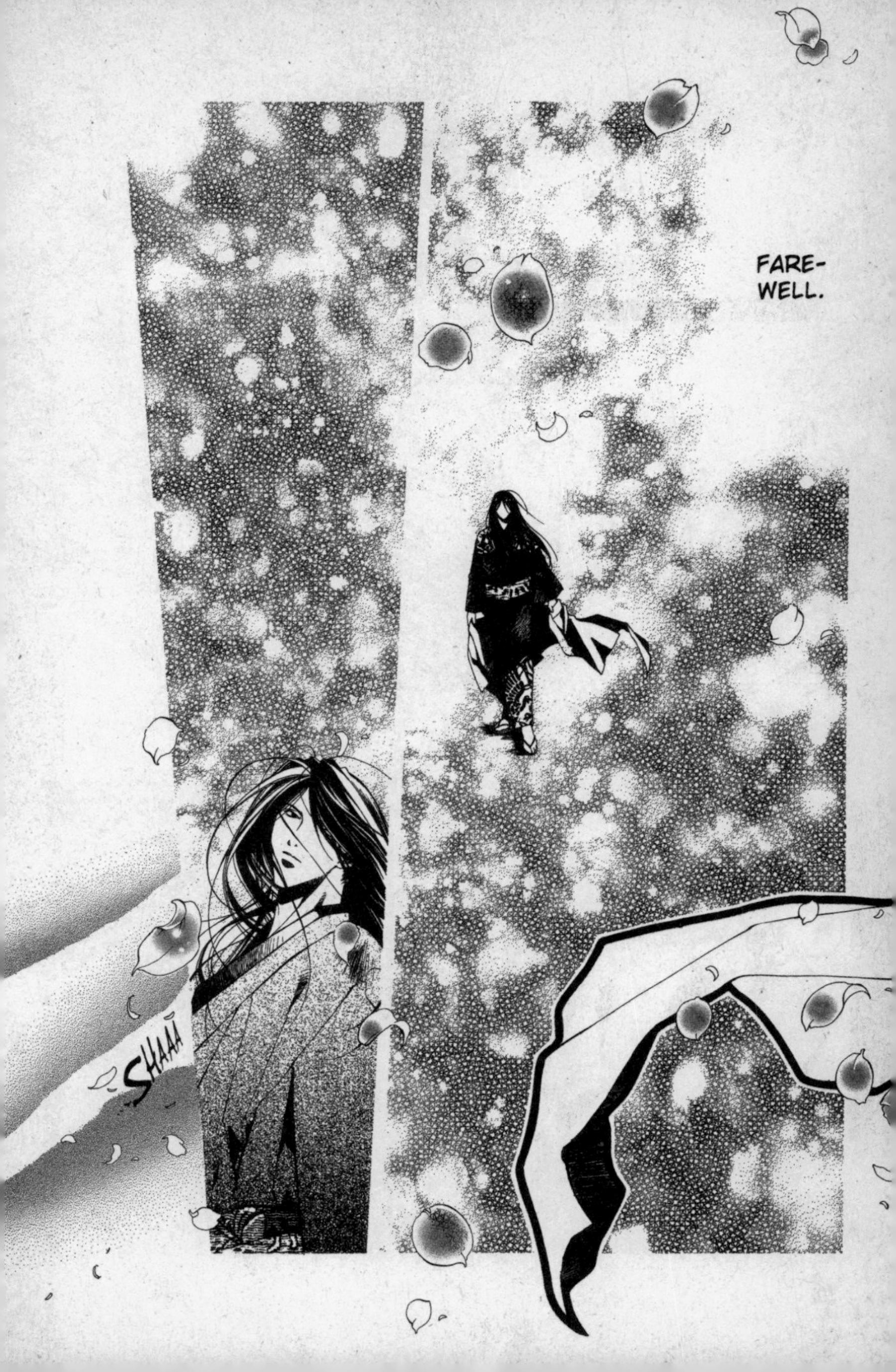
FARE-
WELL.
SHAAA

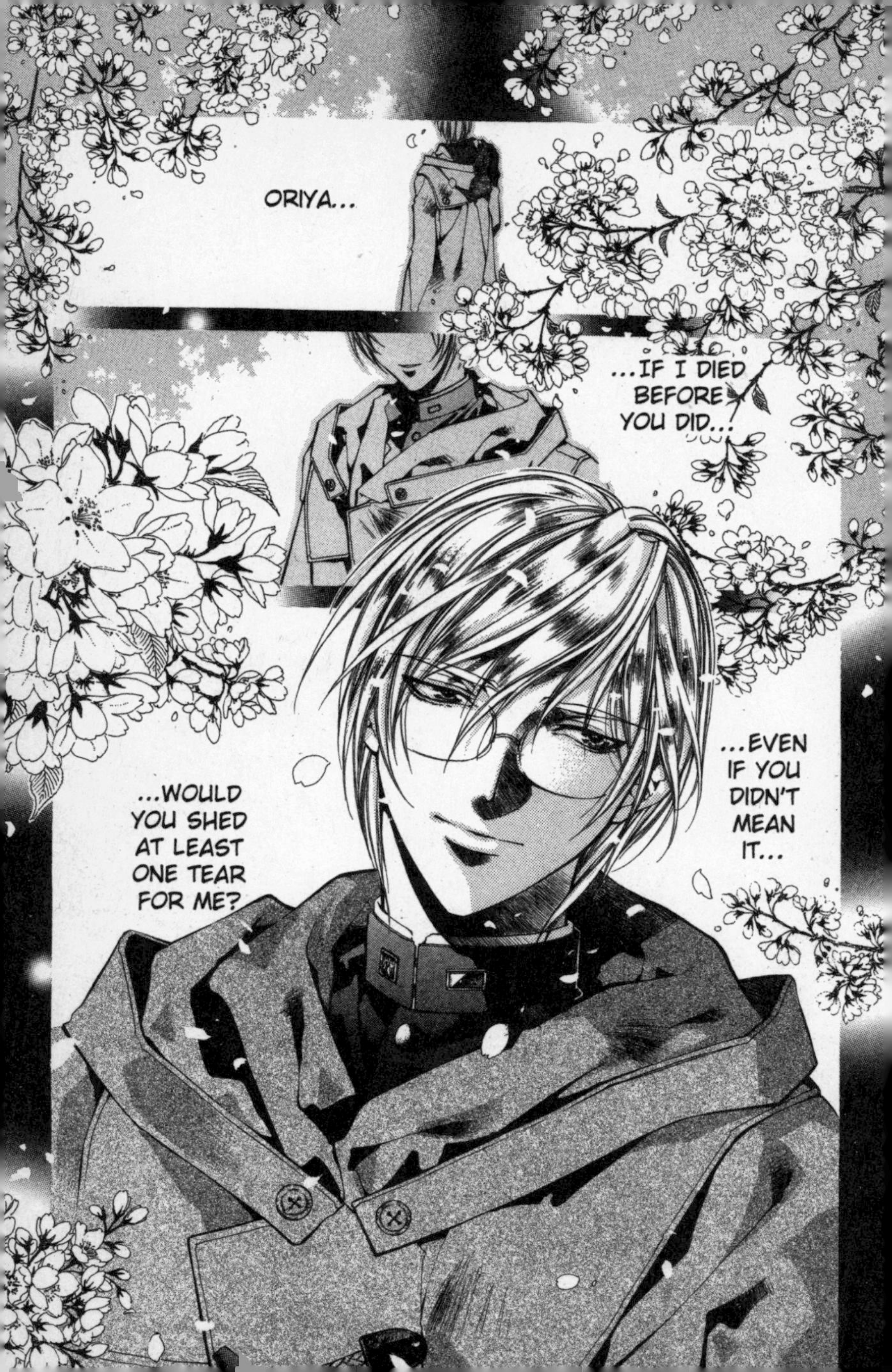
ORIYA...
...IF I DIED BEFORE YOU DID...
...EVEN IF YOU DIDN'T MEAN IT...
...WOULD YOU SHED AT LEAST ONE TEAR FOR ME?

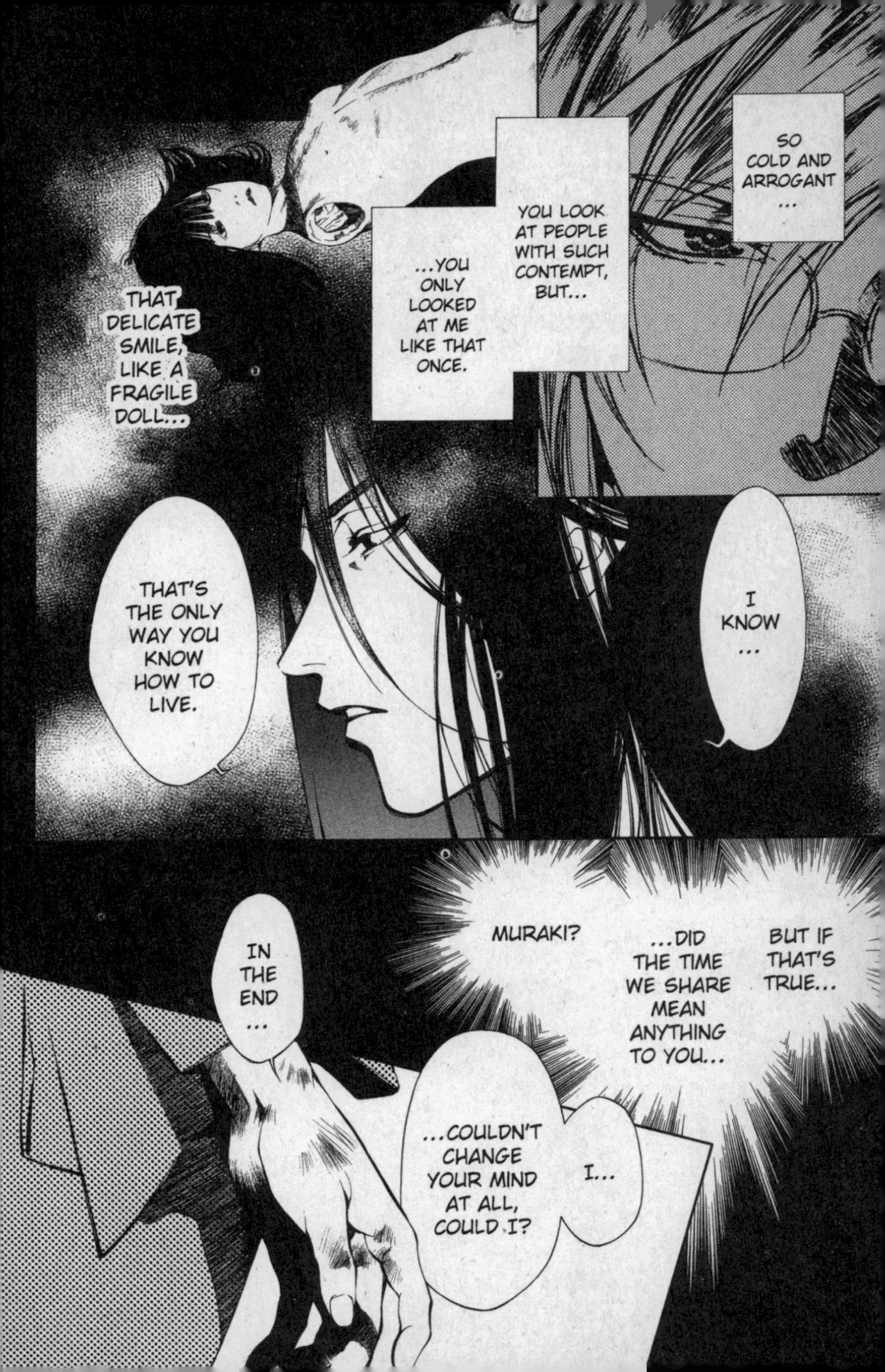
SO COLD AND ARROGANT...
YOU LOOK AT PEOPLE WITH SUCH CONTEMPT, BUT...
...YOU ONLY LOOKED AT ME LIKE THAT ONCE.
THAT DELICATE SMILE, LIKE A FRAGILE DOLL...
I KNOW...
THAT'S THE ONLY WAY YOU KNOW HOW TO LIVE.
BUT IF THAT'S TRUE...
...DID THE TIME WE SHARE MEAN ANYTHING TO YOU...
MURAKI?
IN THE END...
I...
...COULDN'T CHANGE YOUR MIND AT ALL, COULD I?

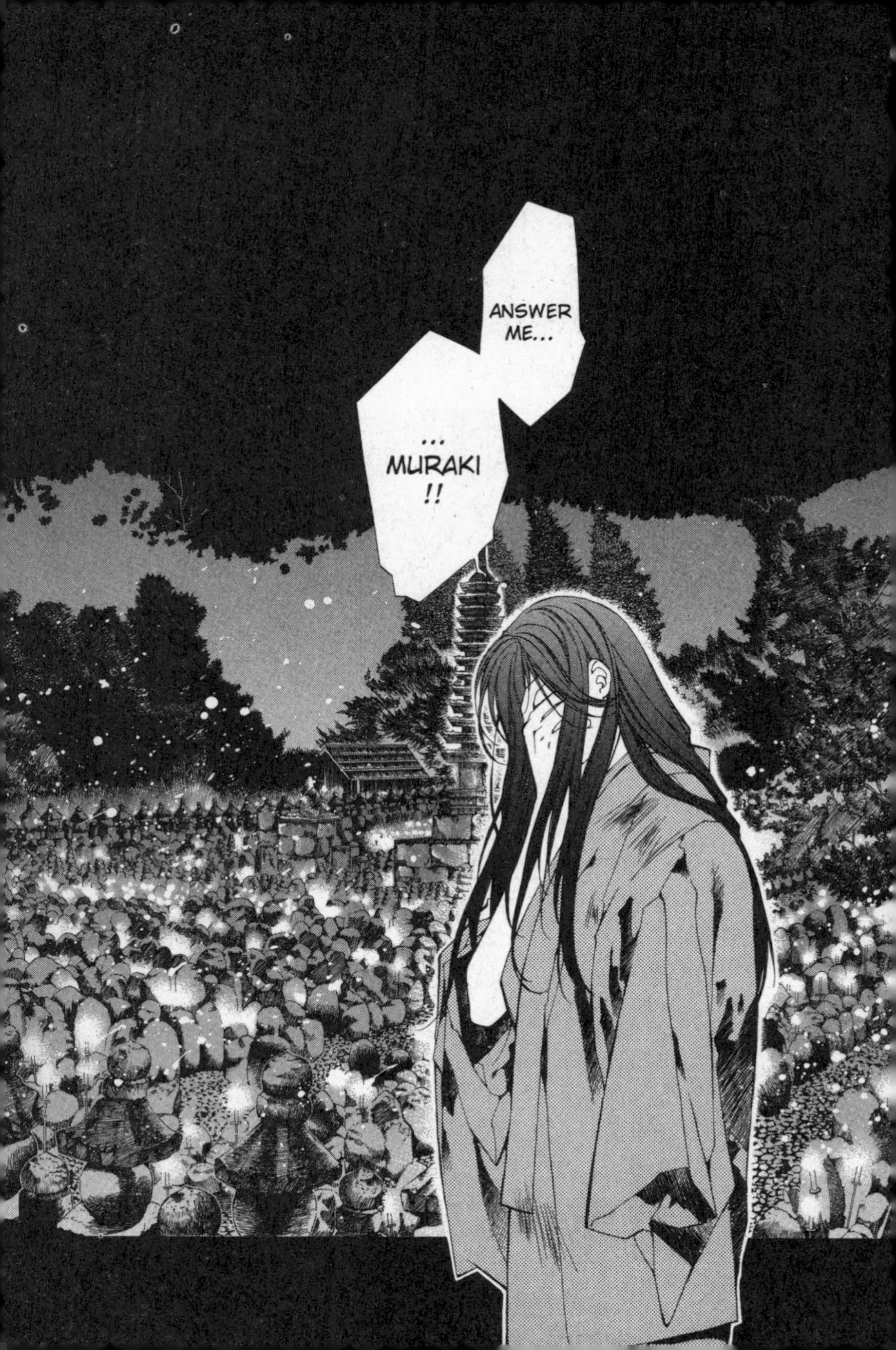
ANSWER ME...
... MURAKI !!

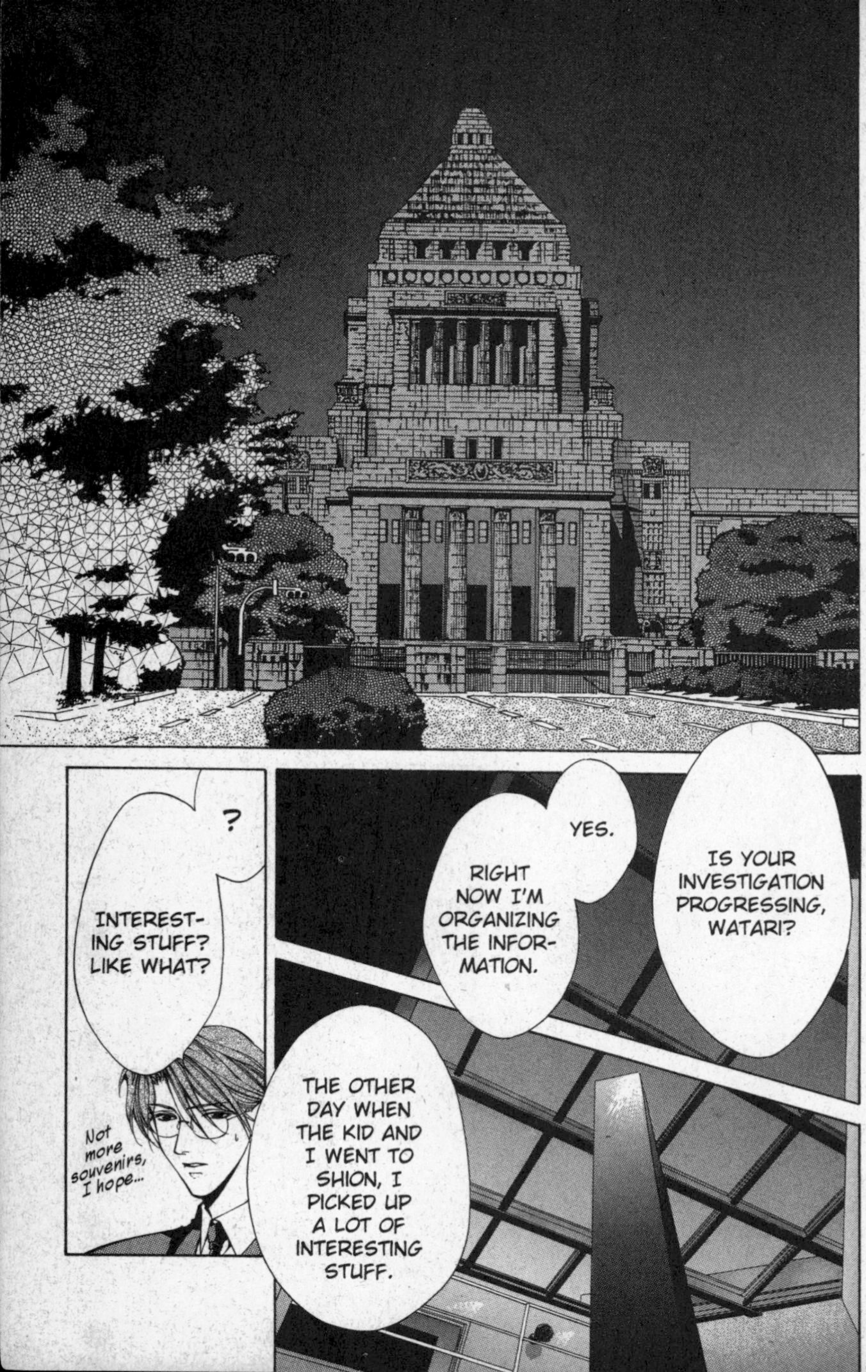
IS YOUR INVESTIGATION PROGRESSING, WATARI?
YES.
RIGHT NOW I'M ORGANIZING THE INFORMATION.
THE OTHER DAY WHEN THE KID AND I WENT TO SHION, I PICKED UP A LOT OF INTERESTING STUFF.
?
INTERESTING STUFF? LIKE WHAT?
Not more souvenirs, I hope...

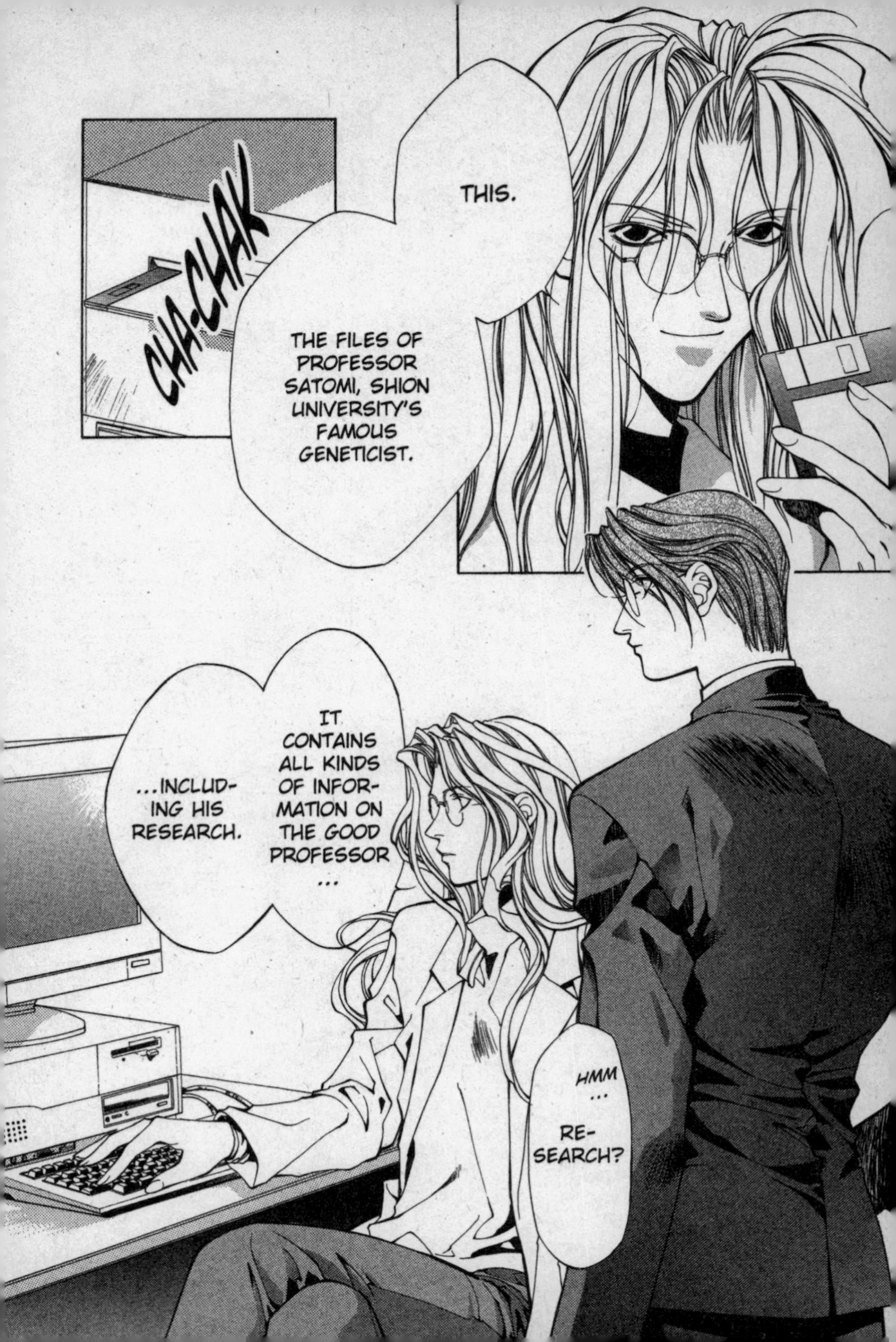
THIS.
CHA-CHAK
THE FILES OF PROFESSOR SATOMI, SHION UNIVERSITY'S FAMOUS GENETICIST.
IT CONTAINS ALL KINDS OF INFORMATION ON THE GOOD PROFESSOR ...
...INCLUDING HIS RESEARCH.
HMM ... RESEARCH?

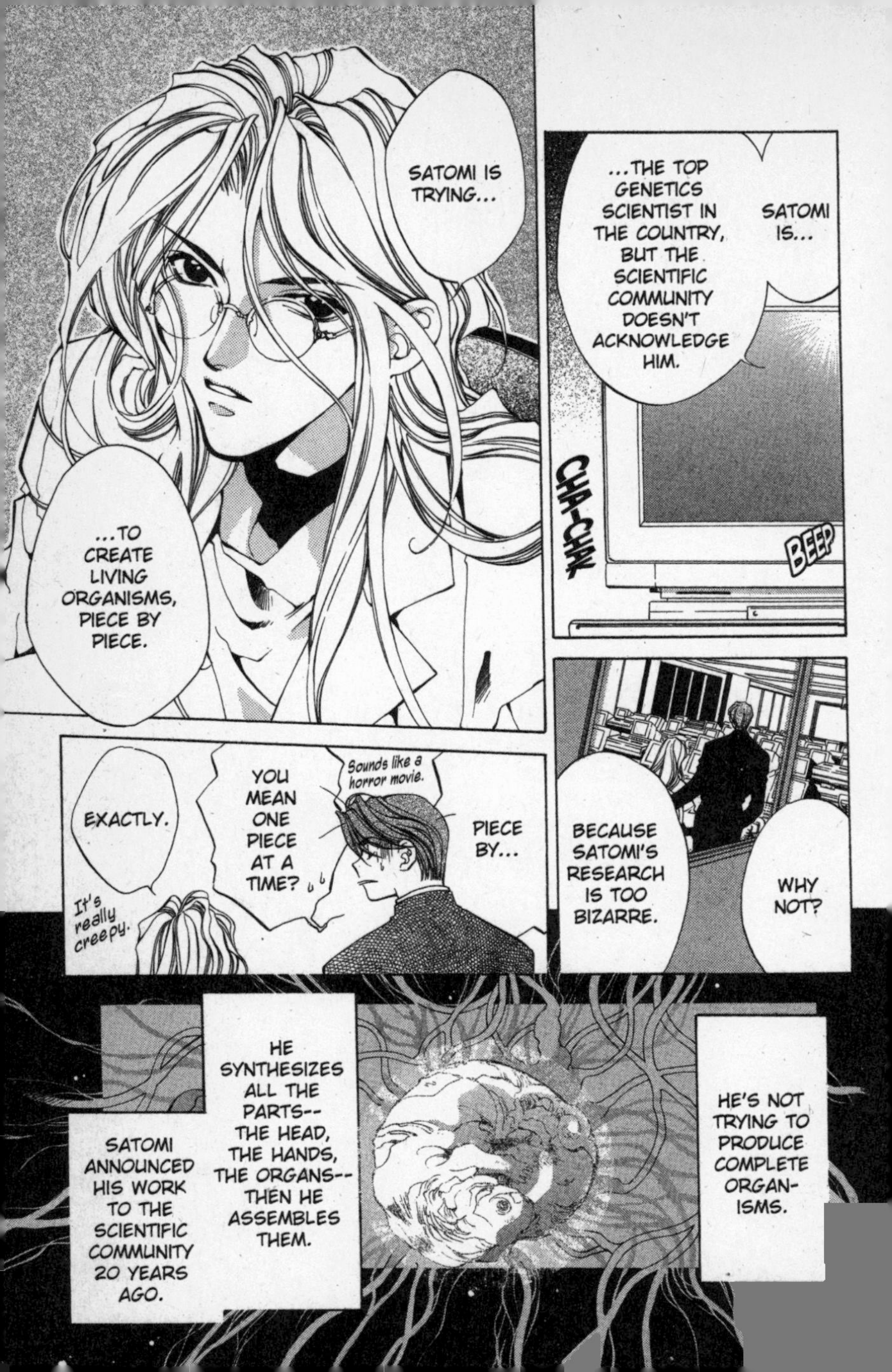
SATOMI IS...
...THE TOP GENETICS SCIENTIST IN THE COUNTRY, BUT THE SCIENTIFIC COMMUNITY DOESN'T ACKNOWLEDGE HIM.
BEEP
CHA-CHAK
WHY NOT?
BECAUSE SATOMI'S RESEARCH IS TOO BIZARRE.
SATOMI IS TRYING...
...TO CREATE LIVING ORGANISMS, PIECE BY PIECE.
PIECE BY...
Sounds like a horror movie.
YOU MEAN ONE PIECE AT A TIME?
EXACTLY.
It's really creepy.
HE'S NOT TRYING TO PRODUCE COMPLETE ORGAN-ISMS.
HE SYNTHESIZES ALL THE PARTS--THE HEAD, THE HANDS, THE ORGANS--THEN HE ASSEMBLES THEM.
SATOMI ANNOUNCED HIS WORK TO THE SCIENTIFIC COMMUNITY 20 YEARS AGO.

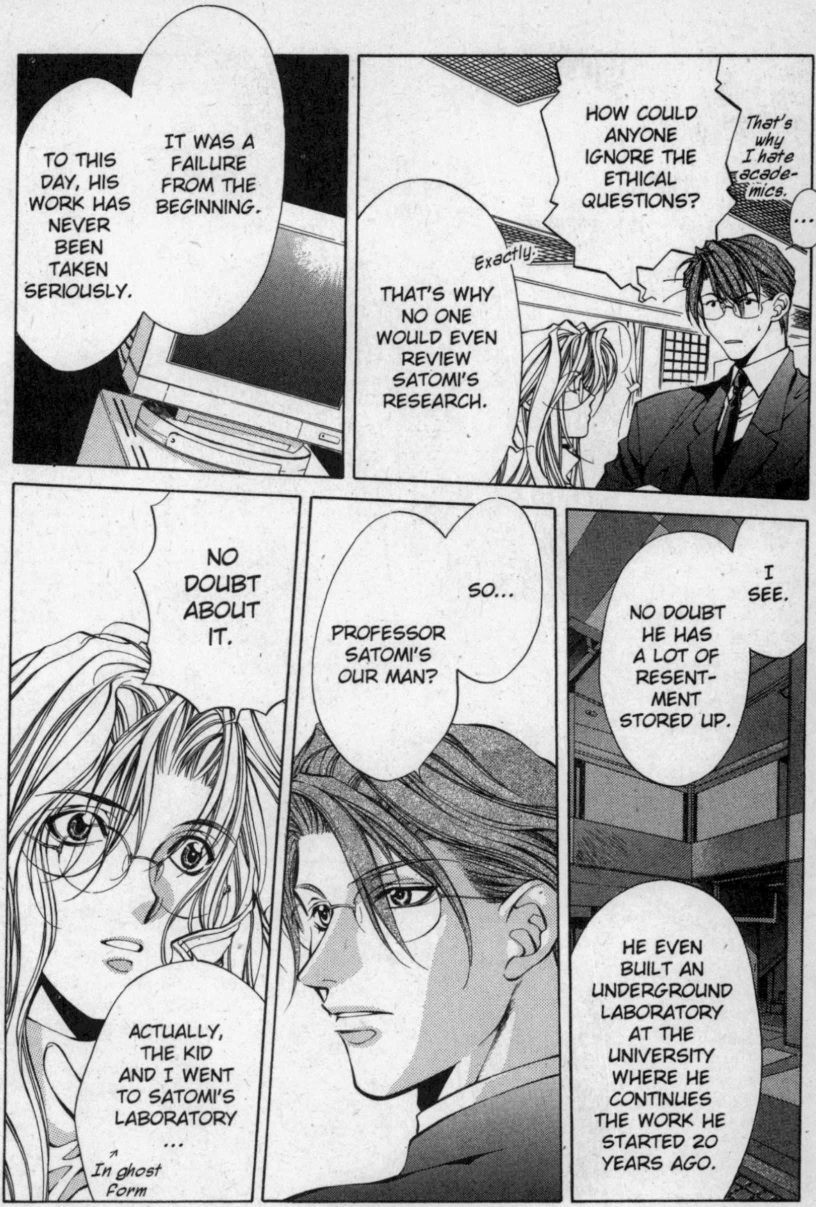
That's why I hate academics.
...
HOW COULD ANYONE IGNORE THE ETHICAL QUESTIONS?
Exactly.
THAT'S WHY NO ONE WOULD EVEN REVIEW SATOMI'S RESEARCH.
IT WAS A FAILURE FROM THE BEGINNING.
TO THIS DAY, HIS WORK HAS NEVER BEEN TAKEN SERIOUSLY.
I SEE.
NO DOUBT HE HAS A LOT OF RESENTMENT STORED UP.
HE EVEN BUILT AN UNDERGROUND LABORATORY AT THE UNIVERSITY WHERE HE CONTINUES THE WORK HE STARTED 20 YEARS AGO.
SO...
PROFESSOR SATOMI'S OUR MAN?
NO DOUBT ABOUT IT.
ACTUALLY, THE KID AND I WENT TO SATOMI'S LABORATORY ...
In ghost form

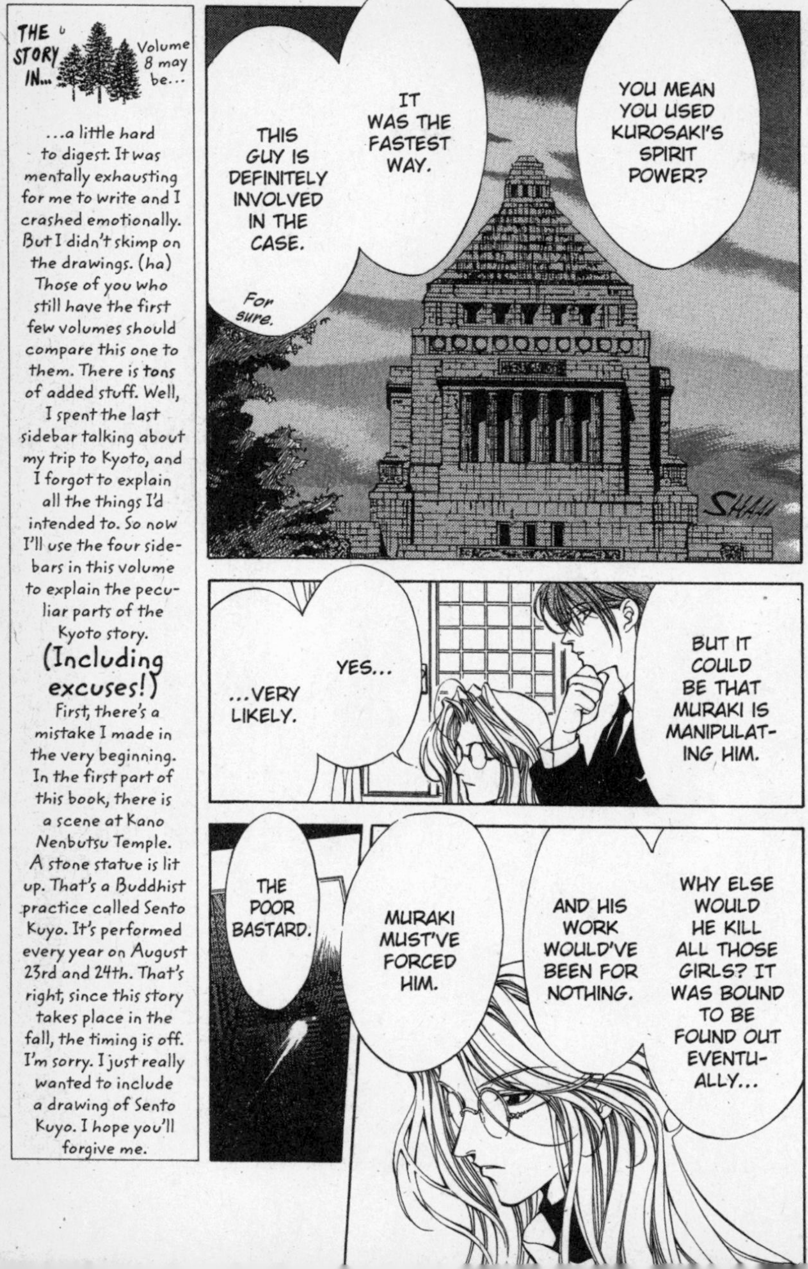
YOU MEAN YOU USED KUROSAKI'S SPIRIT POWER?
IT WAS THE FASTEST WAY.
THIS GUY IS DEFINITELY INVOLVED IN THE CASE.
For sure.
BUT IT COULD BE THAT MURAKI IS MANIPULATING HIM.
YES...
...VERY LIKELY.
WHY ELSE WOULD HE KILL ALL THOSE GIRLS? IT WAS BOUND TO BE FOUND OUT EVENTUALLY...
AND HIS WORK WOULD'VE BEEN FOR NOTHING.
MURAKI MUST'VE FORCED HIM.
THE POOR BASTARD.

THE STORY IN... Volume 8 may be...

...a little hard to digest. It was mentally exhausting for me to write and I crashed emotionally. But I didn't skimp on the drawings. (ha) Those of you who still have the first few volumes should compare this one to them. There is tons of added stuff. Well, I spent the last sidebar talking about my trip to Kyoto, and I forgot to explain all the things I'd intended to. So now I'll use the four sidebars in this volume to explain the peculiar parts of the Kyoto story.

(Including excuses!)

First, there's a mistake I made in the very beginning. In the first part of this book, there is a scene at Kano Nenbutsu Temple. A stone statue is lit up. That's a Buddhist practice called Sento Kuyo. It's performed every year on August 23rd and 24th. That's right, since this story takes place in the fall, the timing is off. I'm sorry. I just really wanted to include a drawing of Sento Kuyo. I hope you'll forgive me.

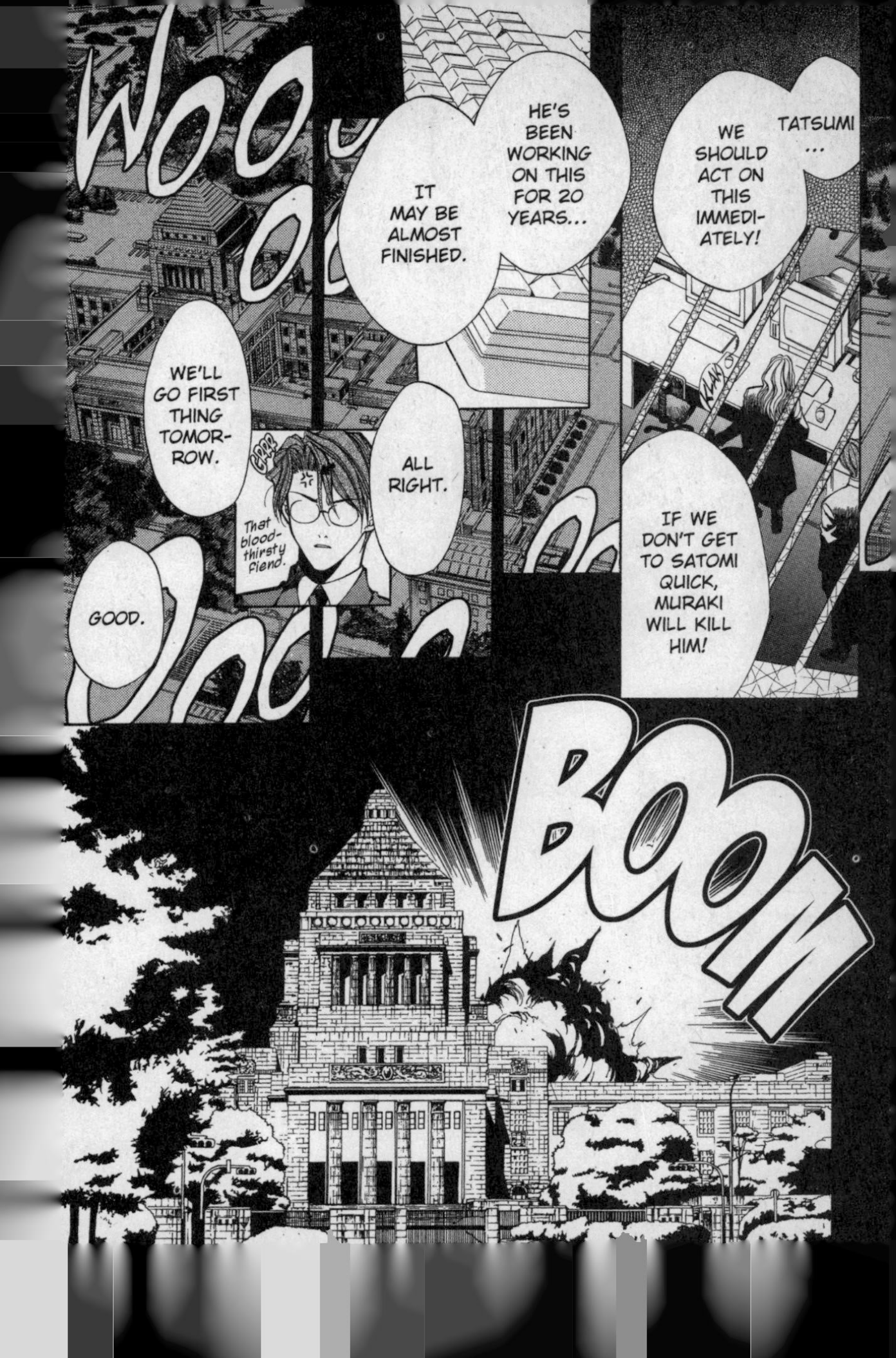
TATSUMI...
WE SHOULD ACT ON THIS IMMEDIATELY!
KLAK
IF WE DON'T GET TO SATOMI QUICK, MURAKI WILL KILL HIM!
HE'S BEEN WORKING ON THIS FOR 20 YEARS...
IT MAY BE ALMOST FINISHED.
ALL RIGHT.
That bloodthirsty fiend.
WE'LL GO FIRST THING TOMORROW.
GOOD.
WOOOOO
BOOM

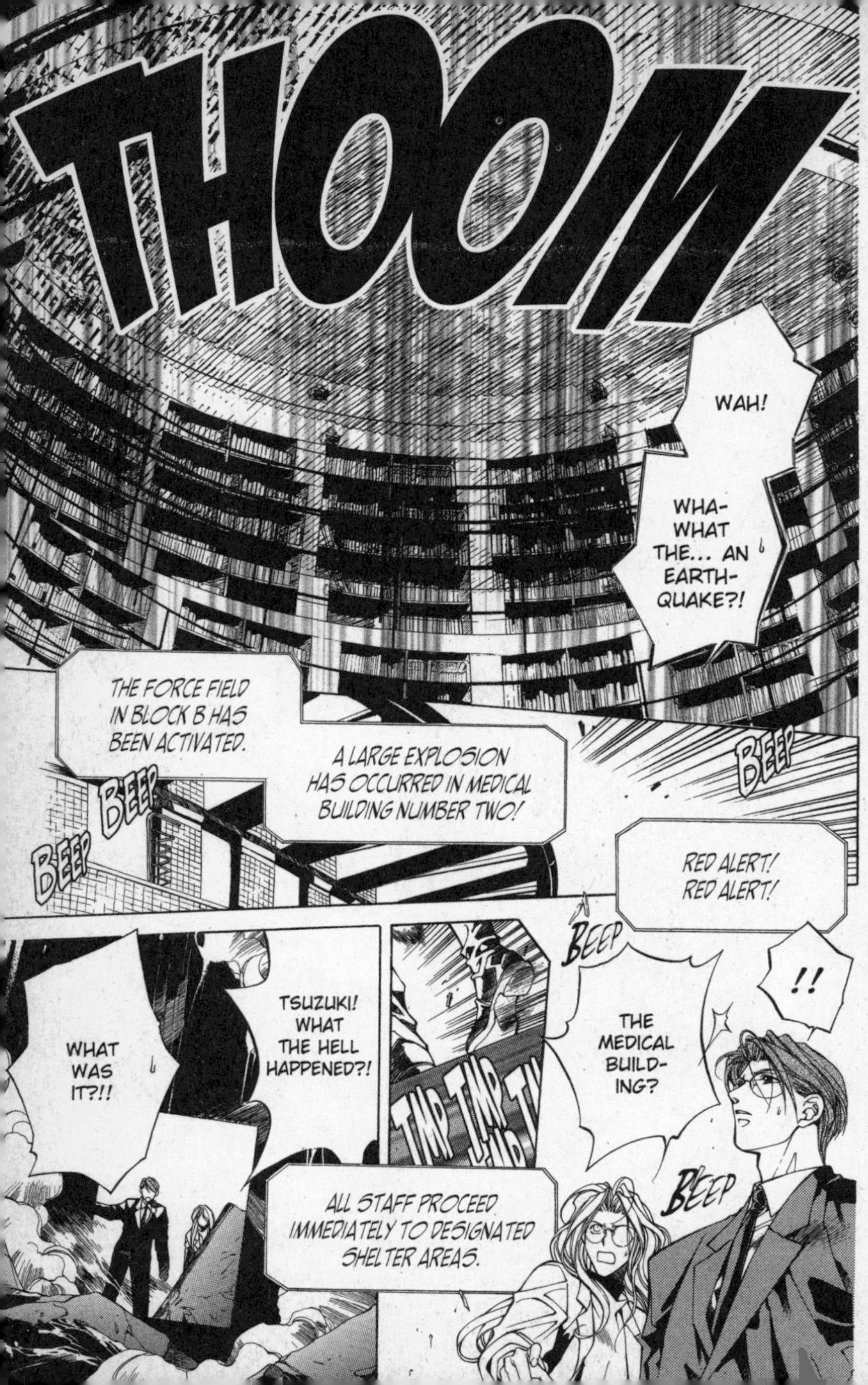

THOOM
WAH!
WHA-WHAT THE... AN EARTHQUAKE?!
THE FORCE FIELD IN BLOCK B HAS BEEN ACTIVATED.
BEEP
A LARGE EXPLOSION HAS OCCURRED IN MEDICAL BUILDING NUMBER TWO!
BEEP
BEEP
RED ALERT! RED ALERT!
BEEP
!!
THE MEDICAL BUILDING?
BEEP
ALL STAFF PROCEED IMMEDIATELY TO DESIGNATED SHELTER AREAS.
TMP TMP TMP
TSUZUKI! WHAT THE HELL HAPPENED?!
WHAT WAS IT?!!

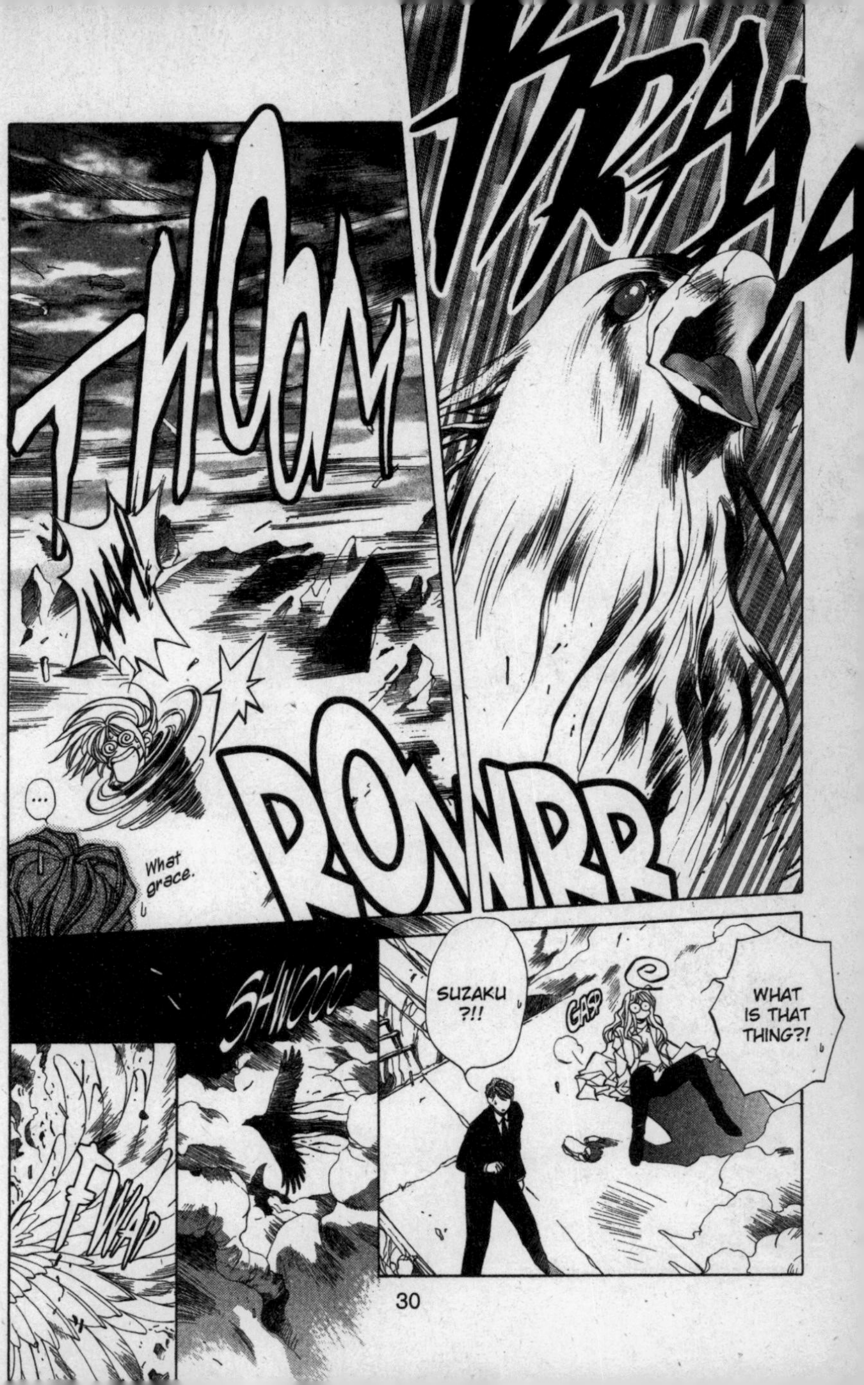
KRAAA
THOOM
...
What grace.
ROWRR
WHAT IS THAT THING?!
GASP
SUZAKU ?!!
SHWOOO
FWAP

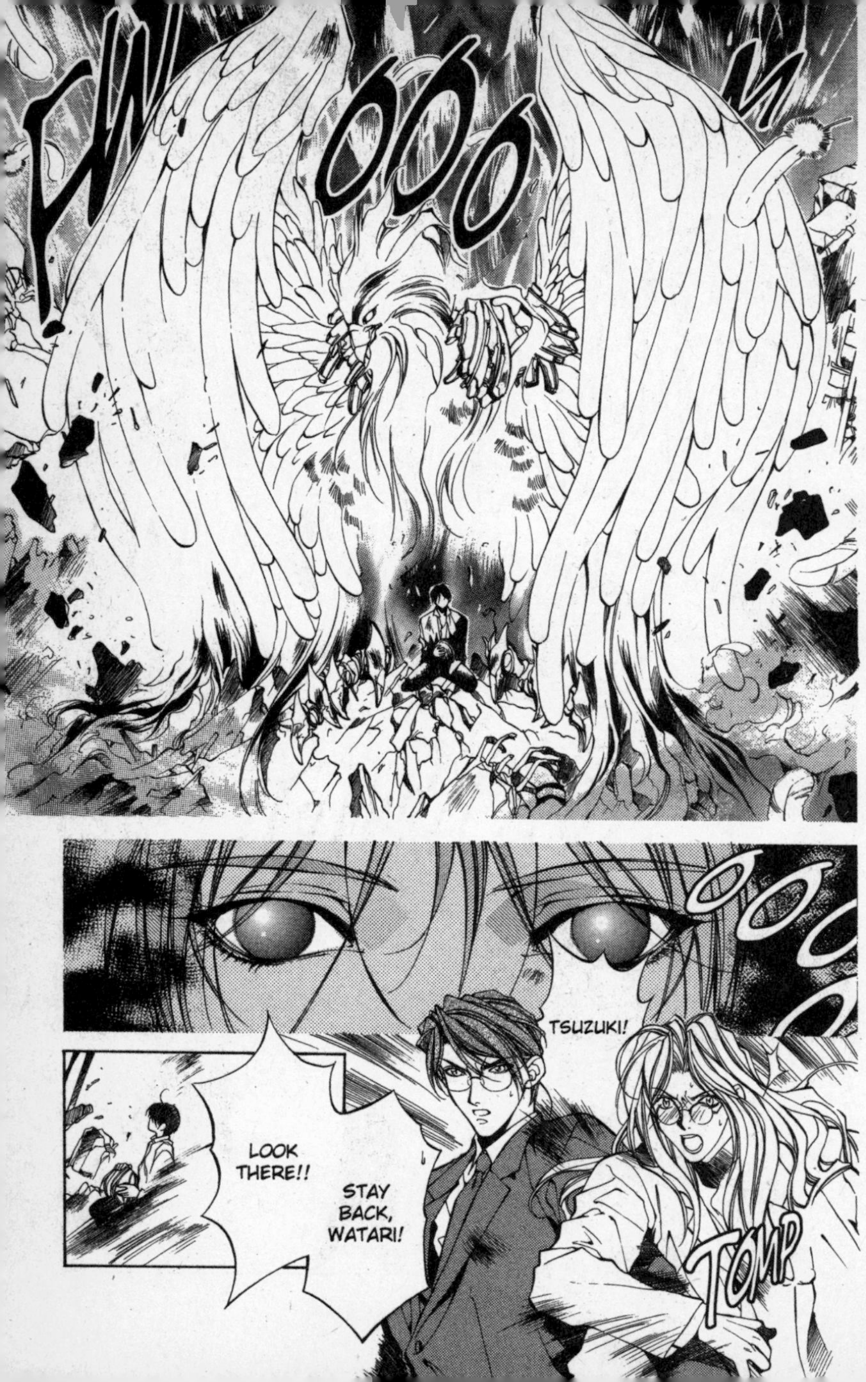
FWOOOM
OOOO
TSUZUKI!
STAY BACK, WATARI!
TOMP
LOOK THERE!!

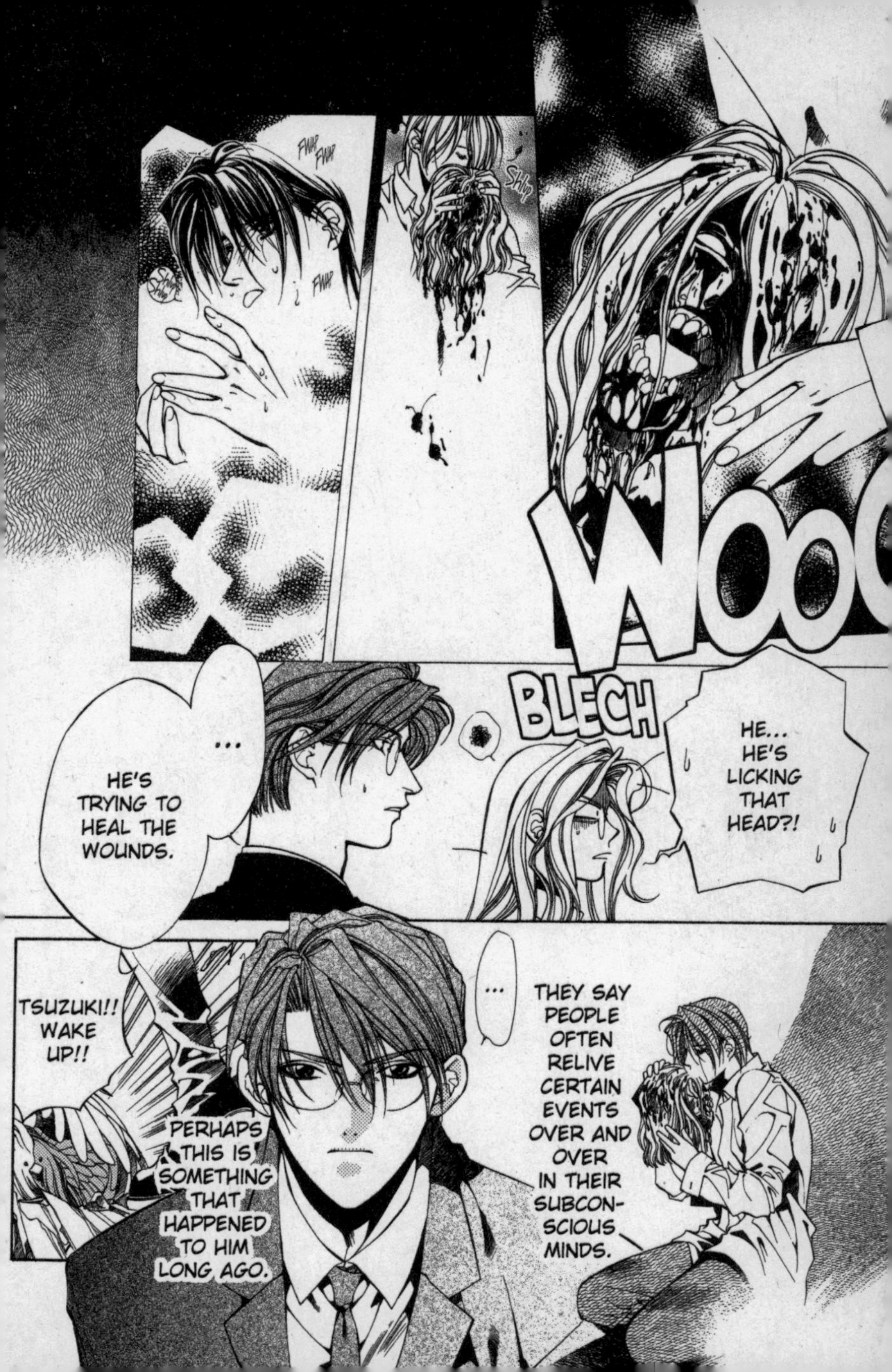
WOO
Shlp
FWAP FWAP
FWAP
Shlp Shlp
BLECH
HE... HE'S LICKING THAT HEAD?!
...
HE'S TRYING TO HEAL THE WOUNDS.
THEY SAY PEOPLE OFTEN RELIVE CERTAIN EVENTS OVER AND OVER IN THEIR SUBCONSCIOUS MINDS.
...
PERHAPS THIS IS SOMETHING THAT HAPPENED TO HIM LONG AGO.
TSUZUKI!! WAKE UP!!

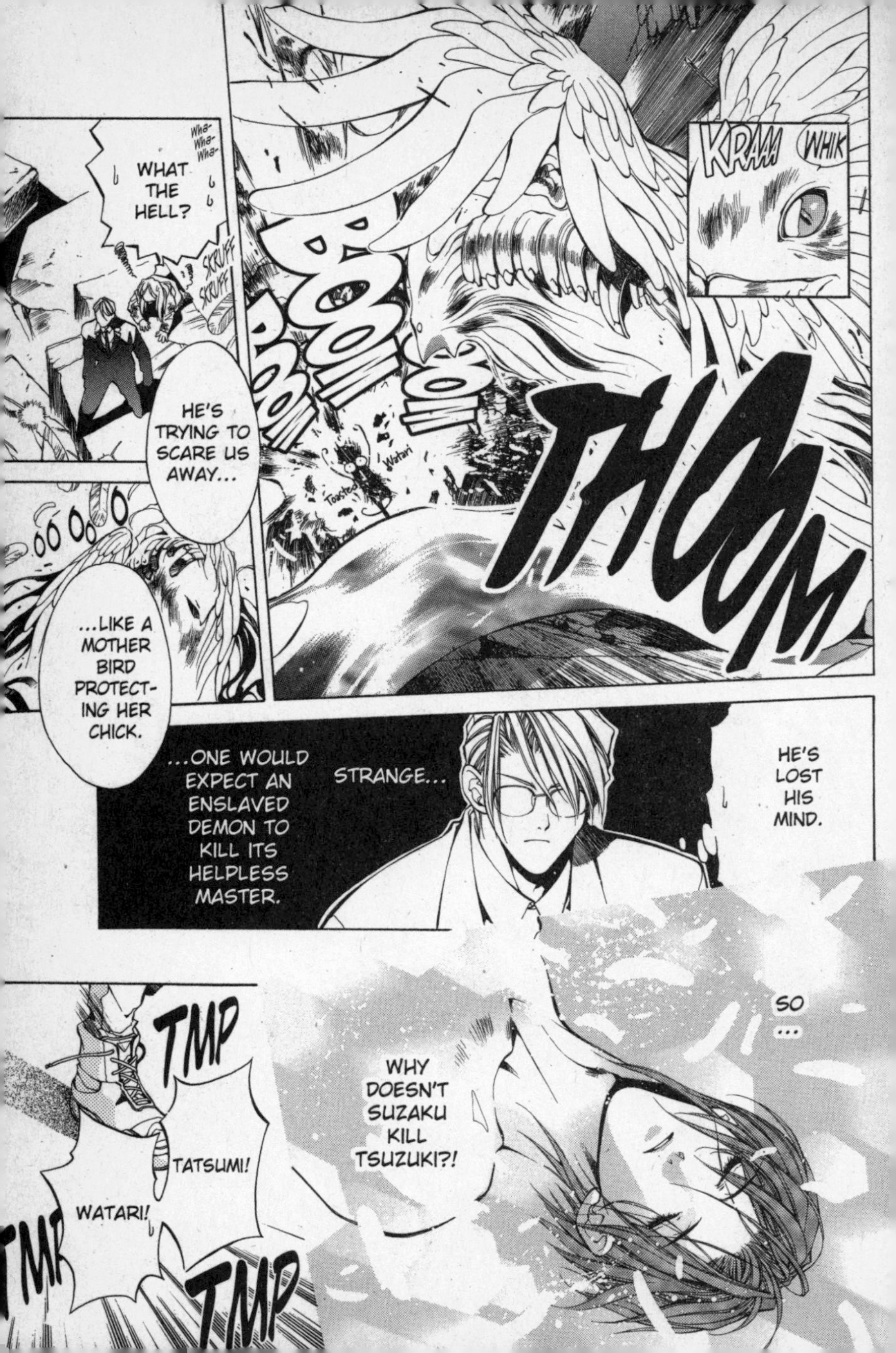
KRAAA
WHIK
BOOOM
BOOOM
THOOM
Watari
Toasted
Wha-Wha-Wha-
WHAT THE HELL?
SKRUFF SKRUFF
HE'S TRYING TO SCARE US AWAY...
...LIKE A MOTHER BIRD PROTECTING HER CHICK.
HE'S LOST HIS MIND.
STRANGE...
...ONE WOULD EXPECT AN ENSLAVED DEMON TO KILL ITS HELPLESS MASTER.
SO...
WHY DOESN'T SUZAKU KILL TSUZUKI?!
TMP
TATSUMI!
WATARI!
TMP
TMP

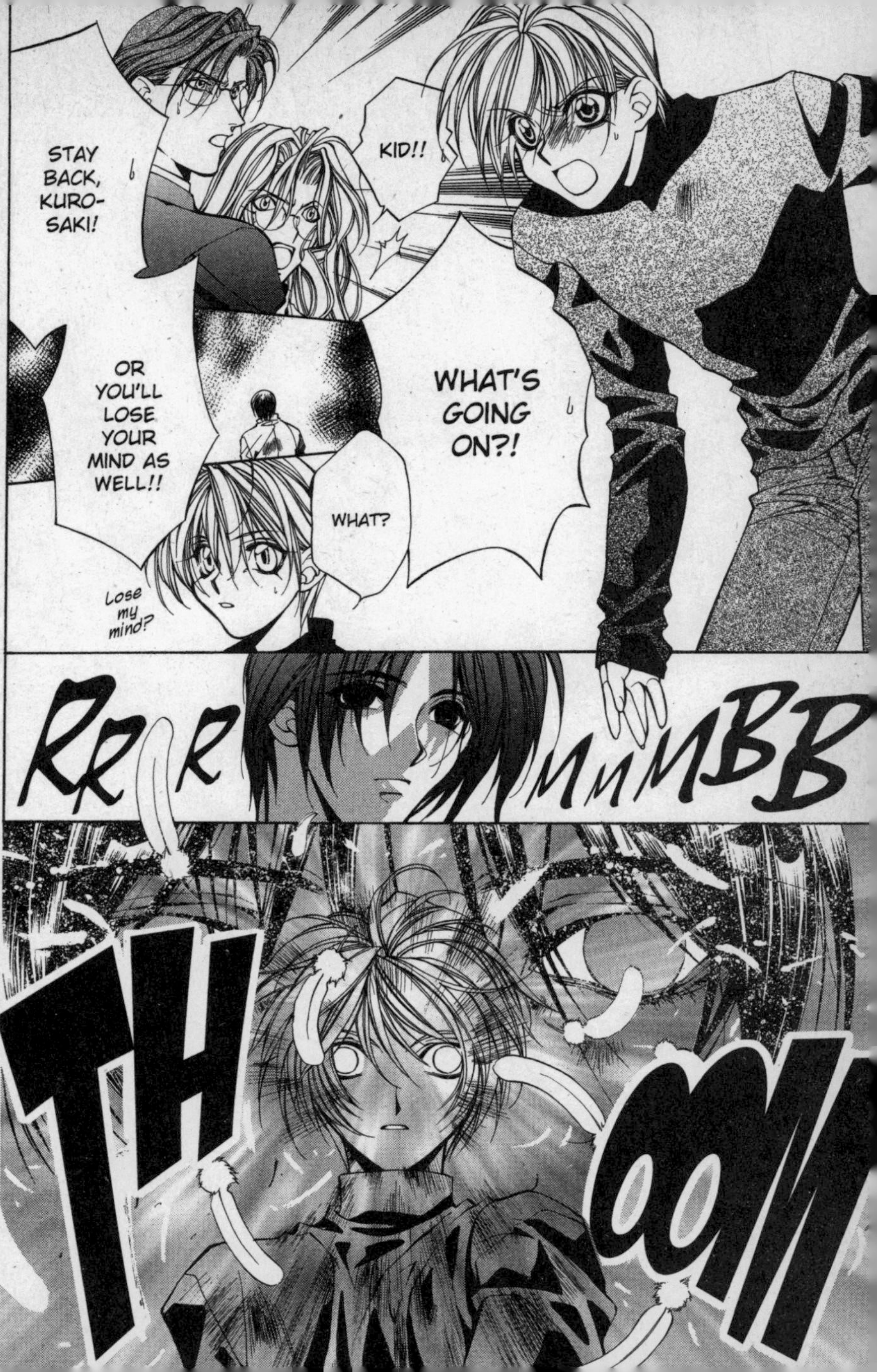
KID!!
WHAT'S GOING ON?!
STAY BACK, KURO-SAKI!
OR YOU'LL LOSE YOUR MIND AS WELL!!
WHAT?
Lose my mind?
RRRMMMBB
THOOM

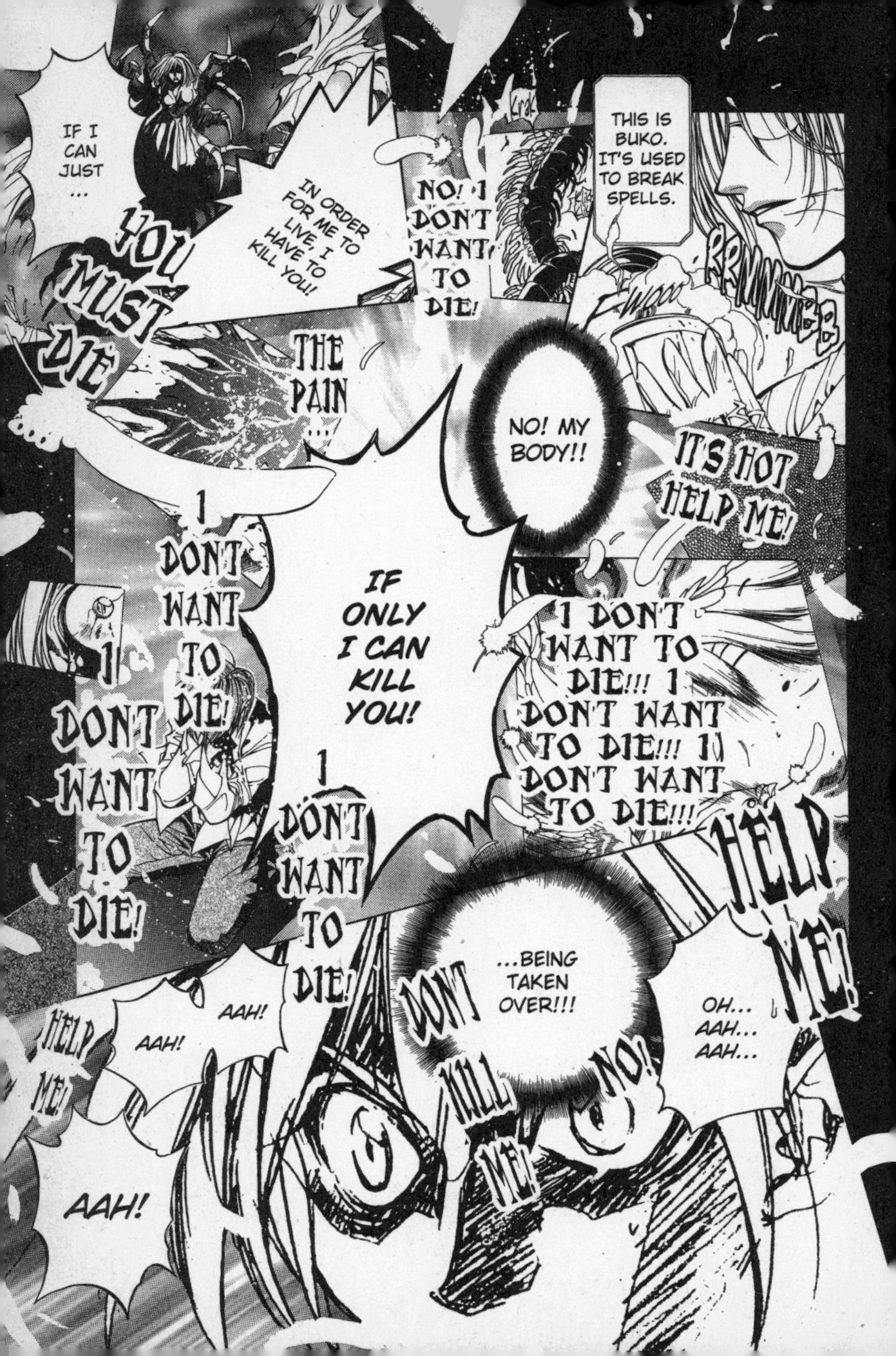
THIS IS BUKO. IT'S USED TO BREAK SPELLS.
KRAK
NO! I DON'T WANT TO DIE!
IN ORDER FOR ME TO LIVE, I HAVE TO KILL YOU!
IF I CAN JUST ...
YOU MUST DIE
IT'S HOT HELP ME!
NO! MY BODY!!
THE PAIN ...
I DON'T WANT TO DIE!!! I DON'T WANT TO DIE!!! I DON'T WANT TO DIE!!!
IF ONLY I CAN KILL YOU!
I DON'T WANT TO DIE!
I DON'T WANT TO DIE!
I DON'T WANT TO DIE!
HELP ME!
OH... AAH... AAH...
NO!
...BEING TAKEN OVER!!!
DON'T KILL ME!
AAH!
AAH!
HELP ME!
AAH!

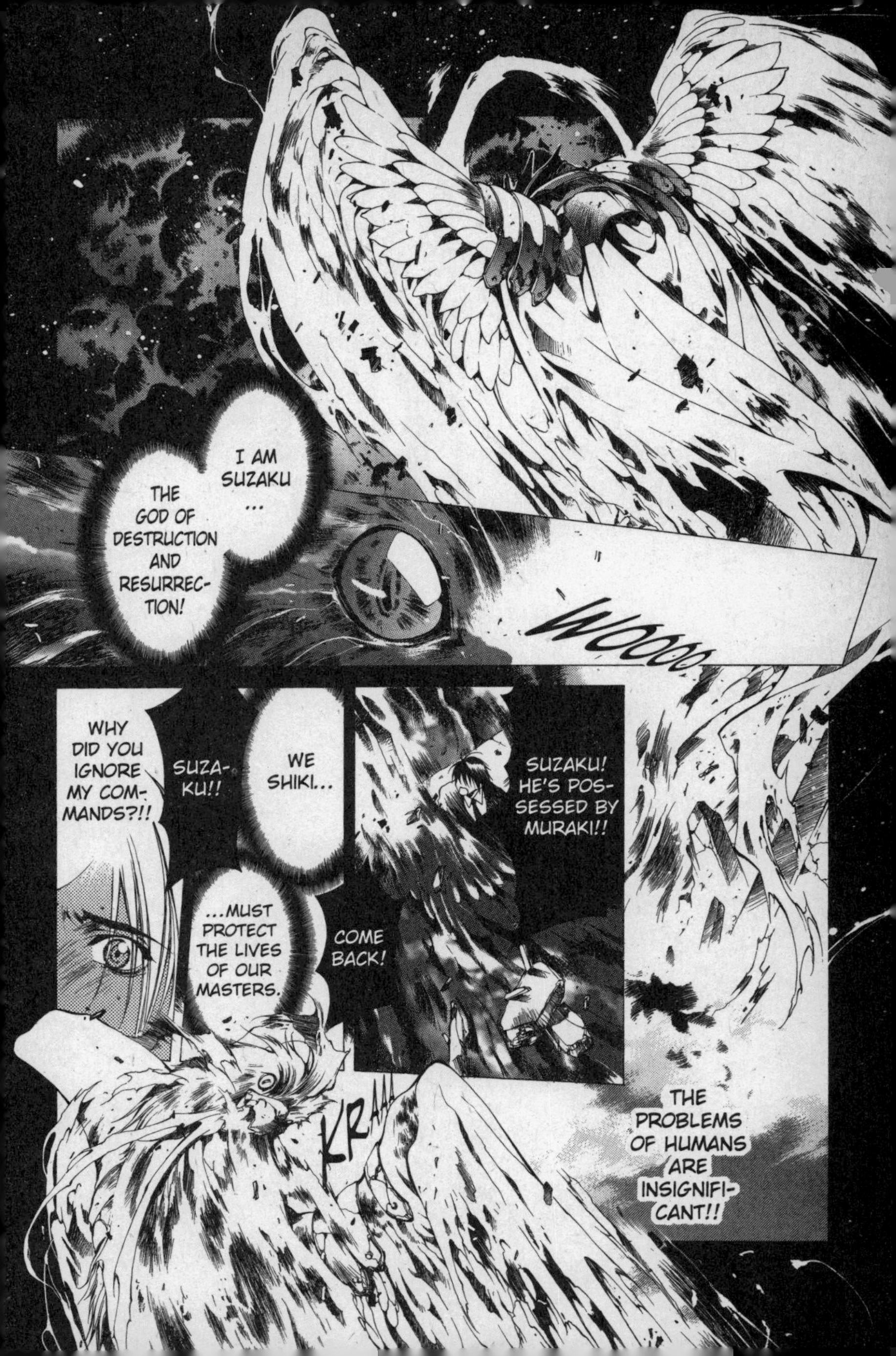
I AM SUZAKU ...
THE GOD OF DESTRUCTION AND RESURRECTION!
WOOOO
SUZAKU! HE'S POSSESSED BY MURAKI!!
COME BACK!
SUZA-KU!!
WHY DID YOU IGNORE MY COM-MANDS?!!
WE SHIKI...
...MUST PROTECT THE LIVES OF OUR MASTERS.
THE PROBLEMS OF HUMANS ARE INSIGNIFI-CANT!!
KRAAA

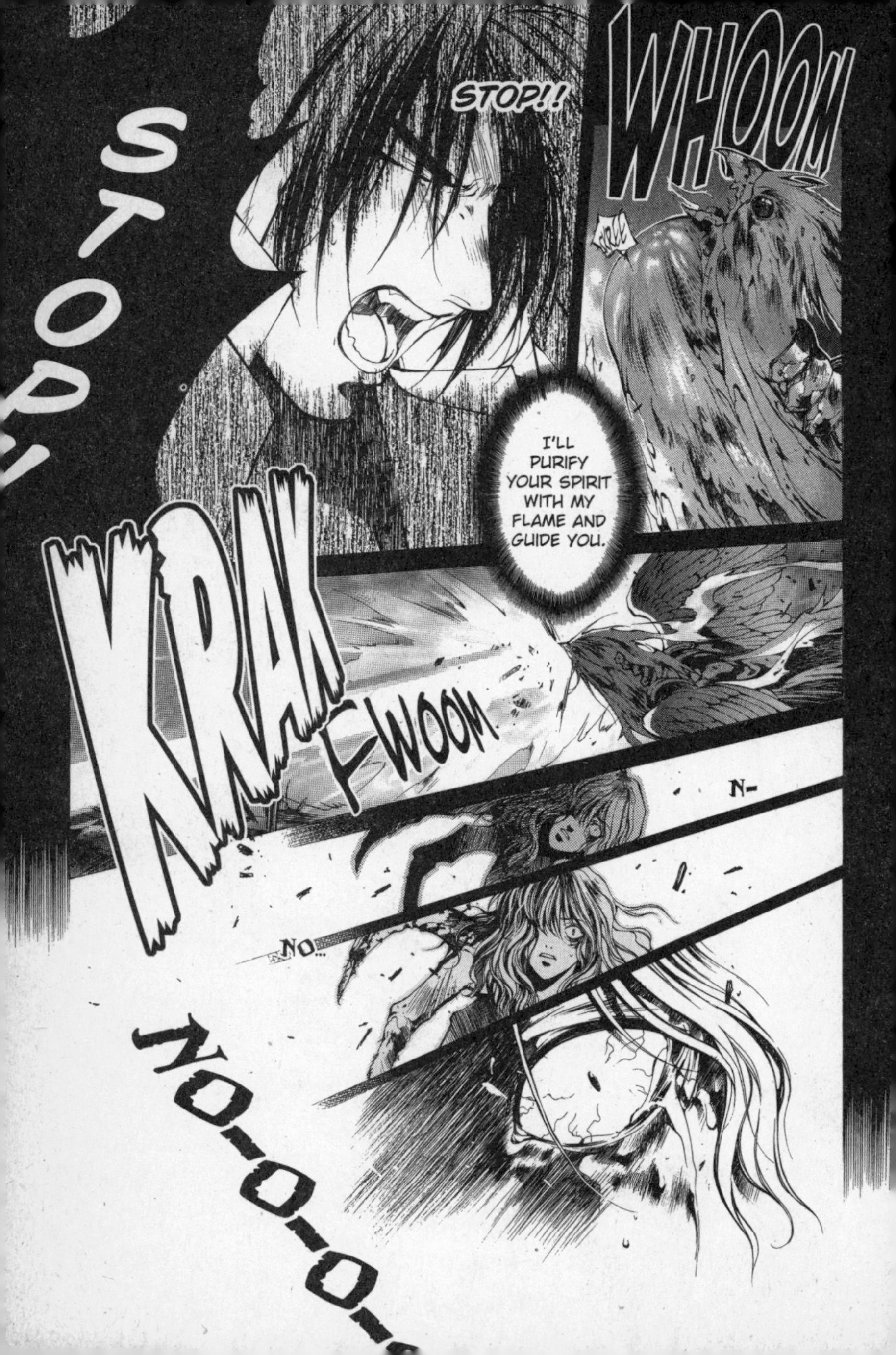

WHOOM
I'LL PURIFY YOUR SPIRIT WITH MY FLAME AND GUIDE YOU.
STOP!!
STOP!!
KRAK
FWOOM
N-
NO...
NO-O-O-O-

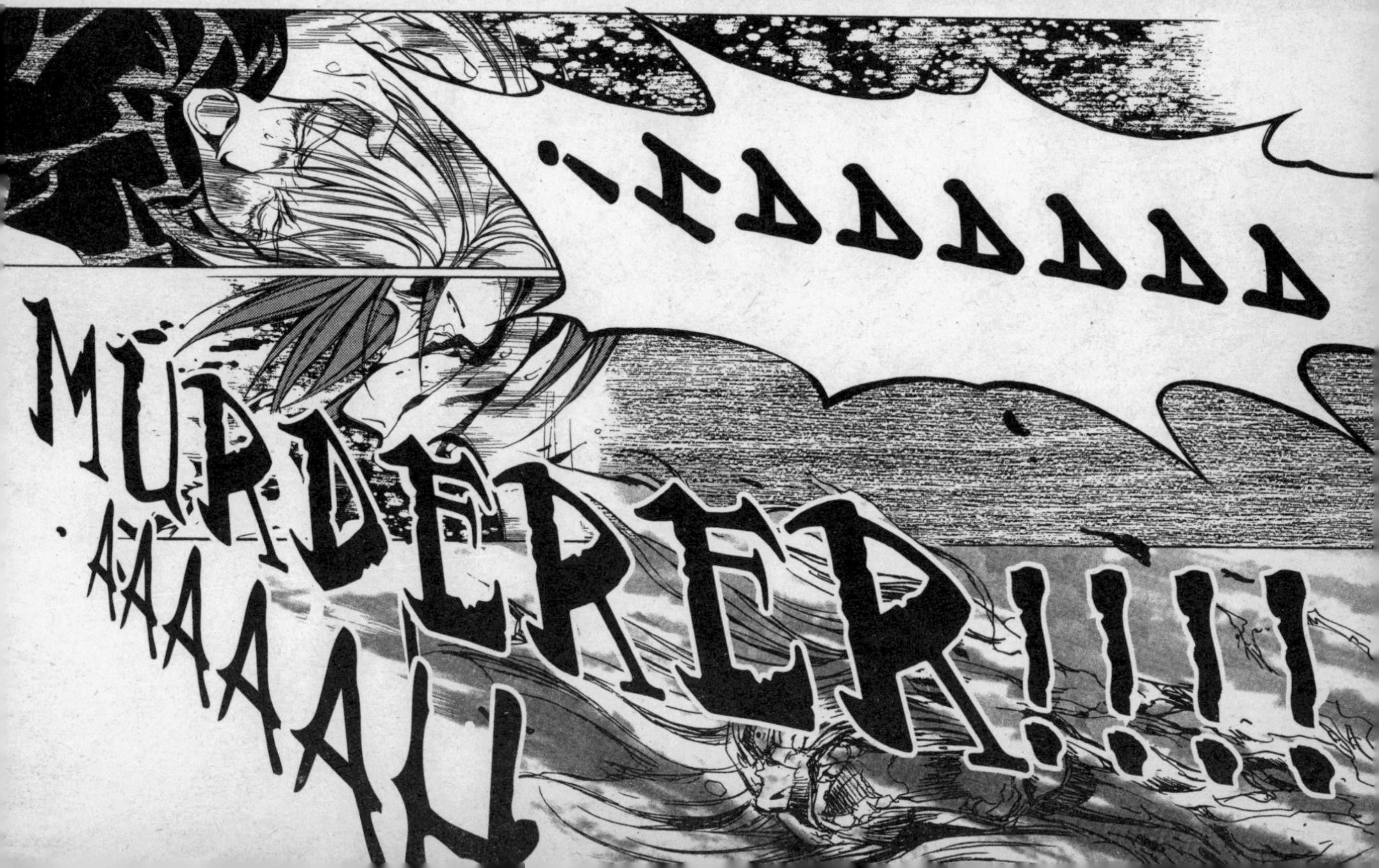

AAAAAAH!
MURDERER!!!!!
AAAAAH

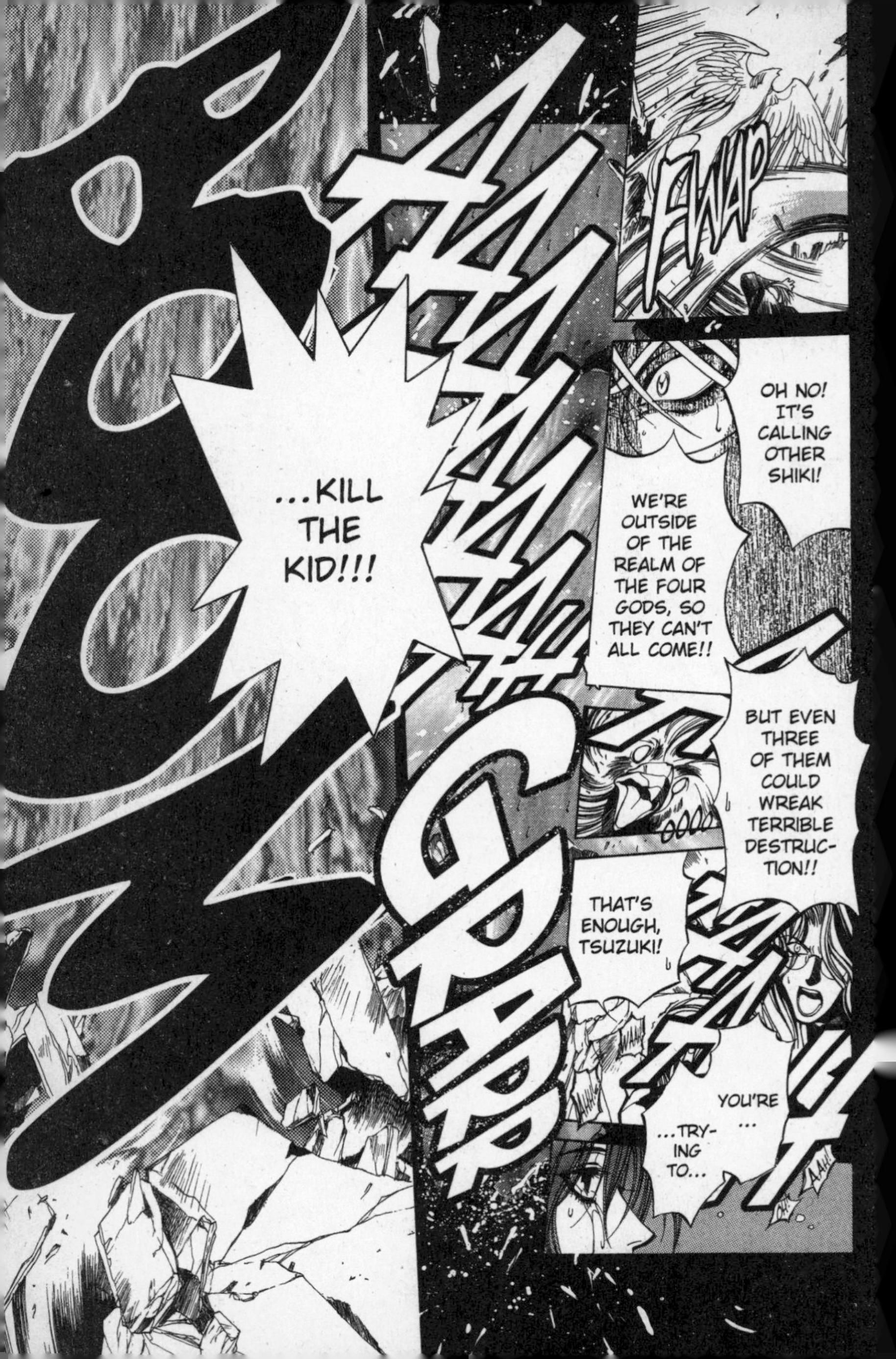
FWAP
OH NO! IT'S CALLING OTHER SHIKI!
WE'RE OUTSIDE OF THE REALM OF THE FOUR GODS, SO THEY CAN'T ALL COME!!
BUT EVEN THREE OF THEM COULD WREAK TERRIBLE DESTRUC-TION!!
THAT'S ENOUGH, TSUZUKI!
YOU'RE ...
...TRY-ING TO...
...KILL THE KID!!!

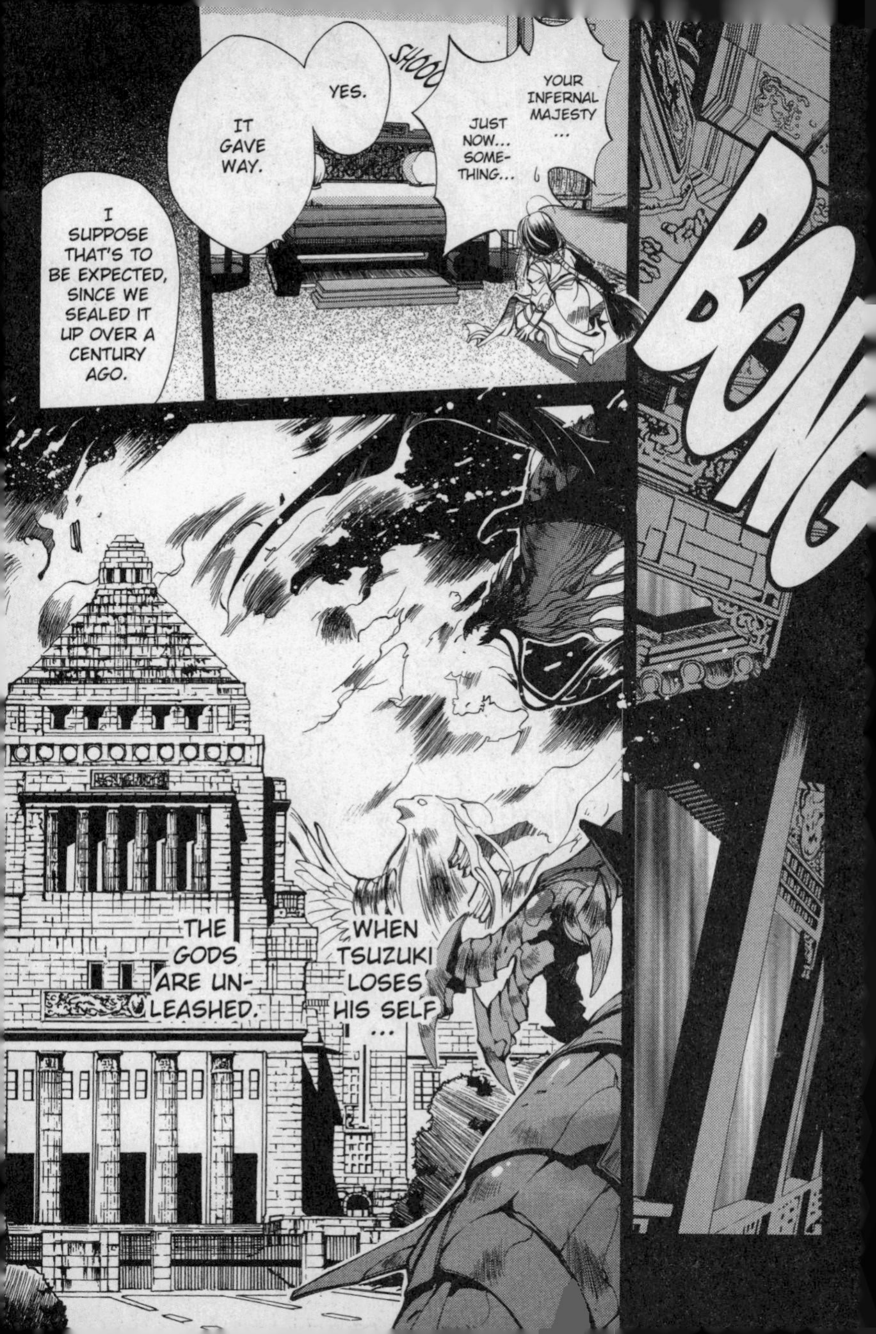
BONG
YOUR INFERNAL MAJESTY ...
JUST NOW... SOMETHING...
SHOOO
YES.
IT GAVE WAY.
I SUPPOSE THAT'S TO BE EXPECTED, SINCE WE SEALED IT UP OVER A CENTURY AGO.
WHEN TSUZUKI LOSES HIS SELF ...
THE GODS ARE UNLEASHED.

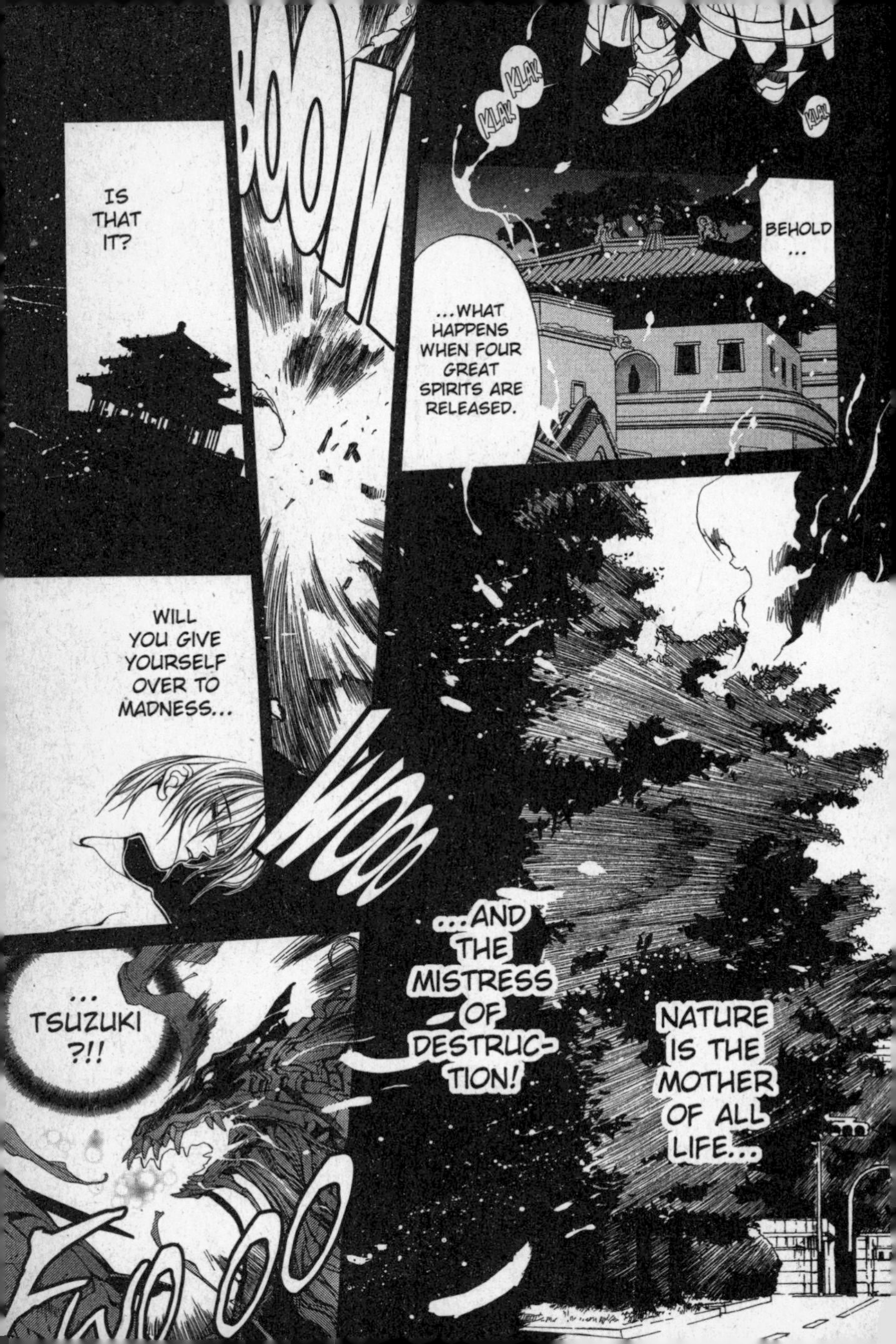
KLAK
KLAK
KLAK
BEHOLD...
...WHAT HAPPENS WHEN FOUR GREAT SPIRITS ARE RELEASED.
BOOM
IS THAT IT?
NATURE IS THE MOTHER OF ALL LIFE...
...AND THE MISTRESS OF DESTRUCTION!
WILL YOU GIVE YOURSELF OVER TO MADNESS...
WOOO
...TSUZUKI?!!
WOOOO

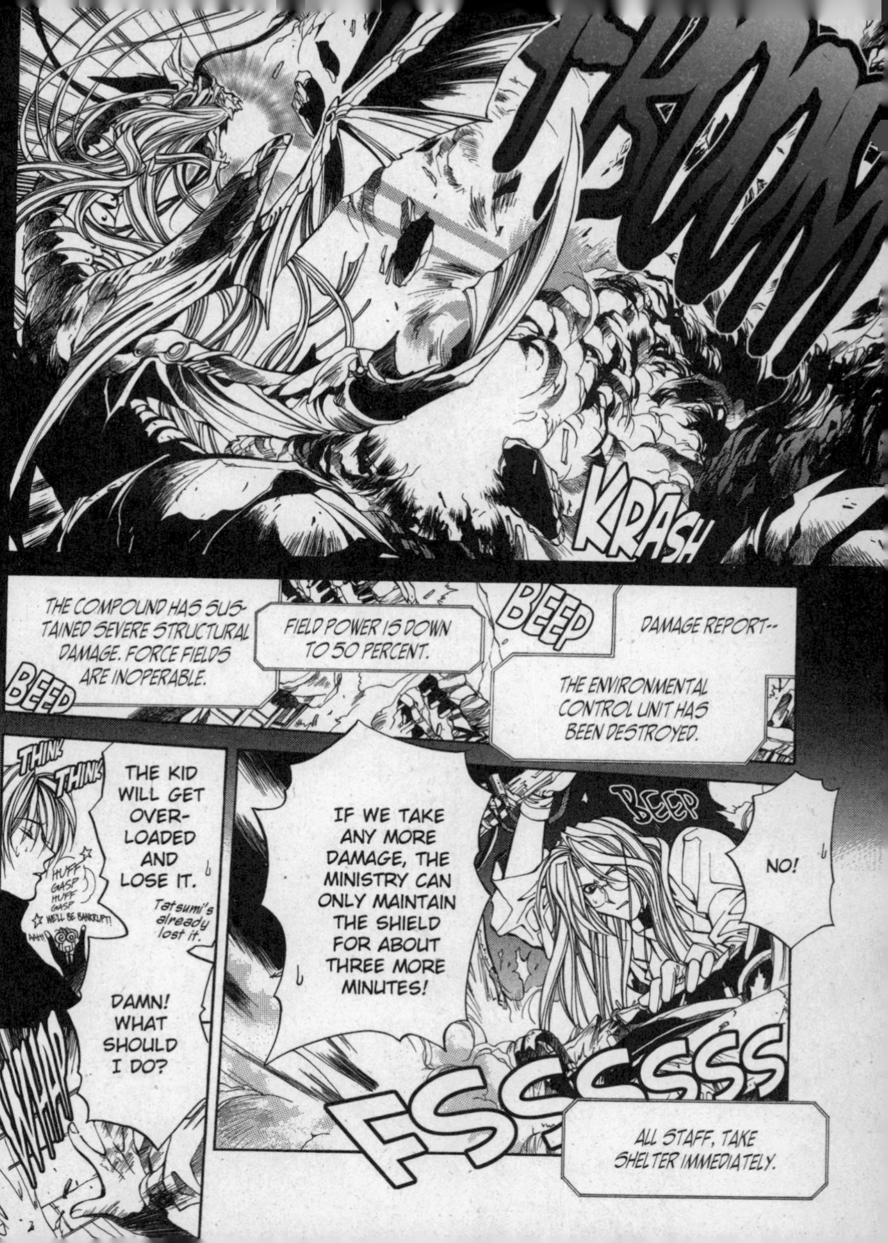
KRASH
DAMAGE REPORT--
BEEP
THE ENVIRONMENTAL CONTROL UNIT HAS BEEN DESTROYED.
FIELD POWER IS DOWN TO 50 PERCENT.
THE COMPOUND HAS SUSTAINED SEVERE STRUCTURAL DAMAGE. FORCE FIELDS ARE INOPERABLE.
BEEP
BEEP
NO!
IF WE TAKE ANY MORE DAMAGE, THE MINISTRY CAN ONLY MAINTAIN THE SHIELD FOR ABOUT THREE MORE MINUTES!
FSSSSSS
ALL STAFF, TAKE SHELTER IMMEDIATELY.
THINK THINK
THE KID WILL GET OVERLOADED AND LOSE IT.
HUFF GASP HUFF GASP
WE'LL BE BANKRUPT!
Tatsumi's already lost it.
DAMN! WHAT SHOULD I DO?

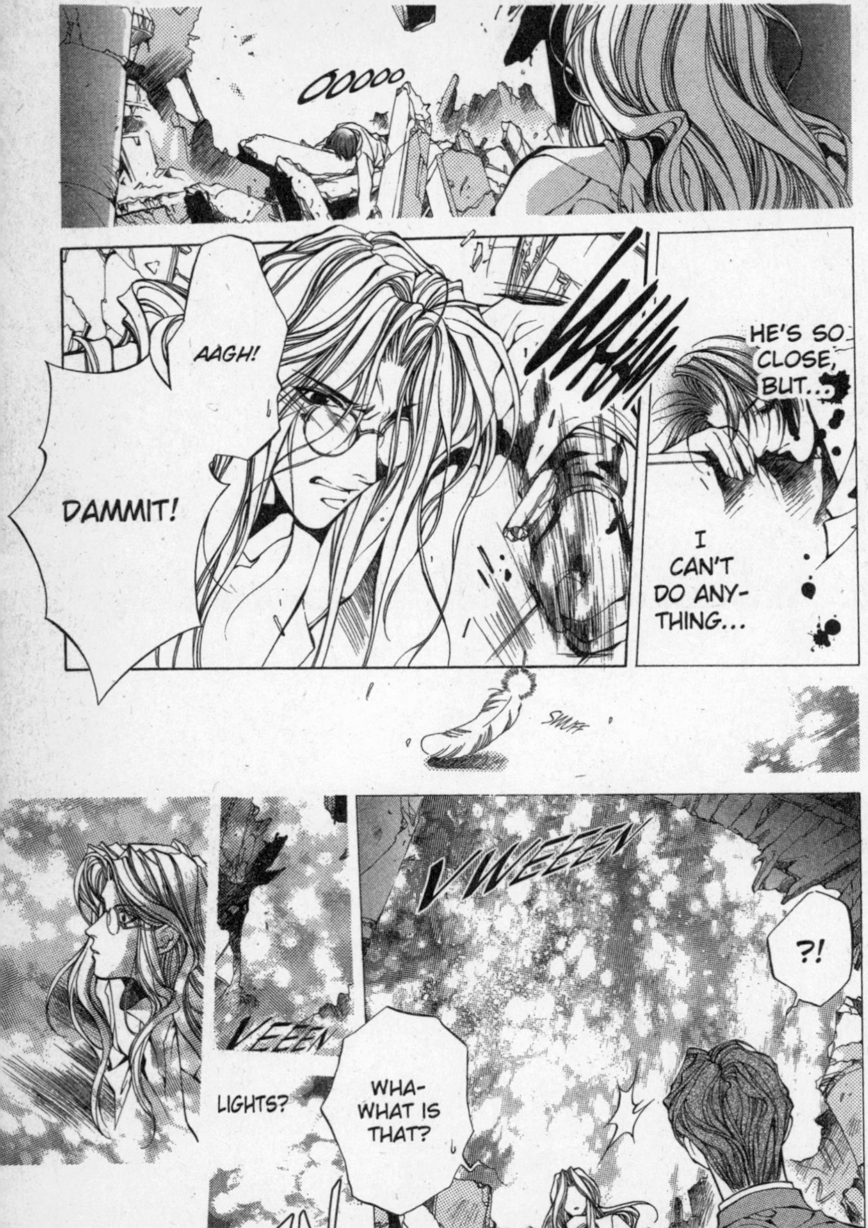
OOOOO
HE'S SO CLOSE, BUT...
I CAN'T DO ANYTHING...
WHAM
AAGH!
DAMMIT!
SWUFF
VWEEEN
?!
WHA- WHAT IS THAT?
VEEEN
VEEEN
LIGHTS?

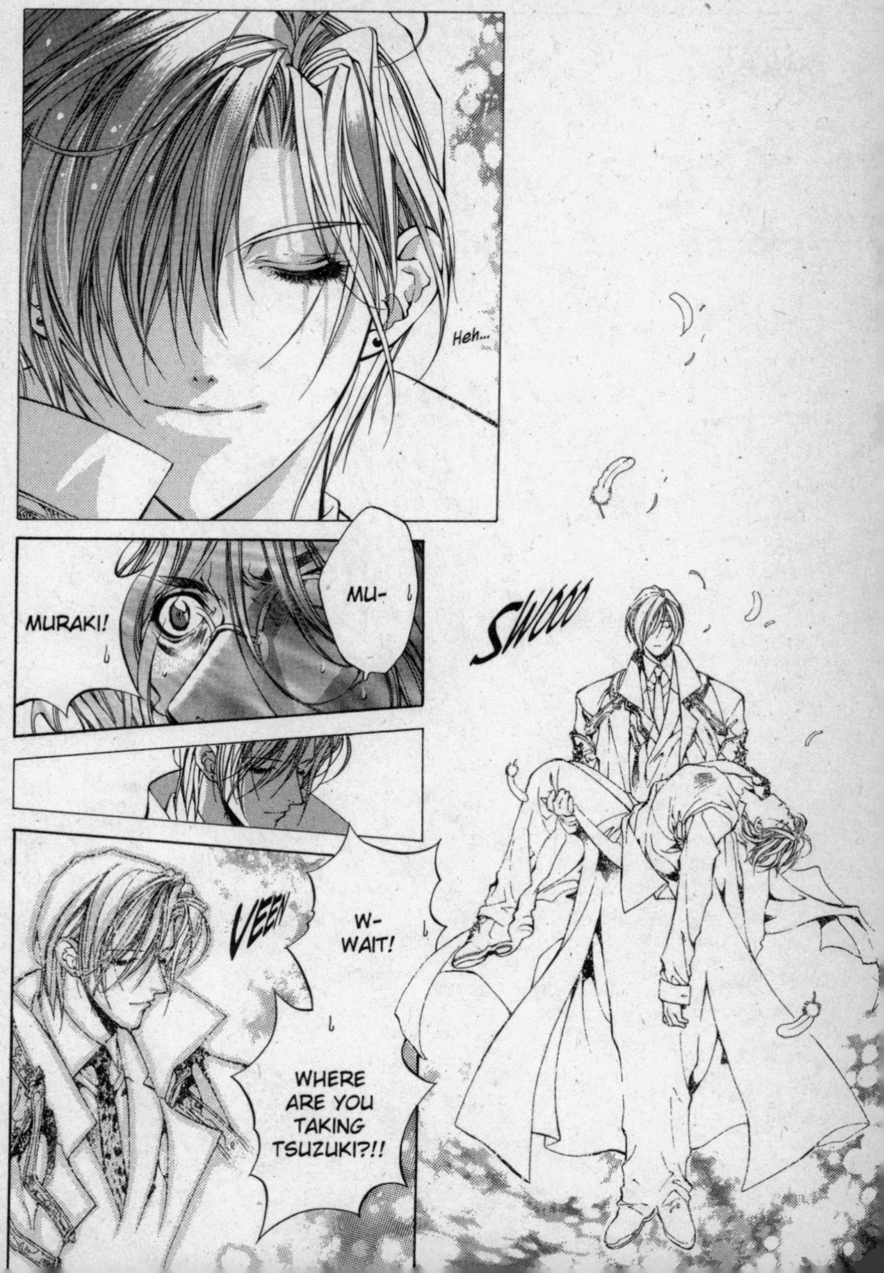
SWOOO
Heh...
MU-
MURAKI!
W-
WAIT!
VEEN
WHERE ARE YOU TAKING TSUZUKI?!!

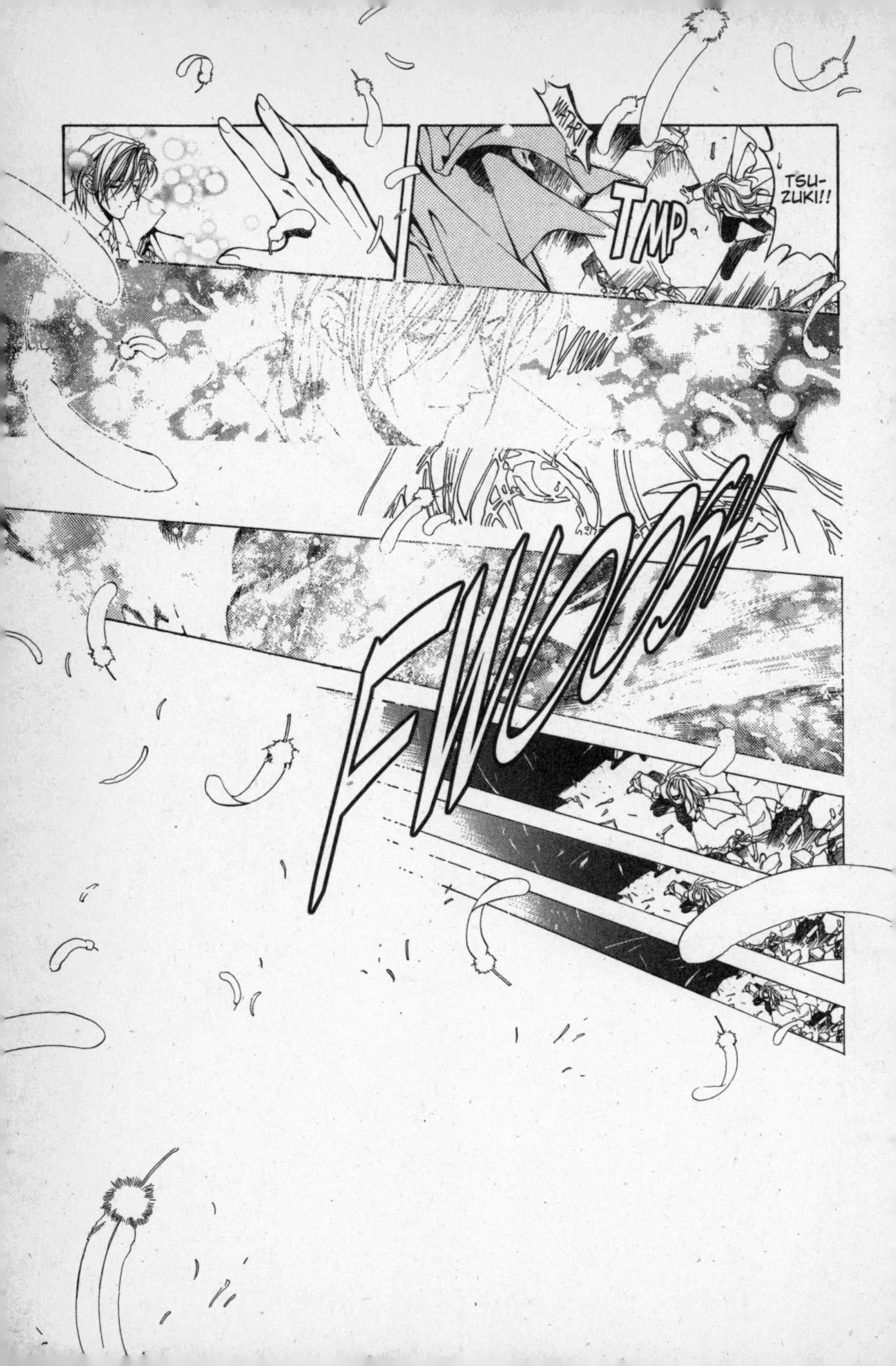
TSU-ZUKI!!
WATARI!!
TMP
FWOOSH

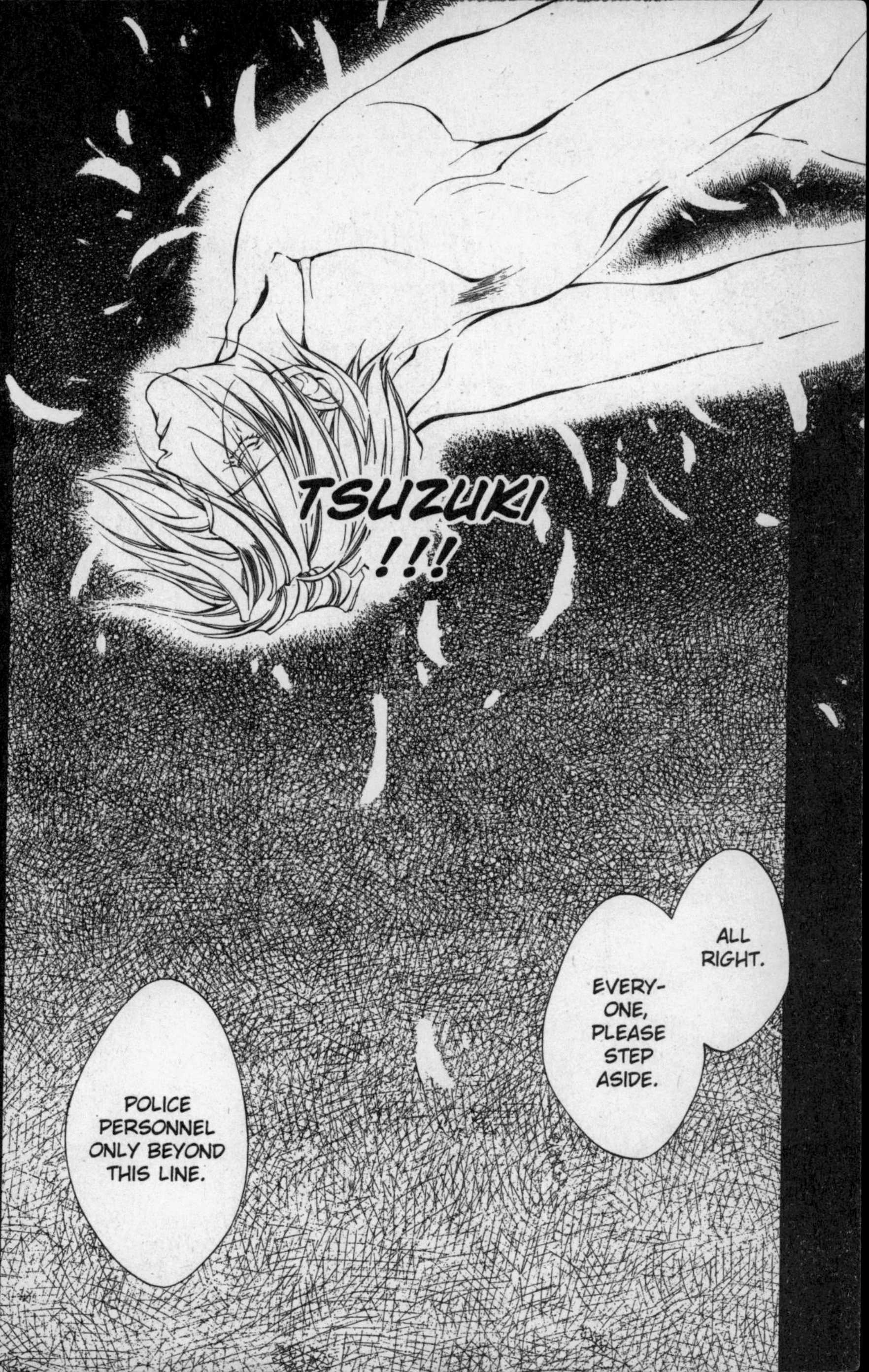
TSUZUKI !!!
ALL RIGHT.
EVERY-ONE, PLEASE STEP ASIDE.
POLICE PERSONNEL ONLY BEYOND THIS LINE.

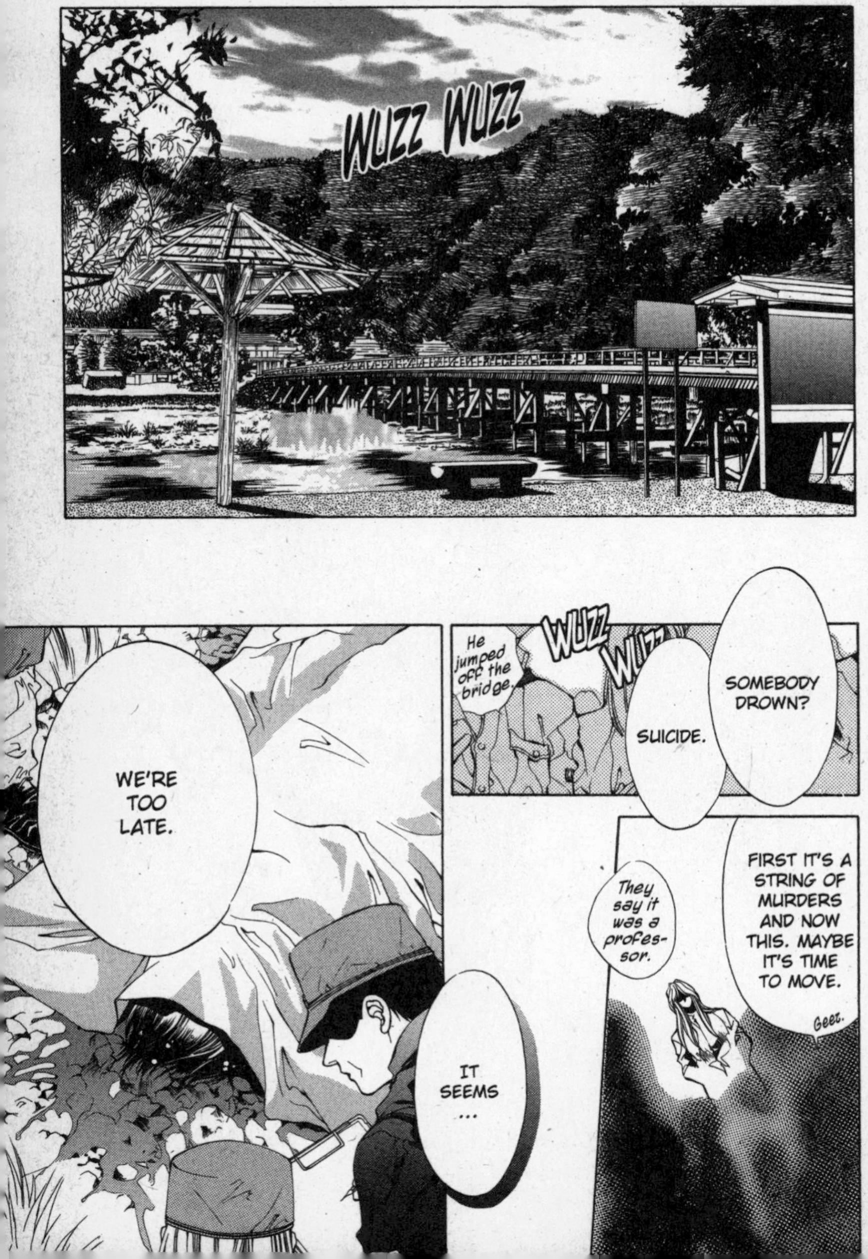
WUZZ WUZZ
WUZZ WUZZ
SOMEBODY DROWN?
SUICIDE.
He jumped off the bridge.
FIRST IT'S A STRING OF MURDERS AND NOW THIS. MAYBE IT'S TIME TO MOVE.
Geez.
They say it was a profes-sor.
WE'RE TOO LATE.
IT SEEMS ...

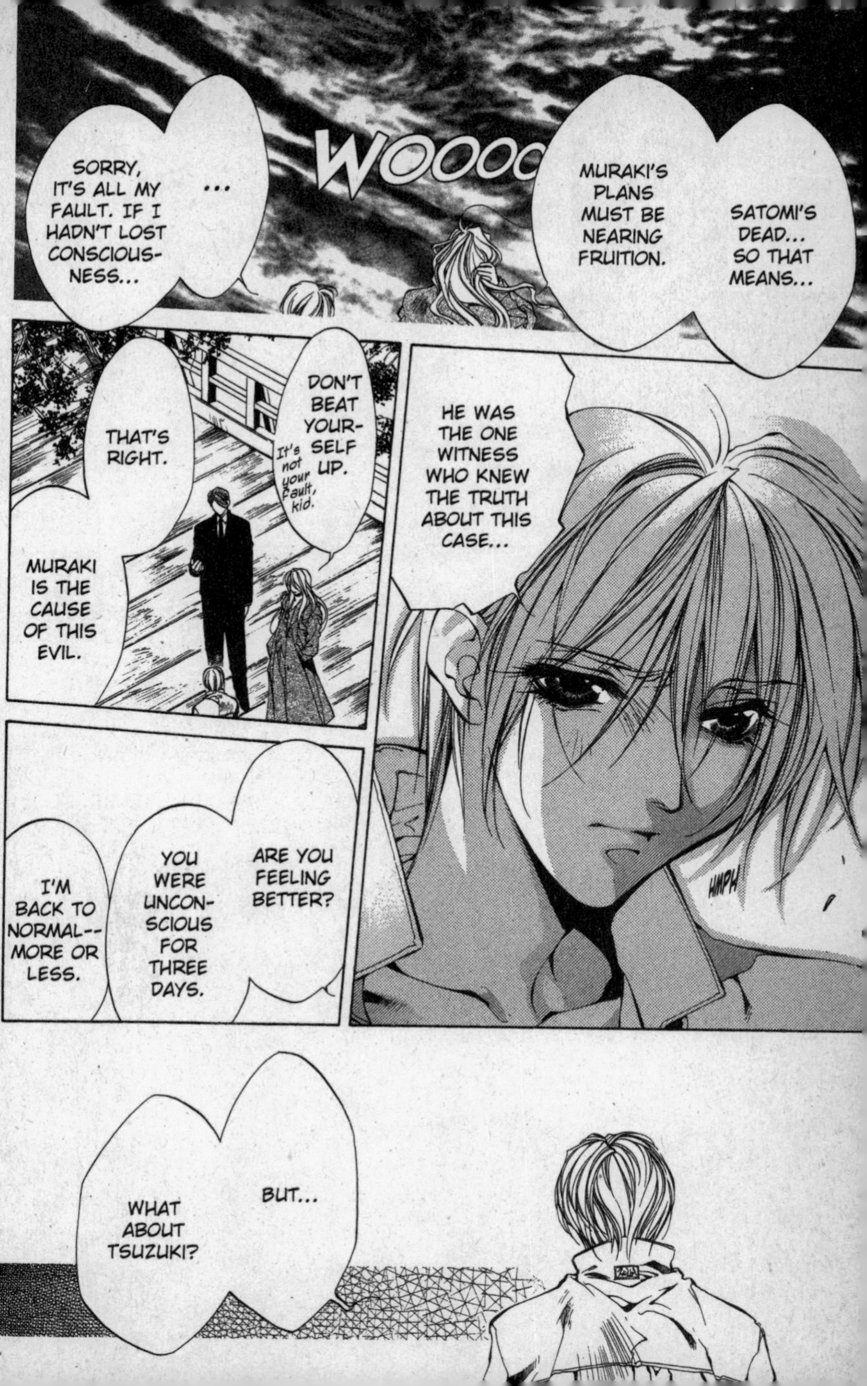
SATOMI'S DEAD... SO THAT MEANS...
MURAKI'S PLANS MUST BE NEARING FRUITION.
WOOOO
...
SORRY, IT'S ALL MY FAULT. IF I HADN'T LOST CONSCIOUS-NESS...
HE WAS THE ONE WITNESS WHO KNEW THE TRUTH ABOUT THIS CASE...
HMPH
DON'T BEAT YOUR-SELF UP.
It's not your fault, kid.
THAT'S RIGHT.
MURAKI IS THE CAUSE OF THIS EVIL.
ARE YOU FEELING BETTER?
YOU WERE UNCON-SCIOUS FOR THREE DAYS.
I'M BACK TO NORMAL--MORE OR LESS.
BUT...
WHAT ABOUT TSUZUKI?

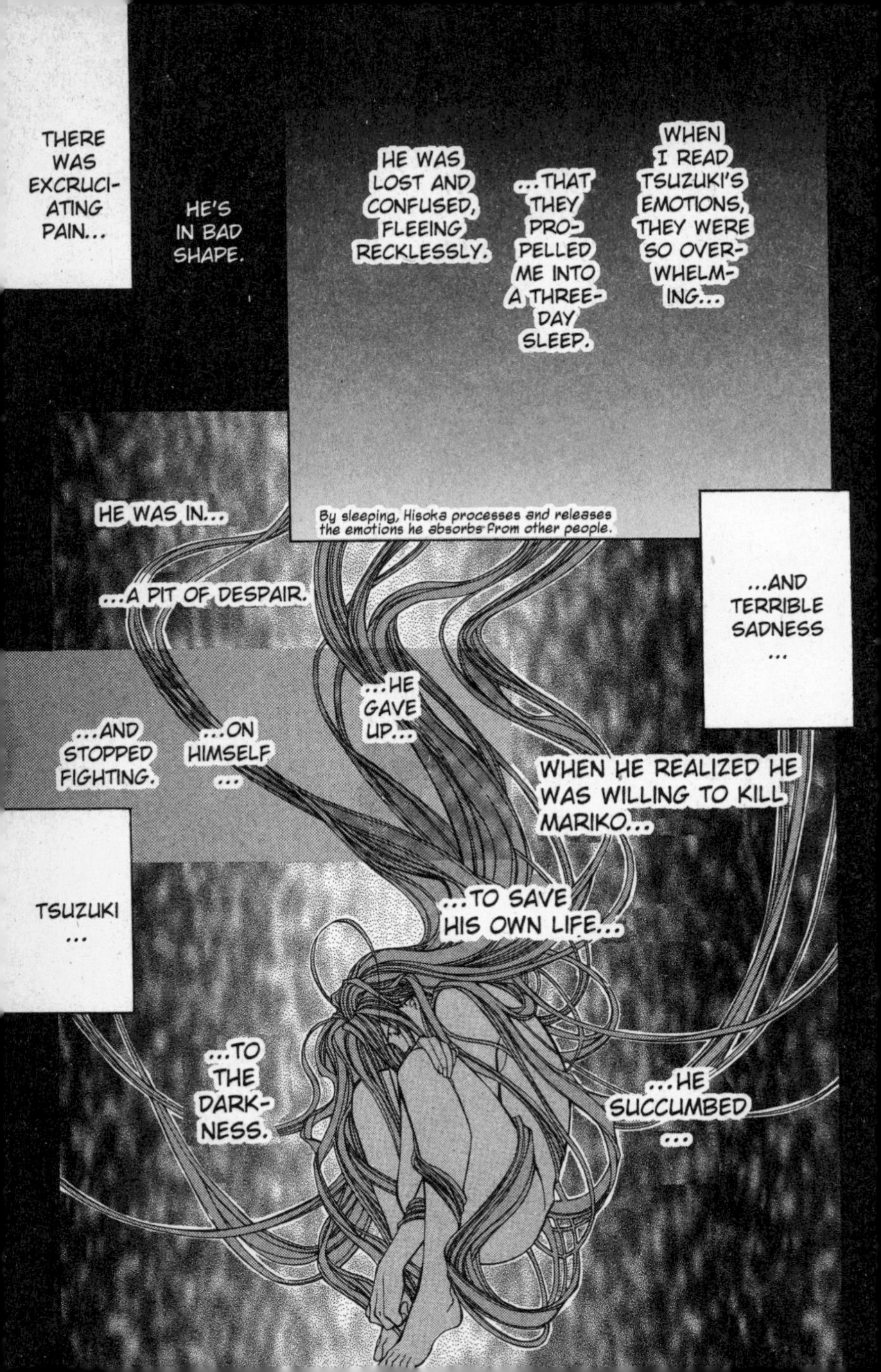
WHEN I READ TSUZUKI'S EMOTIONS, THEY WERE SO OVER-WHELMING...
...THAT THEY PRO-PELLED ME INTO A THREE-DAY SLEEP.
HE WAS LOST AND CONFUSED, FLEEING RECKLESSLY.
By sleeping, Hisoka processes and releases the emotions he absorbs from other people.
HE'S IN BAD SHAPE.
THERE WAS EXCRUCI-ATING PAIN...
...AND TERRIBLE SADNESS ...
HE WAS IN...
...A PIT OF DESPAIR.
...HE GAVE UP...
...ON HIMSELF ...
...AND STOPPED FIGHTING.
WHEN HE REALIZED HE WAS WILLING TO KILL MARIKO...
...TO SAVE HIS OWN LIFE...
...HE SUCCUMBED ...
...TO THE DARK-NESS.
TSUZUKI ...

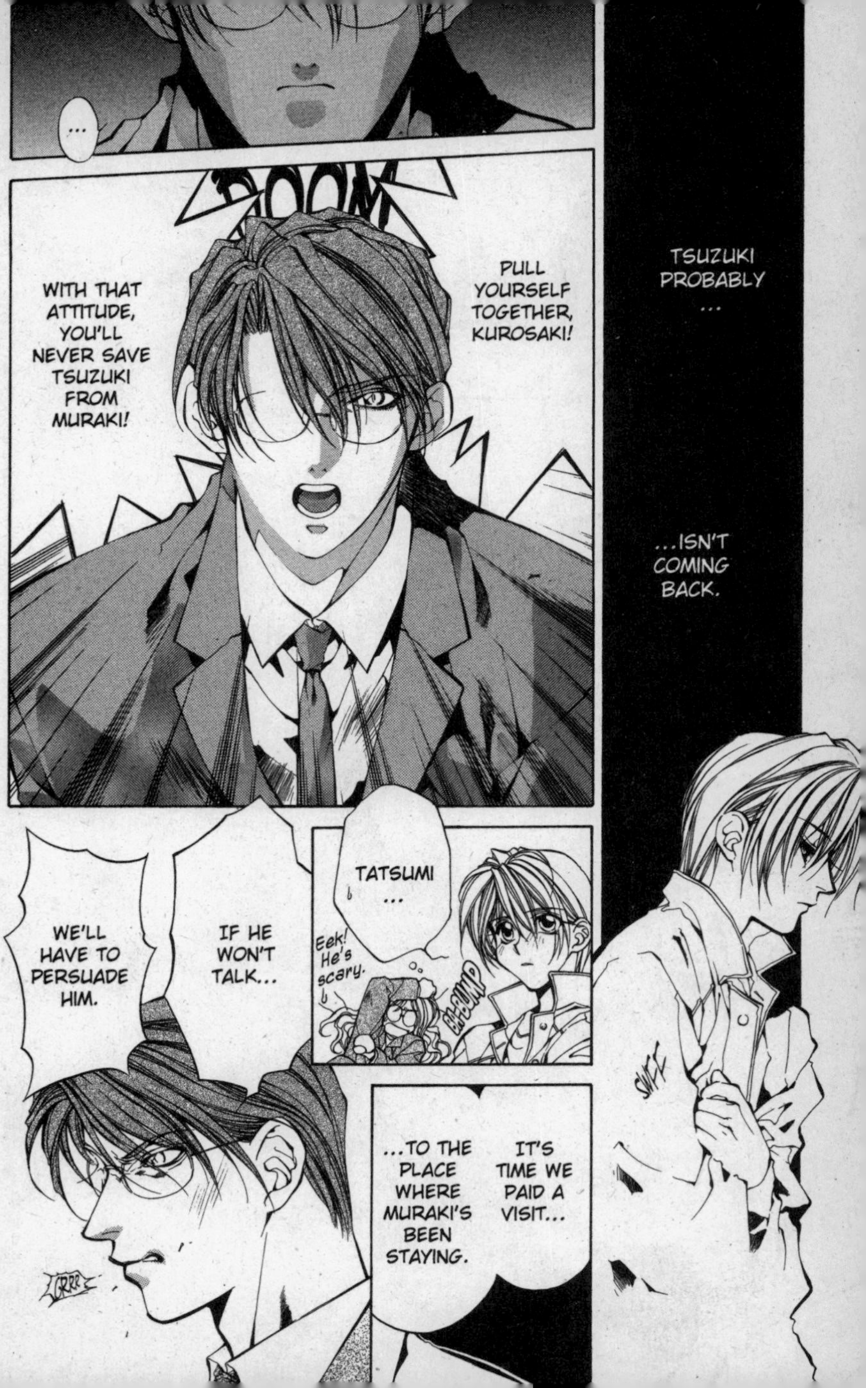

TSUZUKI PROBABLY...
...ISN'T COMING BACK.
SNIFF
...
DOOM
PULL YOURSELF TOGETHER, KUROSAKI!
WITH THAT ATTITUDE, YOU'LL NEVER SAVE TSUZUKI FROM MURAKI!
TATSUMI...
BA-BUMP
Eek! He's scary.
IF HE WON'T TALK...
WE'LL HAVE TO PERSUADE HIM.
GRRR
IT'S TIME WE PAID A VISIT...
...TO THE PLACE WHERE MURAKI'S BEEN STAYING.

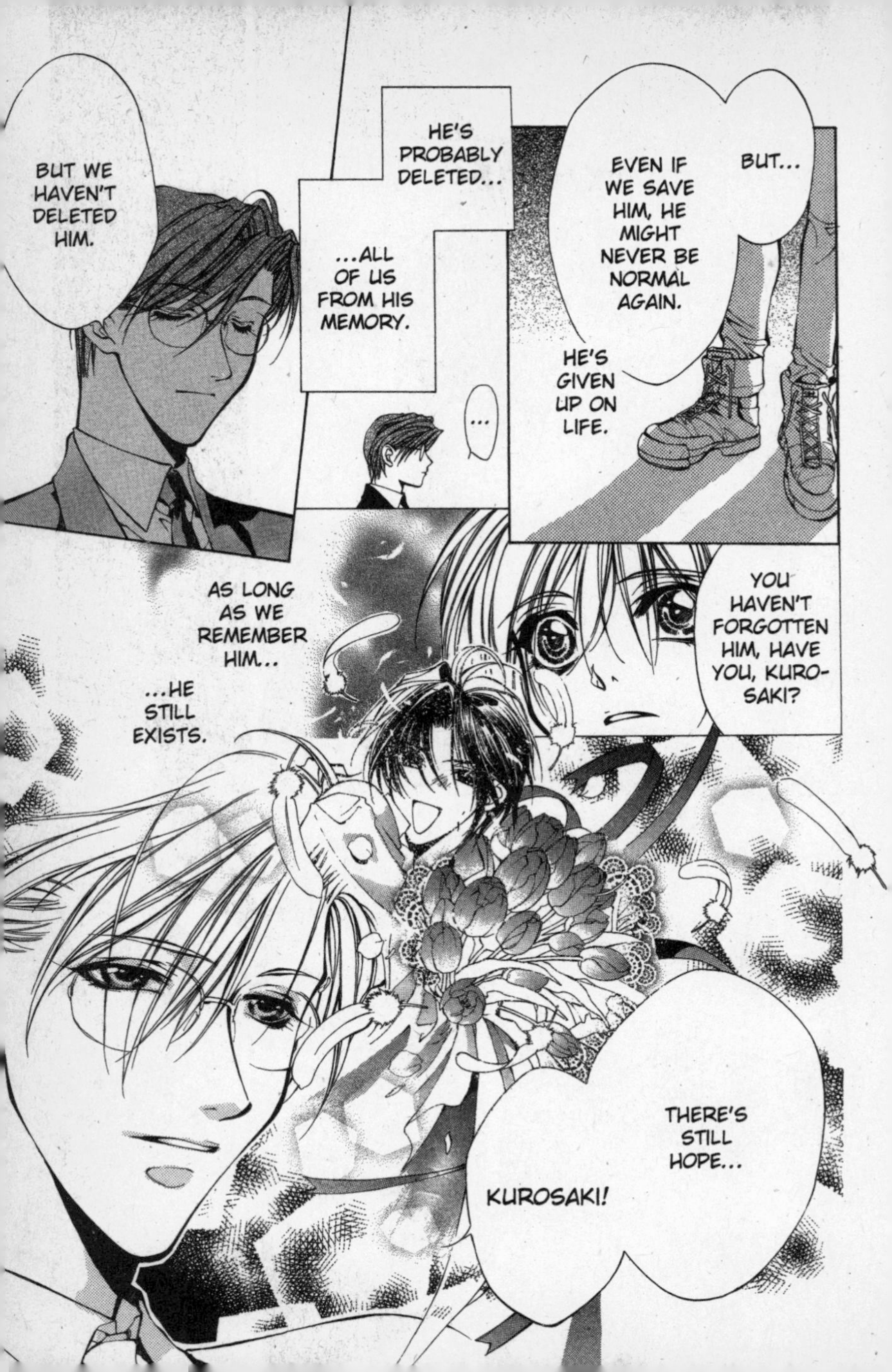
BUT...
EVEN IF WE SAVE HIM, HE MIGHT NEVER BE NORMAL AGAIN.
HE'S GIVEN UP ON LIFE.
HE'S PROBABLY DELETED...
...ALL OF US FROM HIS MEMORY.
...
BUT WE HAVEN'T DELETED HIM.
YOU HAVEN'T FORGOTTEN HIM, HAVE YOU, KURO-SAKI?
AS LONG AS WE REMEMBER HIM...
...HE STILL EXISTS.
THERE'S STILL HOPE...
KUROSAKI!

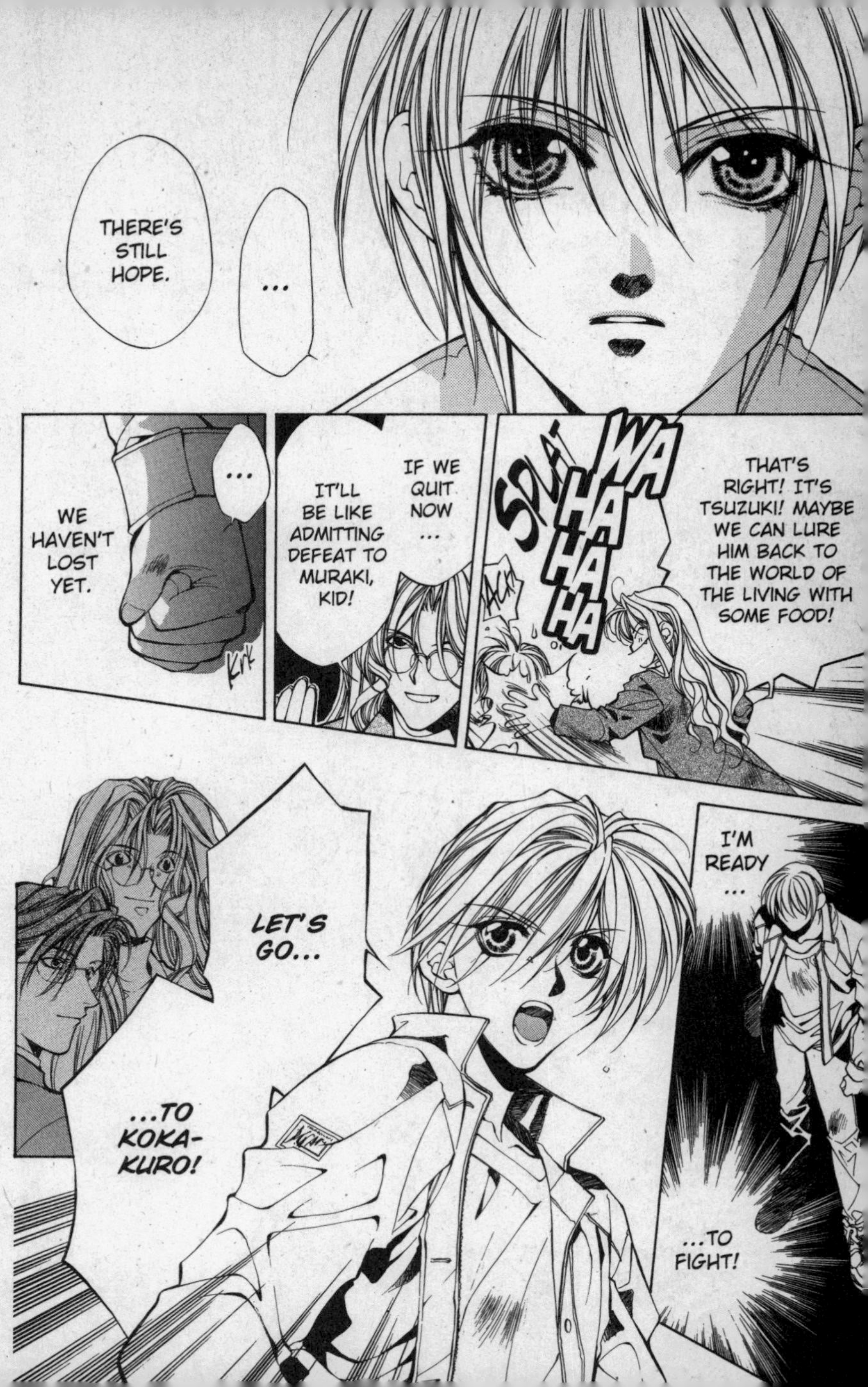
...
THERE'S STILL HOPE.
THAT'S RIGHT! IT'S TSUZUKI! MAYBE WE CAN LURE HIM BACK TO THE WORLD OF THE LIVING WITH SOME FOOD!
WA HA HA HA HA HA
IF WE QUIT NOW ...
IT'LL BE LIKE ADMITTING DEFEAT TO MURAKI, KID!
...
WE HAVEN'T LOST YET.
Krik
I'M READY ...
...TO FIGHT!
LET'S GO...
...TO KOKA-KURO!

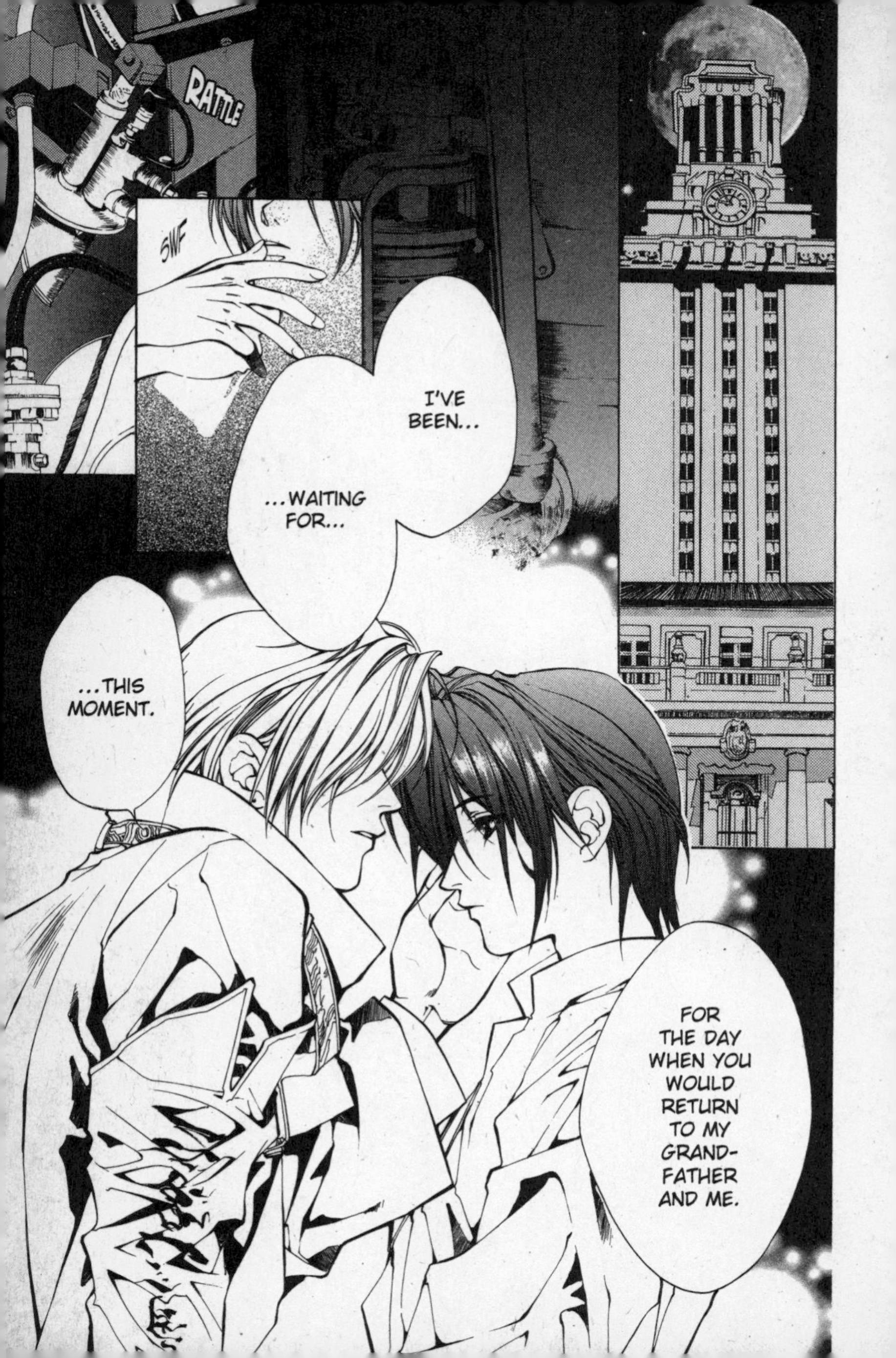
RATTLE
SWF
I'VE BEEN...
...WAITING FOR...
...THIS MOMENT.
FOR THE DAY WHEN YOU WOULD RETURN TO MY GRAND-FATHER AND ME.

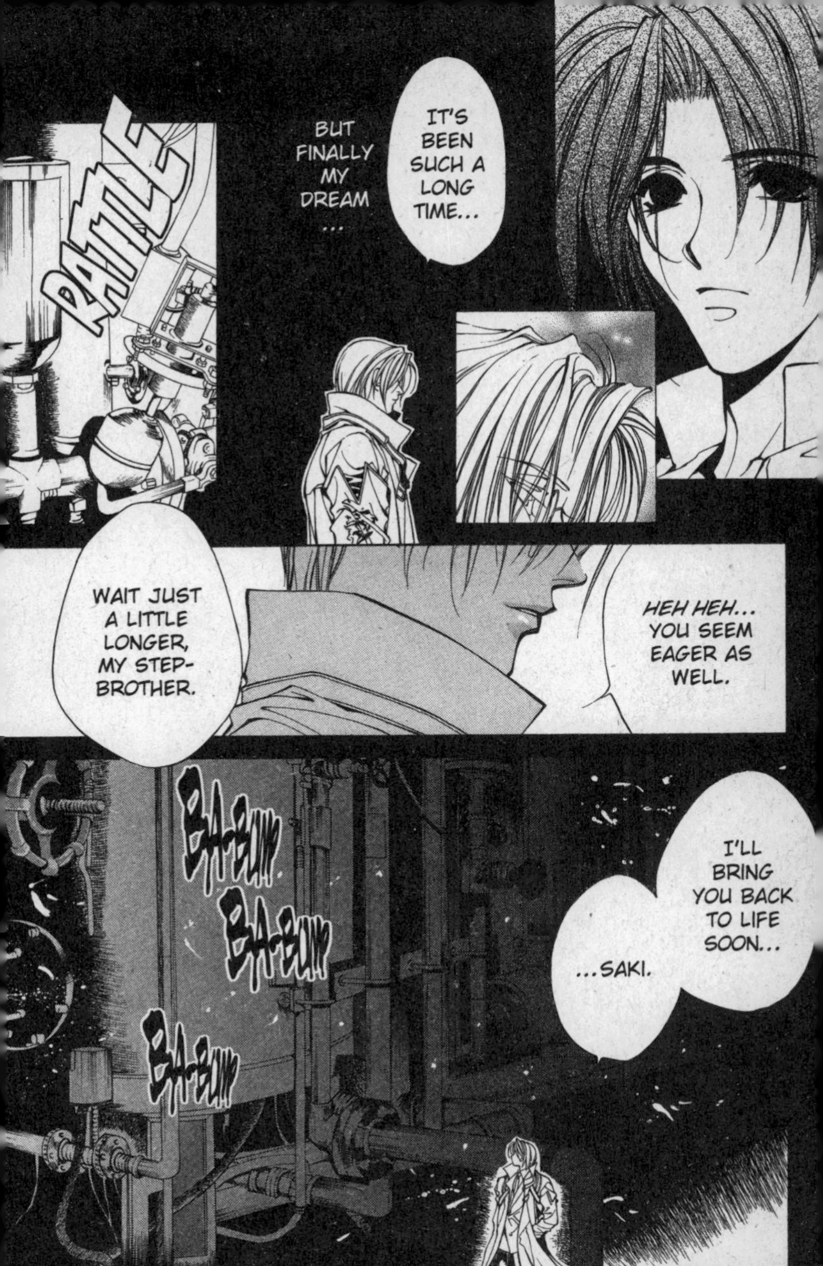
IT'S BEEN SUCH A LONG TIME...
BUT FINALLY MY DREAM...
RATTLE
HEH HEH... YOU SEEM EAGER AS WELL.
WAIT JUST A LITTLE LONGER, MY STEP-BROTHER.
I'LL BRING YOU BACK TO LIFE SOON...
...SAKI.
BA-BUMP
BA-BUMP
BA-BUMP

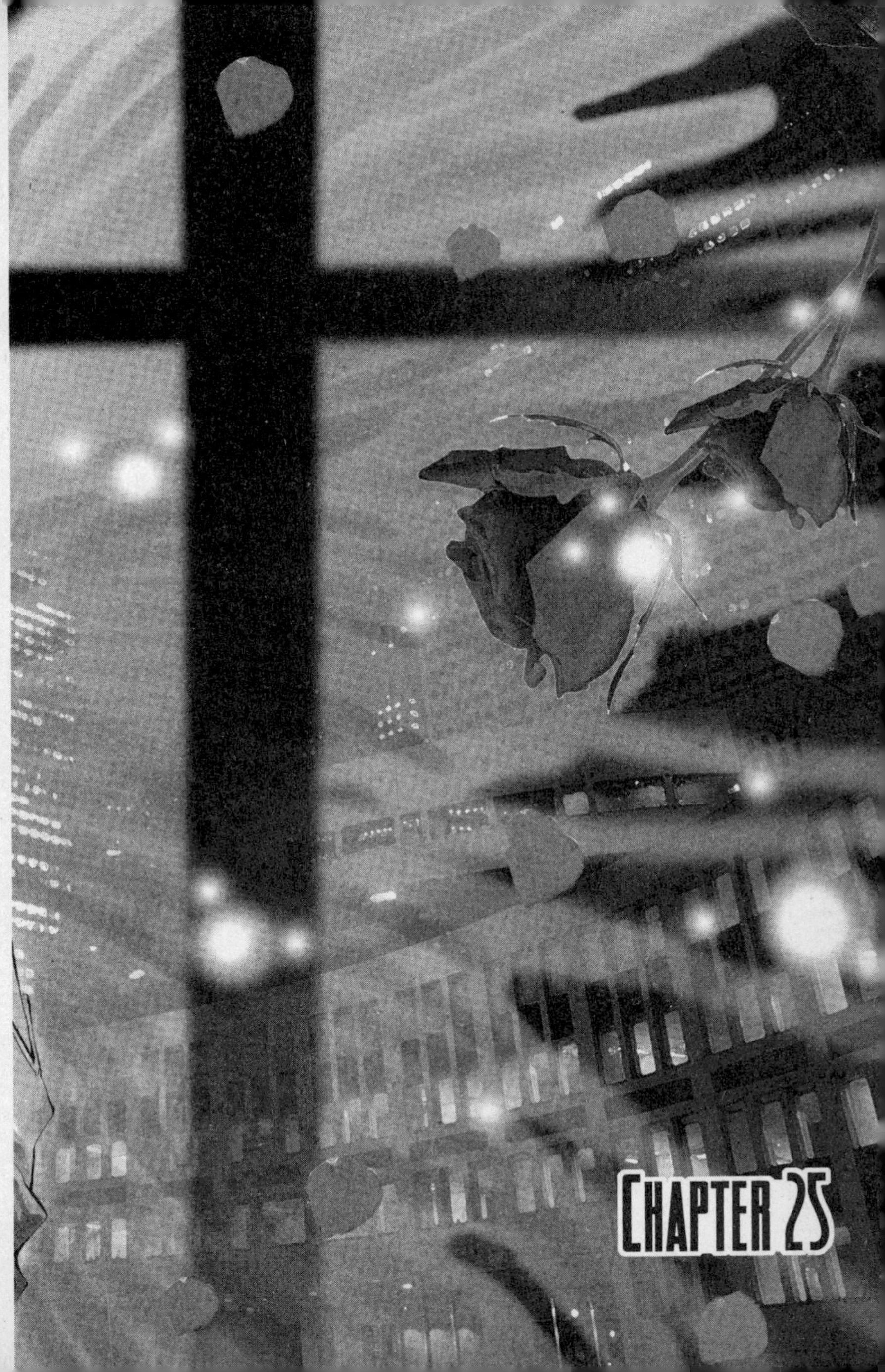
CHAPTER 25

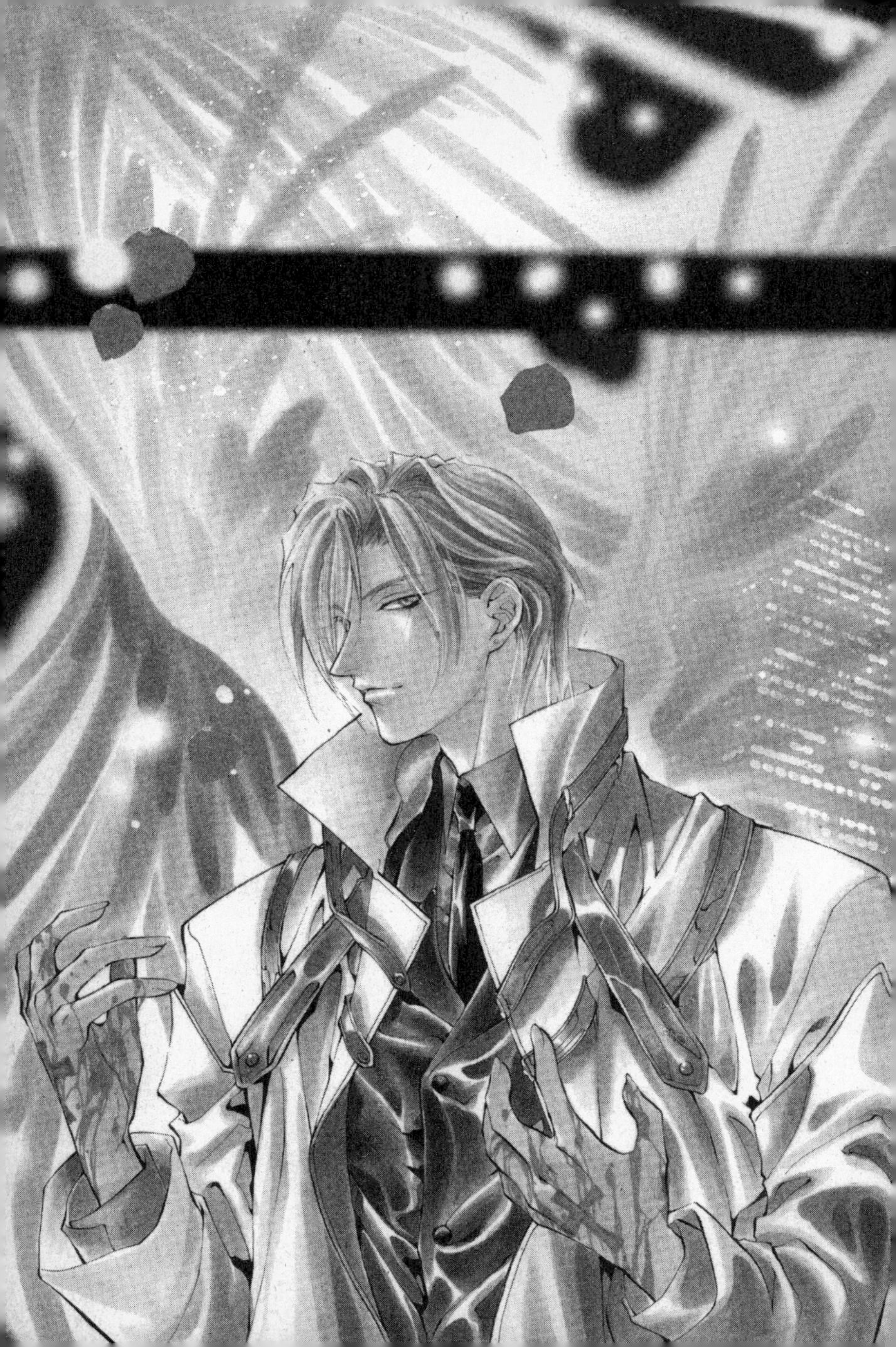

I CAN'T SEE ANYTHING...

I CAN'T HEAR ANYTHING....

DARKNESS FALLS AGAIN...

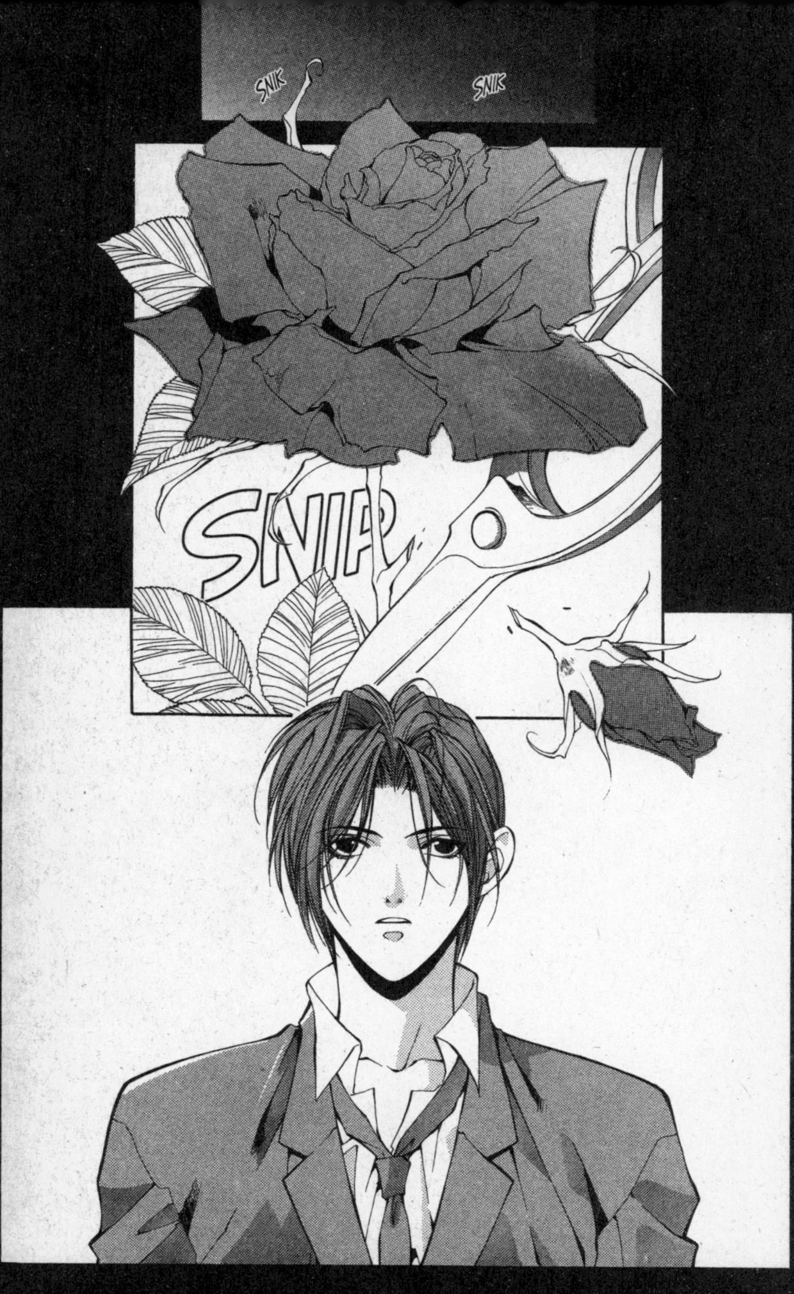
SNIK
SNIK
SNIP

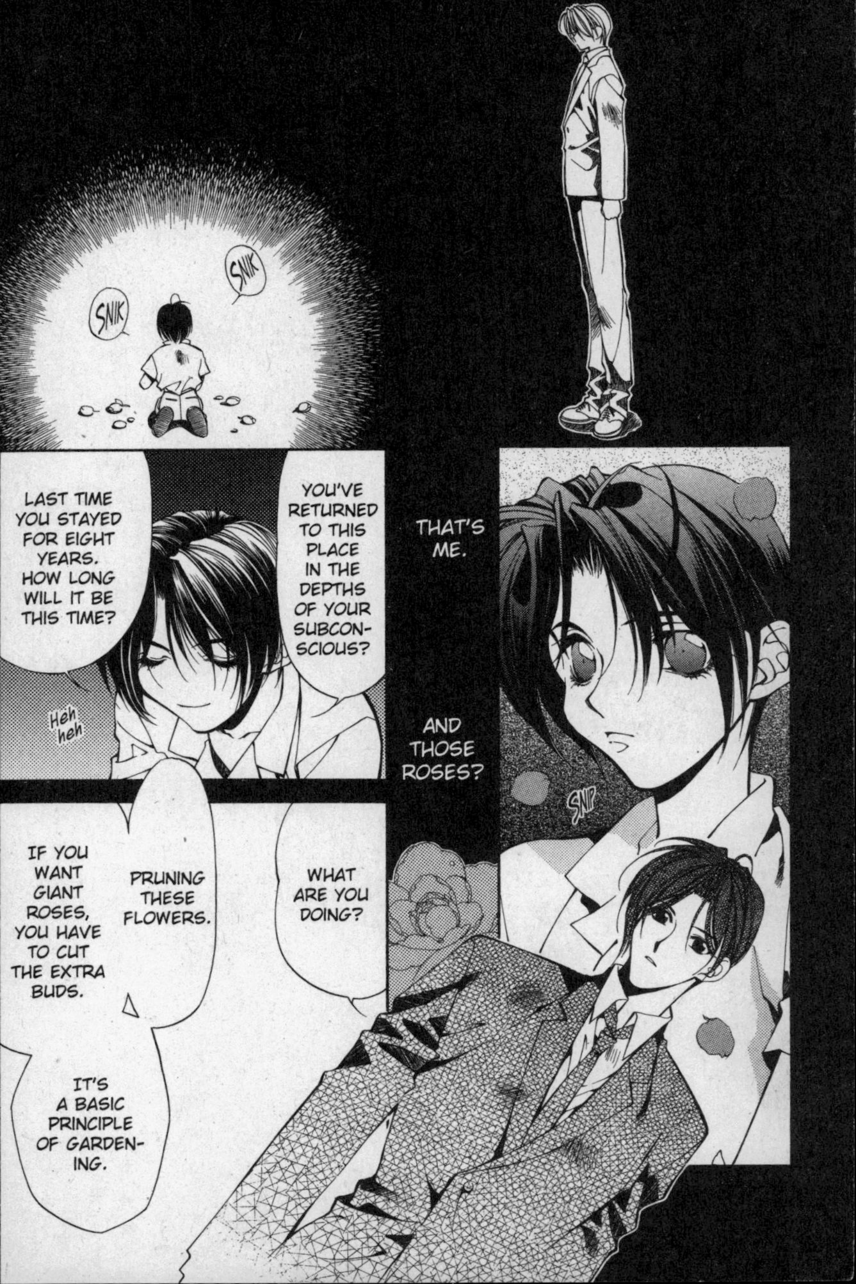
SNIK
SNIK
THAT'S ME.
AND THOSE ROSES?
SNIP
YOU'VE RETURNED TO THIS PLACE IN THE DEPTHS OF YOUR SUBCON-SCIOUS?
LAST TIME YOU STAYED FOR EIGHT YEARS. HOW LONG WILL IT BE THIS TIME?
Heh heh
WHAT ARE YOU DOING?
PRUNING THESE FLOWERS.
IF YOU WANT GIANT ROSES, YOU HAVE TO CUT THE EXTRA BUDS.
IT'S A BASIC PRINCIPLE OF GARDEN-ING.

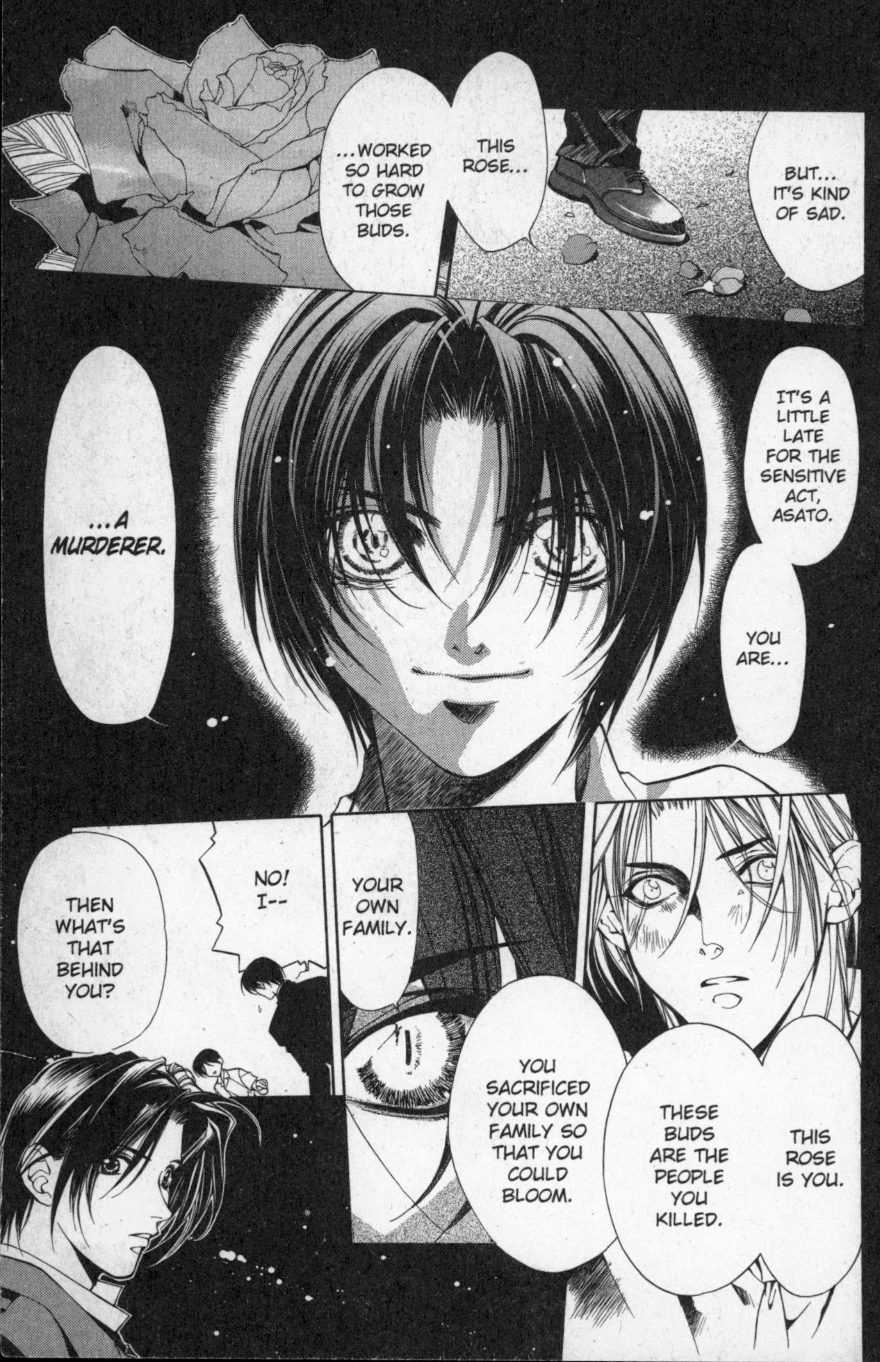
BUT... IT'S KIND OF SAD.
THIS ROSE...
...WORKED SO HARD TO GROW THOSE BUDS.
IT'S A LITTLE LATE FOR THE SENSITIVE ACT, ASATO.
YOU ARE...
...A MURDERER.
THIS ROSE IS YOU.
THESE BUDS ARE THE PEOPLE YOU KILLED.
YOU SACRIFICED YOUR OWN FAMILY SO THAT YOU COULD BLOOM.
YOUR OWN FAMILY.
NO! I--
THEN WHAT'S THAT BEHIND YOU?

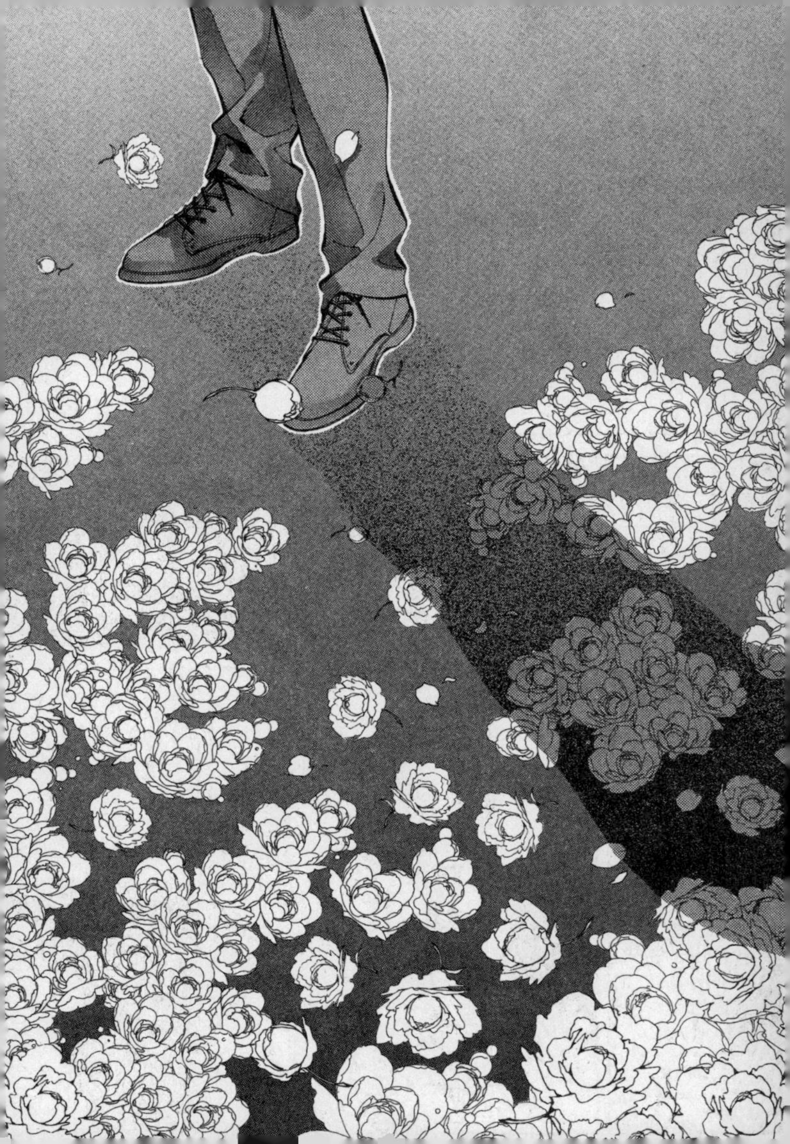

SWP
TUP

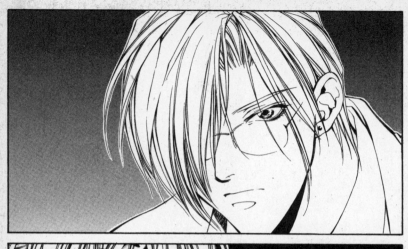

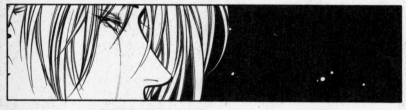

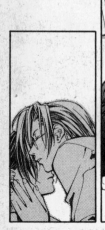

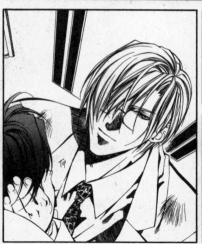

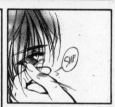

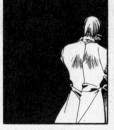

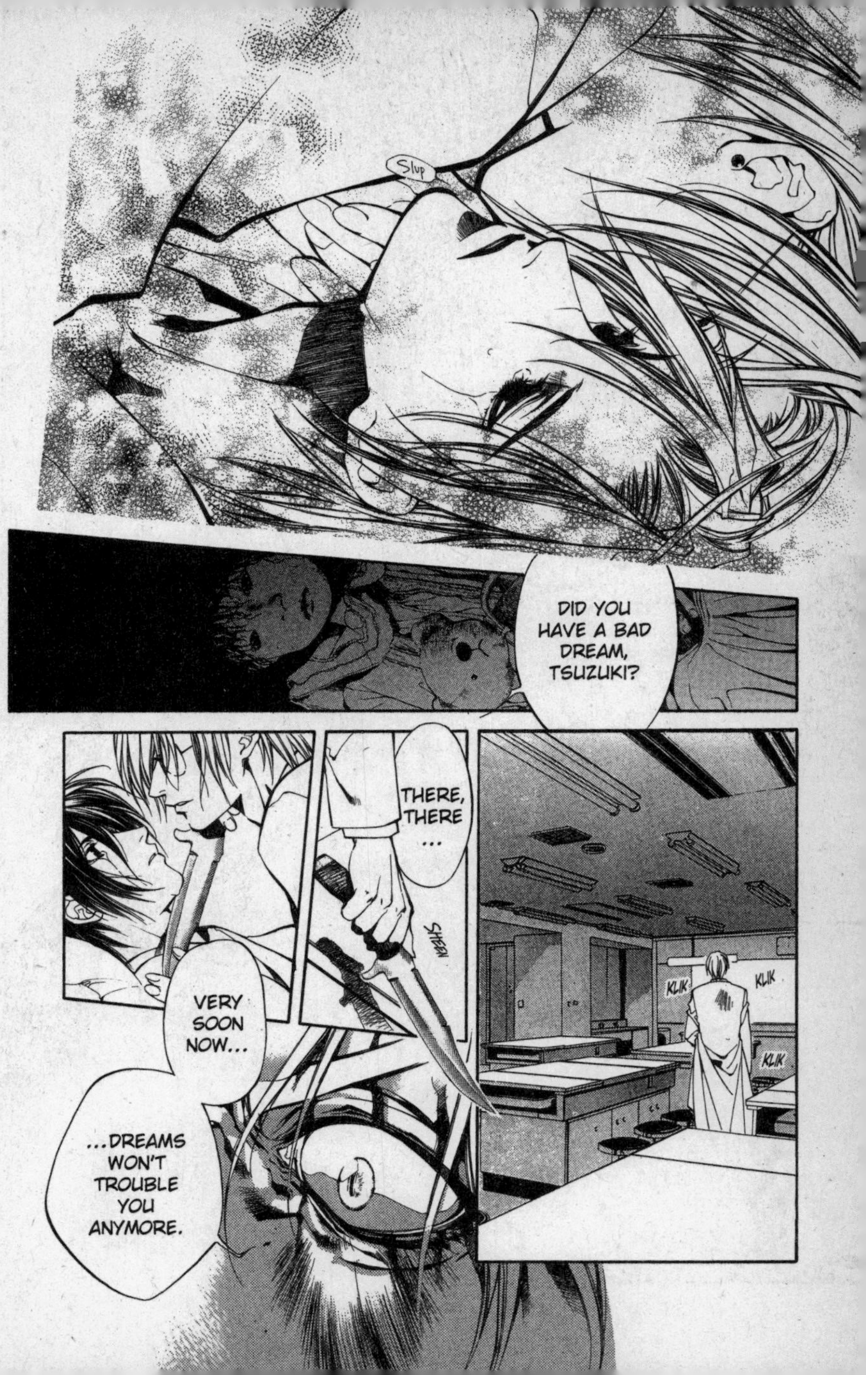
Slup
DID YOU HAVE A BAD DREAM, TSUZUKI?
KLIK
KLIK
KLIK
THERE, THERE ...
SHEEN
VERY SOON NOW...
...DREAMS WON'T TROUBLE YOU ANYMORE.

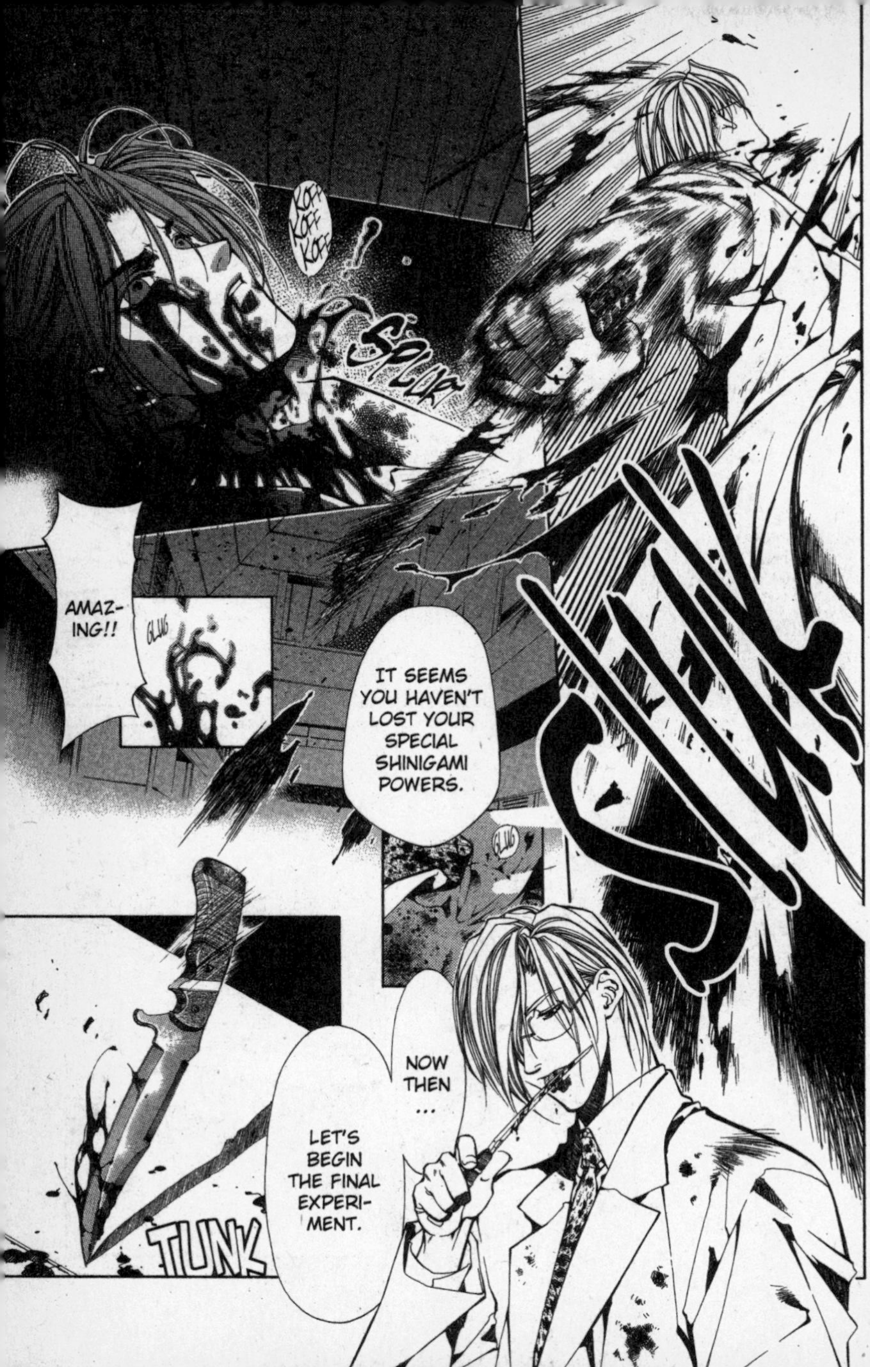

KOFF KOFF KOFF
SPLUR
IT SEEMS YOU HAVEN'T LOST YOUR SPECIAL SHINIGAMI POWERS.
GLUG
AMAZ-ING!!
GLUG
NOW THEN ...
LET'S BEGIN THE FINAL EXPERI-MENT.
TUNK

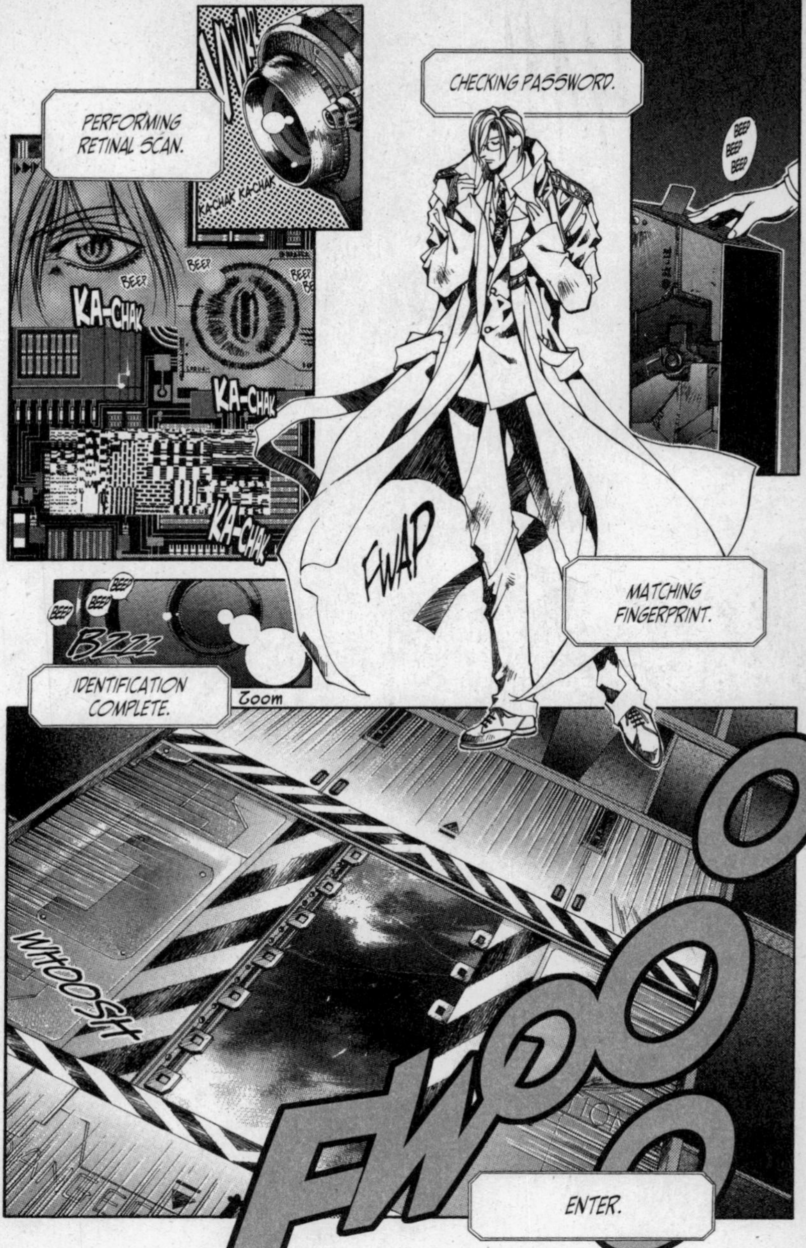
CHECKING PASSWORD.
BEEP BEEP BEEP
PERFORMING RETINAL SCAN.
KA-CHAK KA-CHAK
BEEP
BEEP
BEEP
KA-CHAK
KA-CHAK
KA-CHAK
MATCHING FINGERPRINT.
FWAP
BEEP
BEEP
BEEP
BZZZ
IDENTIFICATION COMPLETE.
ZOOM
FWOOO
WHOOSH
ENTER.

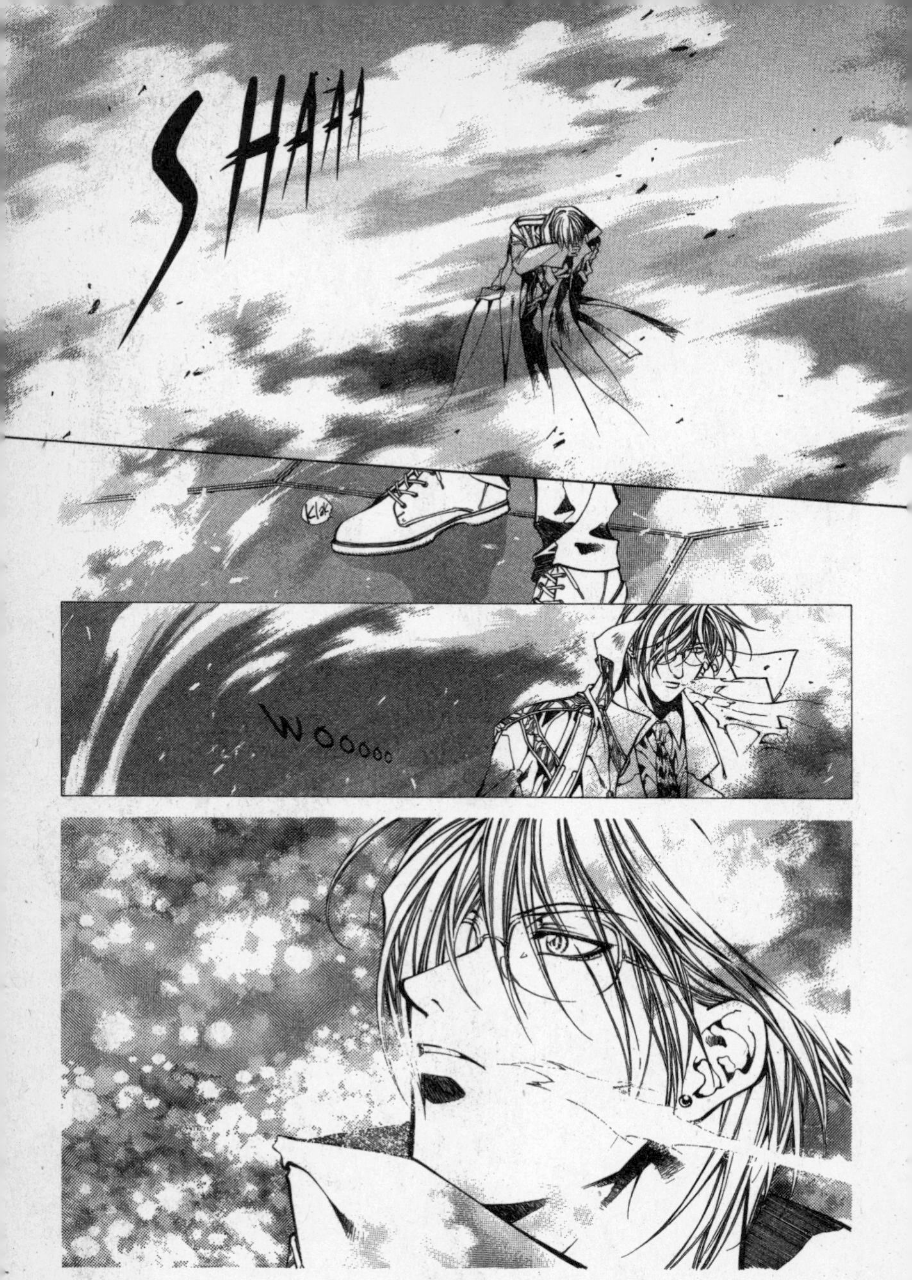
SHAAA
Klak
WOOOOO

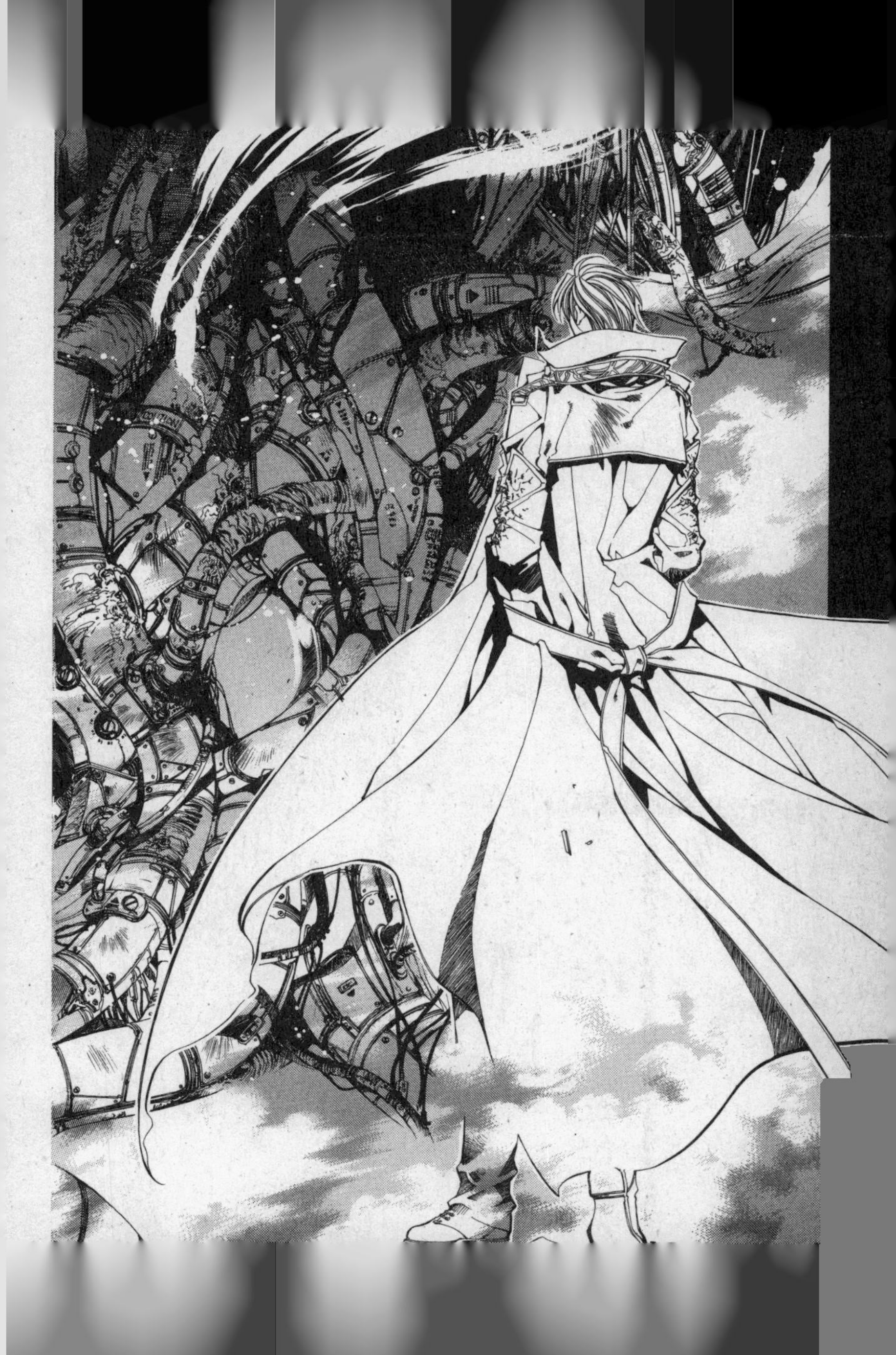

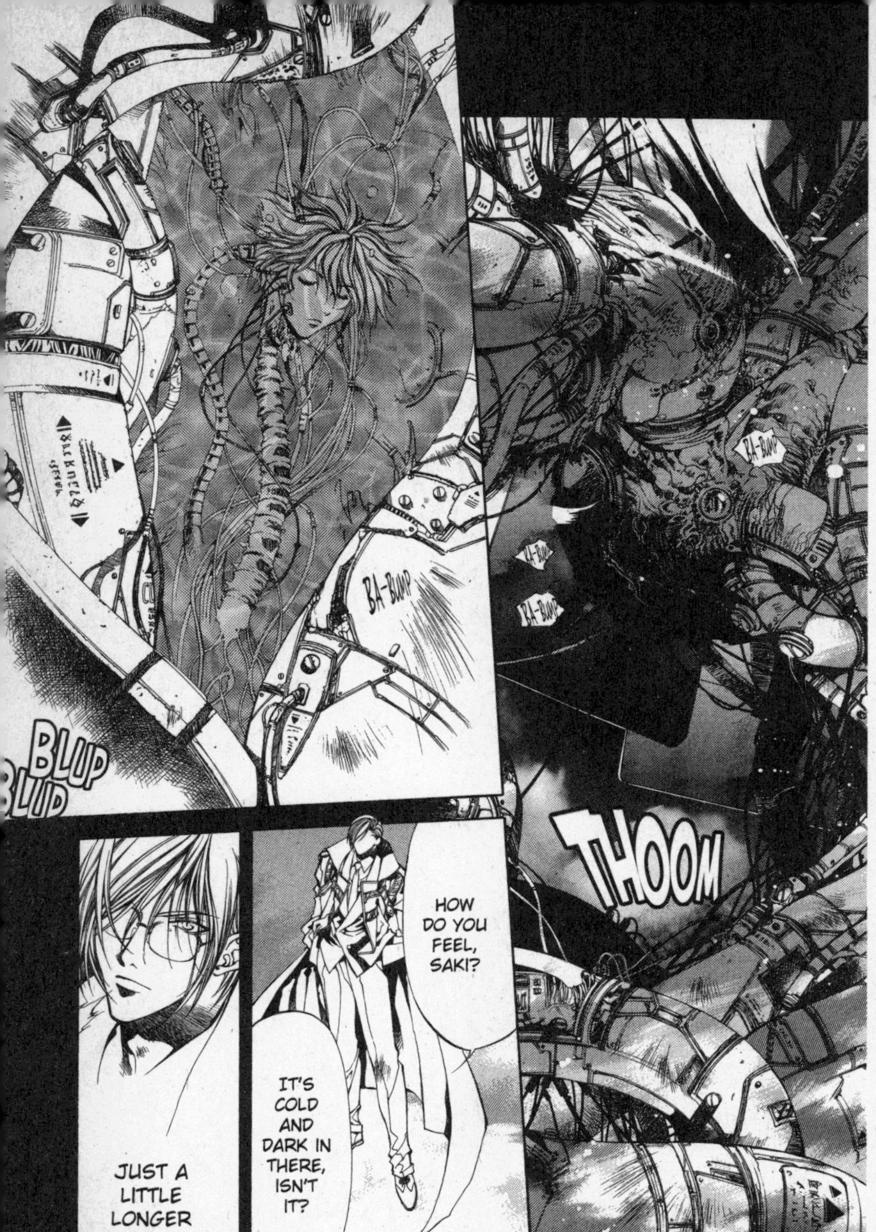
BA-BUMP
BA-BUMP
BA-BUMP
THOOM
BA-BUMP
BLUP BLUP
HOW DO YOU FEEL, SAKI?
IT'S COLD AND DARK IN THERE, ISN'T IT?
JUST A LITTLE LONGER NOW.

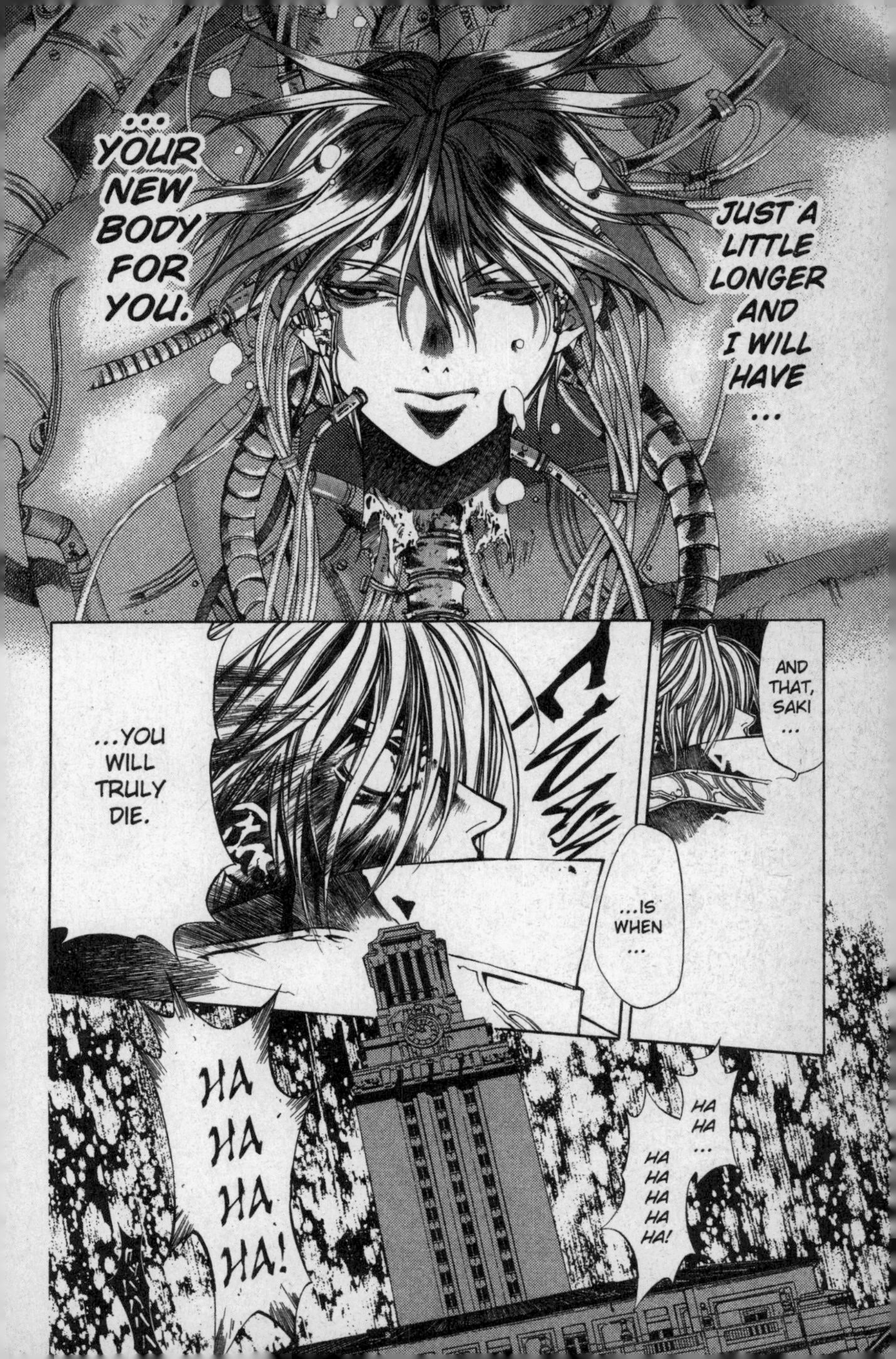
JUST A LITTLE LONGER AND I WILL HAVE ...
... YOUR NEW BODY FOR YOU.
AND THAT, SAKI ...
...IS WHEN ...
...YOU WILL TRULY DIE.
HA HA ...
HA HA HA HA HA!
HA HA HA HA!

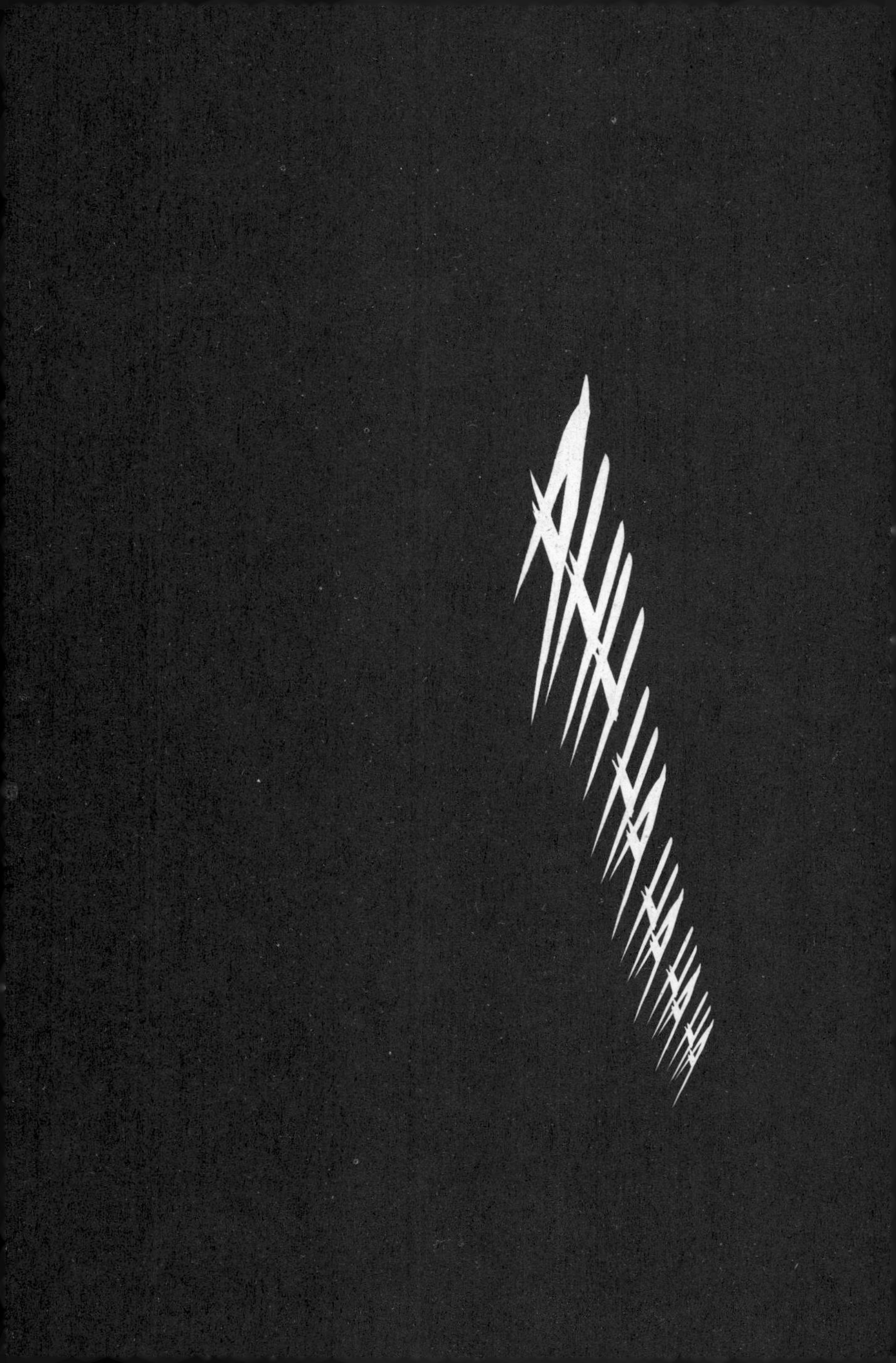

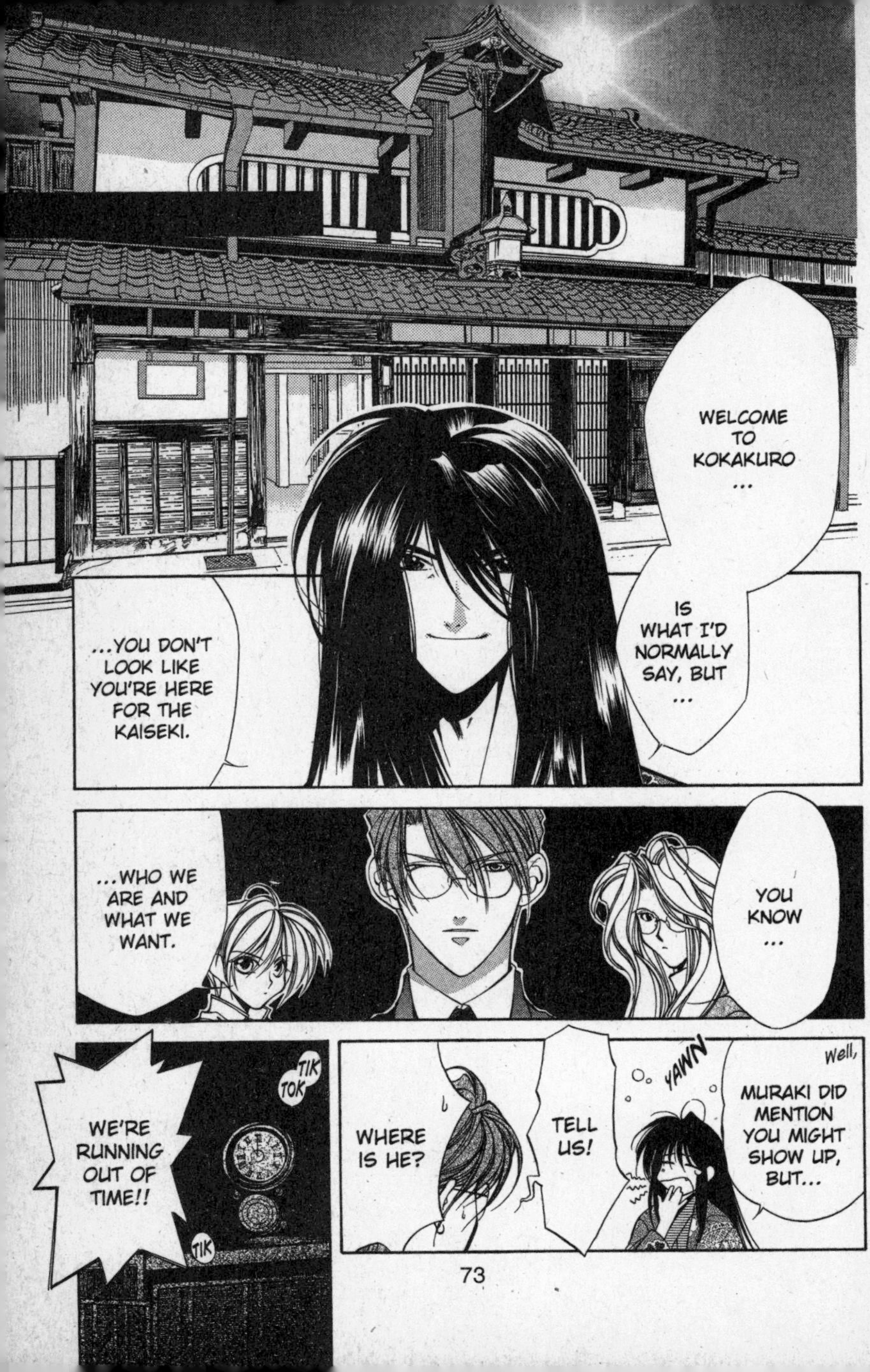
WELCOME TO KOKAKURO ...
IS WHAT I'D NORMALLY SAY, BUT ...
...YOU DON'T LOOK LIKE YOU'RE HERE FOR THE KAISEKI.
YOU KNOW ...
...WHO WE ARE AND WHAT WE WANT.
Well,
MURAKI DID MENTION YOU MIGHT SHOW UP, BUT...
YAWN
TELL US!
WHERE IS HE?
TIK TOK
WE'RE RUNNING OUT OF TIME!!
TIK

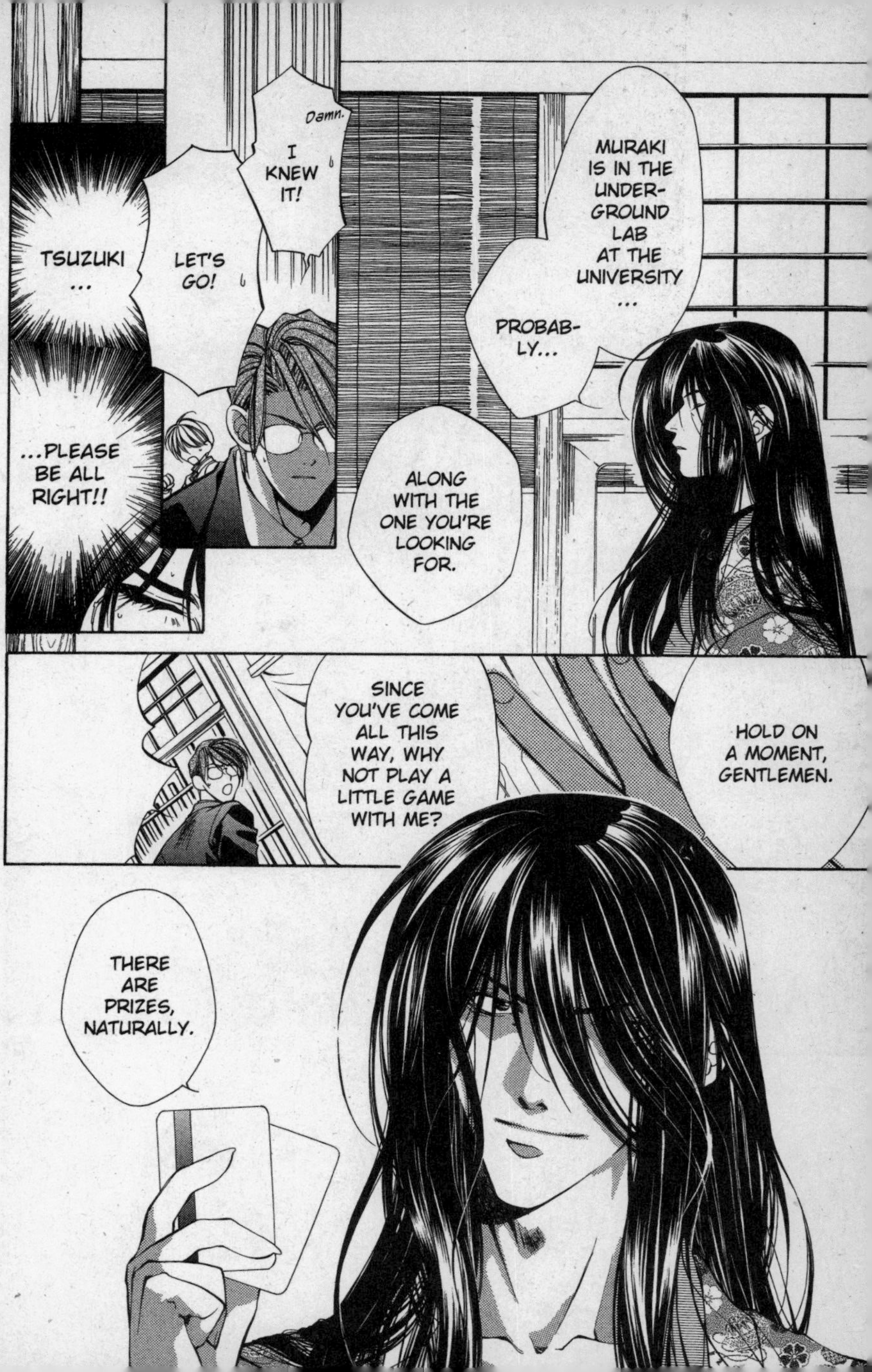
MURAKI IS IN THE UNDER-GROUND LAB AT THE UNIVERSITY ...
PROBAB-LY...
ALONG WITH THE ONE YOU'RE LOOKING FOR.
Damn.
I KNEW IT!
LET'S GO!
TSUZUKI ...
...PLEASE BE ALL RIGHT!!
HOLD ON A MOMENT, GENTLEMEN.
SINCE YOU'VE COME ALL THIS WAY, WHY NOT PLAY A LITTLE GAME WITH ME?
THERE ARE PRIZES, NATURALLY.

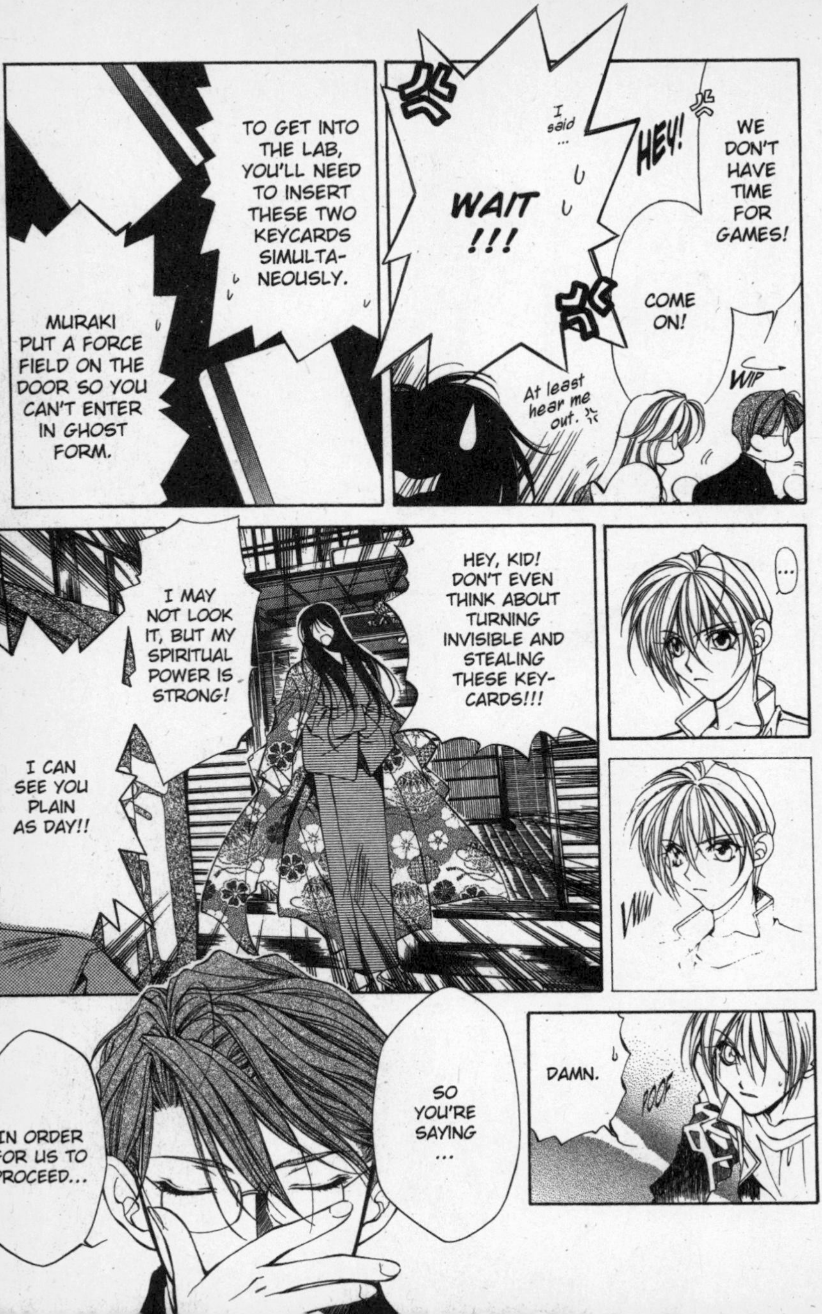
WE DON'T HAVE TIME FOR GAMES!
HEY!
I said ...
WAIT!!!
COME ON!
WIP
At least hear me out.
TO GET INTO THE LAB, YOU'LL NEED TO INSERT THESE TWO KEYCARDS SIMULTA-NEOUSLY.
MURAKI PUT A FORCE FIELD ON THE DOOR SO YOU CAN'T ENTER IN GHOST FORM.
...
HEY, KID! DON'T EVEN THINK ABOUT TURNING INVISIBLE AND STEALING THESE KEY-CARDS!!!
I MAY NOT LOOK IT, BUT MY SPIRITUAL POWER IS STRONG!
I CAN SEE YOU PLAIN AS DAY!!
DAMN.
SO YOU'RE SAYING ...
IN ORDER FOR US TO PROCEED...

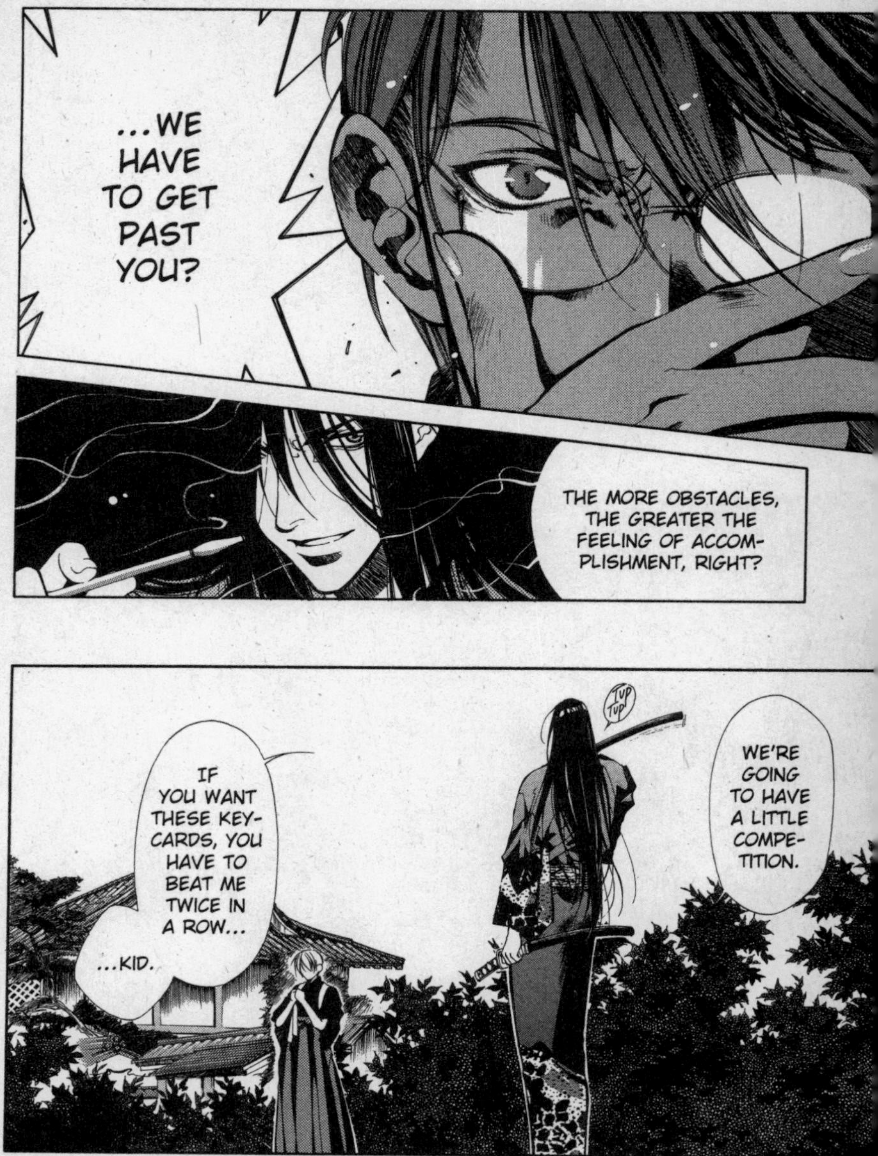
...WE HAVE TO GET PAST YOU?
THE MORE OBSTACLES, THE GREATER THE FEELING OF ACCOMPLISHMENT, RIGHT?
WE'RE GOING TO HAVE A LITTLE COMPETITION.
TUP TUP!
IF YOU WANT THESE KEYCARDS, YOU HAVE TO BEAT ME TWICE IN A ROW...
...KID.

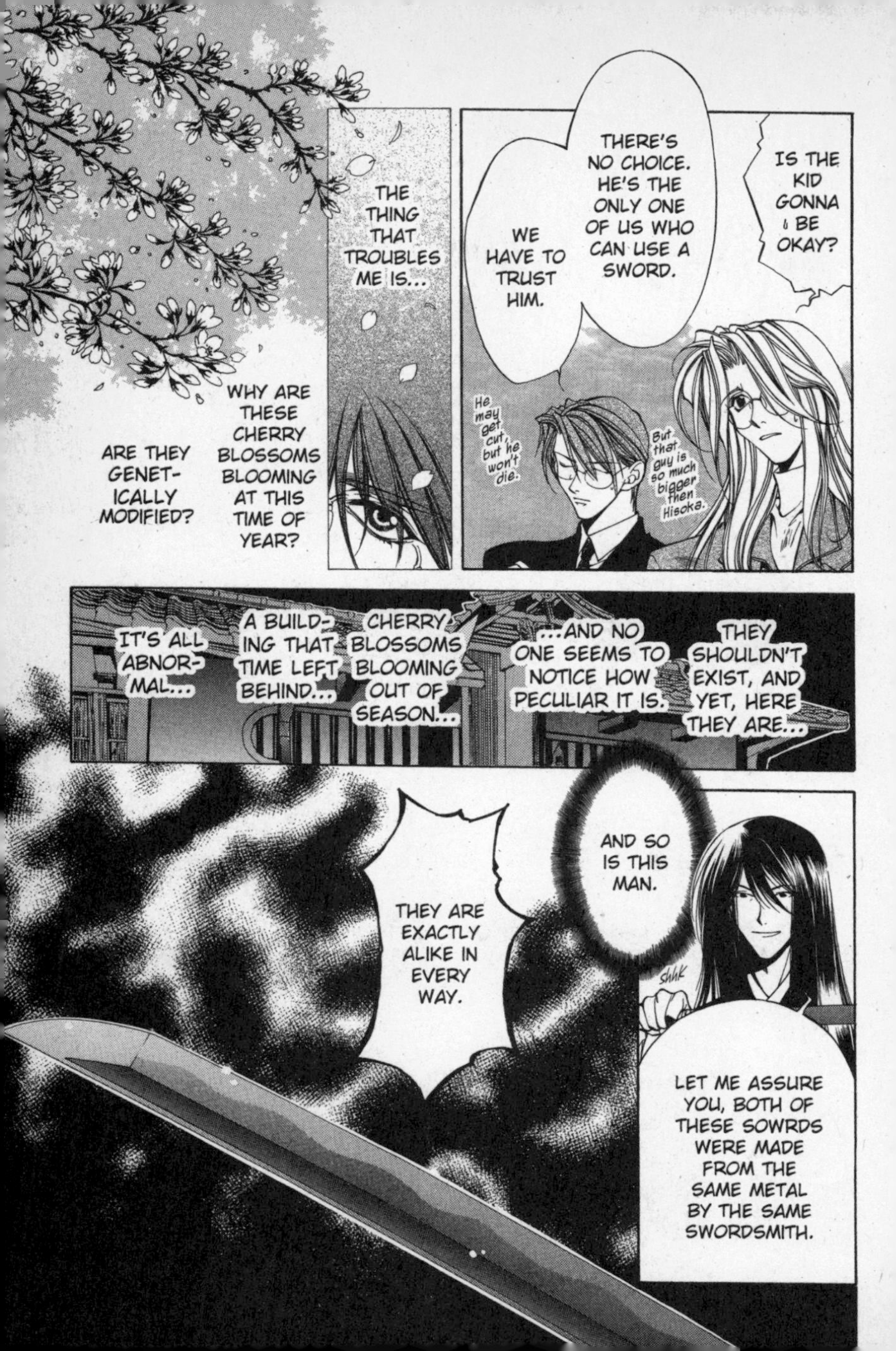
IS THE KID GONNA BE OKAY?
THERE'S NO CHOICE. HE'S THE ONLY ONE OF US WHO CAN USE A SWORD.
WE HAVE TO TRUST HIM.
But that guy is so much bigger then Hisoka.
He may get cut, but he won't die.
THE THING THAT TROUBLES ME IS...
WHY ARE THESE CHERRY BLOSSOMS BLOOMING AT THIS TIME OF YEAR?
ARE THEY GENET-ICALLY MODIFIED?
THEY SHOULDN'T EXIST, AND YET, HERE THEY ARE...
...AND NO ONE SEEMS TO NOTICE HOW PECULIAR IT IS.
CHERRY BLOSSOMS BLOOMING OUT OF SEASON...
A BUILD-ING THAT TIME LEFT BEHIND...
IT'S ALL ABNOR-MAL...
AND SO IS THIS MAN.
shhk
LET ME ASSURE YOU, BOTH OF THESE SOWRDS WERE MADE FROM THE SAME METAL BY THE SAME SWORDSMITH.
THEY ARE EXACTLY ALIKE IN EVERY WAY.

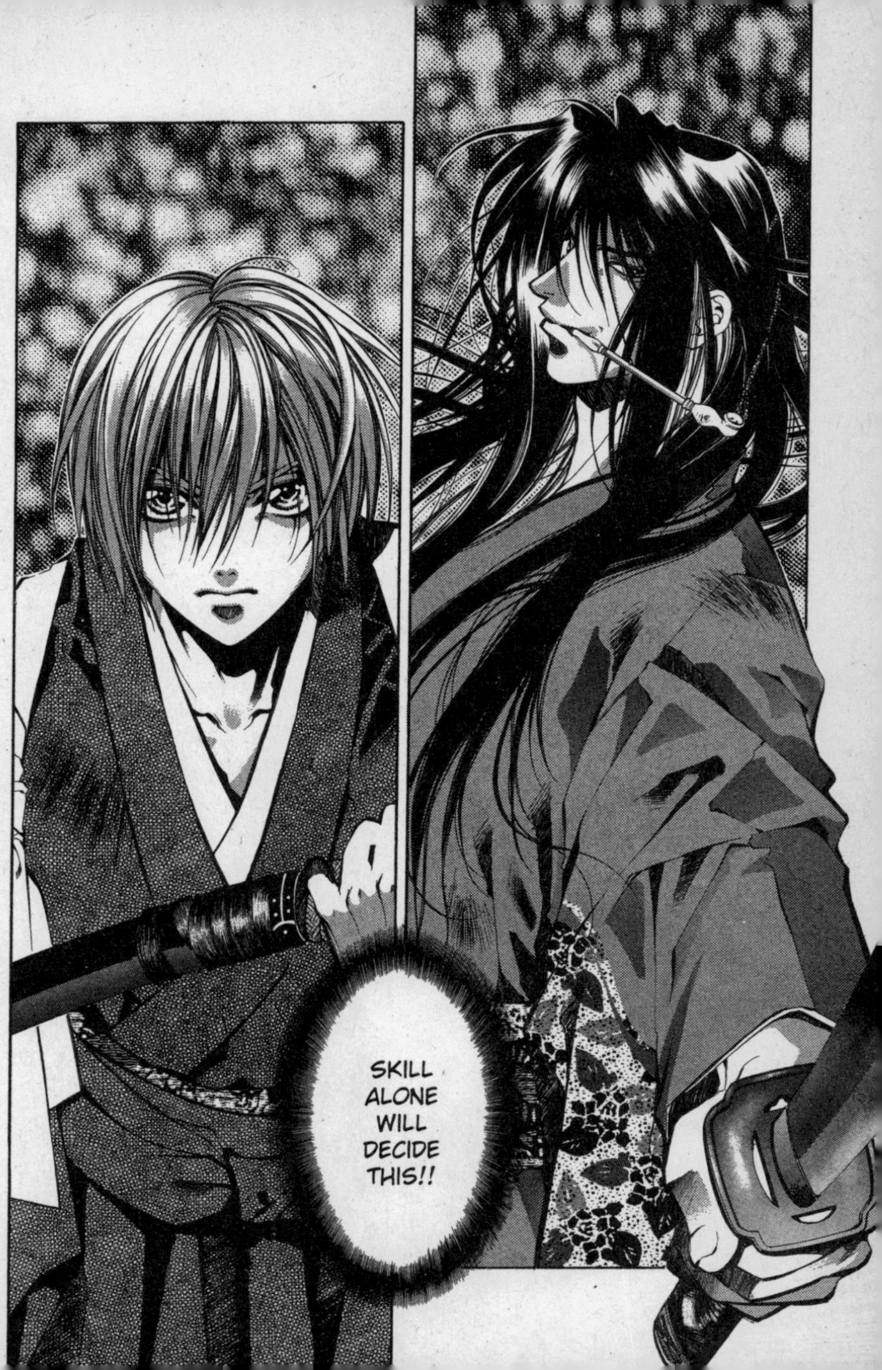
SKILL ALONE WILL DECIDE THIS!!

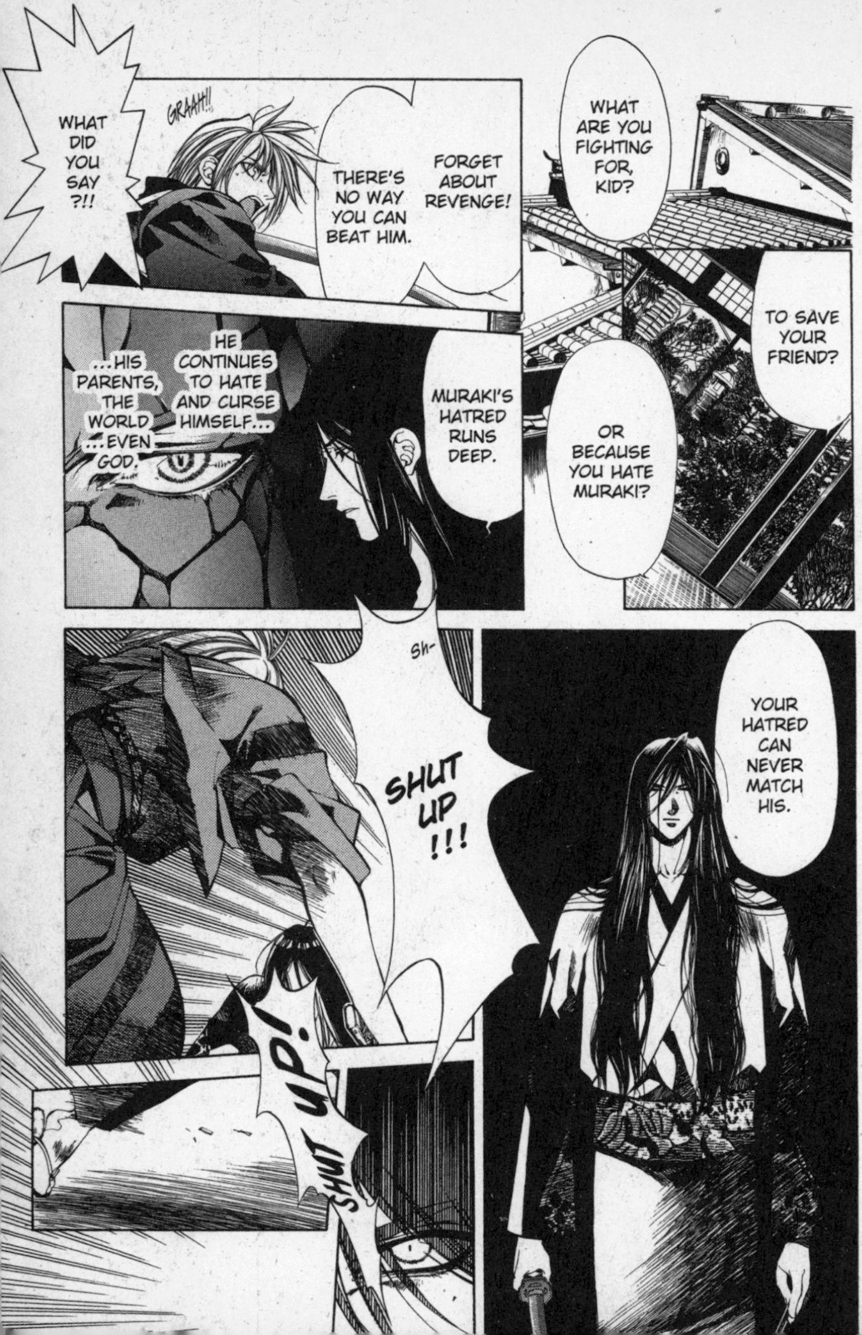
WHAT ARE YOU FIGHTING FOR, KID?
TO SAVE YOUR FRIEND?
OR BECAUSE YOU HATE MURAKI?
FORGET ABOUT REVENGE!
THERE'S NO WAY YOU CAN BEAT HIM.
GRAAH!!
WHAT DID YOU SAY ?!!
MURAKI'S HATRED RUNS DEEP.
HE CONTINUES TO HATE AND CURSE HIMSELF...
...HIS PARENTS, THE WORLD ...EVEN GOD.
YOUR HATRED CAN NEVER MATCH HIS.
Sh-
SHUT UP !!!
SHUT UP!

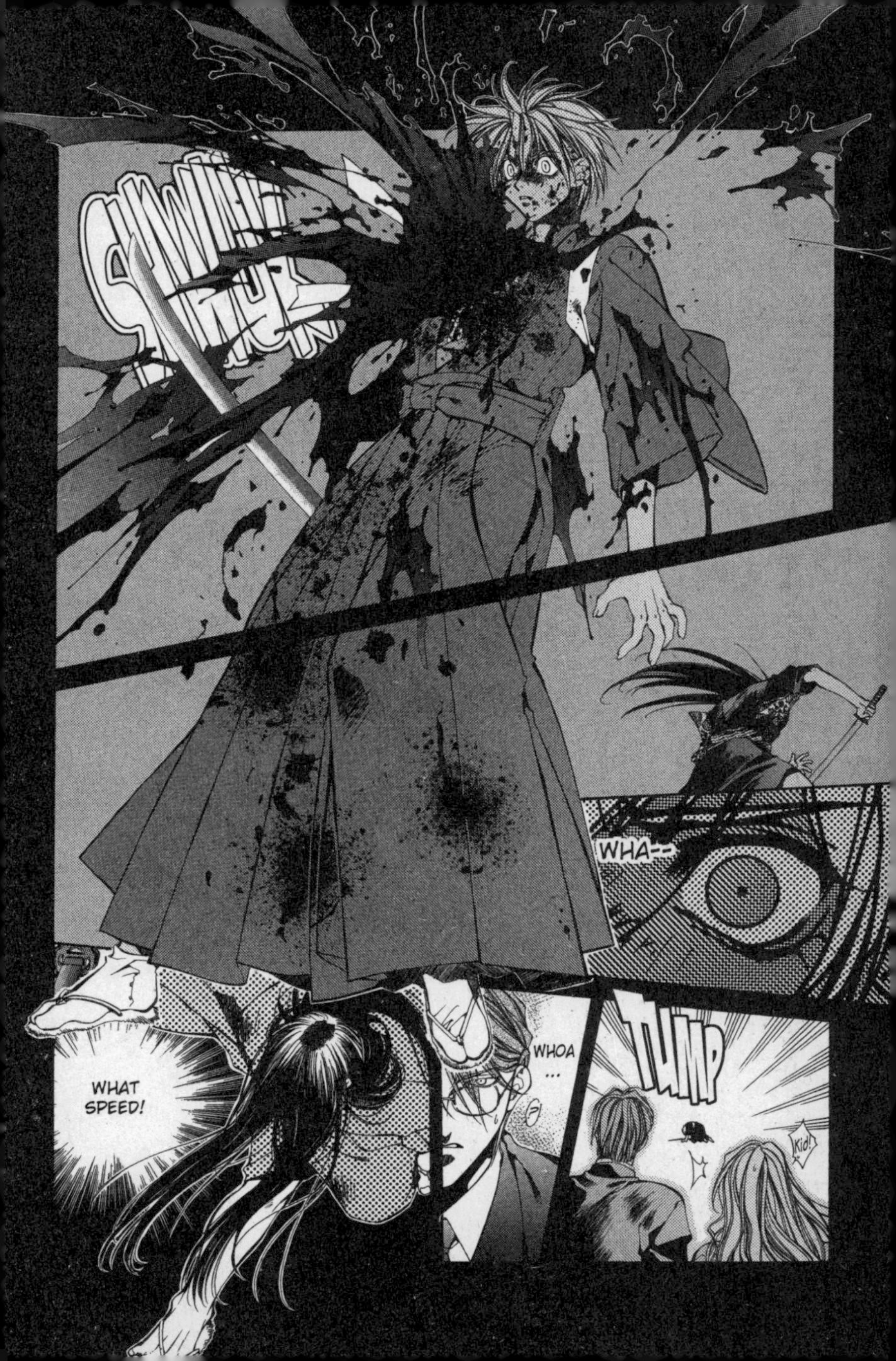
WHA--
TUMP
Kid!
WHOA ...
WHAT SPEED!

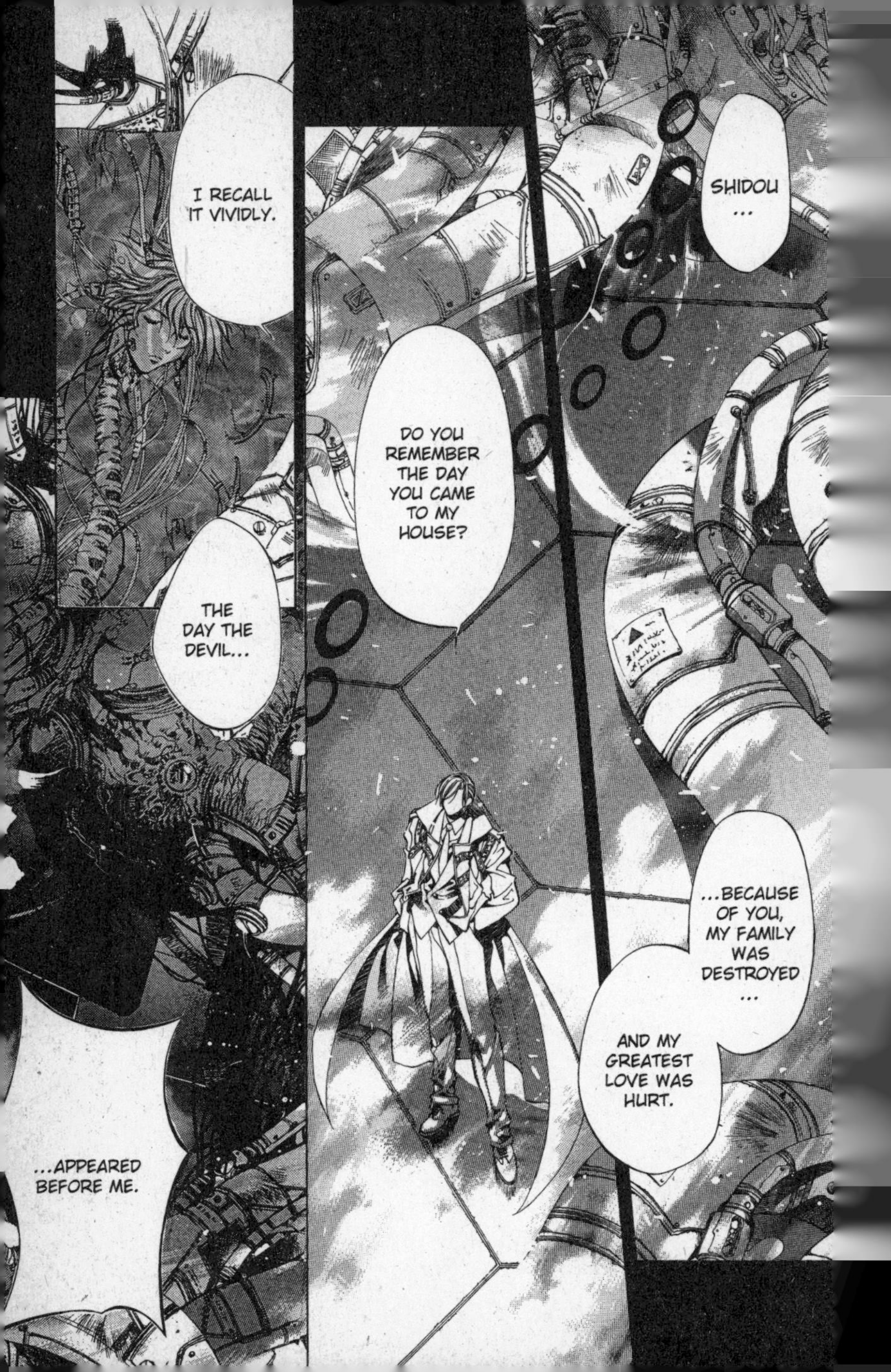
SHIDOU ...
DO YOU REMEMBER THE DAY YOU CAME TO MY HOUSE?
...BECAUSE OF YOU, MY FAMILY WAS DESTROYED ...
AND MY GREATEST LOVE WAS HURT.
I RECALL IT VIVIDLY.
THE DAY THE DEVIL...
...
...APPEARED BEFORE ME.

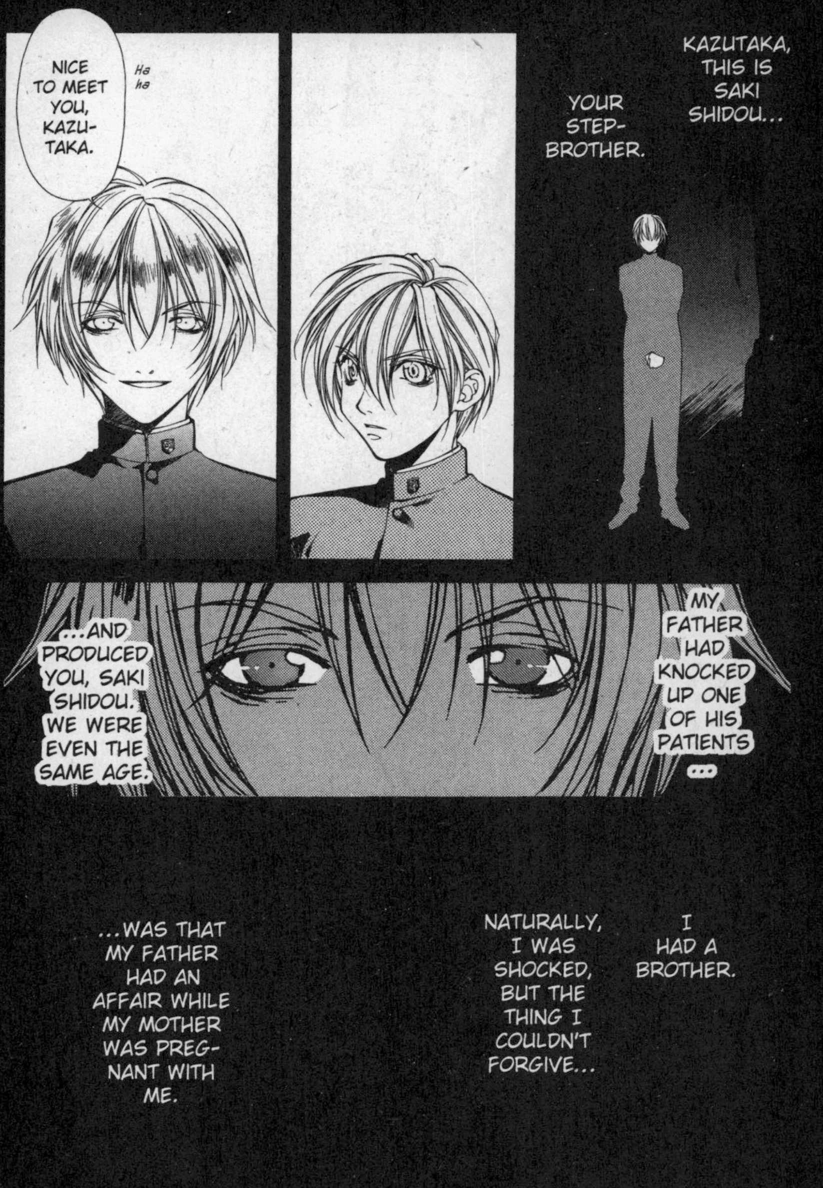
KAZUTAKA, THIS IS SAKI SHIDOU...
YOUR STEP-BROTHER.
NICE TO MEET YOU, KAZU-TAKA.
Ha ha
MY FATHER HAD KNOCKED UP ONE OF HIS PATIENTS...
...AND PRODUCED YOU, SAKI SHIDOU. WE WERE EVEN THE SAME AGE.
I HAD A BROTHER.
NATURALLY, I WAS SHOCKED, BUT THE THING I COULDN'T FORGIVE...
...WAS THAT MY FATHER HAD AN AFFAIR WHILE MY MOTHER WAS PREG-NANT WITH ME.

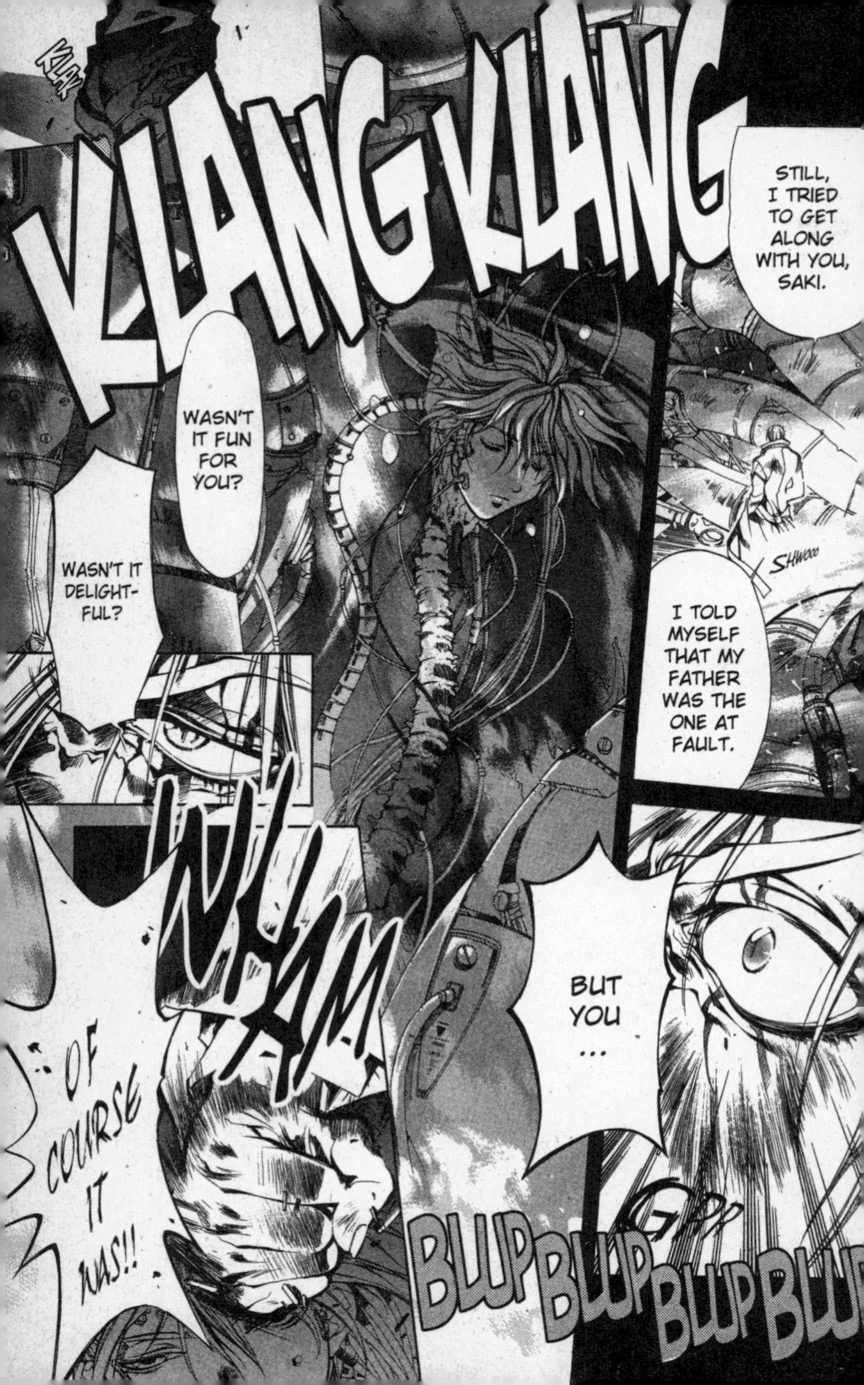
STILL, I TRIED TO GET ALONG WITH YOU, SAKI.
KLANG KLANG
KLAK
SHWOOO
I TOLD MYSELF THAT MY FATHER WAS THE ONE AT FAULT.
WASN'T IT FUN FOR YOU?
WASN'T IT DELIGHT-FUL?
BUT YOU ...
BLUP BLUP BLUP BLUP
GPP
WHAM
OF COURSE IT WAS!!

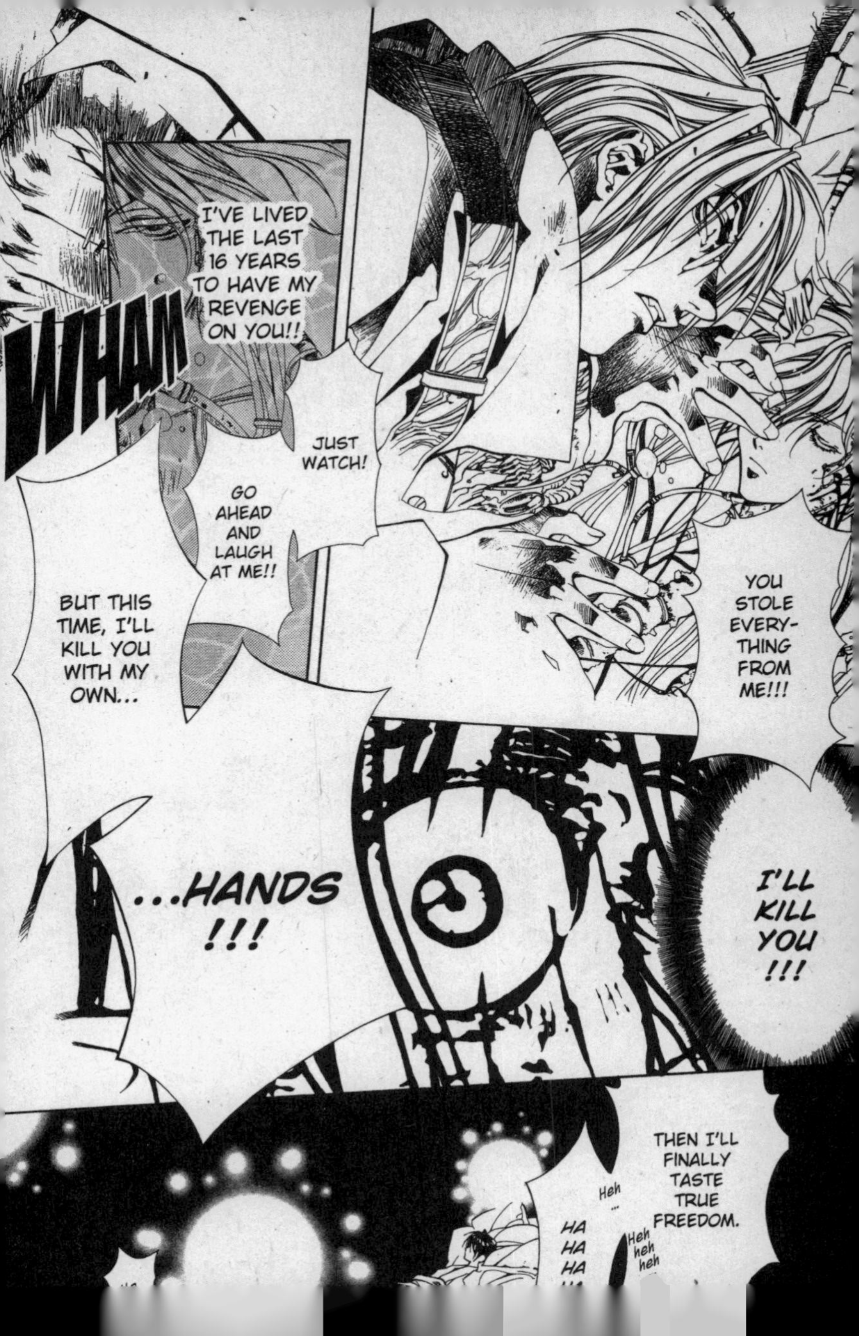
SWP
YOU STOLE EVERYTHING FROM ME!!!
I'VE LIVED THE LAST 16 YEARS TO HAVE MY REVENGE ON YOU!!
WHAM
JUST WATCH!
GO AHEAD AND LAUGH AT ME!!
BUT THIS TIME, I'LL KILL YOU WITH MY OWN...
...HANDS!!!
I'LL KILL YOU!!!
THEN I'LL FINALLY TASTE TRUE FREEDOM.
Heh ...
Heh heh heh
HA HA HA

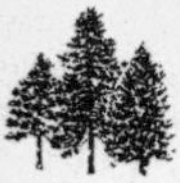

Weird Things About the Kyoto Story
Part 2

Please don't read "Professor Watari's easy course on cloning" and think "Oh, so that's how cloning is done." Apparently the course was totally wrong. To really learn about cloning, read a book by an expert. I don't understand it--it's too complicated. You see, while I was drawing that segment, I took my photo trip to Kyoto and a relative died. It was a difficult time, so I didn't have time to do research. I was hoping to fix it before the manga came out, but I just didn't have time. So I ended up printing something with false information. I'm really sorry. And to those scientists out there who sent me letters saying, "This is wrong," I'm sorry I didn't get to make use of your knowledge. (boo-hoo)

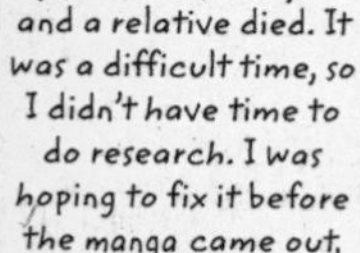
Baa baa
DOLLY

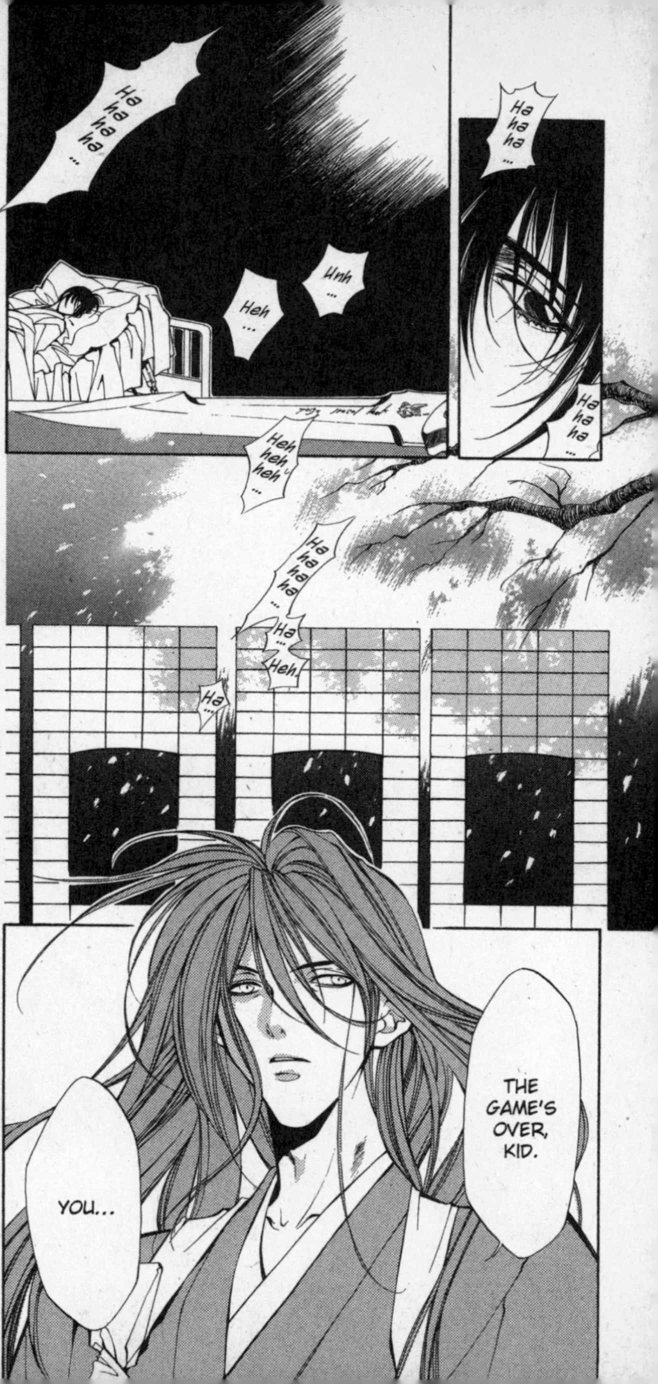
Ha ha ha ...
Ha ha ha ...
Ha ha ha ha ...
Unh ...
Heh ...
Heh heh heh ...
Ha ha ha ha ha ...
Ha ...
Heh.
Ha ...
THE GAME'S OVER, KID.
YOU...

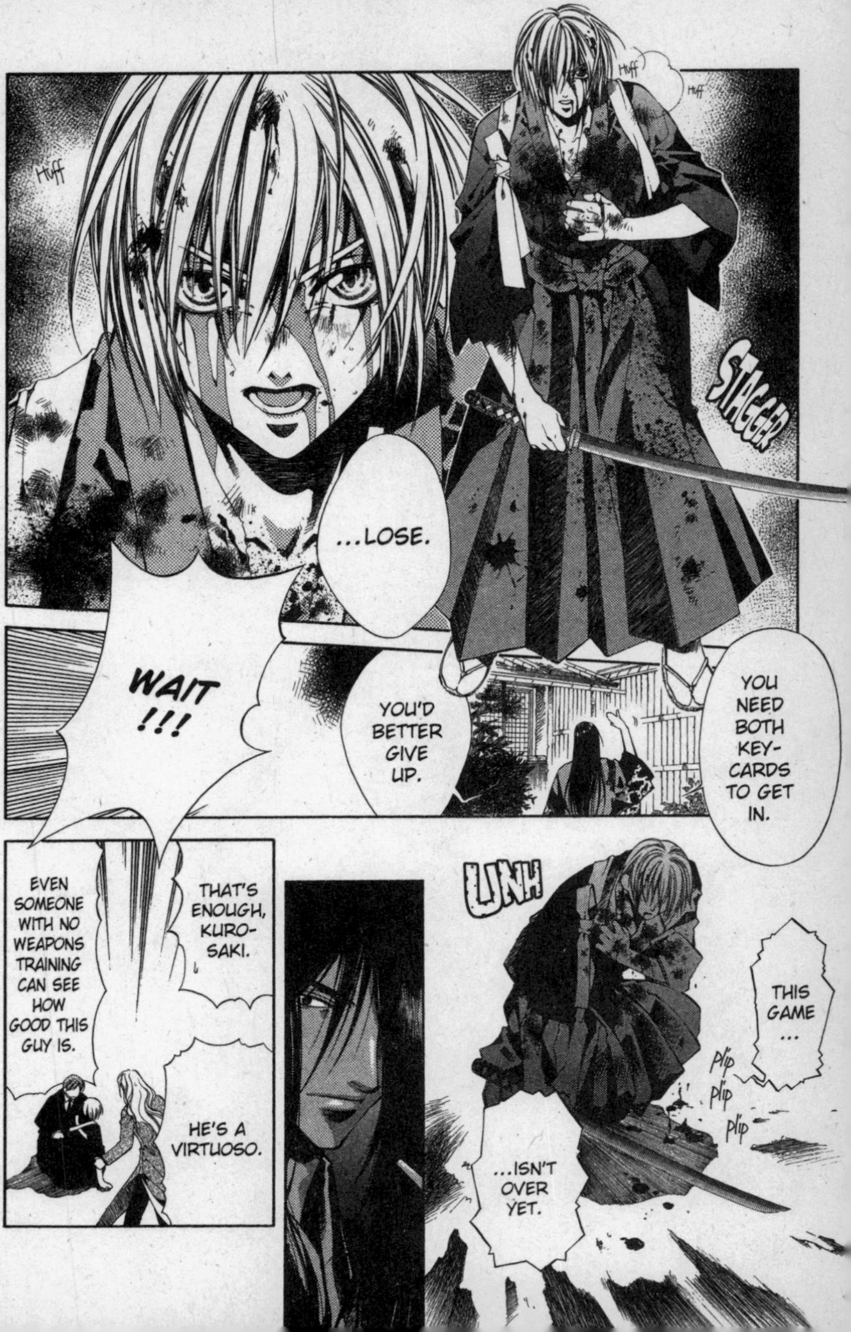
Huff
Huff
STAGGER
Huff
...LOSE.
YOU NEED BOTH KEY-CARDS TO GET IN.
YOU'D BETTER GIVE UP.
WAIT !!!
UNH
THIS GAME ...
plip plip plip
...ISN'T OVER YET.
THAT'S ENOUGH, KURO-SAKI.
EVEN SOMEONE WITH NO WEAPONS TRAINING CAN SEE HOW GOOD THIS GUY IS.
HE'S A VIRTUOSO.

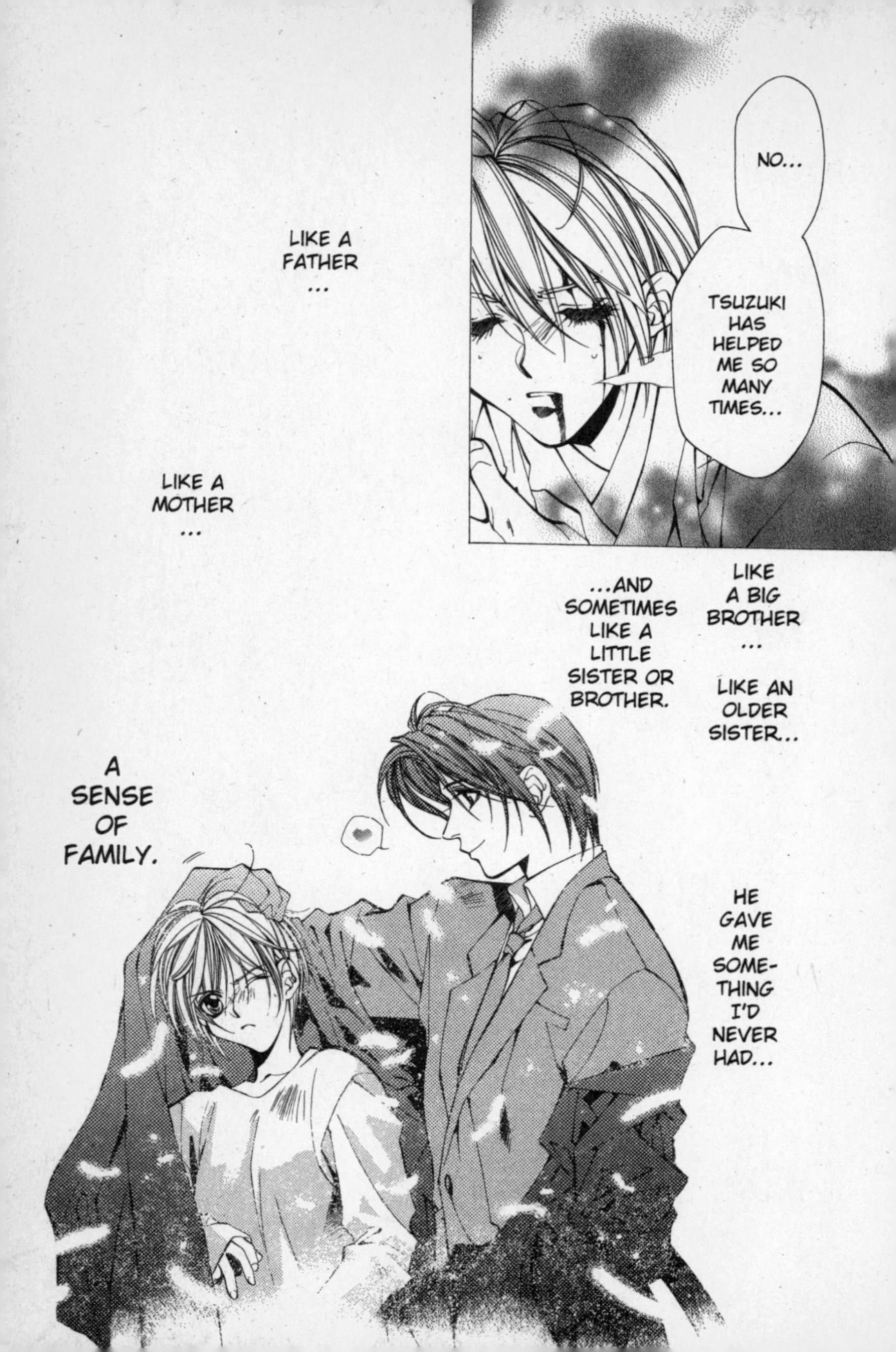
NO...
TSUZUKI HAS HELPED ME SO MANY TIMES...
LIKE A FATHER ...
LIKE A MOTHER ...
LIKE A BIG BROTHER ...
LIKE AN OLDER SISTER...
...AND SOMETIMES LIKE A LITTLE SISTER OR BROTHER.
HE GAVE ME SOME-THING I'D NEVER HAD...
A SENSE OF FAMILY.

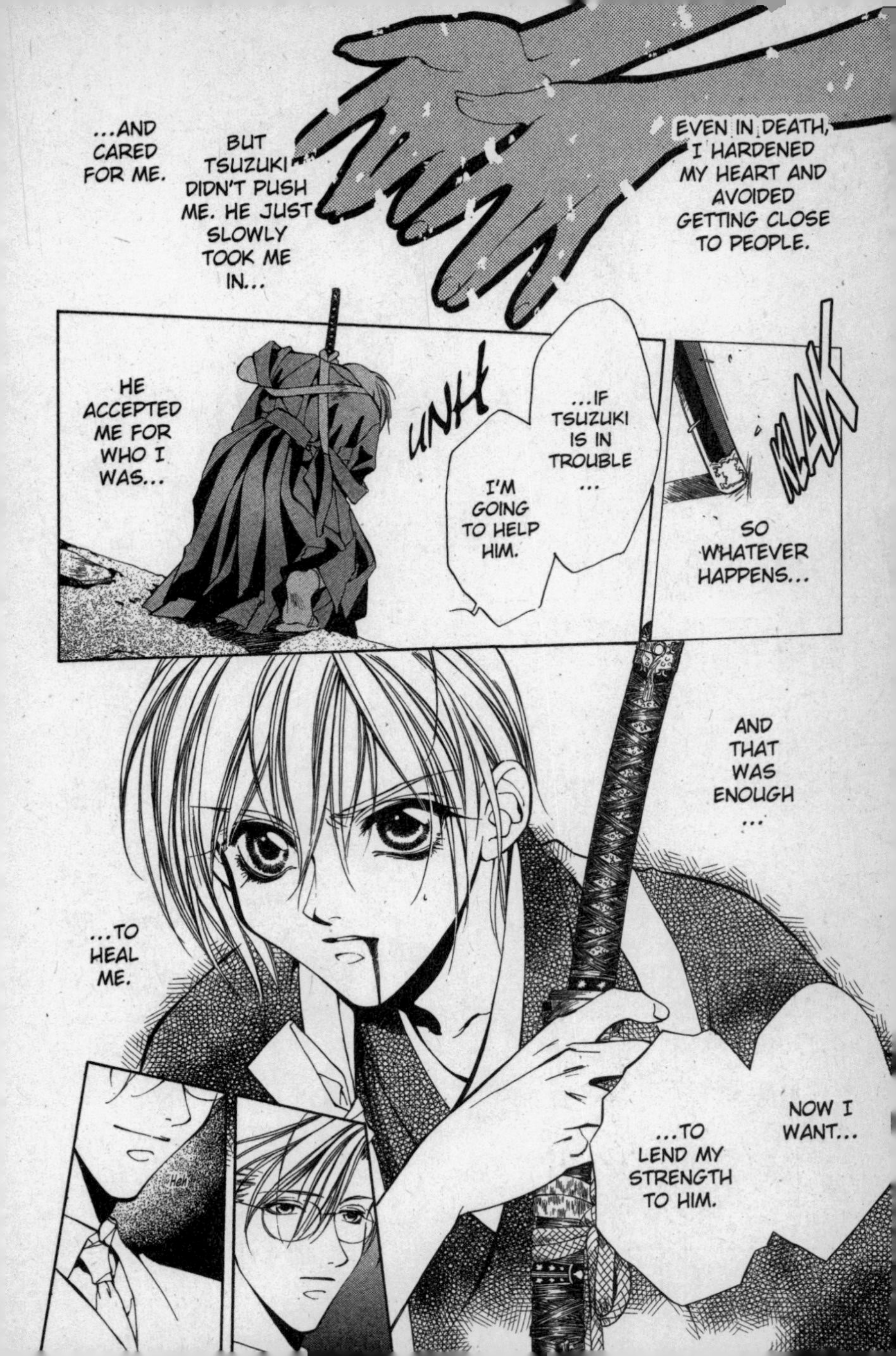
EVEN IN DEATH, I HARDENED MY HEART AND AVOIDED GETTING CLOSE TO PEOPLE.
BUT TSUZUKI DIDN'T PUSH ME. HE JUST SLOWLY TOOK ME IN...
...AND CARED FOR ME.
KLAK
SO WHATEVER HAPPENS...
...IF TSUZUKI IS IN TROUBLE...
I'M GOING TO HELP HIM.
UNH
HE ACCEPTED ME FOR WHO I WAS...
AND THAT WAS ENOUGH...
...TO HEAL ME.
NOW I WANT...
...TO LEND MY STRENGTH TO HIM.
Heh

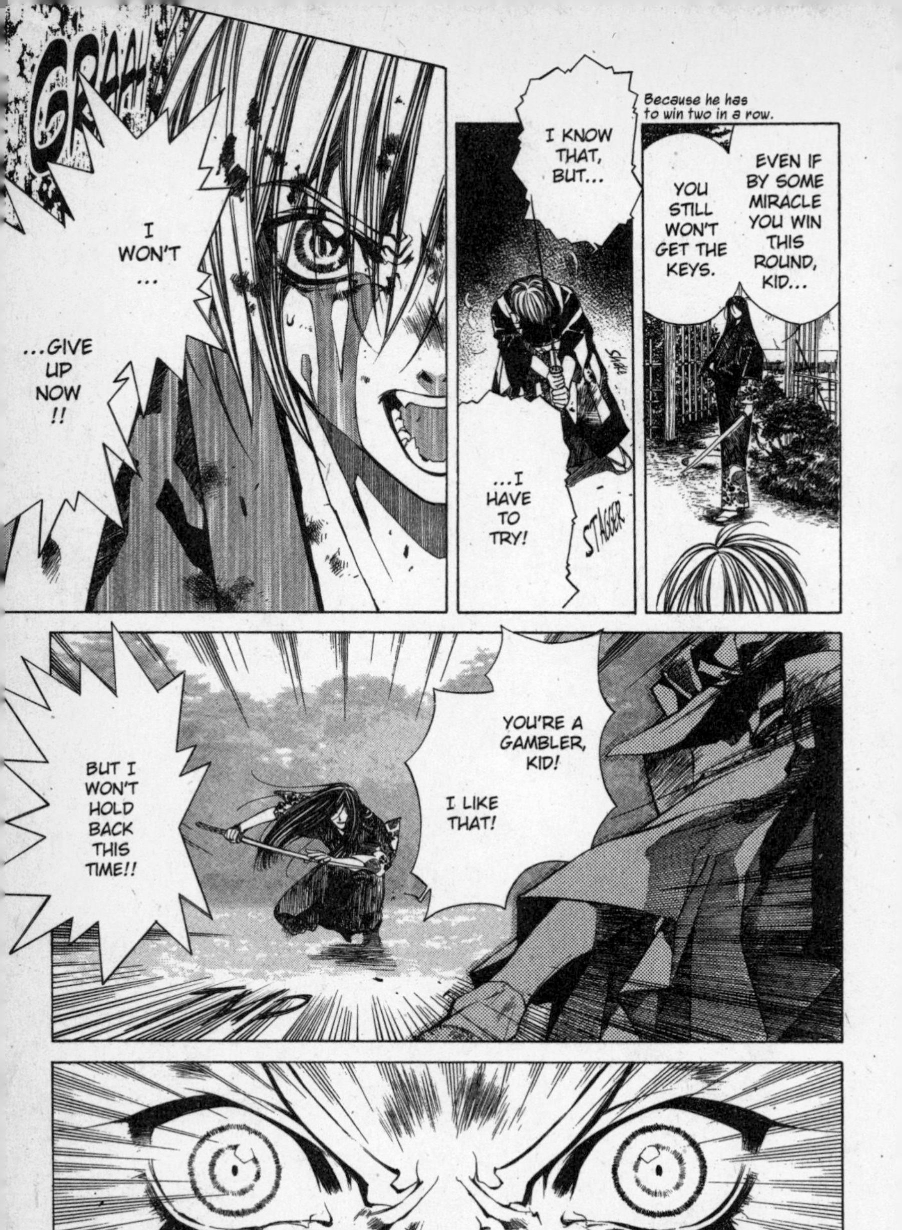
Because he has to win two in a row.
EVEN IF BY SOME MIRACLE YOU WIN THIS ROUND, KID...
YOU STILL WON'T GET THE KEYS.
I KNOW THAT, BUT...
STAGGER
...I HAVE TO TRY!
GRAAH
I WON'T ...
...GIVE UP NOW !!
YOU'RE A GAMBLER, KID!
I LIKE THAT!
BUT I WON'T HOLD BACK THIS TIME!!
TMP

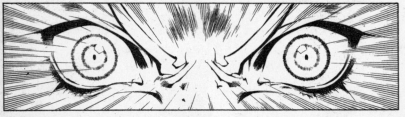

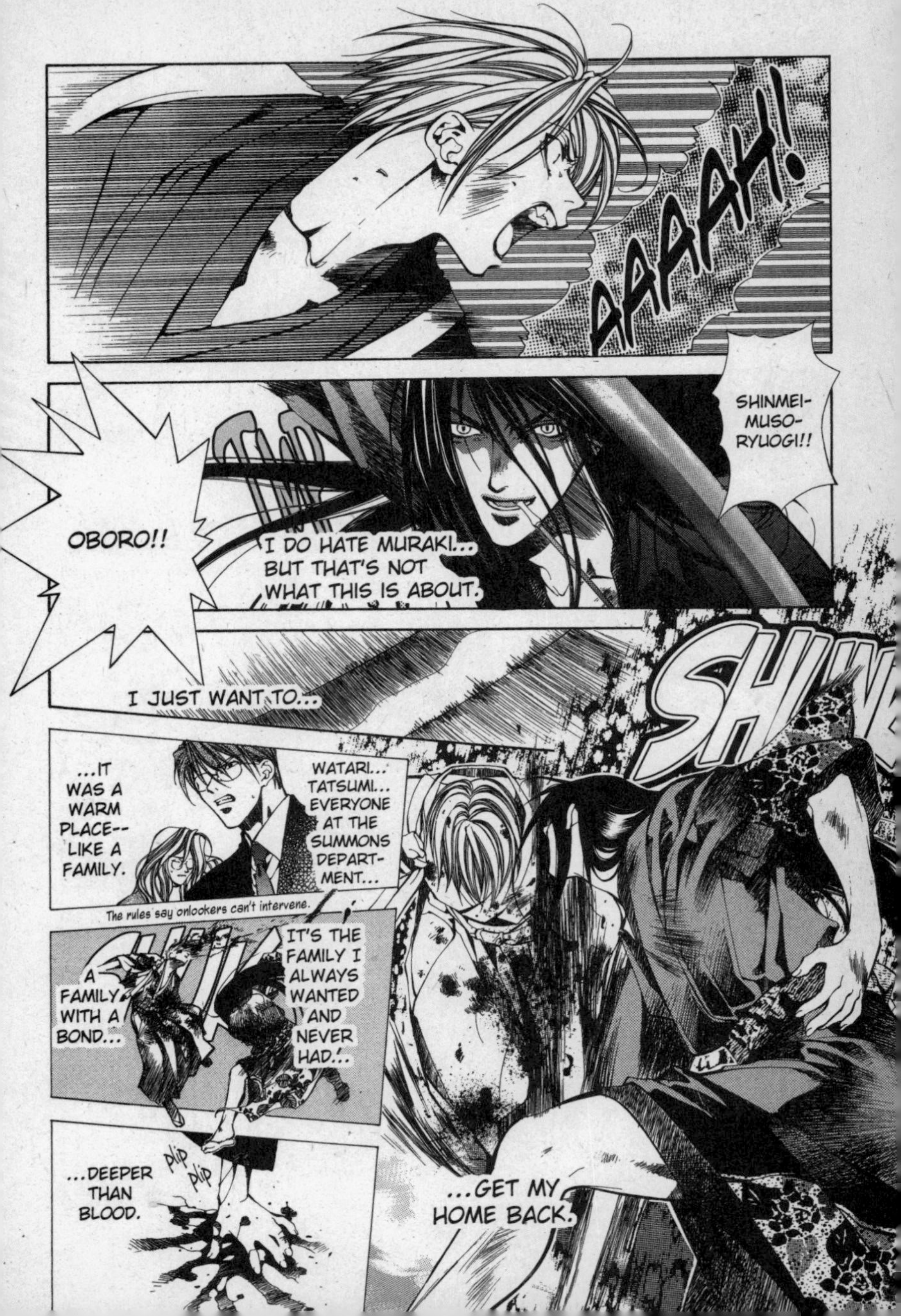
AAAAH!
SHINMEI-MUSO-RYUOGI!!
I DO HATE MURAKI... BUT THAT'S NOT WHAT THIS IS ABOUT.
OBORO!!
SHIN
I JUST WANT TO...
...GET MY HOME BACK.
WATARI... TATSUMI... EVERYONE AT THE SUMMONS DEPARTMENT...
...IT WAS A WARM PLACE--LIKE A FAMILY.
The rules say onlookers can't intervene.
IT'S THE FAMILY I ALWAYS WANTED AND NEVER HAD...
A FAMILY WITH A BOND...
plip plip
...DEEPER THAN BLOOD.

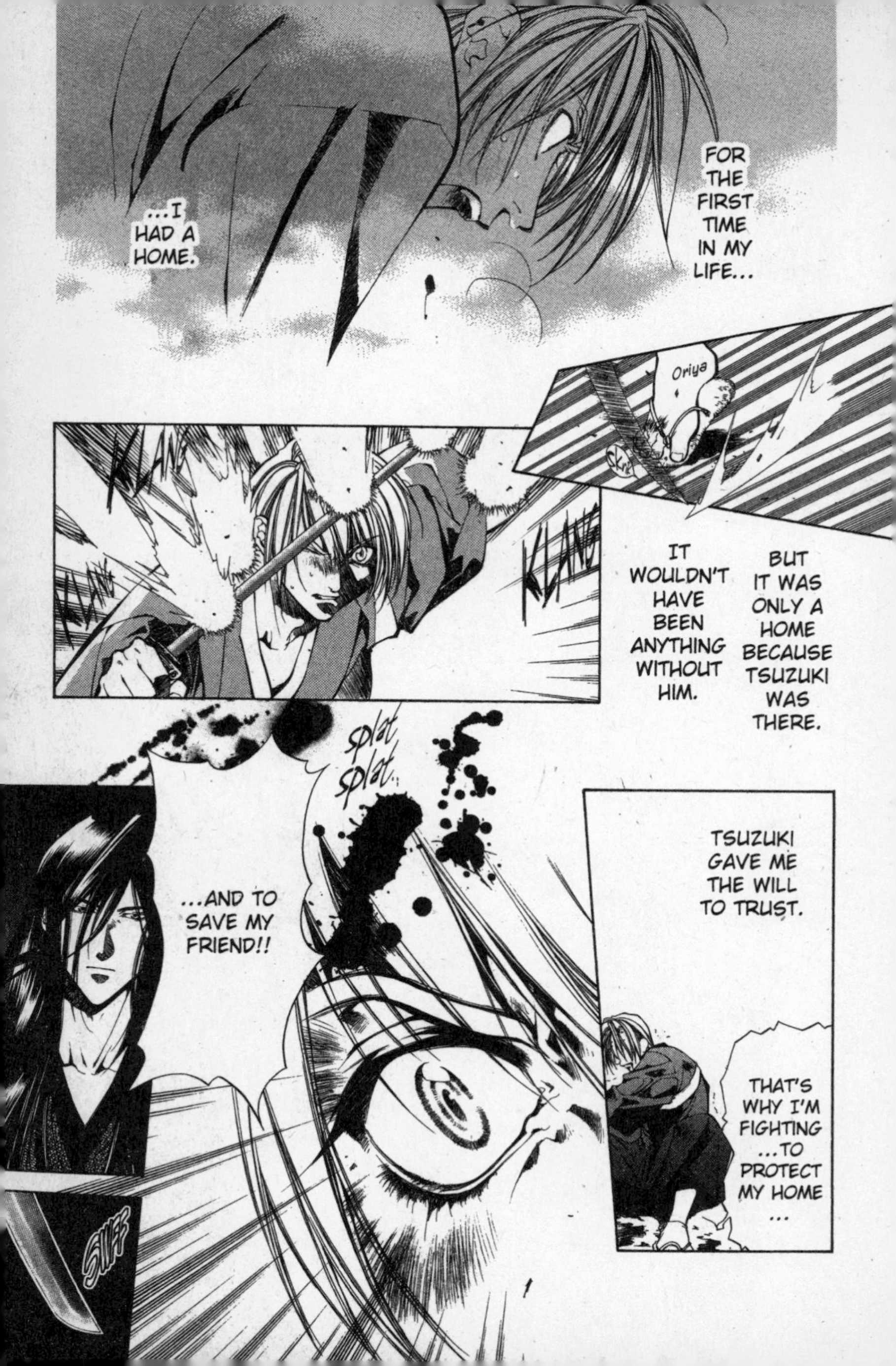
FOR THE FIRST TIME IN MY LIFE...
...I HAD A HOME.
Oriya
KLANG
KLANG
BUT IT WAS ONLY A HOME BECAUSE TSUZUKI WAS THERE.
IT WOULDN'T HAVE BEEN ANYTHING WITHOUT HIM.
TSUZUKI GAVE ME THE WILL TO TRUST.
THAT'S WHY I'M FIGHTING ...TO PROTECT MY HOME ...
splat splat
...AND TO SAVE MY FRIEND!!

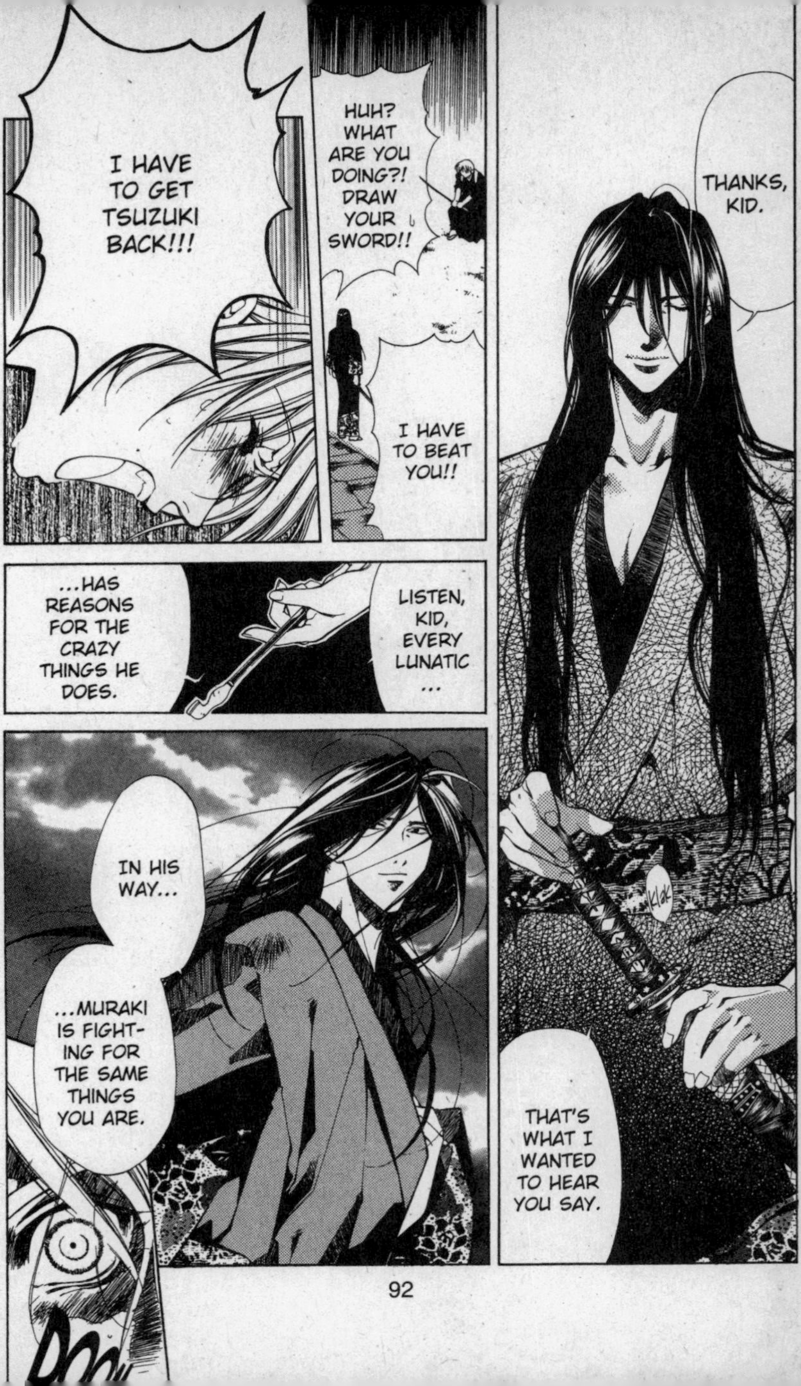
THANKS, KID.
KLAK
THAT'S WHAT I WANTED TO HEAR YOU SAY.
HUH? WHAT ARE YOU DOING?! DRAW YOUR SWORD!!
I HAVE TO BEAT YOU!!
I HAVE TO GET TSUZUKI BACK!!!
LISTEN, KID, EVERY LUNATIC ...
...HAS REASONS FOR THE CRAZY THINGS HE DOES.
IN HIS WAY...
...MURAKI IS FIGHT-ING FOR THE SAME THINGS YOU ARE.

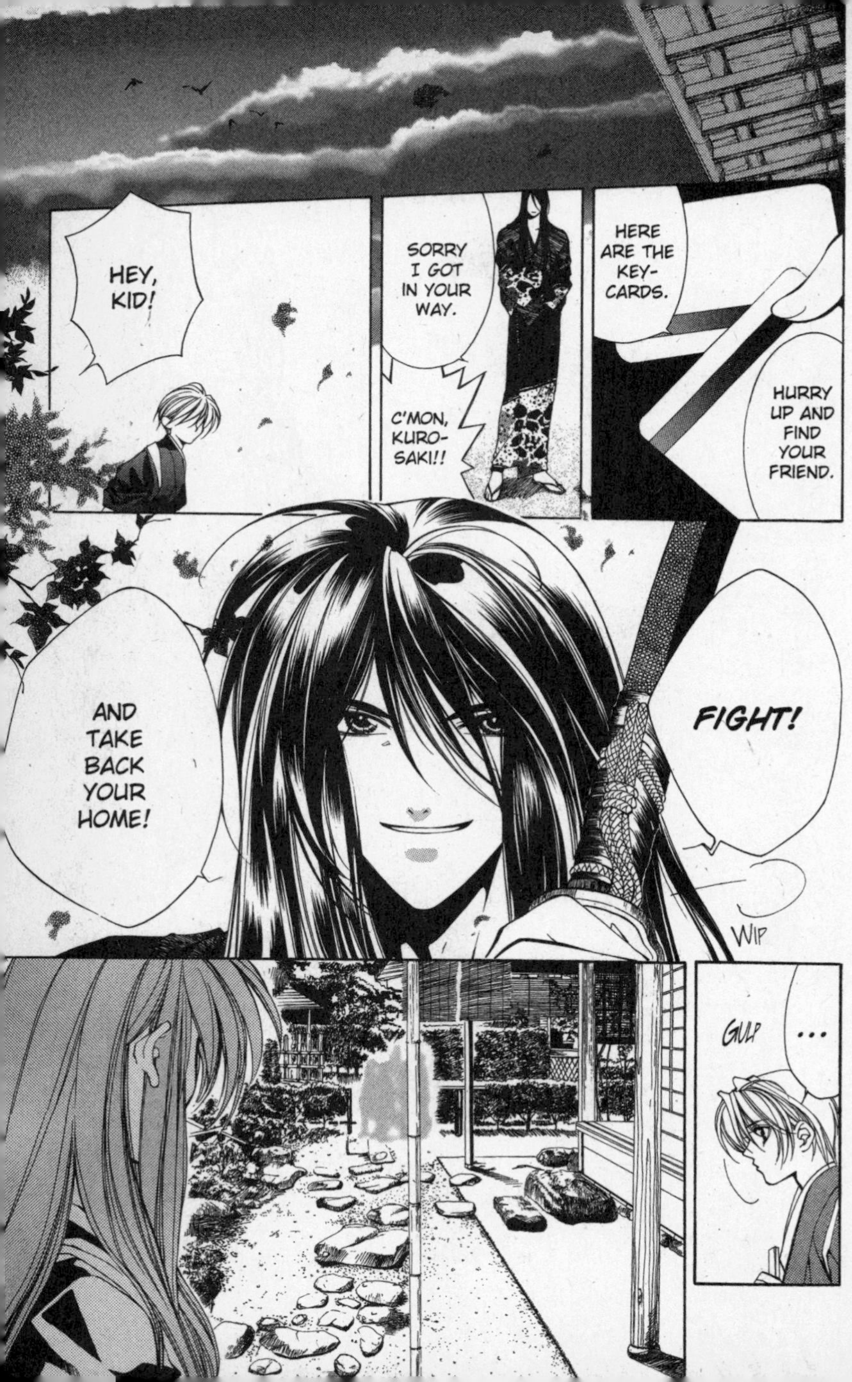
HERE ARE THE KEY-CARDS.
HURRY UP AND FIND YOUR FRIEND.
SORRY I GOT IN YOUR WAY.
C'MON, KURO-SAKI!!
HEY, KID!
FIGHT!
AND TAKE BACK YOUR HOME!
WIP
...
GULP

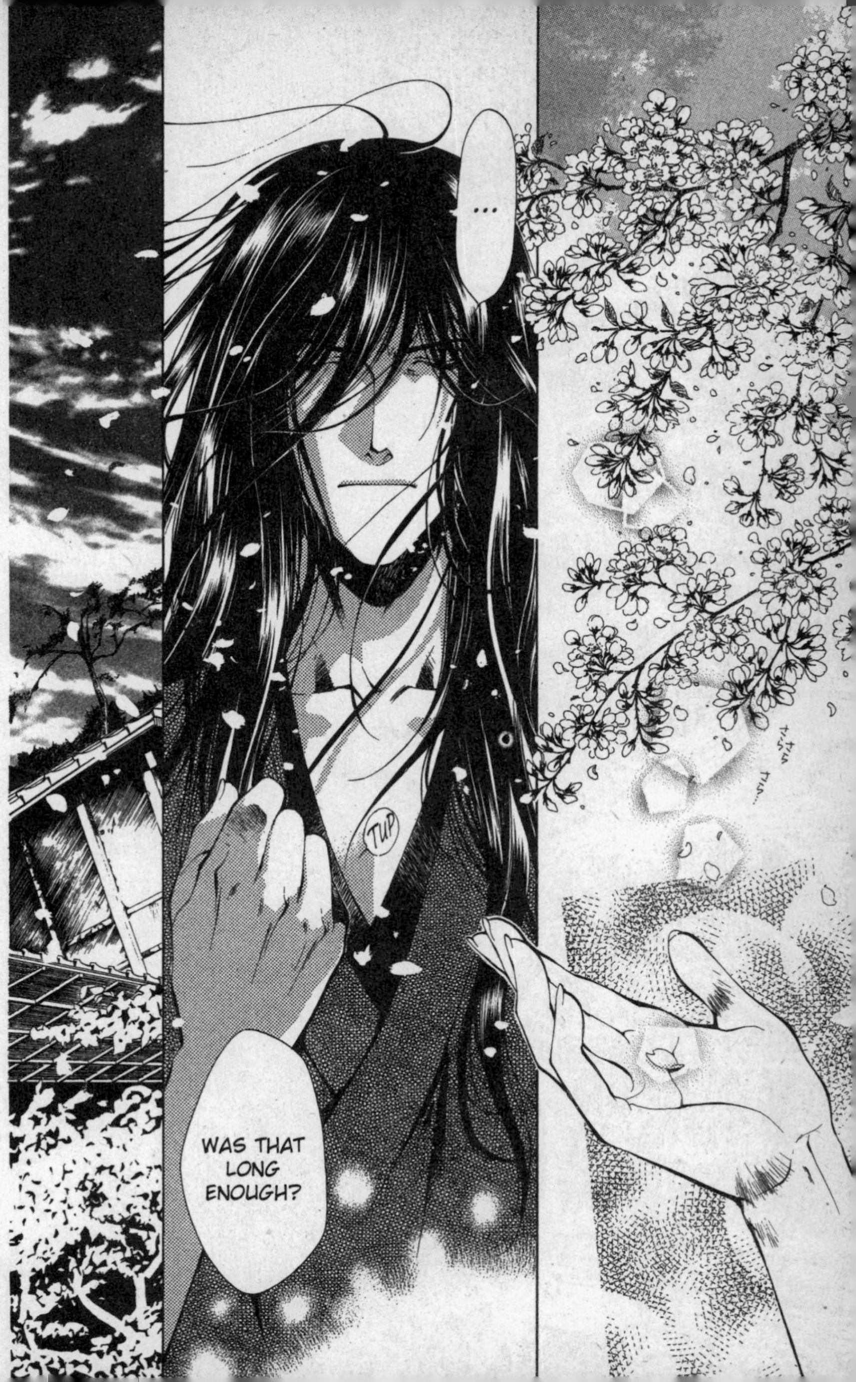
TIP TIP
TIP...
...
TUP
WAS THAT LONG ENOUGH?

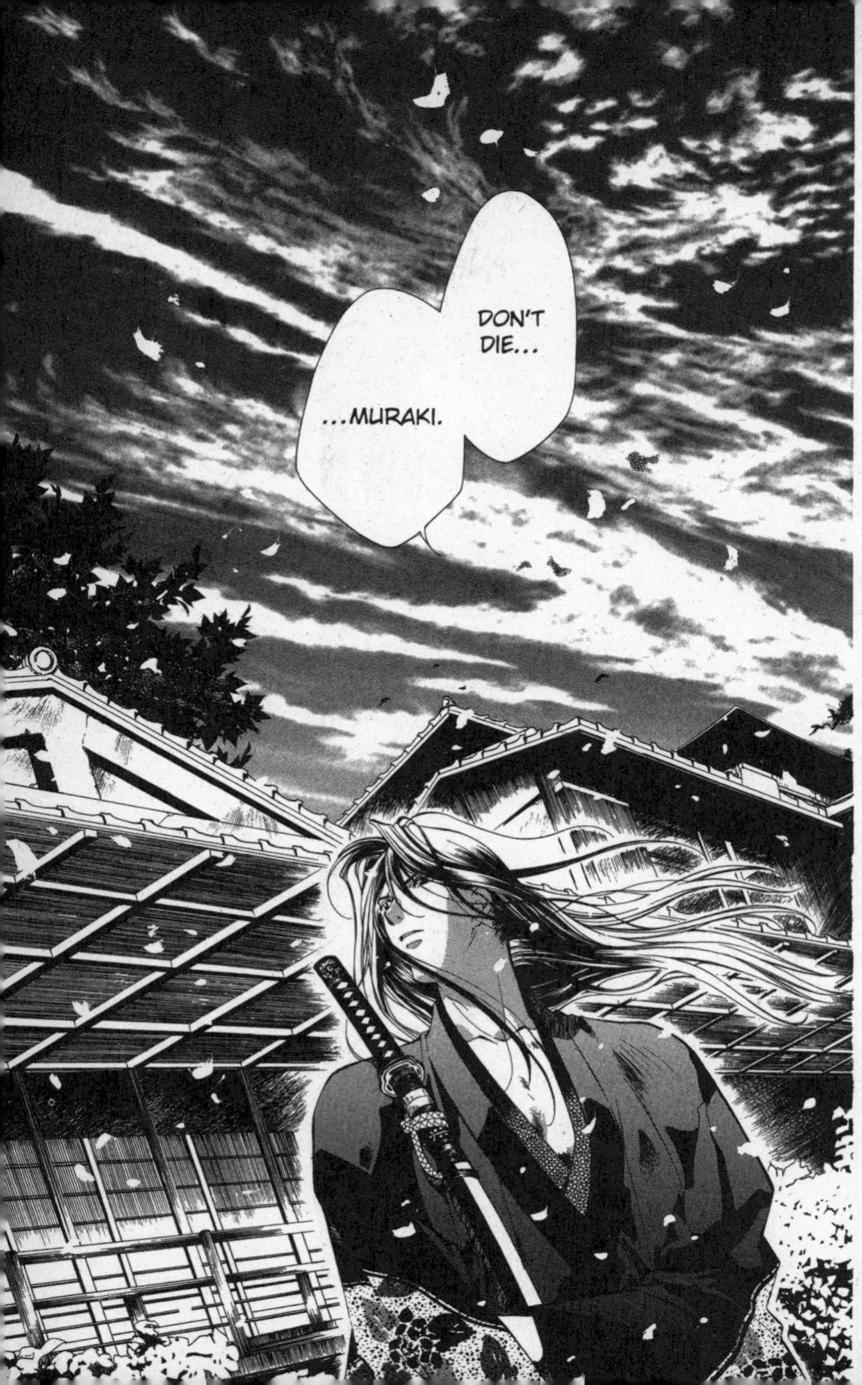
DON'T DIE...
...MURAKI.

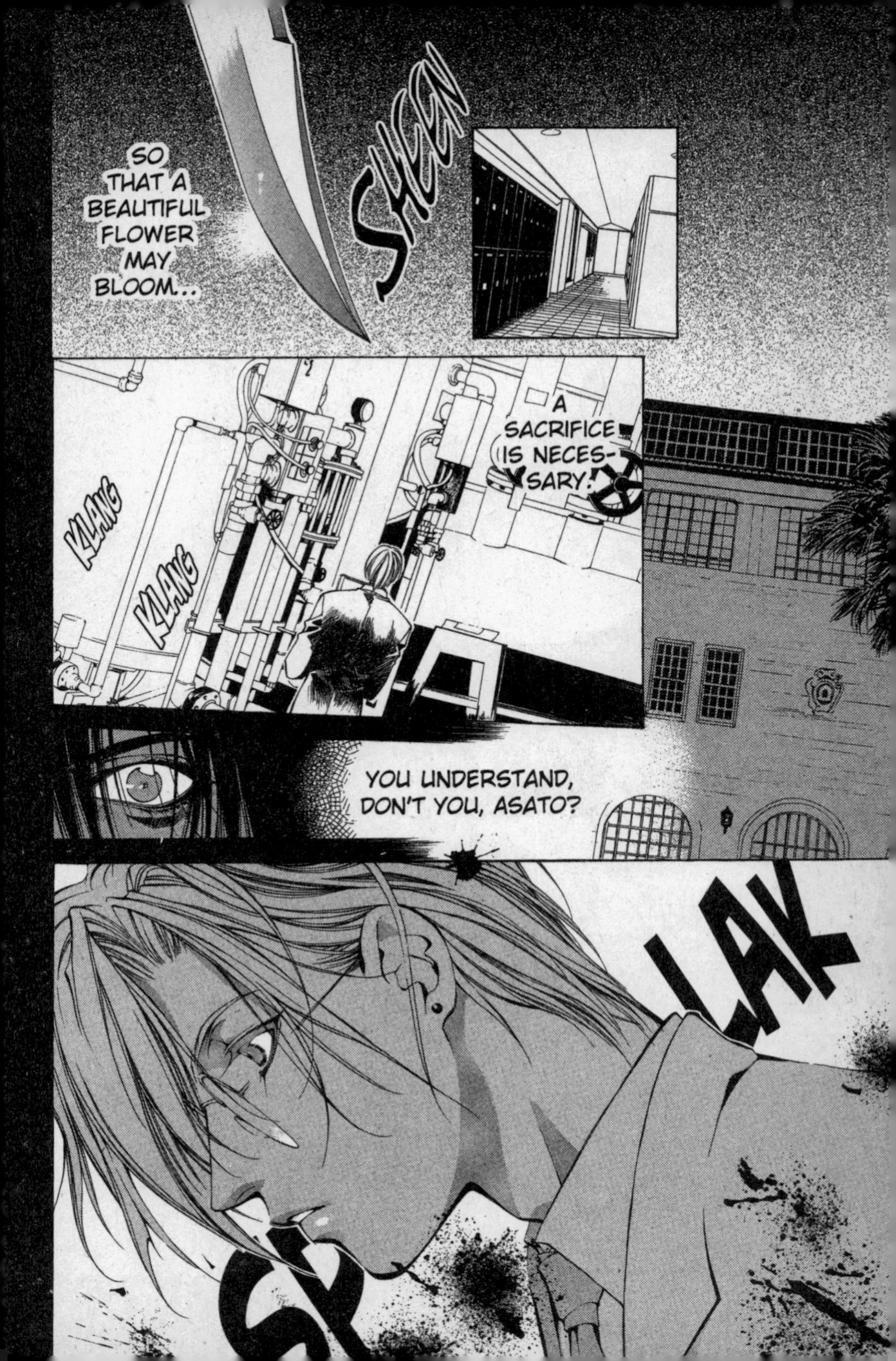
SHEEN
SO THAT A BEAUTIFUL FLOWER MAY BLOOM...
A SACRIFICE IS NECES-SARY.
KLANG
KLANG
YOU UNDERSTAND, DON'T YOU, ASATO?
LAK

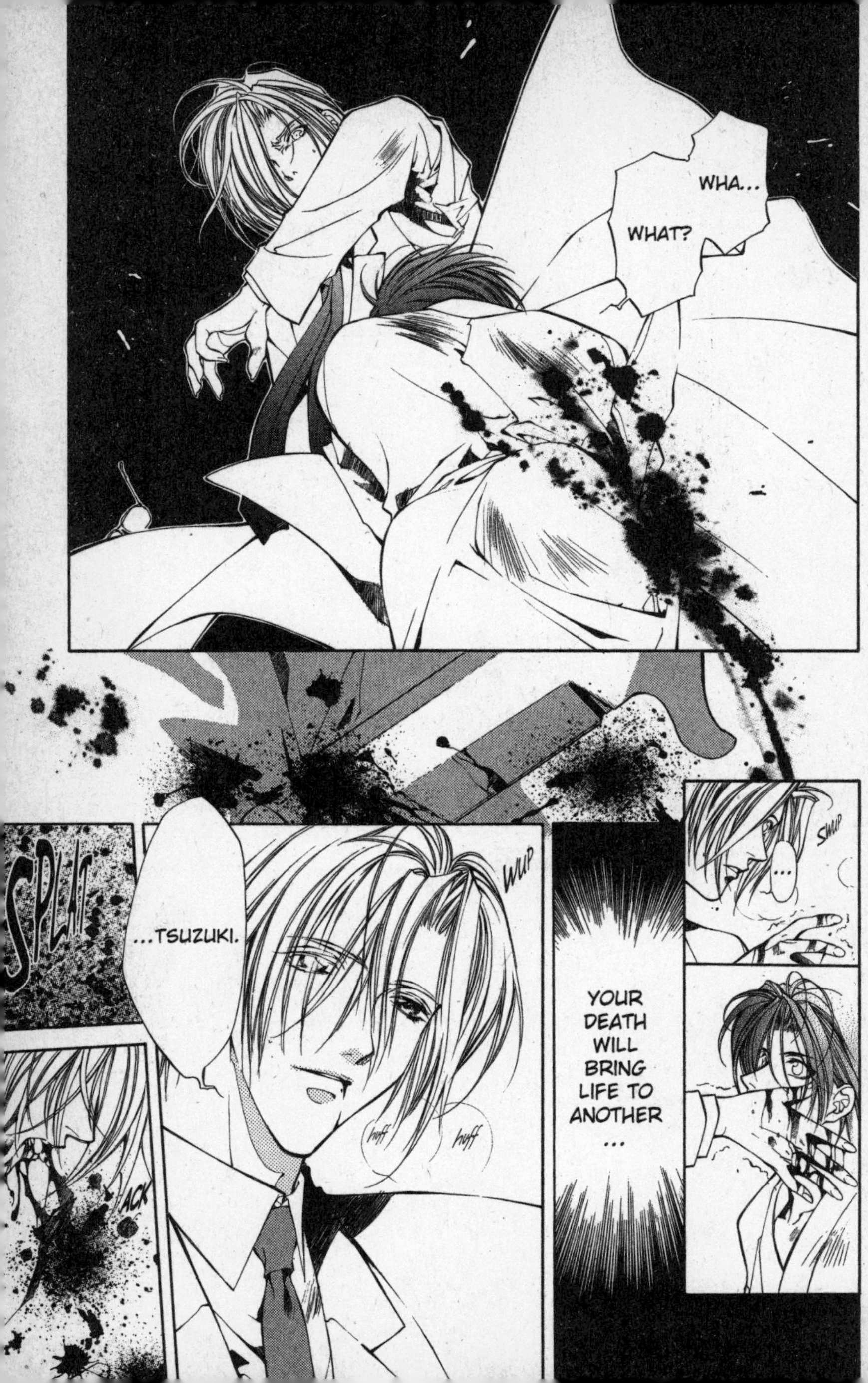
WHA...
WHAT?
SWIP
...
YOUR DEATH WILL BRING LIFE TO ANOTHER ...
WUP
...TSUZUKI.
huff
huff
SPLAT
ACK

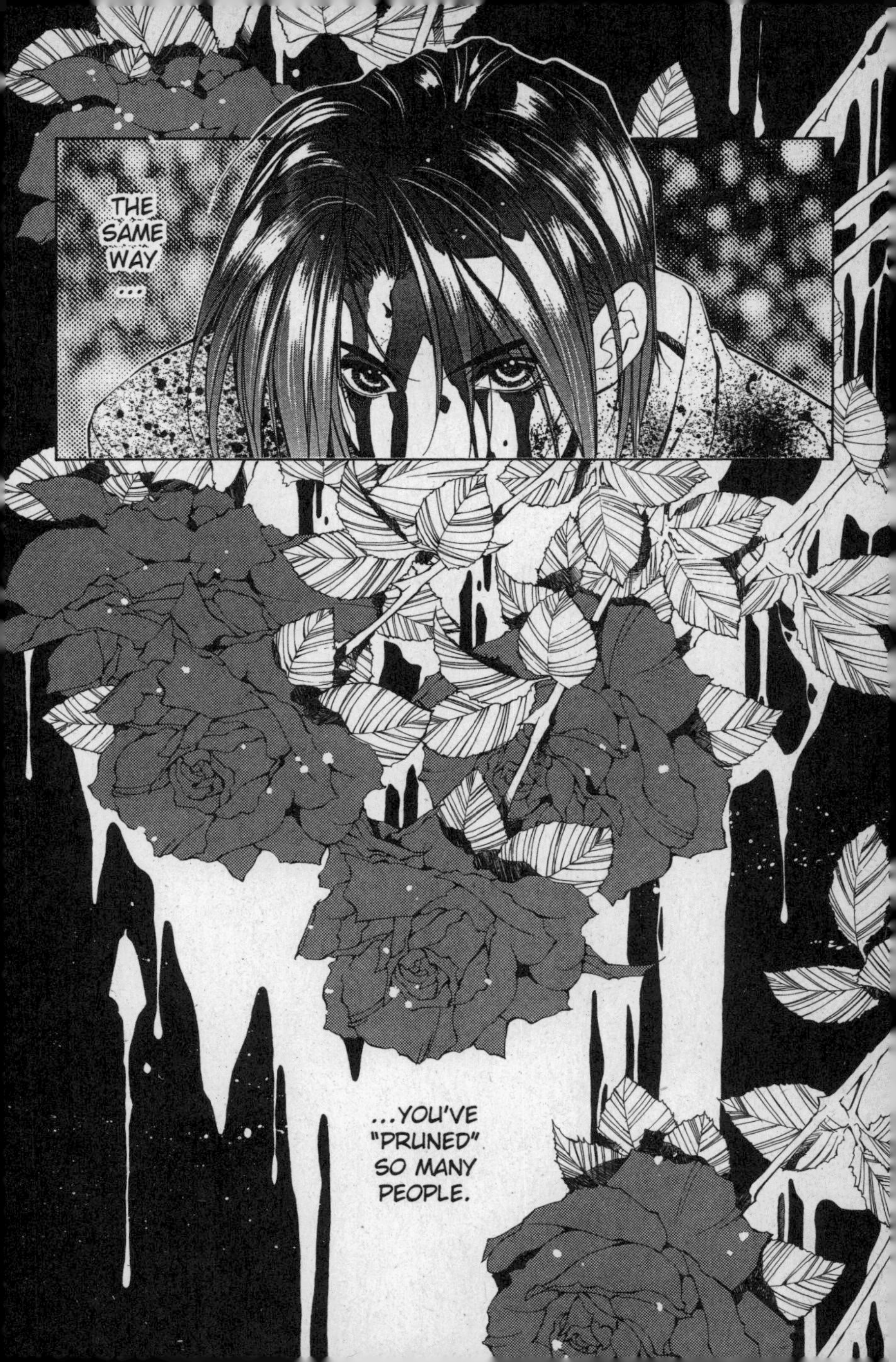
THE SAME WAY ...
...YOU'VE "PRUNED" SO MANY PEOPLE.

I AM A
MURDERER..

I AM
THE SON OF
A CRIMINAL.

WE WERE
CREATED TO KILL...

OURS IS AN ARTIFICIAL LIFE....

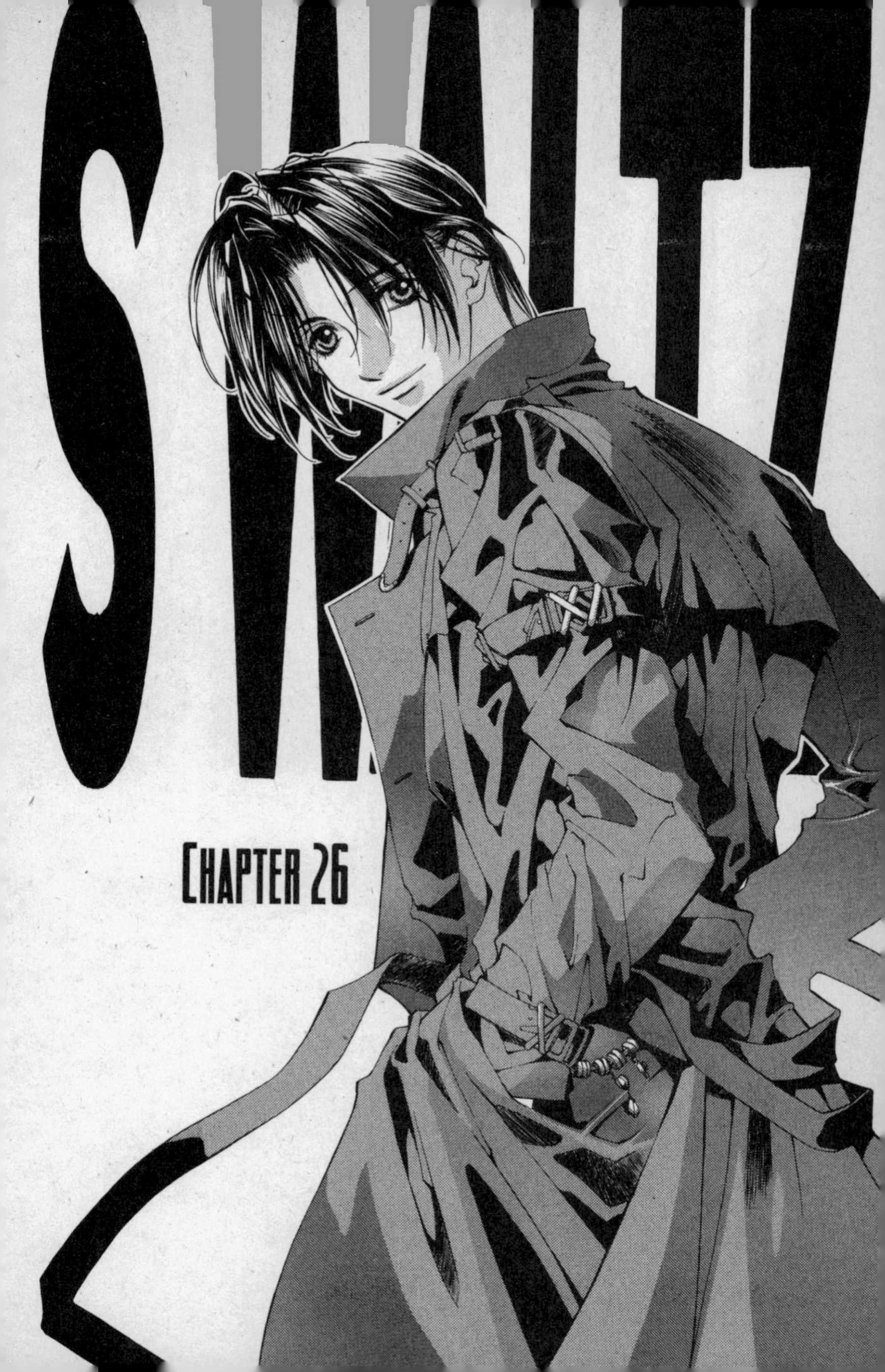
CHAPTER 26

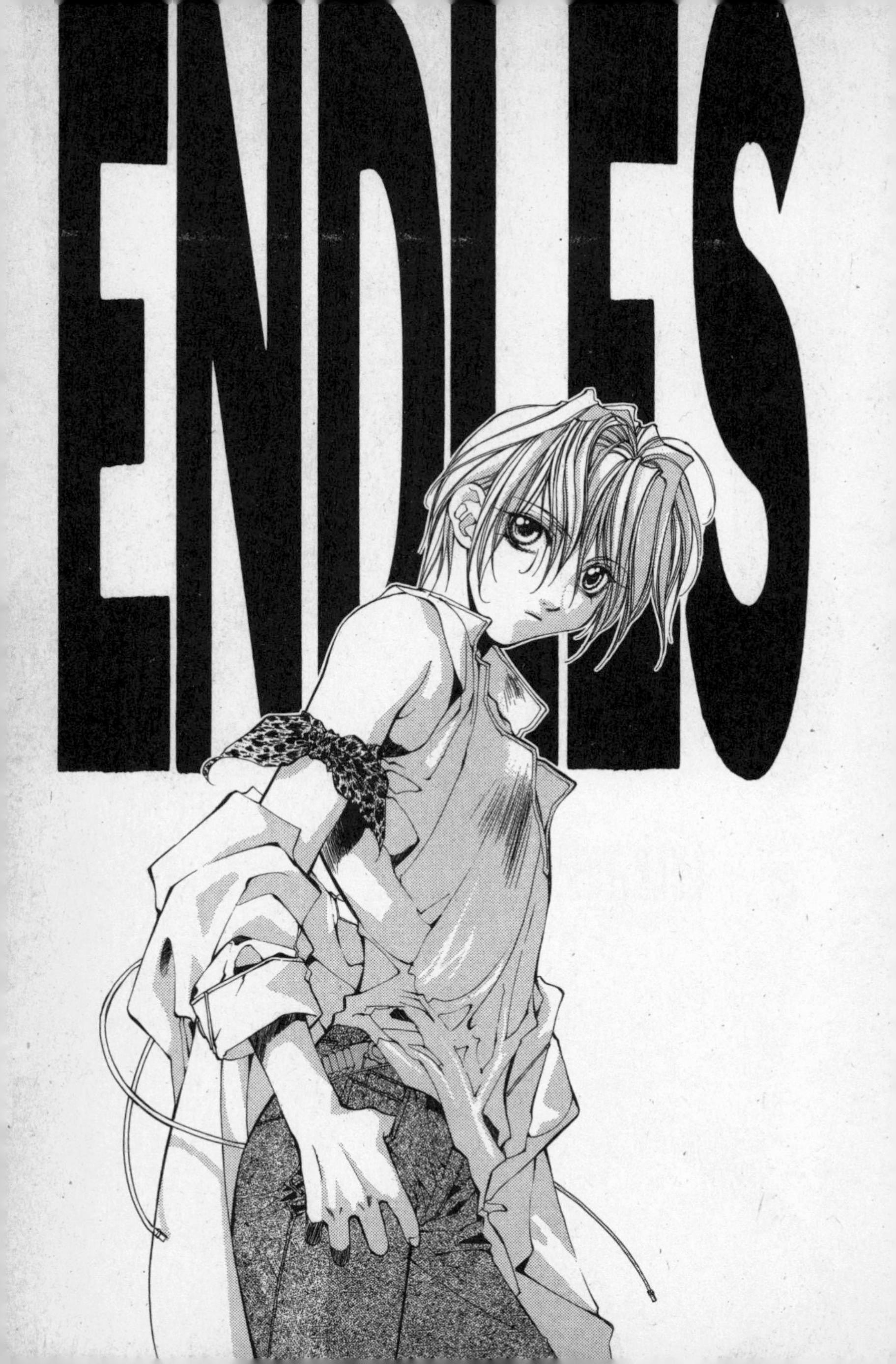
ENDLES

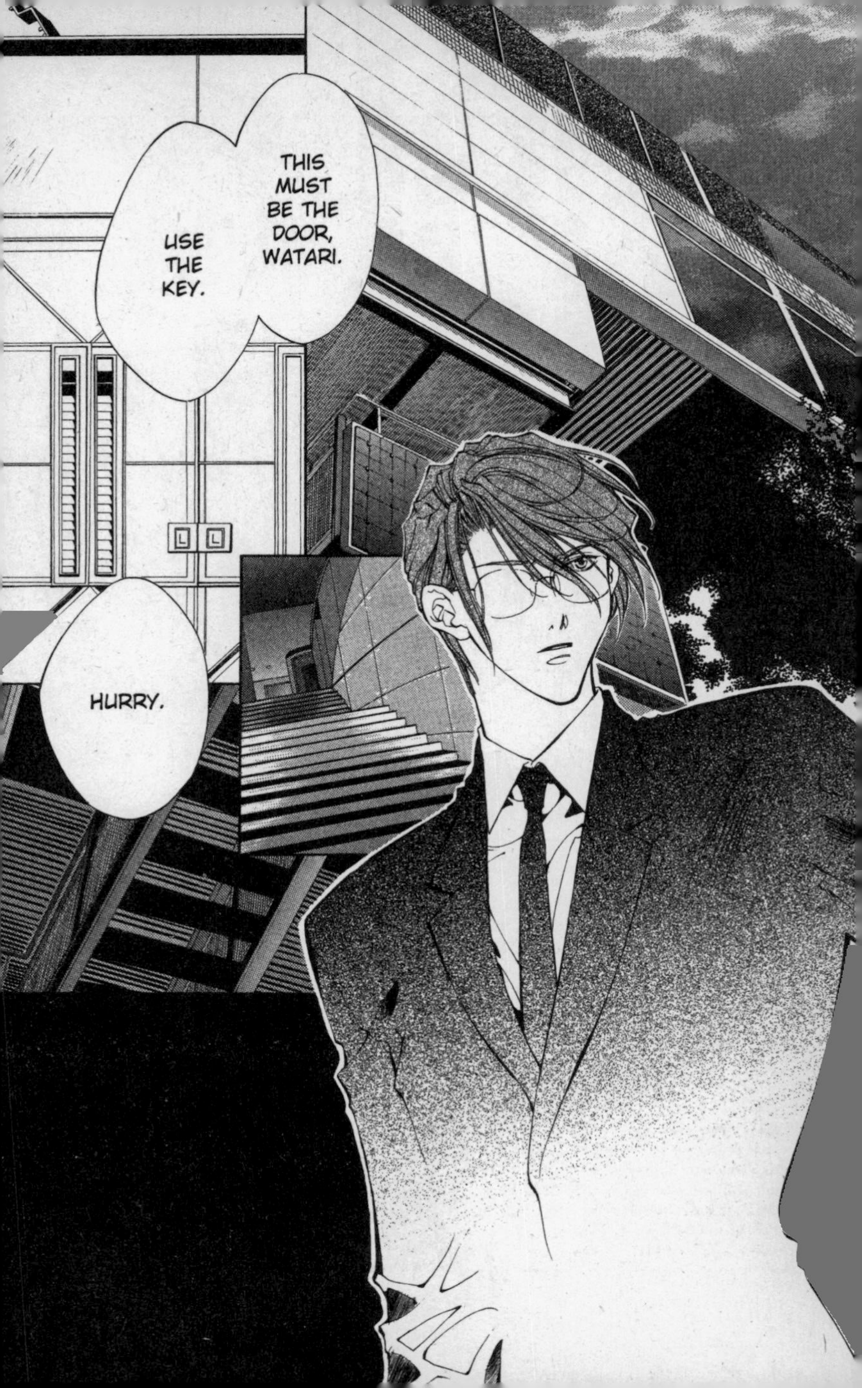
THIS MUST BE THE DOOR, WATARI.
USE THE KEY.
HURRY.

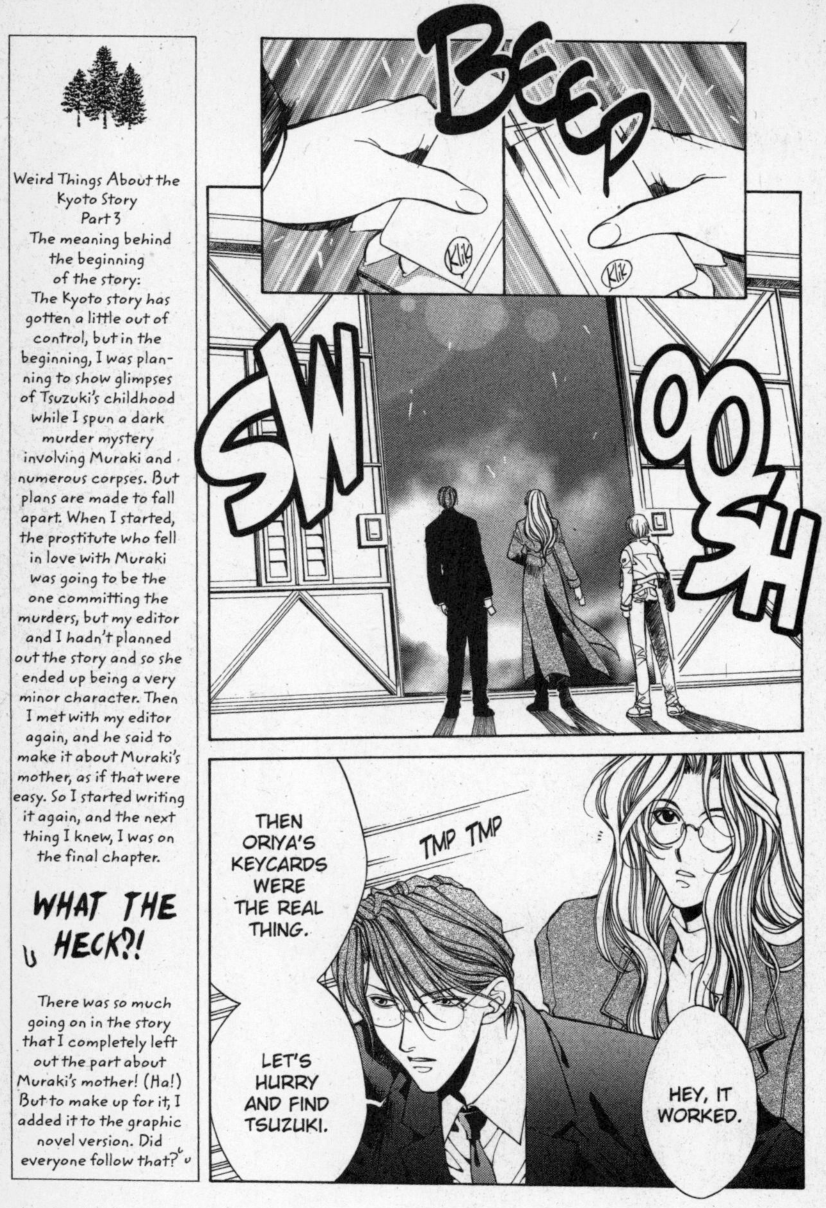
BEEP
Klik
Klik
SWOOSH
HEY, IT WORKED.
TMP TMP
THEN ORIYA'S KEYCARDS WERE THE REAL THING.
LET'S HURRY AND FIND TSUZUKI.

Weird Things About the Kyoto Story Part 3

The meaning behind the beginning of the story: The Kyoto story has gotten a little out of control, but in the beginning, I was planning to show glimpses of Tsuzuki's childhood while I spun a dark murder mystery involving Muraki and numerous corpses. But plans are made to fall apart. When I started, the prostitute who fell in love with Muraki was going to be the one committing the murders, but my editor and I hadn't planned out the story and so she ended up being a very minor character. Then I met with my editor again, and he said to make it about Muraki's mother, as if that were easy. So I started writing it again, and the next thing I knew, I was on the final chapter.

WHAT THE HECK?!

There was so much going on in the story that I completely left out the part about Muraki's mother! (Ha!) But to make up for it, I added it to the graphic novel version. Did everyone follow that?

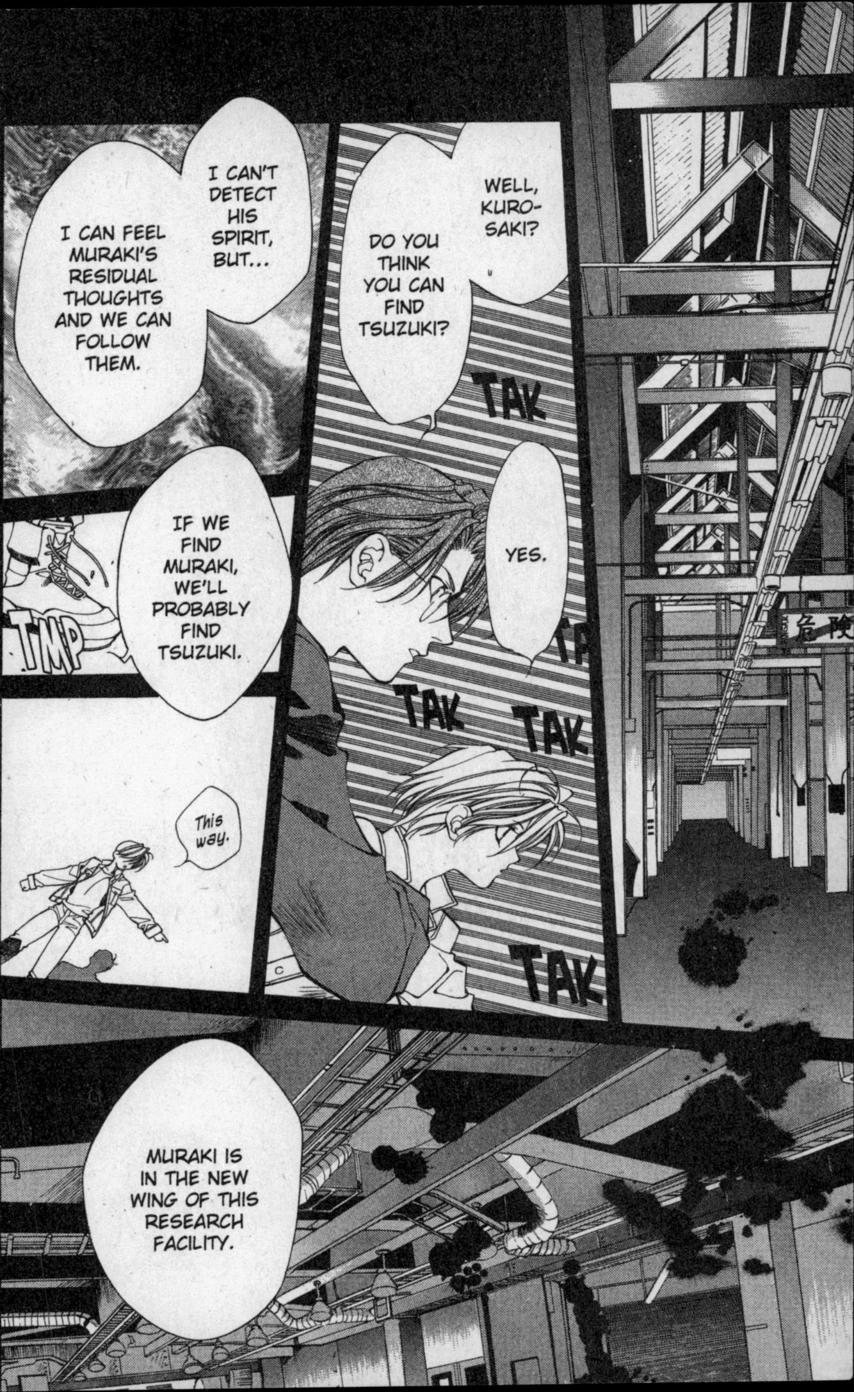
危険
WELL, KURO-SAKI?
DO YOU THINK YOU CAN FIND TSUZUKI?
TAK
YES.
TA
TAK
TAK
TAK
I CAN'T DETECT HIS SPIRIT, BUT...
I CAN FEEL MURAKI'S RESIDUAL THOUGHTS AND WE CAN FOLLOW THEM.
IF WE FIND MURAKI, WE'LL PROBABLY FIND TSUZUKI.
TMP
This way.
MURAKI IS IN THE NEW WING OF THIS RESEARCH FACILITY.

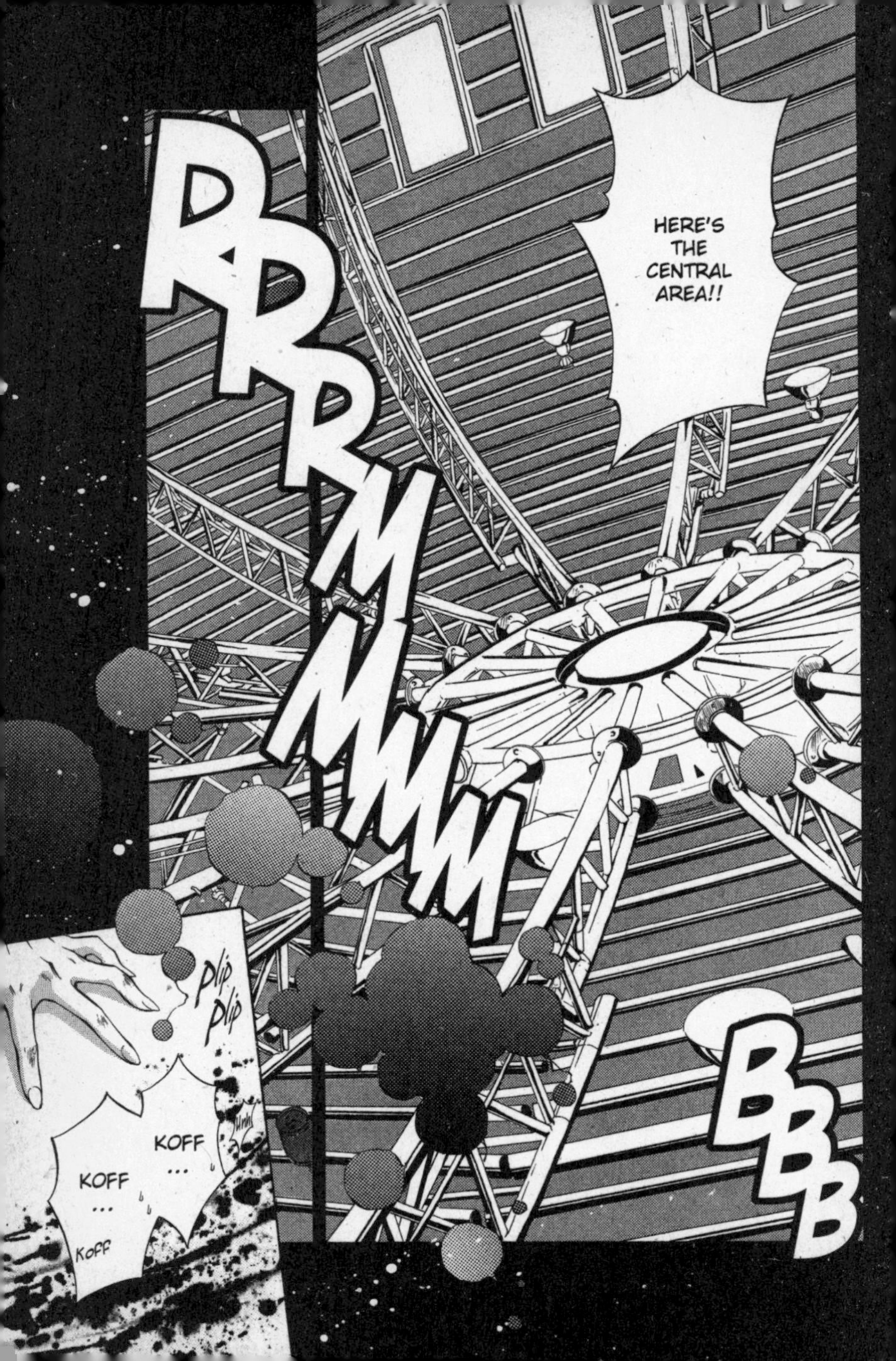
HERE'S THE CENTRAL AREA!!
DRRMMMMM
BBB
plip
plip
KOFF ...
KOFF ...
Koff

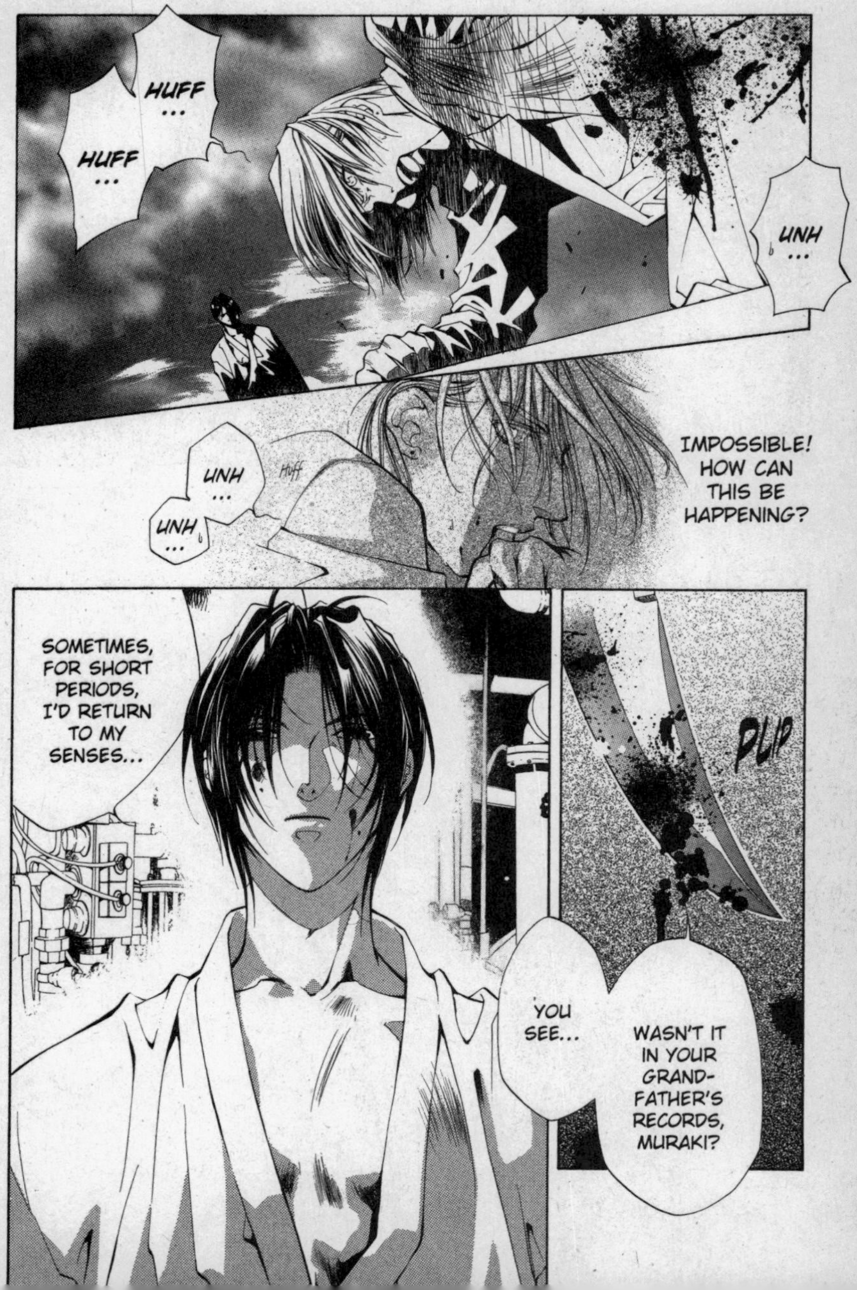
UNH...
HUFF...
HUFF...
IMPOSSIBLE! HOW CAN THIS BE HAPPENING?
Huff
UNH...
UNH...
DLIP
SOMETIMES, FOR SHORT PERIODS, I'D RETURN TO MY SENSES...
YOU SEE...
WASN'T IT IN YOUR GRAND-FATHER'S RECORDS, MURAKI?

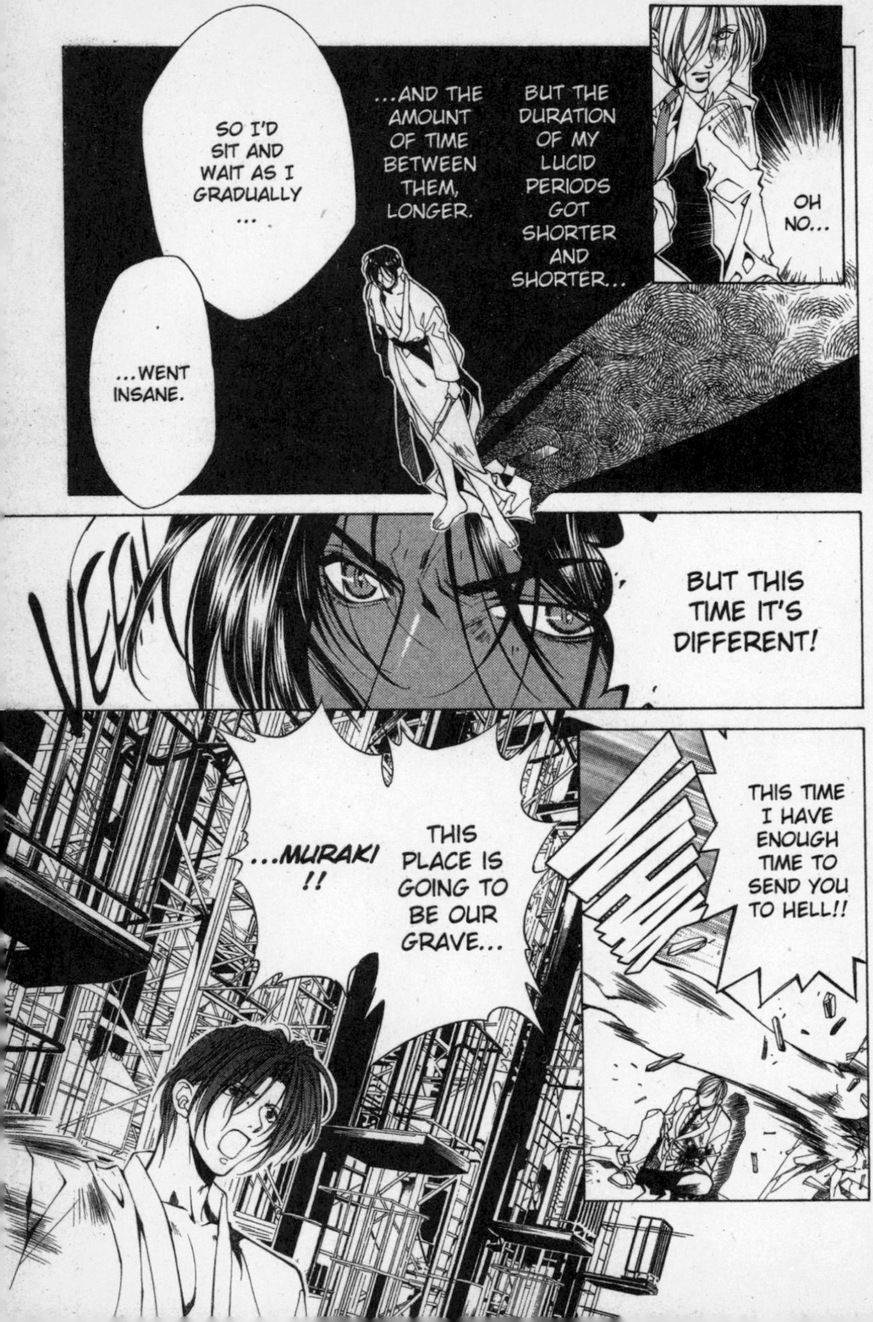
OH NO...
BUT THE DURATION OF MY LUCID PERIODS GOT SHORTER AND SHORTER...
...AND THE AMOUNT OF TIME BETWEEN THEM, LONGER.
SO I'D SIT AND WAIT AS I GRADUALLY ...
...WENT INSANE.
BUT THIS TIME IT'S DIFFERENT!
THIS TIME I HAVE ENOUGH TIME TO SEND YOU TO HELL!!
THIS PLACE IS GOING TO BE OUR GRAVE...
...MURAKI !!

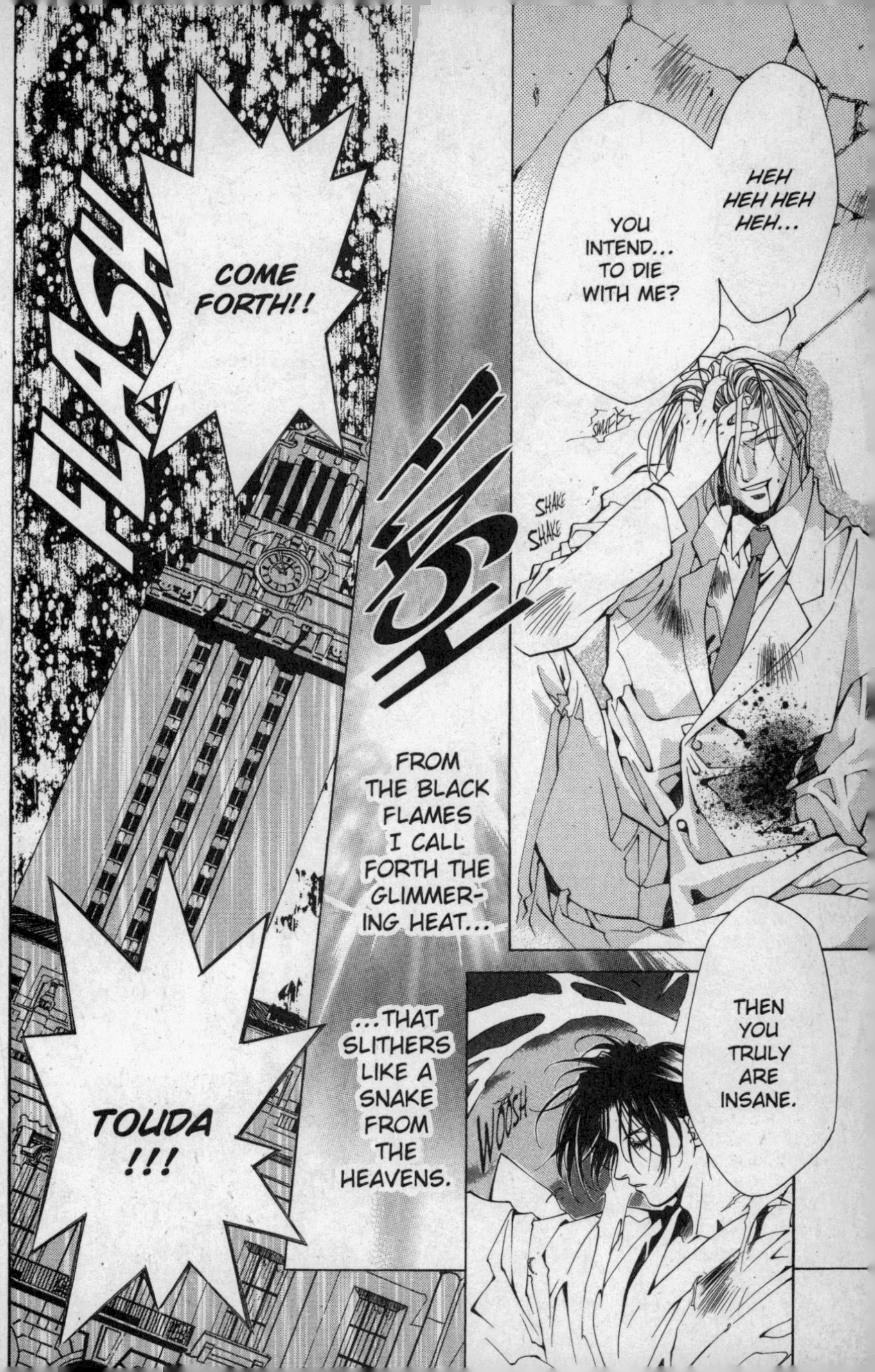

HEH HEH HEH HEH...
YOU INTEND... TO DIE WITH ME?
SHAKE SHAKE
THEN YOU TRULY ARE INSANE.
WOOSH
FLASH
FROM THE BLACK FLAMES I CALL FORTH THE GLIMMERING HEAT...
...THAT SLITHERS LIKE A SNAKE FROM THE HEAVENS.
COME FORTH!!
FLASH
TOUDA!!!

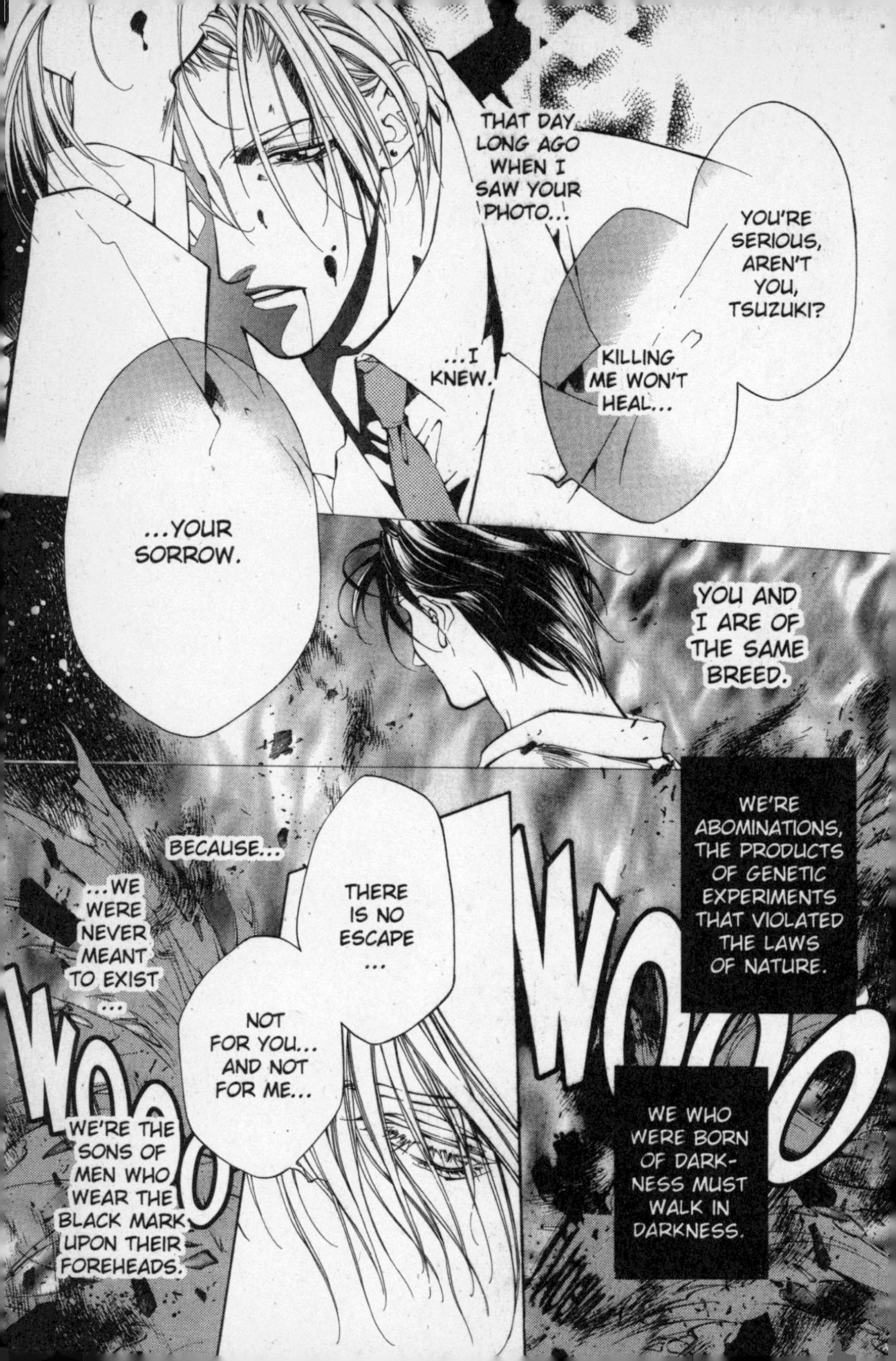
YOU'RE SERIOUS, AREN'T YOU, TSUZUKI?
THAT DAY LONG AGO WHEN I SAW YOUR PHOTO...
...I KNEW.
KILLING ME WON'T HEAL...
...YOUR SORROW.
YOU AND I ARE OF THE SAME BREED.
WE'RE ABOMINATIONS, THE PRODUCTS OF GENETIC EXPERIMENTS THAT VIOLATED THE LAWS OF NATURE.
WOOO
WE WHO WERE BORN OF DARK-NESS MUST WALK IN DARKNESS.
THERE IS NO ESCAPE...
NOT FOR YOU... AND NOT FOR ME...
BECAUSE...
...WE WERE NEVER MEANT TO EXIST...
WOOO
WE'RE THE SONS OF MEN WHO WEAR THE BLACK MARK UPON THEIR FOREHEADS.

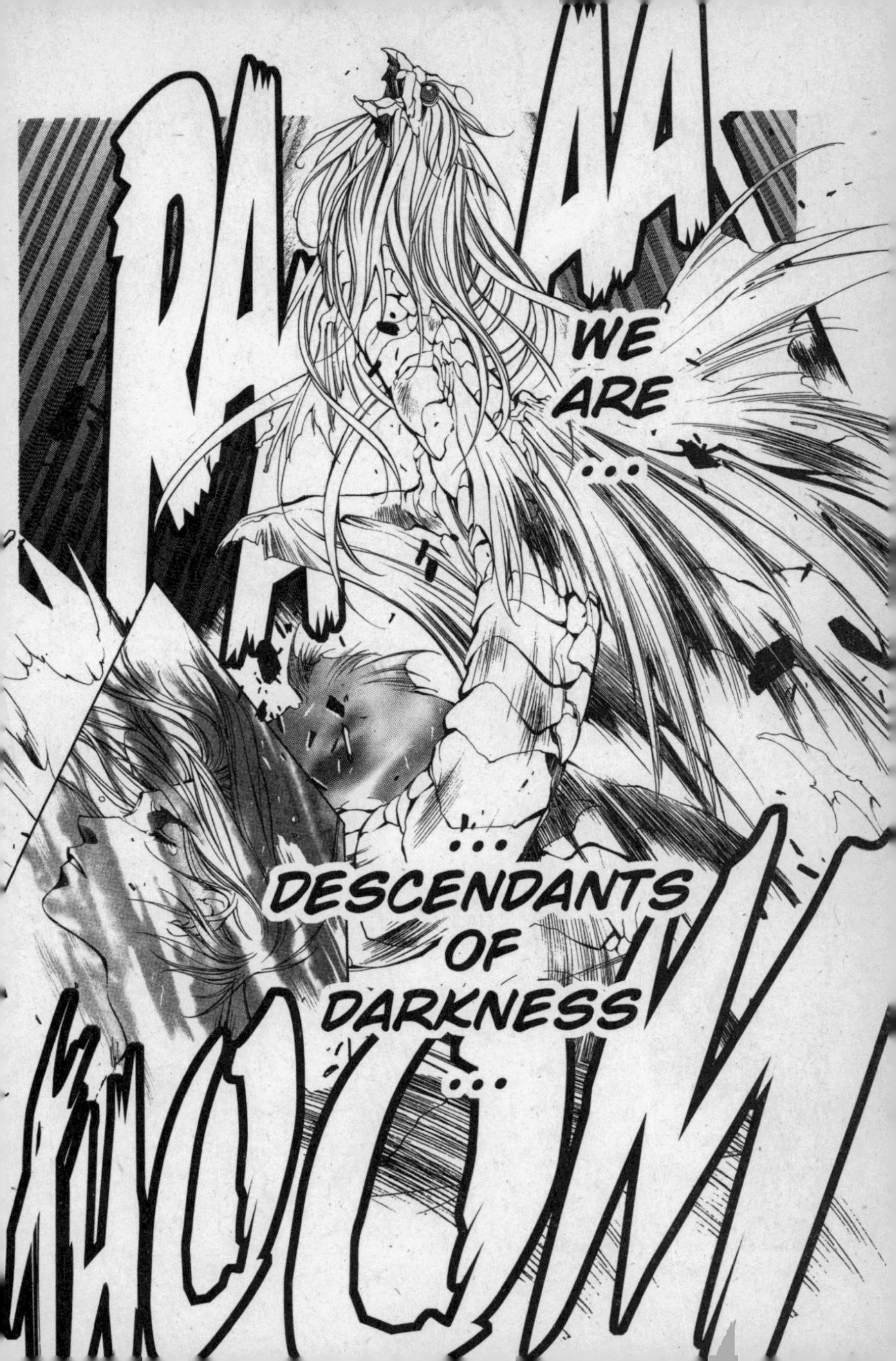
WE ARE ...
... DESCENDANTS OF DARKNESS ...

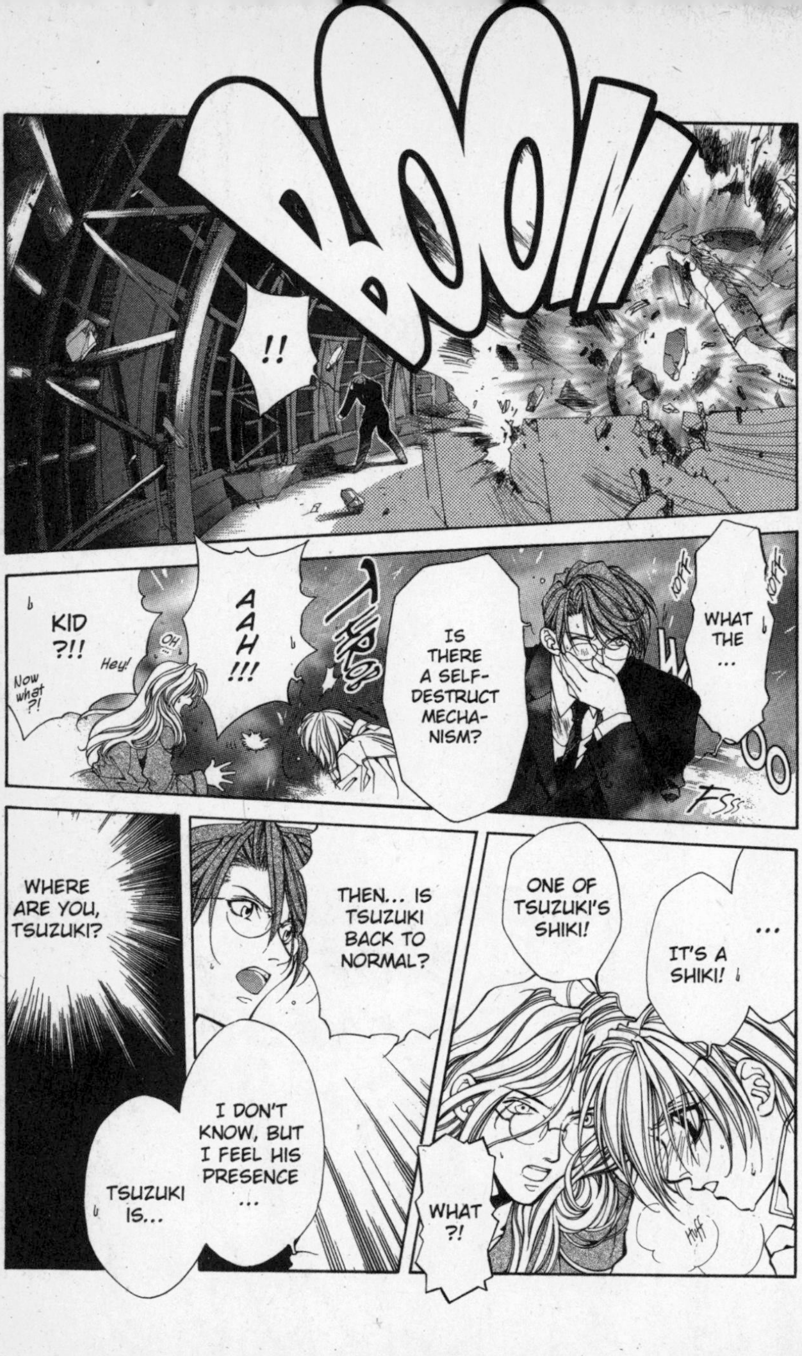
BOOM
!!
KOFF
KOFF
WHAT THE ...
FSSS
IS THERE A SELF-DESTRUCT MECHANISM?
THROB
AAH!!!
OH...
Hey!
KID?!!
Now what?!
...
IT'S A SHIKI!
ONE OF TSUZUKI'S SHIKI!
Huff
WHAT?!
THEN... IS TSUZUKI BACK TO NORMAL?
I DON'T KNOW, BUT I FEEL HIS PRESENCE ...
TSUZUKI IS...
WHERE ARE YOU, TSUZUKI?

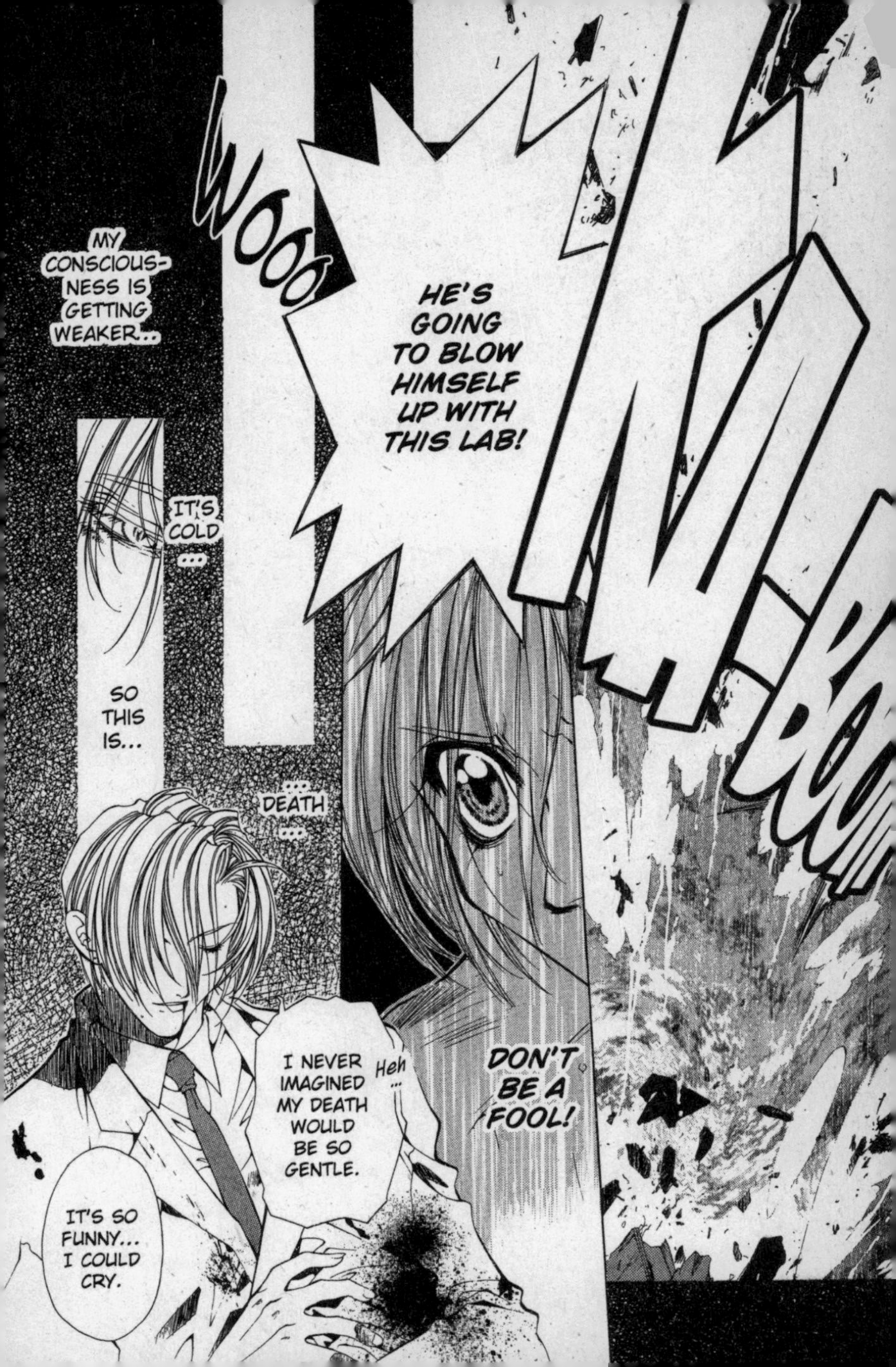
WOOOM-BOO
HE'S GOING TO BLOW HIMSELF UP WITH THIS LAB!
DON'T BE A FOOL!
MY CONSCIOUSNESS IS GETTING WEAKER...
IT'S COLD...
SO THIS IS...
...DEATH...
Heh...
I NEVER IMAGINED MY DEATH WOULD BE SO GENTLE.
IT'S SO FUNNY... I COULD CRY.

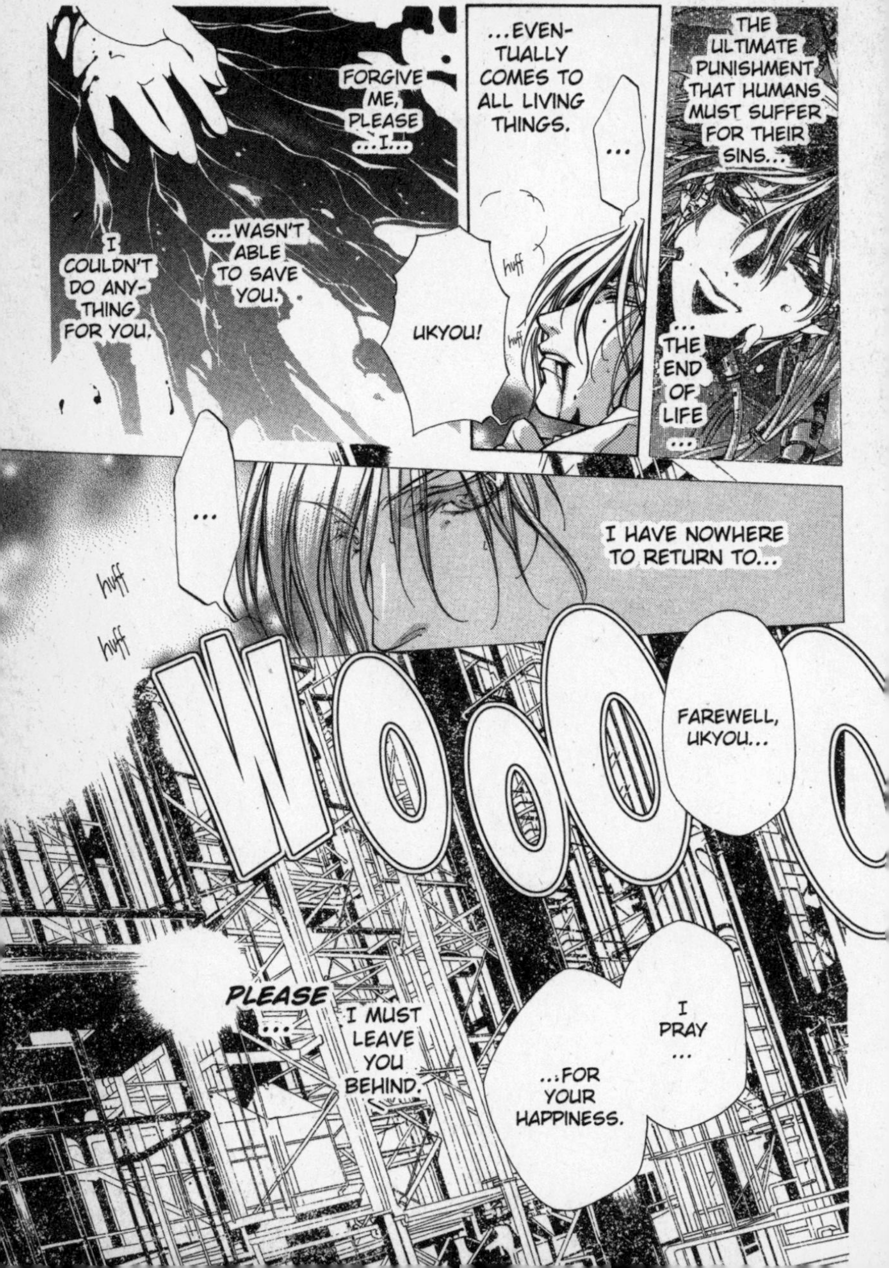
THE ULTIMATE PUNISHMENT THAT HUMANS MUST SUFFER FOR THEIR SINS...
...THE END OF LIFE...
...EVEN-TUALLY COMES TO ALL LIVING THINGS.
...
huff
huff
UKYOU!
FORGIVE ME, PLEASE ...I...
...WASN'T ABLE TO SAVE YOU.
I COULDN'T DO ANY-THING FOR YOU.
I HAVE NOWHERE TO RETURN TO...
...
huff
huff
FAREWELL, UKYOU...
WOOOOO
I PRAY...
...FOR YOUR HAPPINESS.
I MUST LEAVE YOU BEHIND.
PLEASE...

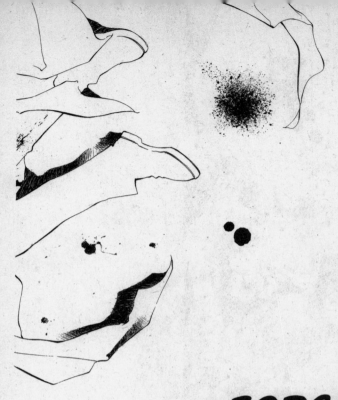

...FORGIVE
ME.

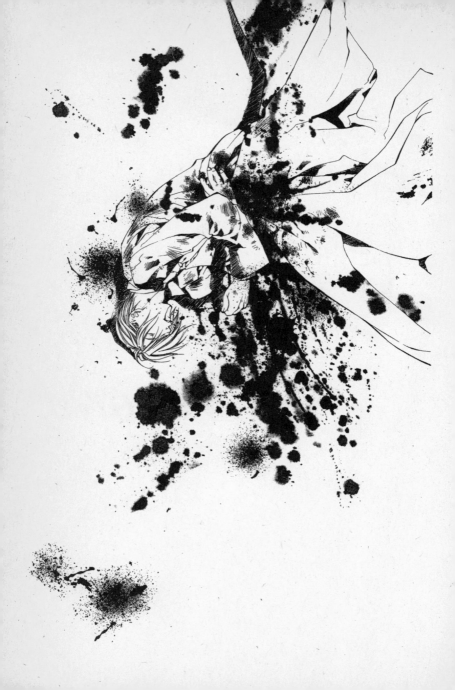

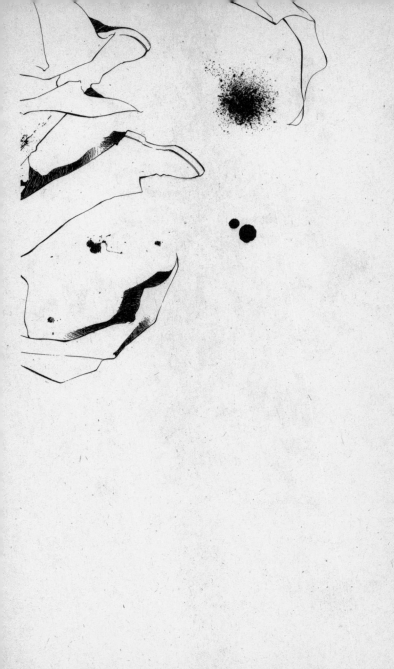

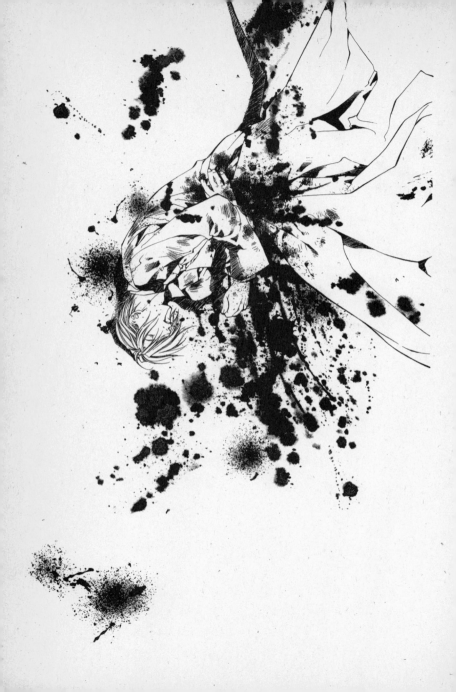

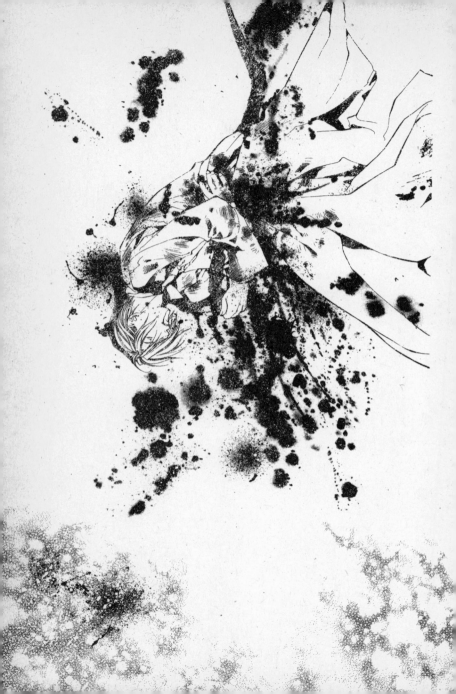

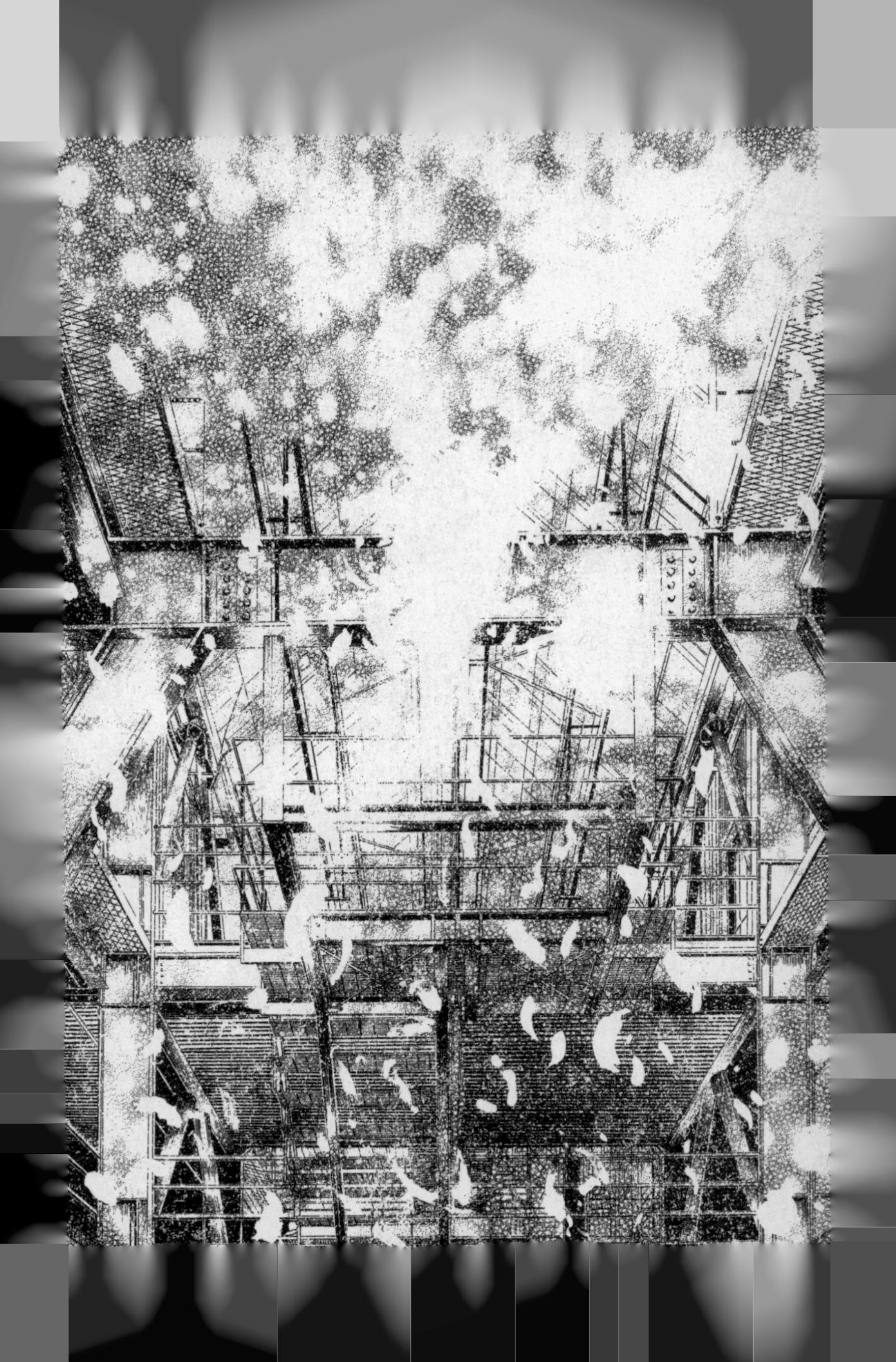

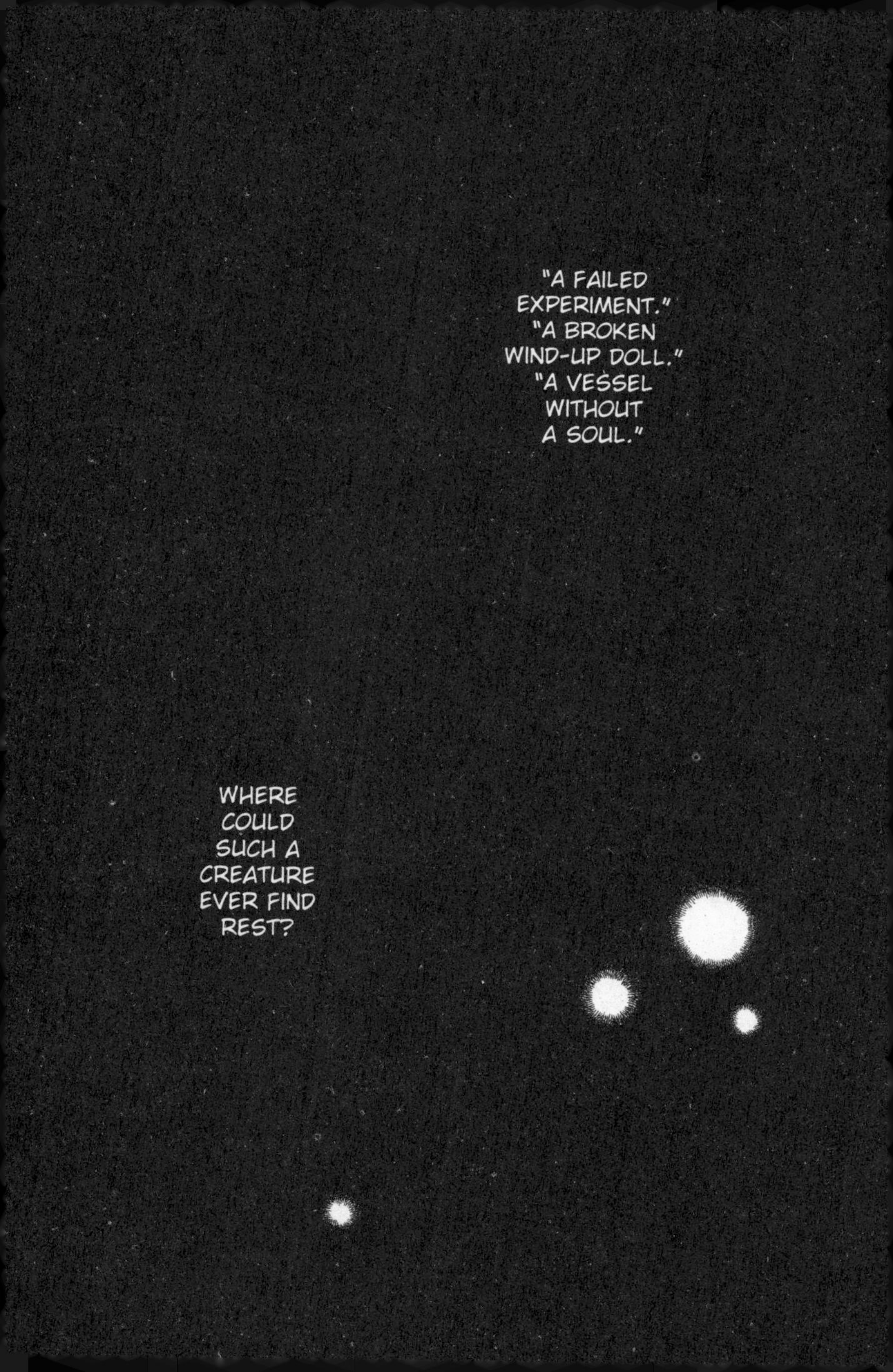
"A FAILED EXPERIMENT." "A BROKEN WIND-UP DOLL." "A VESSEL WITHOUT A SOUL."
WHERE COULD SUCH A CREATURE EVER FIND REST?

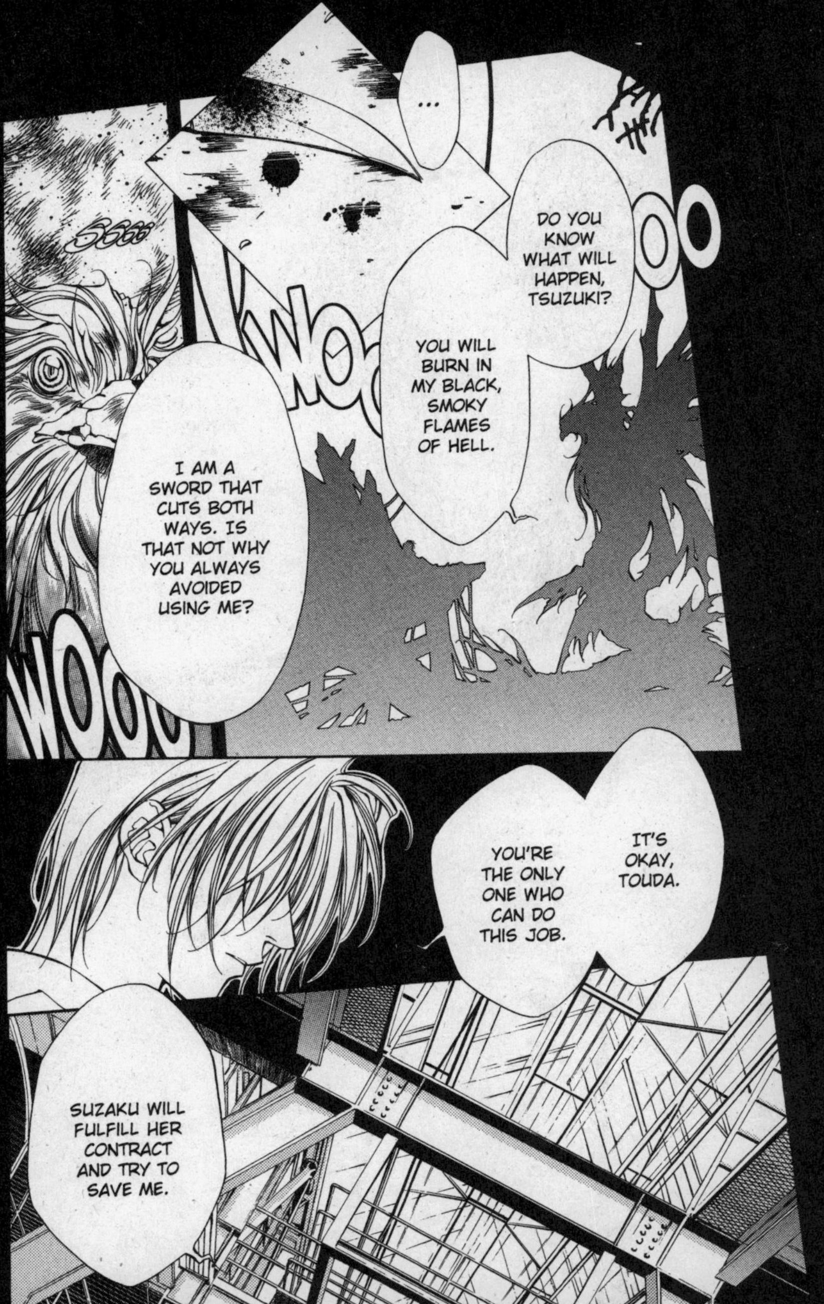
...
DO YOU KNOW WHAT WILL HAPPEN, TSUZUKI?
YOU WILL BURN IN MY BLACK, SMOKY FLAMES OF HELL.
I AM A SWORD THAT CUTS BOTH WAYS. IS THAT NOT WHY YOU ALWAYS AVOIDED USING ME?
IT'S OKAY, TOUDA.
YOU'RE THE ONLY ONE WHO CAN DO THIS JOB.
SUZAKU WILL FULFILL HER CONTRACT AND TRY TO SAVE ME.

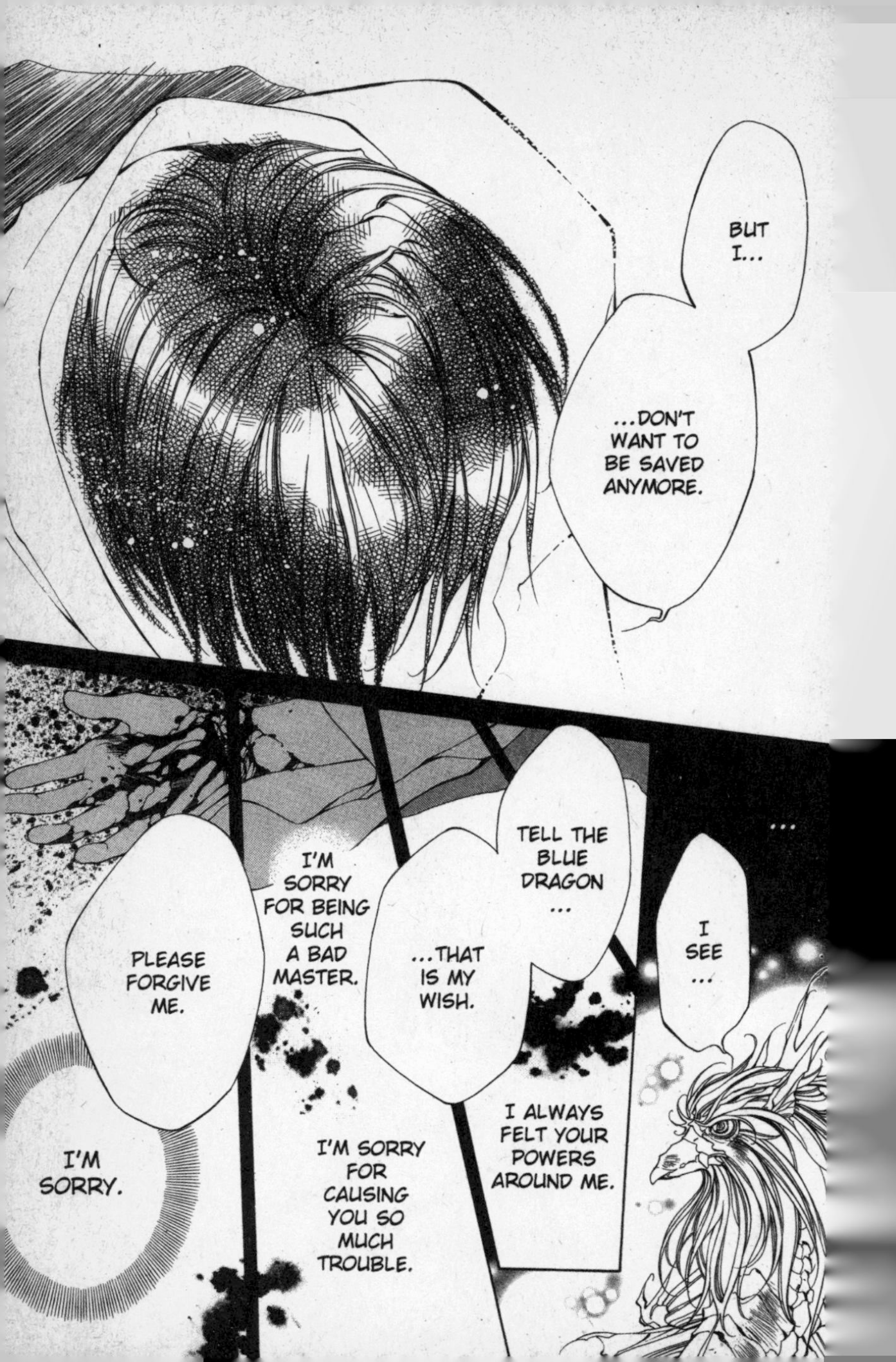
BUT I...
...DON'T WANT TO BE SAVED ANYMORE.
...
I SEE ...
TELL THE BLUE DRAGON ...
...THAT IS MY WISH.
I'M SORRY FOR BEING SUCH A BAD MASTER.
PLEASE FORGIVE ME.
I ALWAYS FELT YOUR POWERS AROUND ME.
I'M SORRY FOR CAUSING YOU SO MUCH TROUBLE.
I'M SORRY.

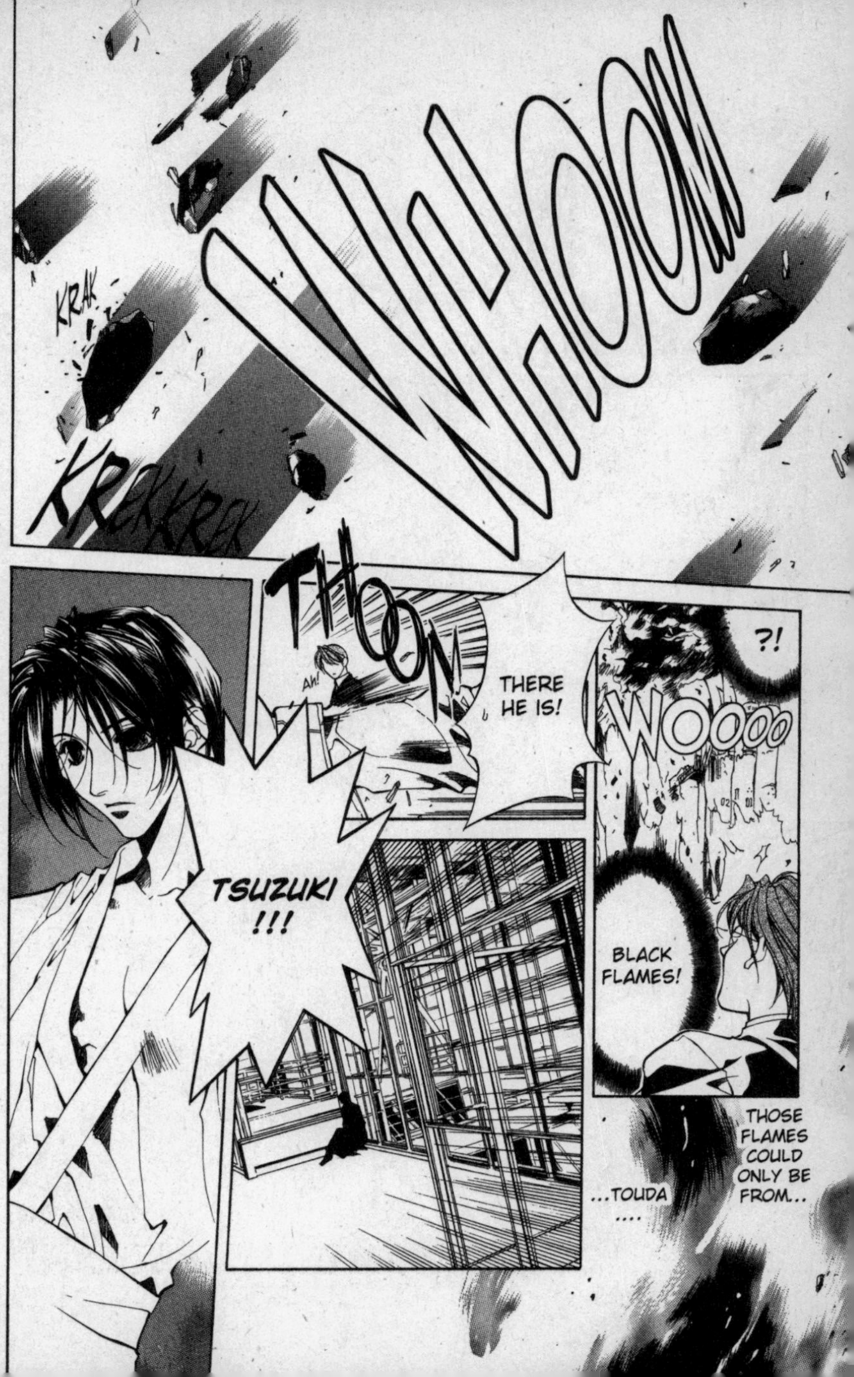
WHOOOM
KRAK
KRAKKRAK
?!
WOOOO
BLACK FLAMES!
THOSE FLAMES COULD ONLY BE FROM...
...TOUDA ....
THOOOM
AH!
THERE HE IS!
TSUZUKI !!!

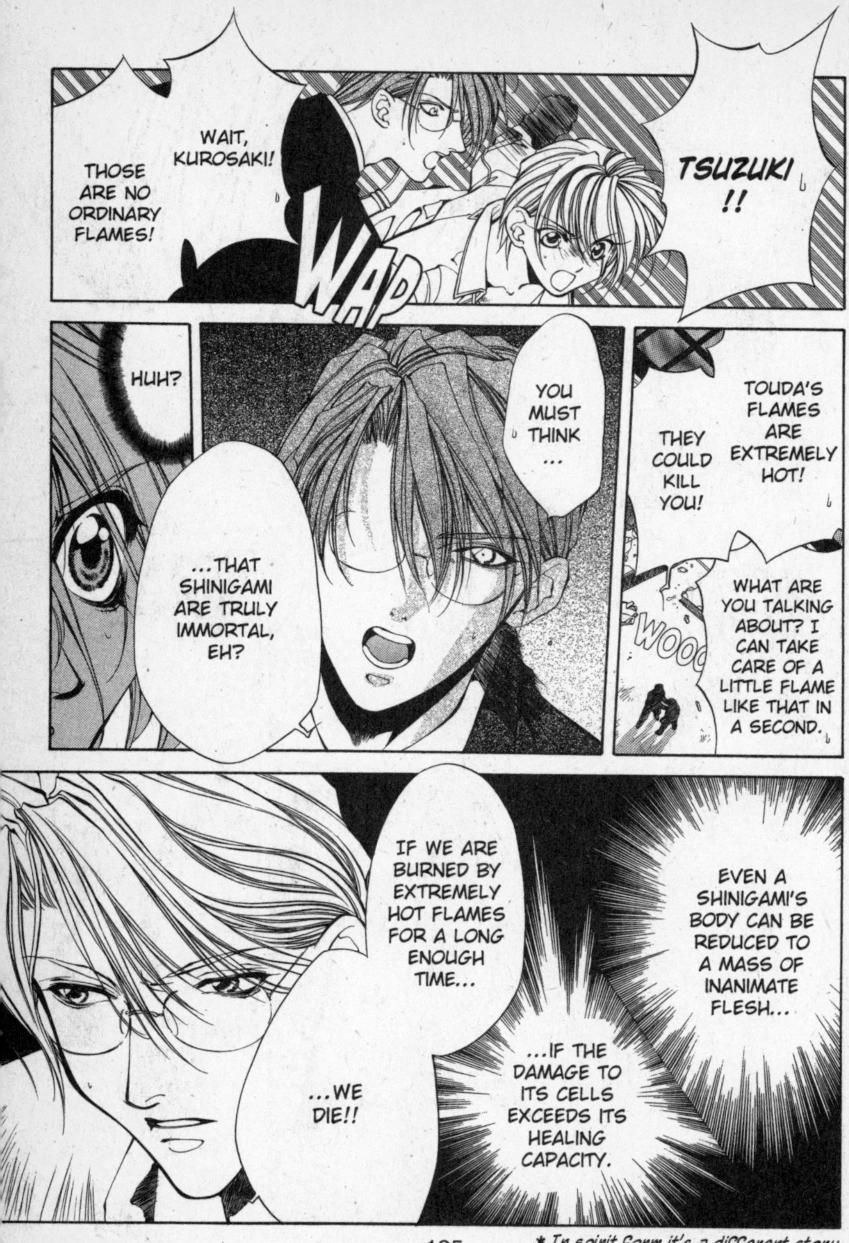
TSUZUKI !!
WAIT, KUROSAKI!
THOSE ARE NO ORDINARY FLAMES!
WAP
TOUDA'S FLAMES ARE EXTREMELY HOT!
THEY COULD KILL YOU!
WHAT ARE YOU TALKING ABOUT? I CAN TAKE CARE OF A LITTLE FLAME LIKE THAT IN A SECOND.
YOU MUST THINK...
...THAT SHINIGAMI ARE TRULY IMMORTAL, EH?
HUH?
EVEN A SHINIGAMI'S BODY CAN BE REDUCED TO A MASS OF INANIMATE FLESH...
...IF THE DAMAGE TO ITS CELLS EXCEEDS ITS HEALING CAPACITY.
IF WE ARE BURNED BY EXTREMELY HOT FLAMES FOR A LONG ENOUGH TIME...
...WE DIE!!

* In spirit form it's a different story.

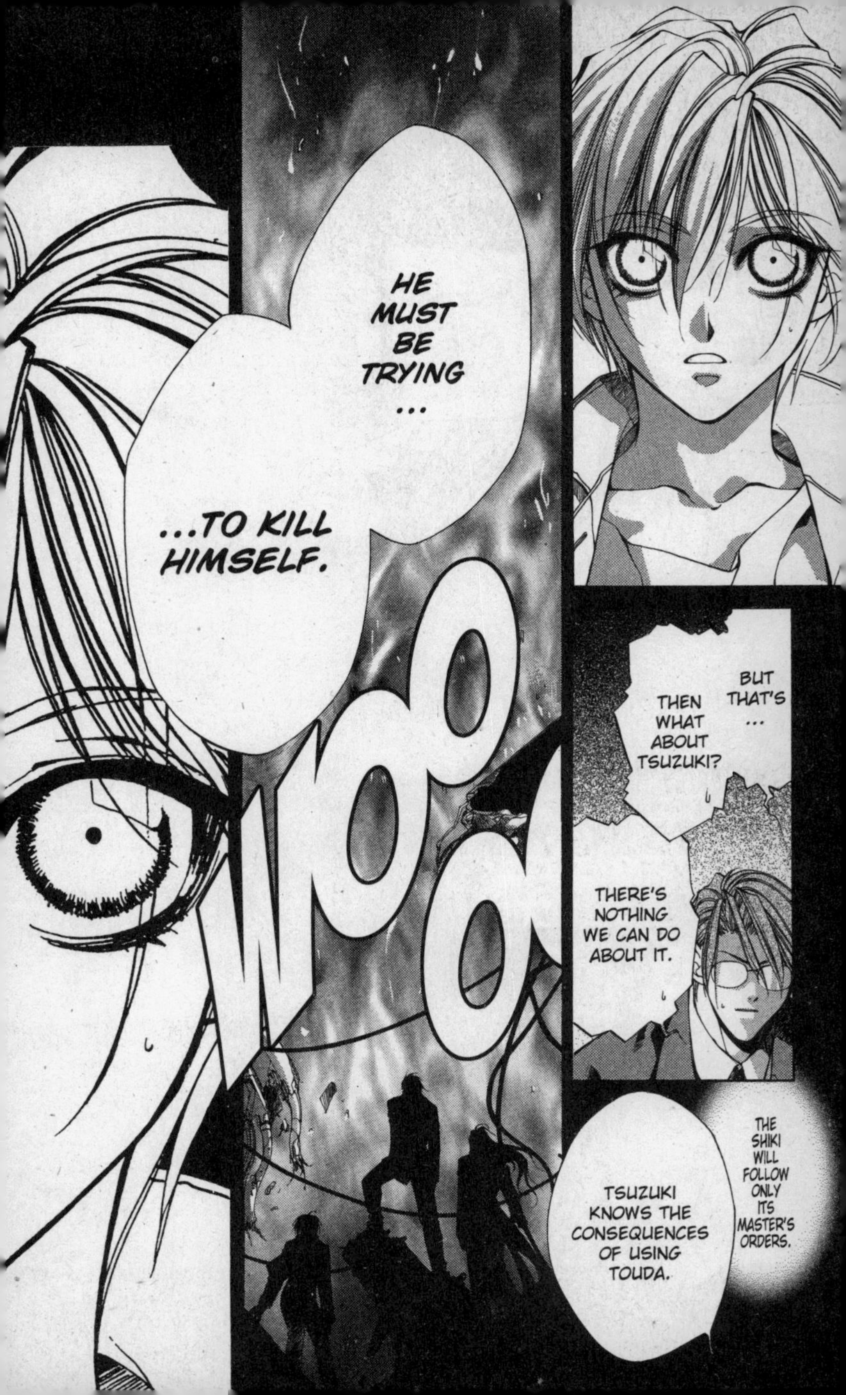
BUT THAT'S ...
THEN WHAT ABOUT TSUZUKI?
THERE'S NOTHING WE CAN DO ABOUT IT.
THE SHIKI WILL FOLLOW ONLY ITS MASTER'S ORDERS.
TSUZUKI KNOWS THE CONSEQUENCES OF USING TOUDA.
HE MUST BE TRYING ...
...TO KILL HIMSELF.
WOOO

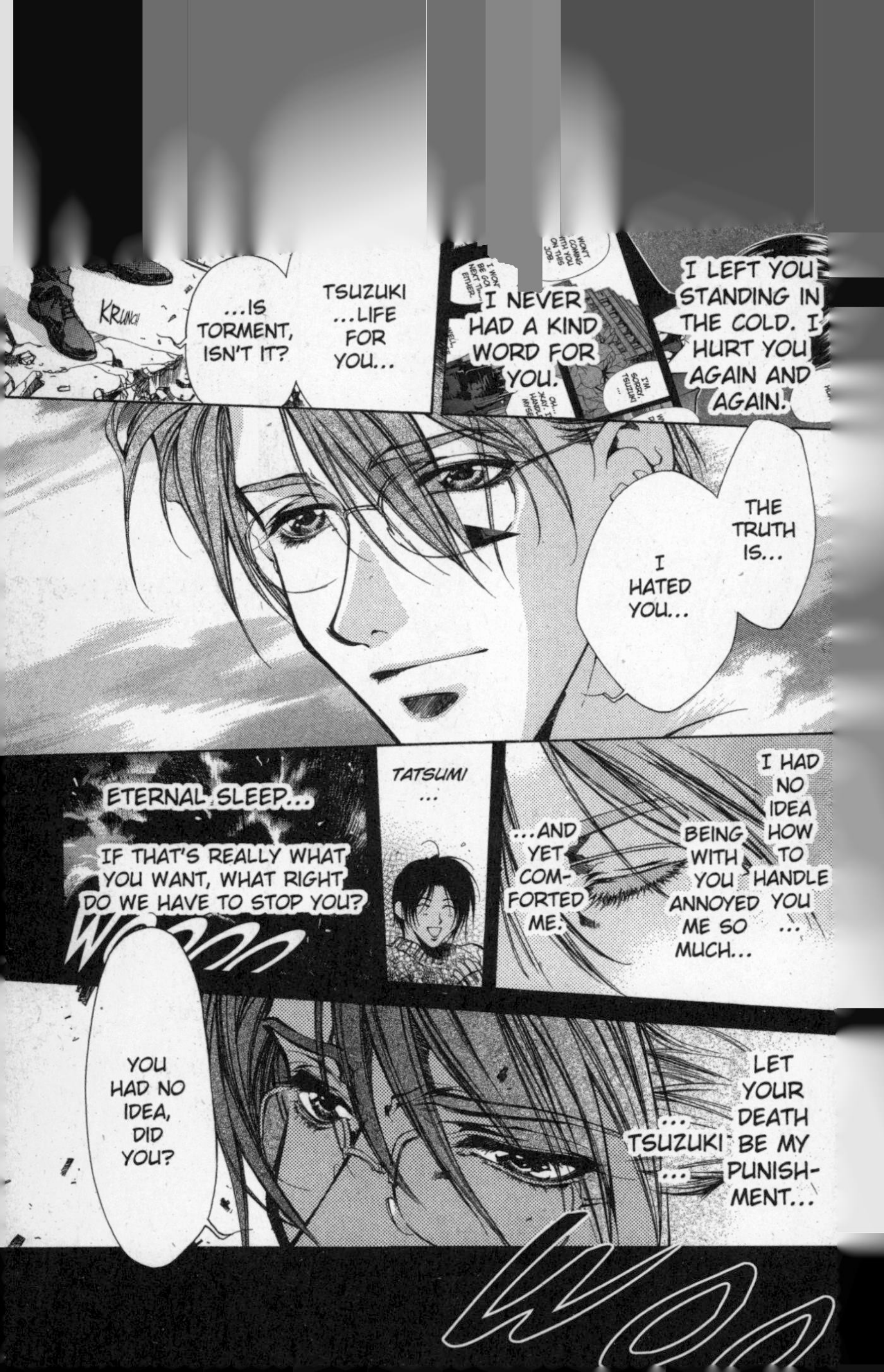
I LEFT YOU STANDING IN THE COLD. I HURT YOU AGAIN AND AGAIN.
I'M SORRY, TSUZUKI...
I NEVER HAD A KIND WORD FOR YOU.
TSUZUKI ...LIFE FOR YOU...
...IS TORMENT, ISN'T IT?
KRUNCH
THE TRUTH IS...
I HATED YOU...
I HAD NO IDEA HOW TO HANDLE YOU...
BEING WITH YOU ANNOYED ME SO MUCH...
...AND YET COMFORTED ME.
TATSUMI...
ETERNAL SLEEP...
IF THAT'S REALLY WHAT YOU WANT, WHAT RIGHT DO WE HAVE TO STOP YOU?
WOOOO
LET YOUR DEATH BE MY PUNISHMENT...
...TSUZUKI...
YOU HAD NO IDEA, DID YOU?
WOO

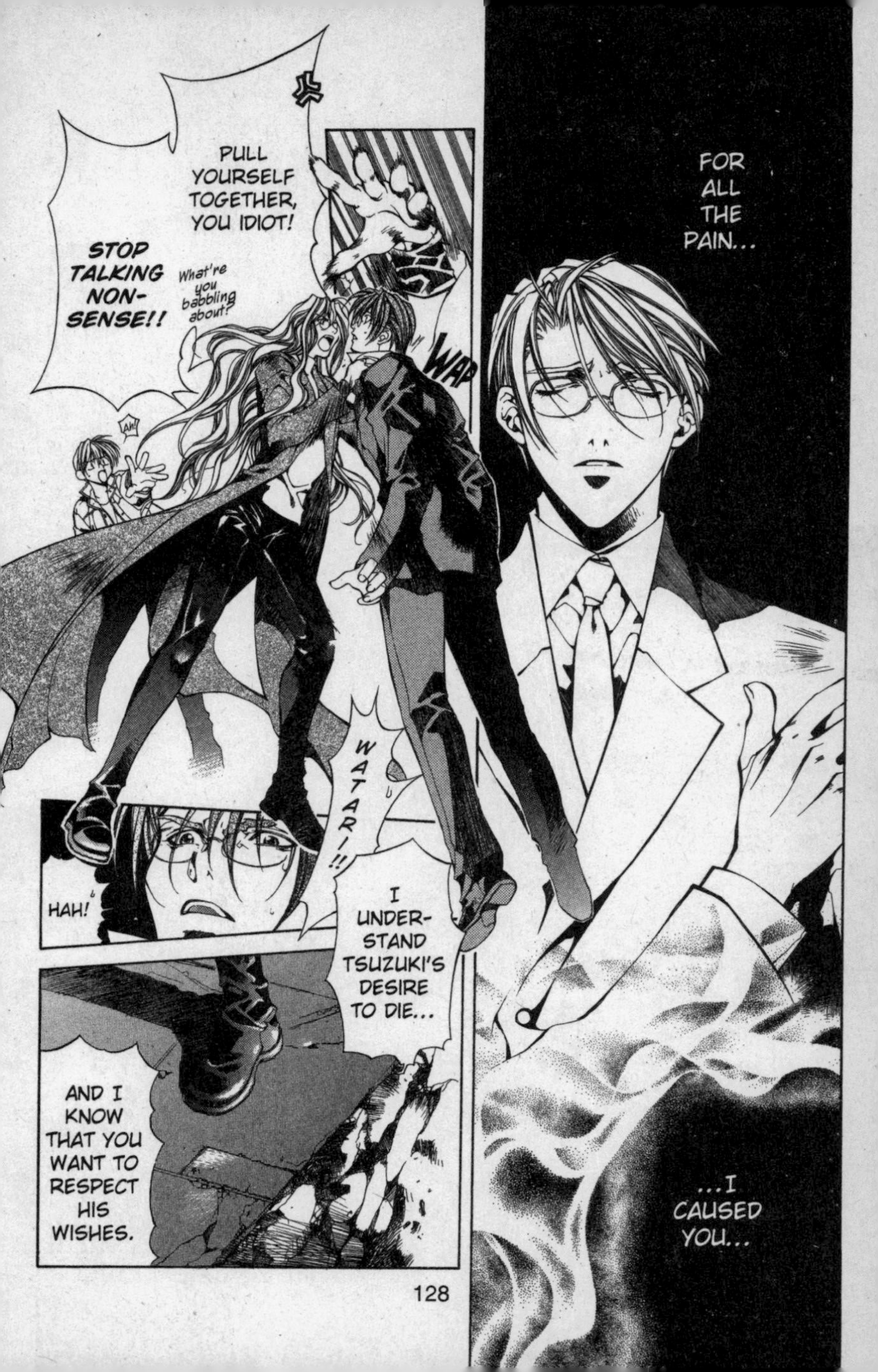
FOR ALL THE PAIN...
...I CAUSED YOU...
PULL YOURSELF TOGETHER, YOU IDIOT!
What're you babbling about?
STOP TALKING NON-SENSE!!
WAP
Ah!
WATARI!!!
HAH!
I UNDER-STAND TSUZUKI'S DESIRE TO DIE...
AND I KNOW THAT YOU WANT TO RESPECT HIS WISHES.

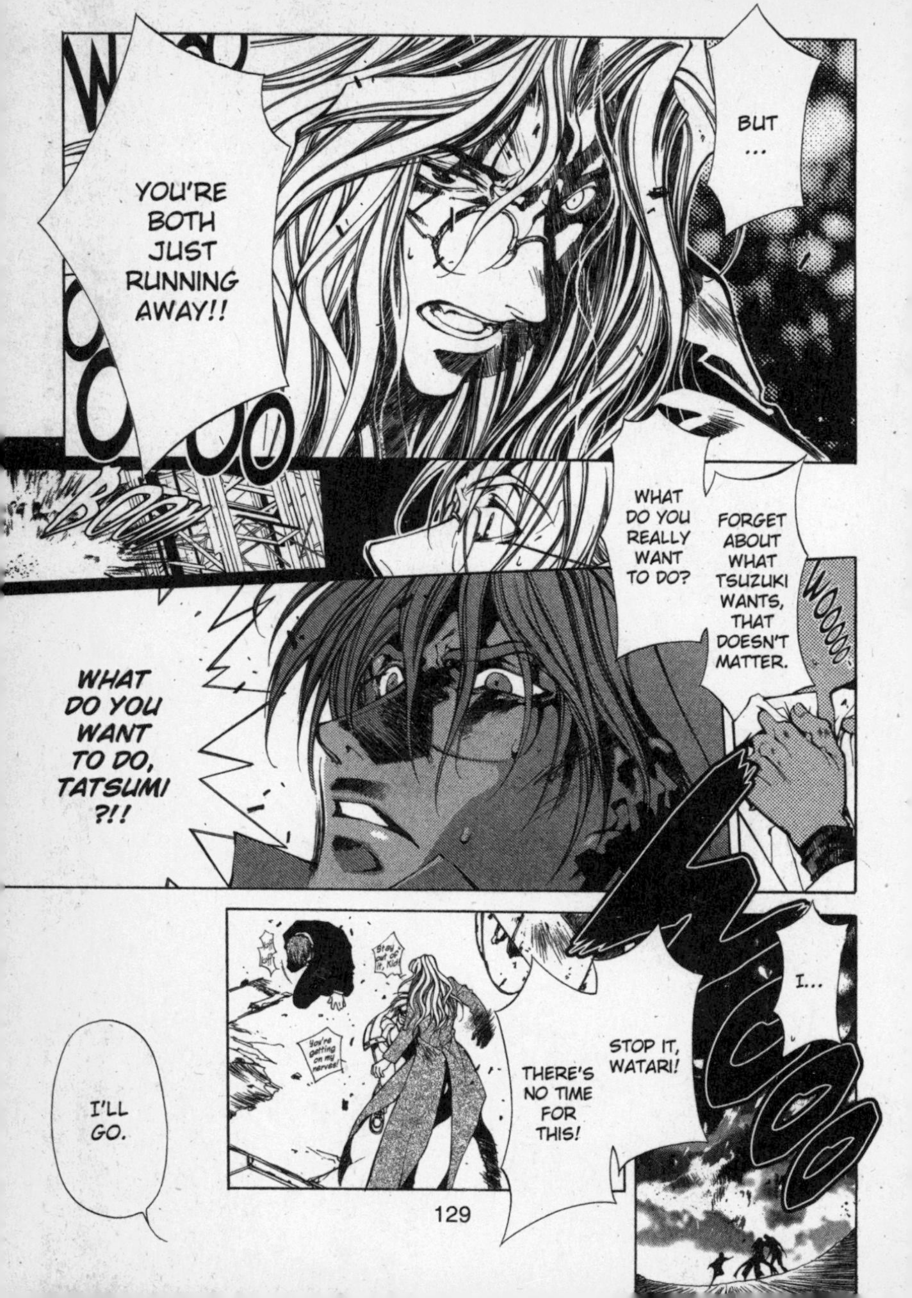
BUT ...
YOU'RE BOTH JUST RUNNING AWAY!!
FORGET ABOUT WHAT TSUZUKI WANTS, THAT DOESN'T MATTER.
WHAT DO YOU REALLY WANT TO DO?
WOOO
WHAT DO YOU WANT TO DO, TATSUMI ?!!
I...
STOP IT, WATARI!
THERE'S NO TIME FOR THIS!
Stay out of it, Kid!
You're getting on my nerves!
I'LL GO.

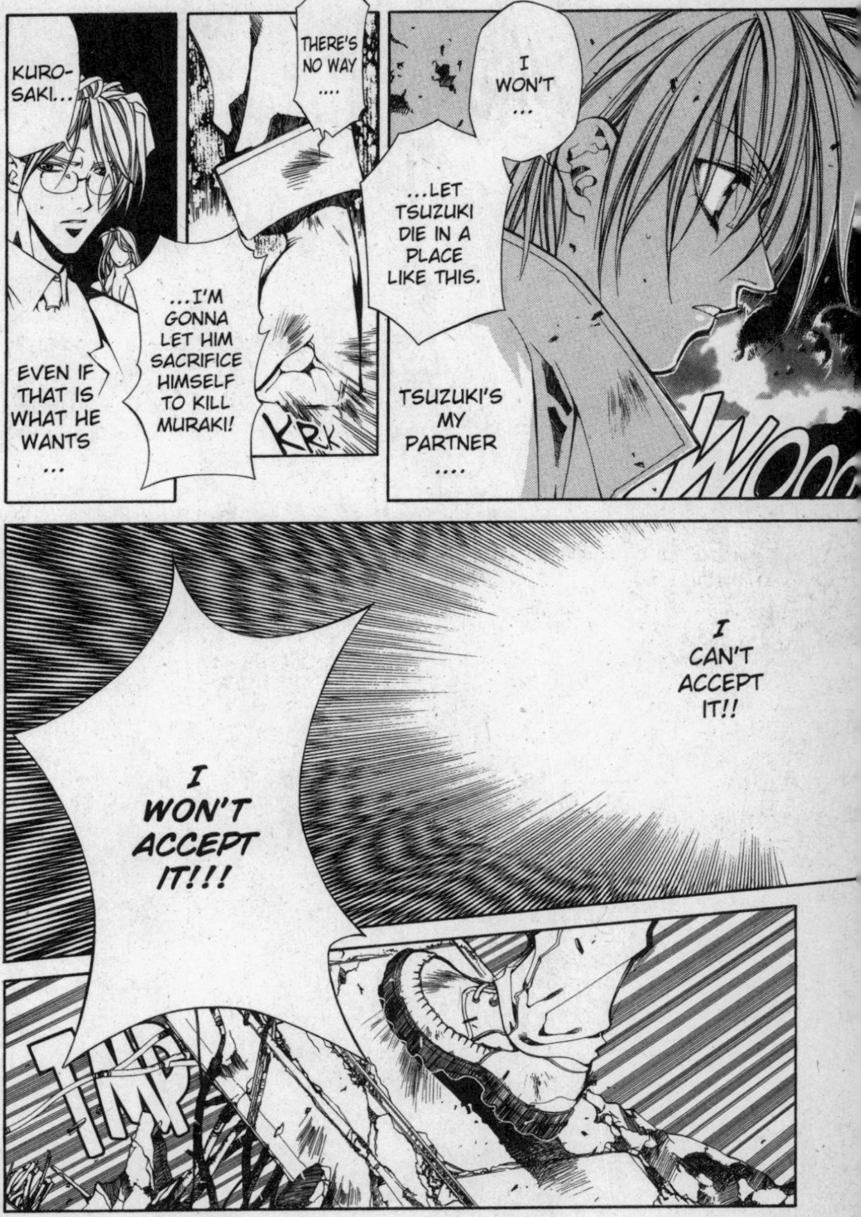
I WON'T ...
...LET TSUZUKI DIE IN A PLACE LIKE THIS.
TSUZUKI'S MY PARTNER ....
THERE'S NO WAY ....
...I'M GONNA LET HIM SACRIFICE HIMSELF TO KILL MURAKI!
KRK
KURO-SAKI...
EVEN IF THAT IS WHAT HE WANTS ...
I CAN'T ACCEPT IT!!
I WON'T ACCEPT IT!!!

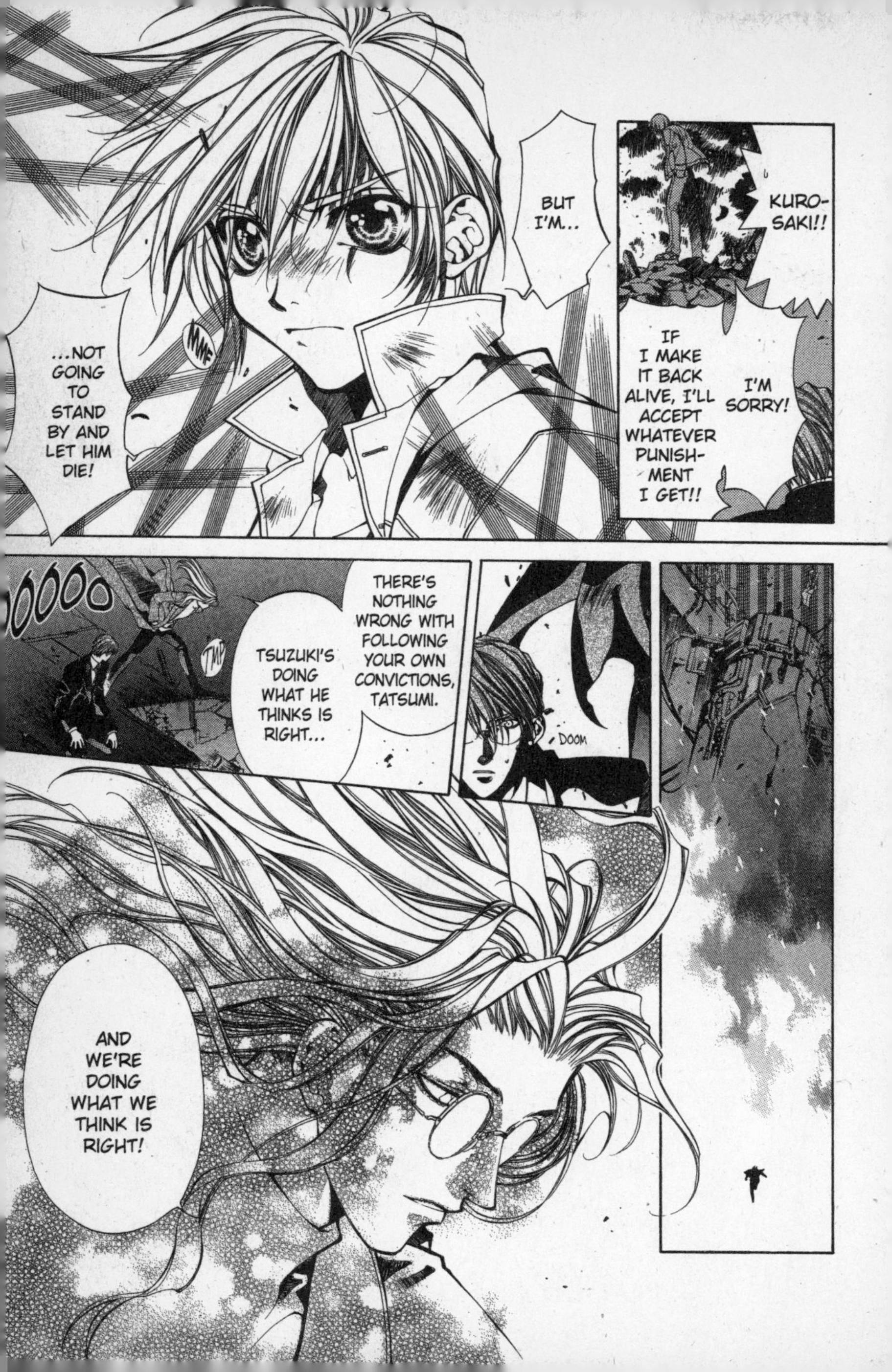

KURO-SAKI!!
I'M SORRY!
IF I MAKE IT BACK ALIVE, I'LL ACCEPT WHATEVER PUNISH-MENT I GET!!
BUT I'M...
MMF
...NOT GOING TO STAND BY AND LET HIM DIE!
DOOM
THERE'S NOTHING WRONG WITH FOLLOWING YOUR OWN CONVICTIONS, TATSUMI.
TSUZUKI'S DOING WHAT HE THINKS IS RIGHT...
TMP
OOOOO
AND WE'RE DOING WHAT WE THINK IS RIGHT!

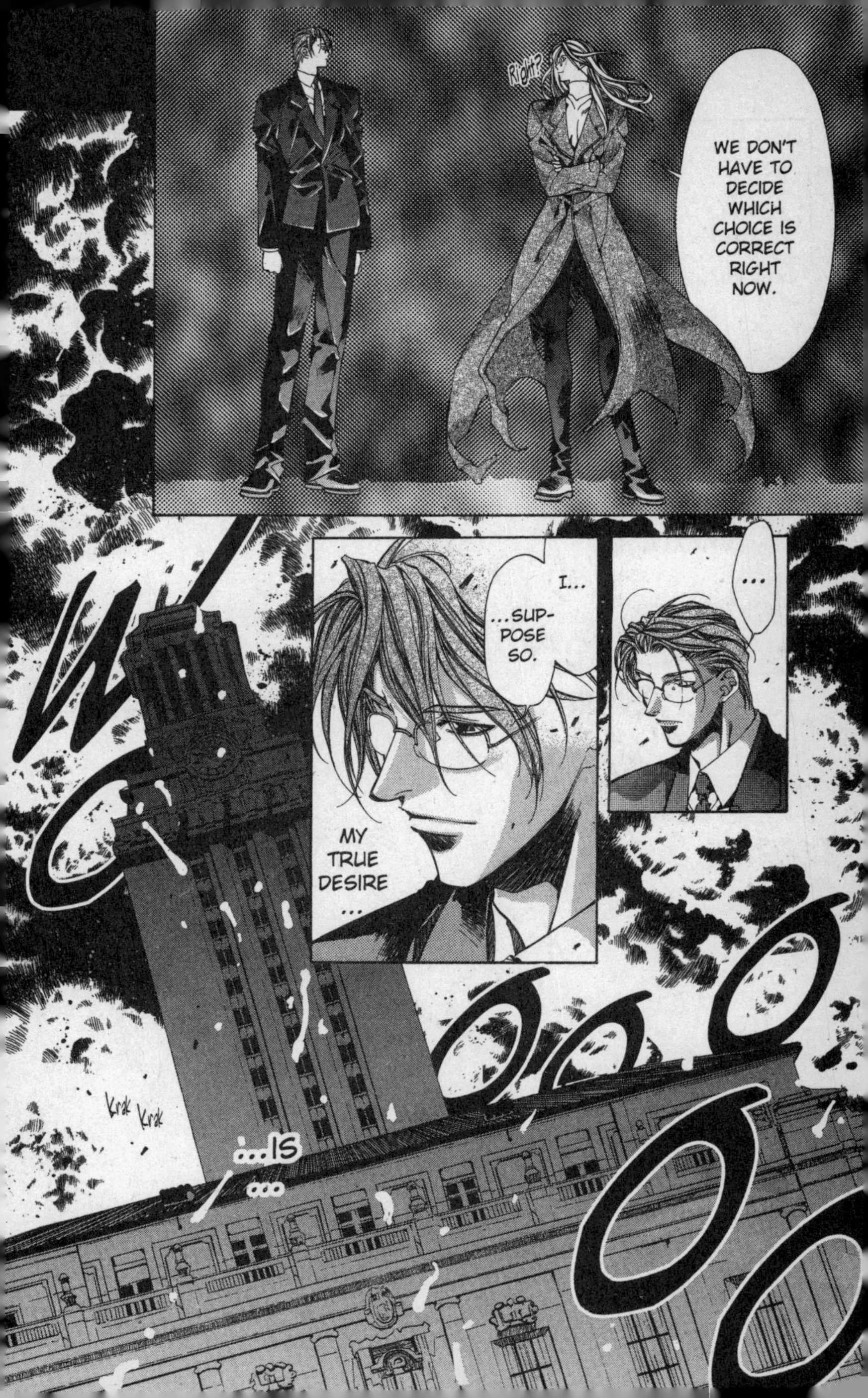
Right?
WE DON'T HAVE TO DECIDE WHICH CHOICE IS CORRECT RIGHT NOW.
...
I...
...SUP-POSE SO.
MY TRUE DESIRE ...
Krak Krak
...IS
...

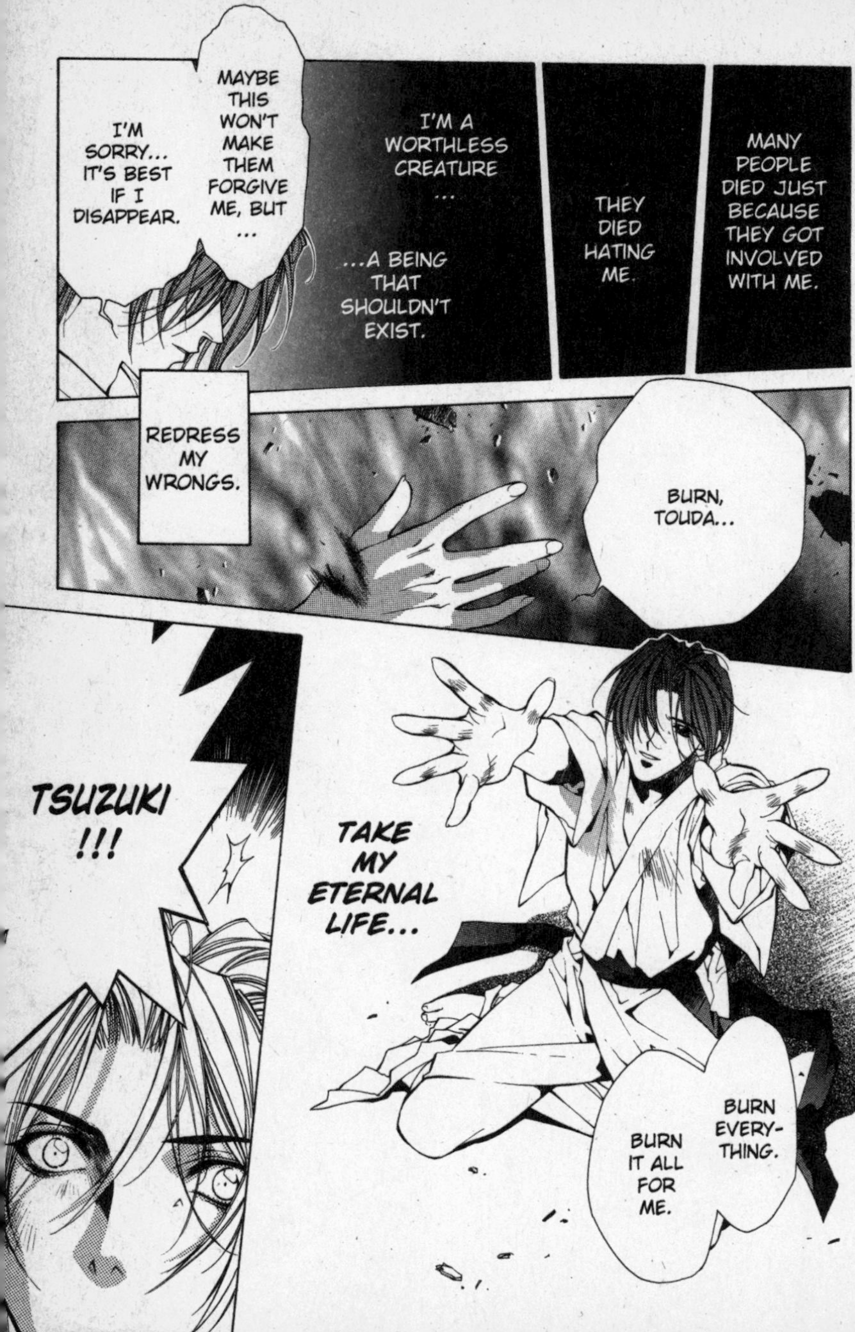
MANY PEOPLE DIED JUST BECAUSE THEY GOT INVOLVED WITH ME.
THEY DIED HATING ME.
I'M A WORTHLESS CREATURE...
...A BEING THAT SHOULDN'T EXIST.
MAYBE THIS WON'T MAKE THEM FORGIVE ME, BUT...
I'M SORRY... IT'S BEST IF I DISAPPEAR.
REDRESS MY WRONGS.
BURN, TOUDA...
BURN EVERY-THING.
BURN IT ALL FOR ME.
TAKE MY ETERNAL LIFE...
TSUZUKI !!!

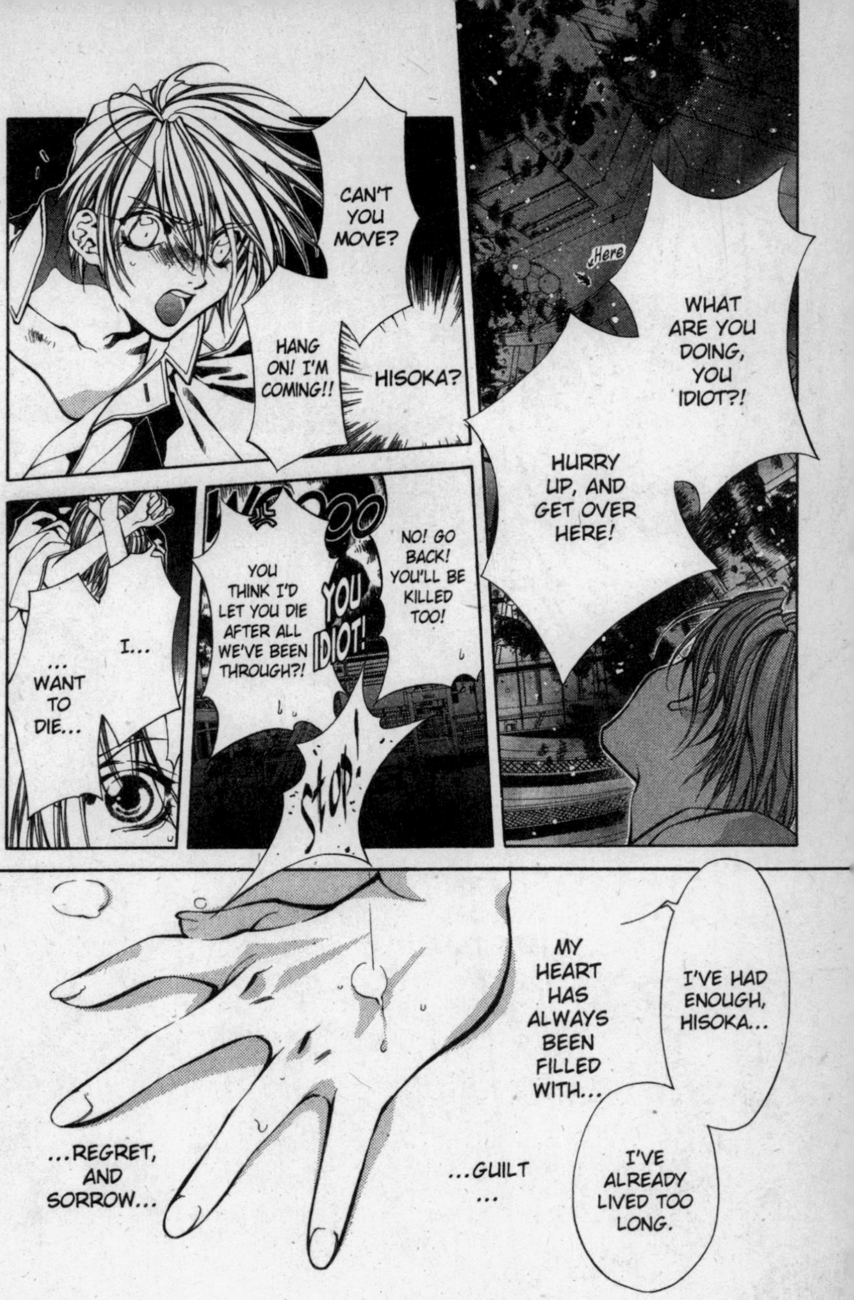

Here
WHAT ARE YOU DOING, YOU IDIOT?!
HURRY UP, AND GET OVER HERE!
CAN'T YOU MOVE?
HISOKA?
HANG ON! I'M COMING!!
NO! GO BACK! YOU'LL BE KILLED TOO!
YOU IDIOT!
YOU THINK I'D LET YOU DIE AFTER ALL WE'VE BEEN THROUGH?!
STOP!
I...
...WANT TO DIE...
I'VE HAD ENOUGH, HISOKA...
I'VE ALREADY LIVED TOO LONG.
MY HEART HAS ALWAYS BEEN FILLED WITH...
...GUILT ...
...REGRET, AND SORROW...

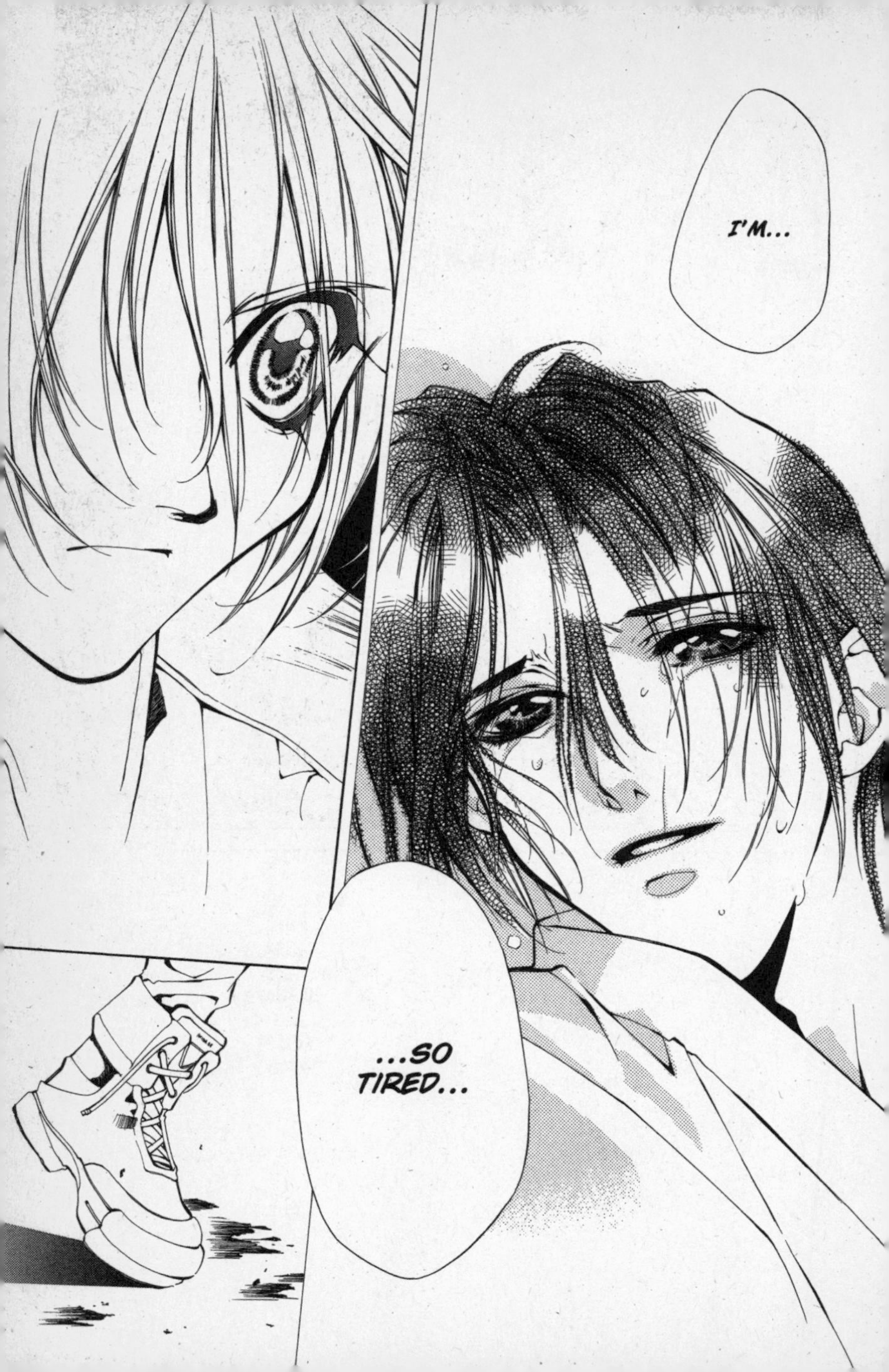
I'M...
...SO TIRED...

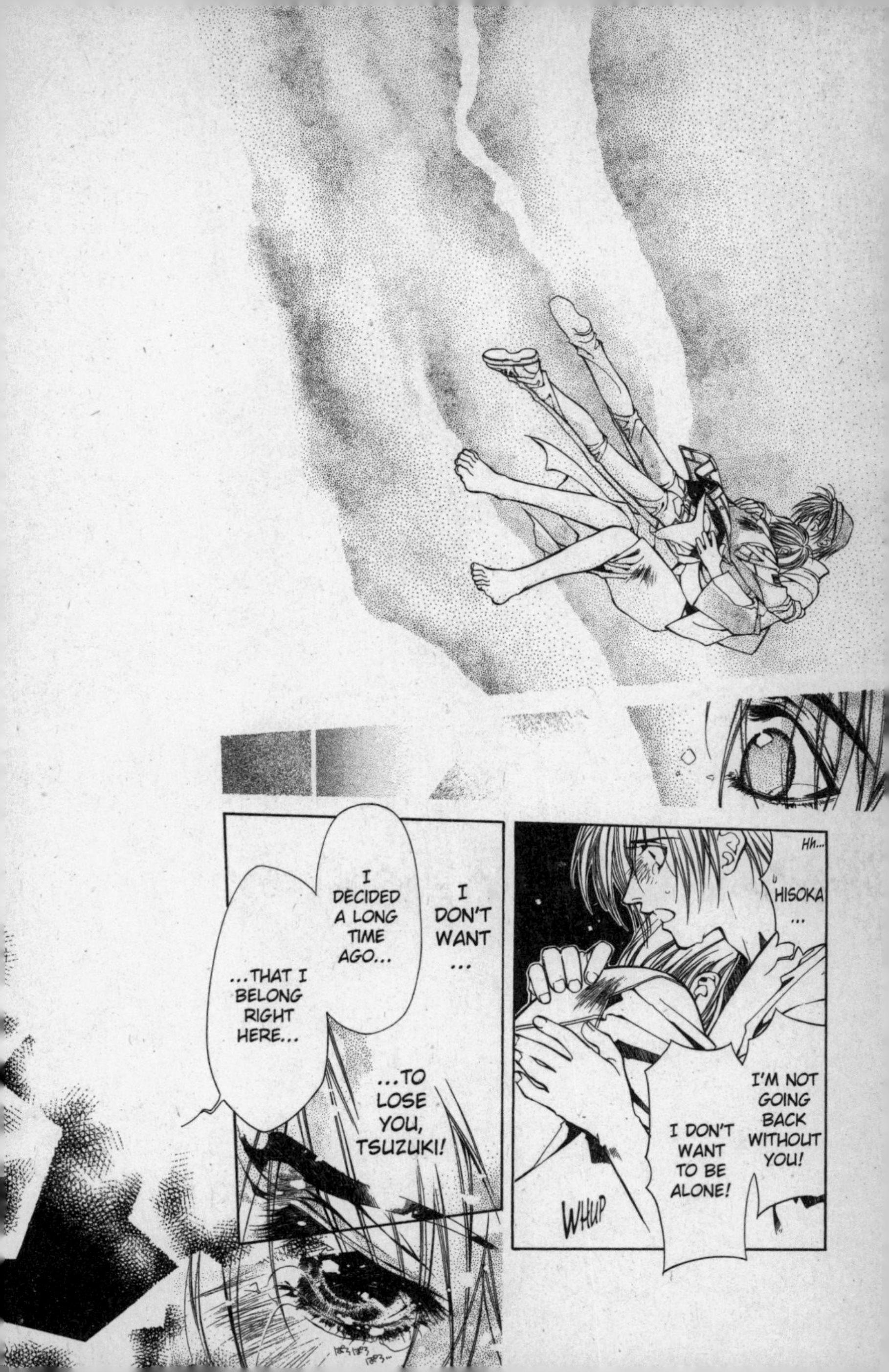
Hh...
HISOKA...
I'M NOT GOING BACK WITHOUT YOU!
I DON'T WANT TO BE ALONE!
WHUP
I DON'T WANT...
I DECIDED A LONG TIME AGO...
...THAT I BELONG RIGHT HERE...
...TO LOSE YOU, TSUZUKI!

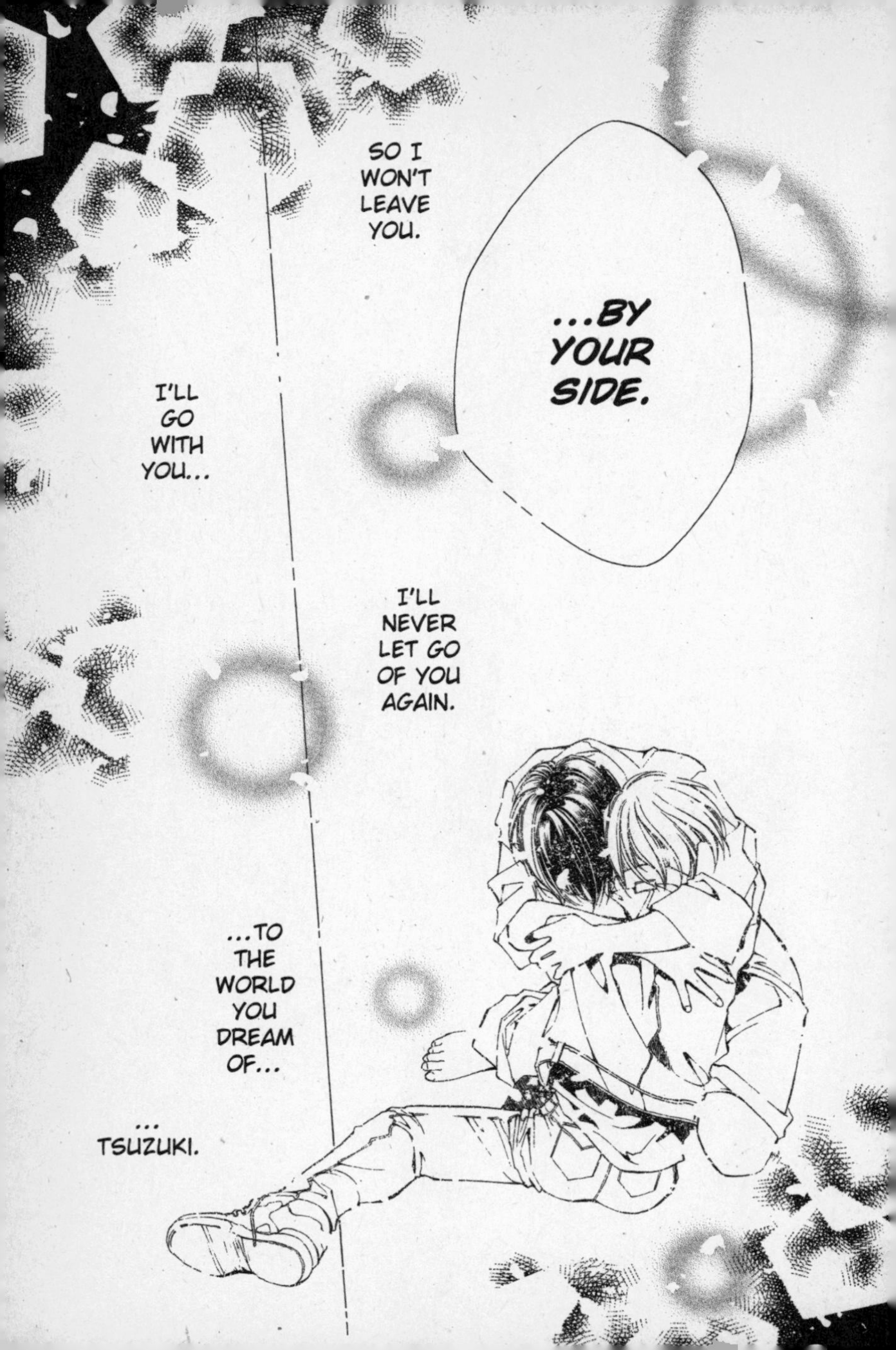
SO I WON'T LEAVE YOU.
...BY YOUR SIDE.
I'LL NEVER LET GO OF YOU AGAIN.
I'LL GO WITH YOU...
...TO THE WORLD YOU DREAM OF...
...TSUZUKI.

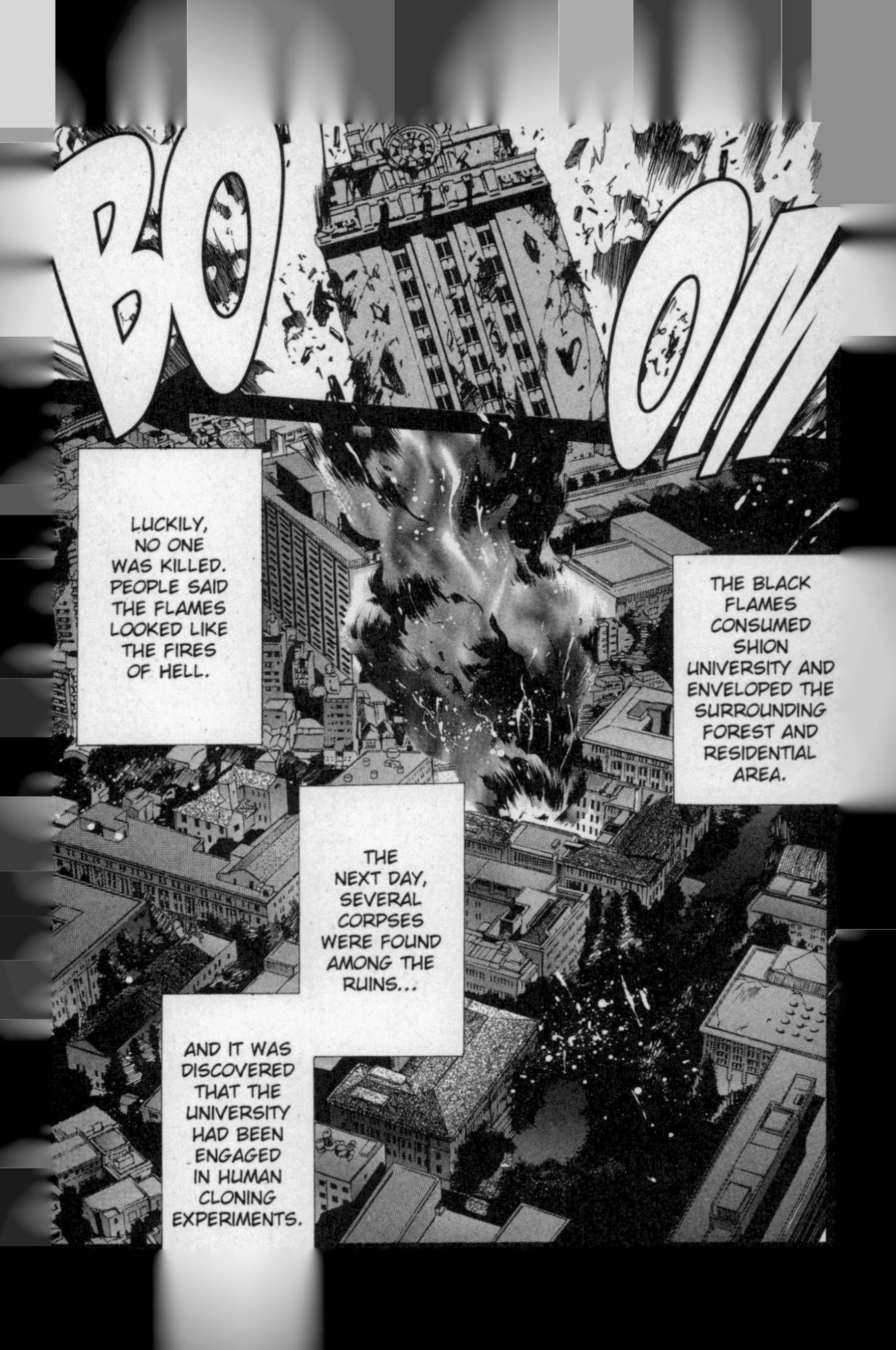
BOOM
THE BLACK FLAMES CONSUMED SHION UNIVERSITY AND ENVELOPED THE SURROUNDING FOREST AND RESIDENTIAL AREA.
LUCKILY, NO ONE WAS KILLED. PEOPLE SAID THE FLAMES LOOKED LIKE THE FIRES OF HELL.
THE NEXT DAY, SEVERAL CORPSES WERE FOUND AMONG THE RUINS...
AND IT WAS DISCOVERED THAT THE UNIVERSITY HAD BEEN ENGAGED IN HUMAN CLONING EXPERIMENTS.

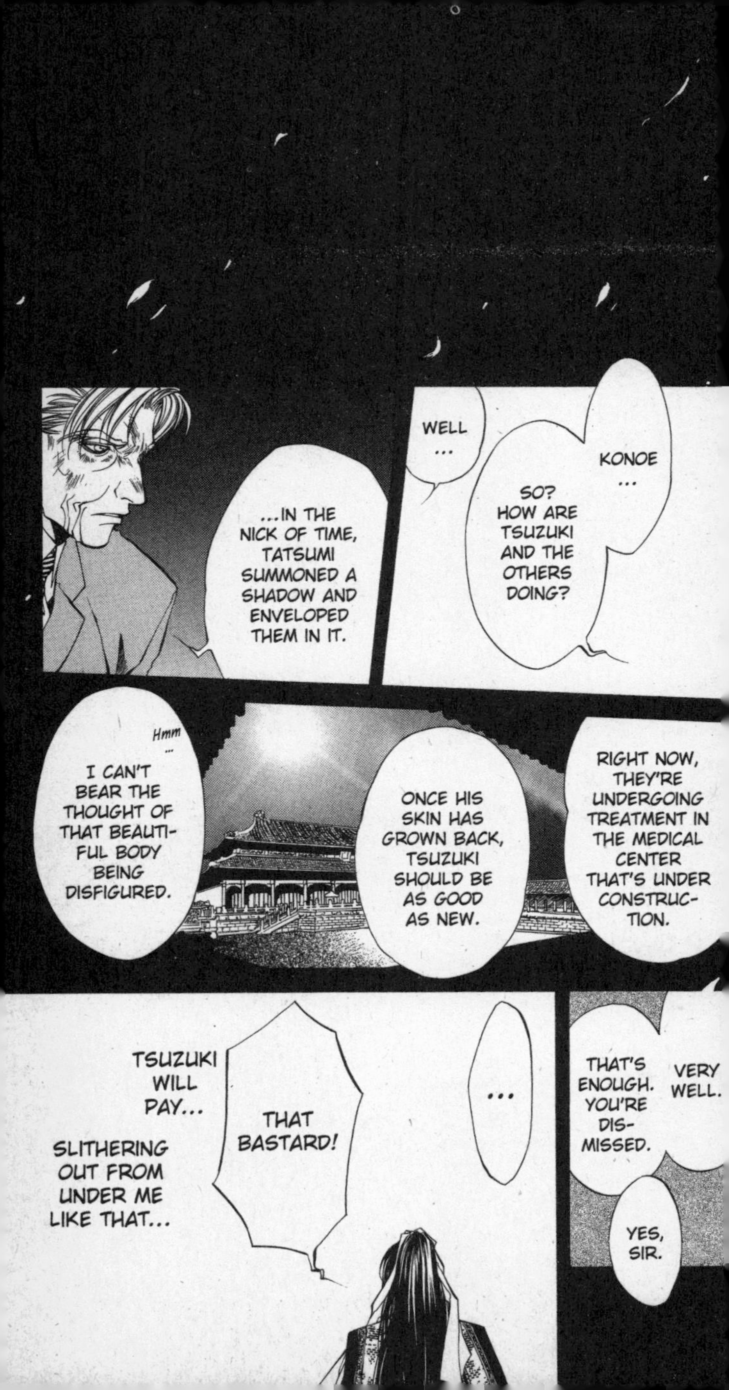
KONOE ...
SO? HOW ARE TSUZUKI AND THE OTHERS DOING?
WELL ...
...IN THE NICK OF TIME, TATSUMI SUMMONED A SHADOW AND ENVELOPED THEM IN IT.
RIGHT NOW, THEY'RE UNDERGOING TREATMENT IN THE MEDICAL CENTER THAT'S UNDER CONSTRUCTION.
ONCE HIS SKIN HAS GROWN BACK, TSUZUKI SHOULD BE AS GOOD AS NEW.
Hmm ...
I CAN'T BEAR THE THOUGHT OF THAT BEAUTIFUL BODY BEING DISFIGURED.
VERY WELL.
THAT'S ENOUGH. YOU'RE DISMISSED.
YES, SIR.
...
THAT BASTARD!
TSUZUKI WILL PAY...
SLITHERING OUT FROM UNDER ME LIKE THAT...

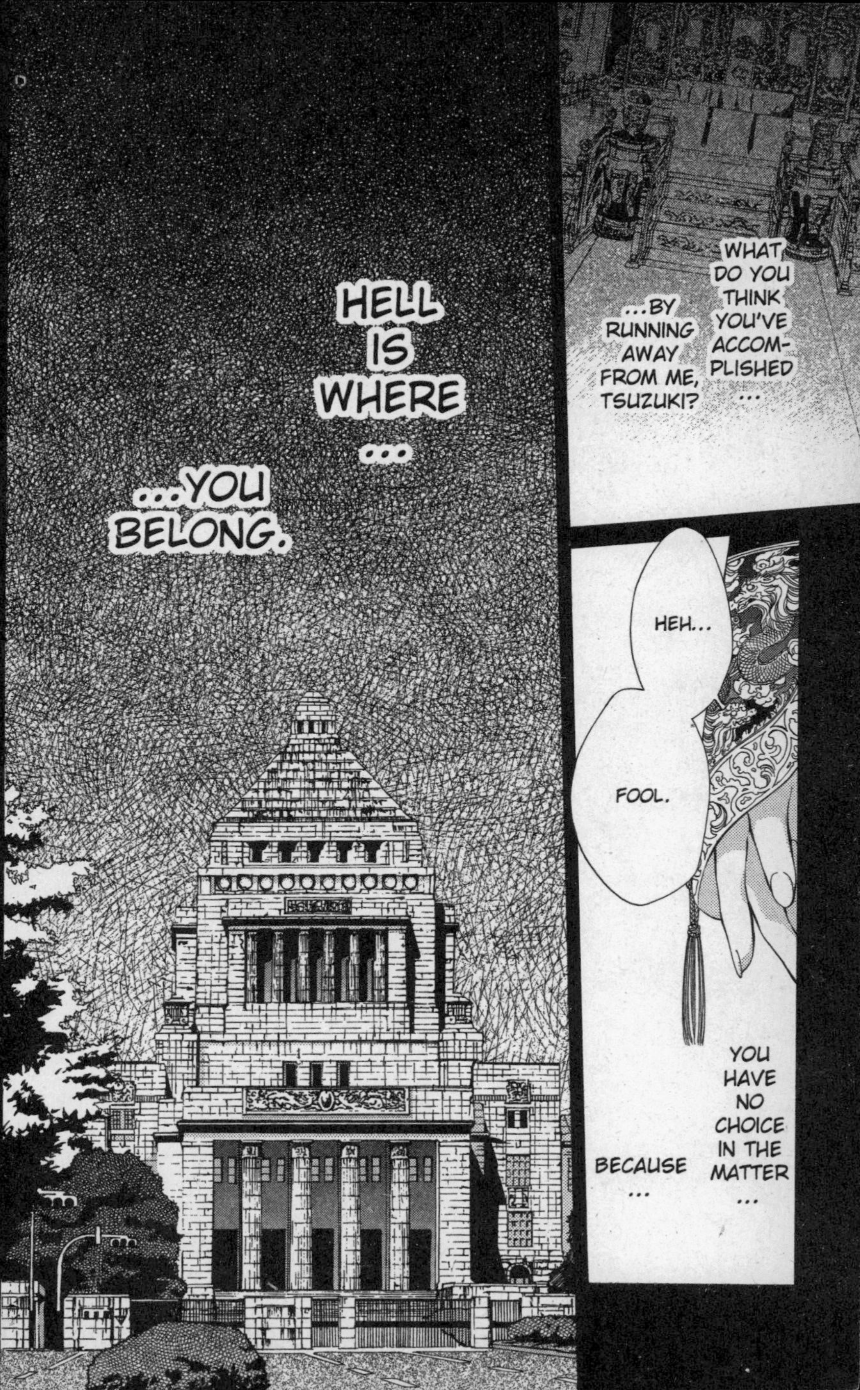
WHAT DO YOU THINK YOU'VE ACCOMPLISHED ...
...BY RUNNING AWAY FROM ME, TSUZUKI?
HEH...
FOOL.
YOU HAVE NO CHOICE IN THE MATTER ...
BECAUSE ...
HELL IS WHERE ...
...YOU BELONG.

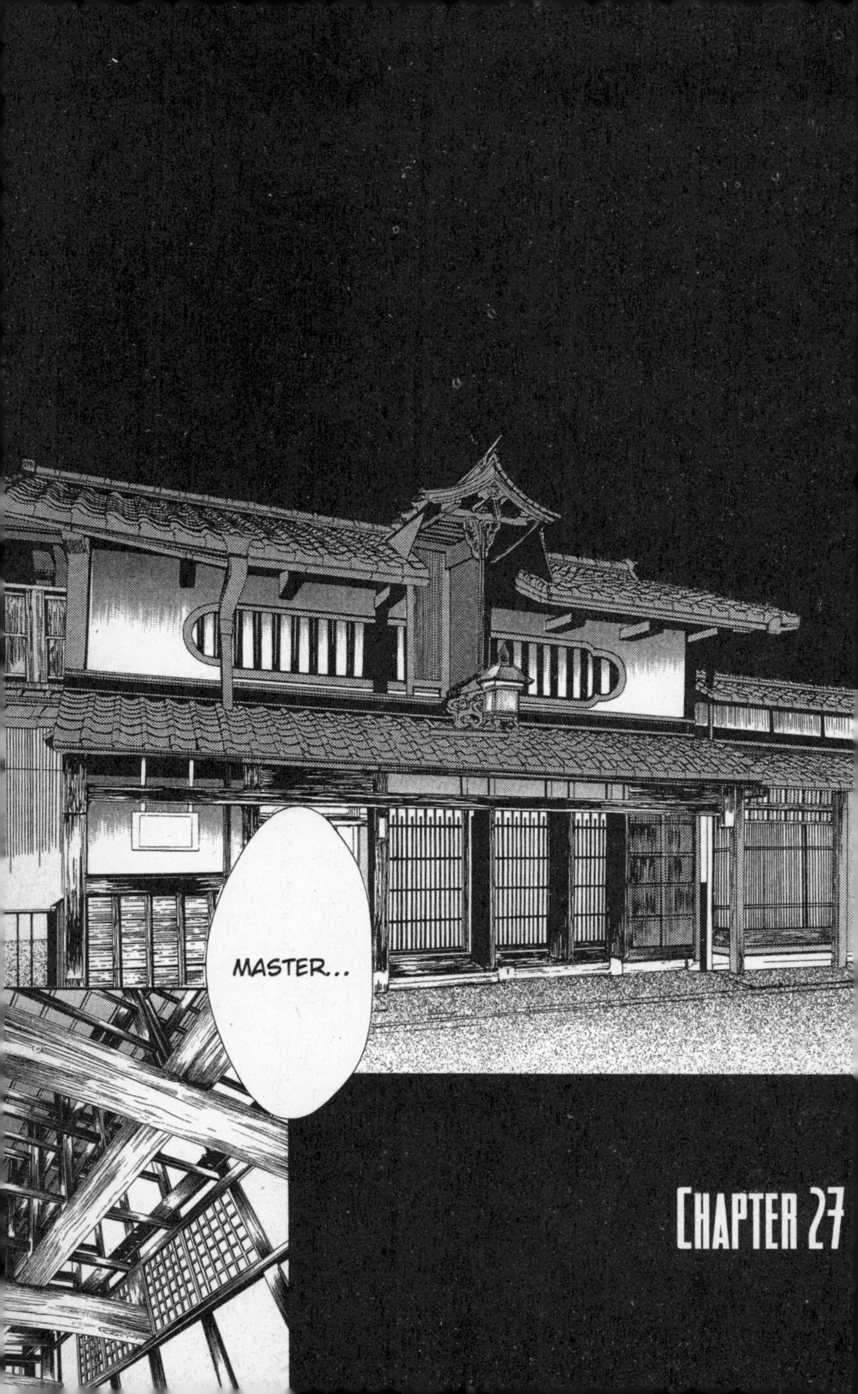
MASTER...
CHAPTER 27

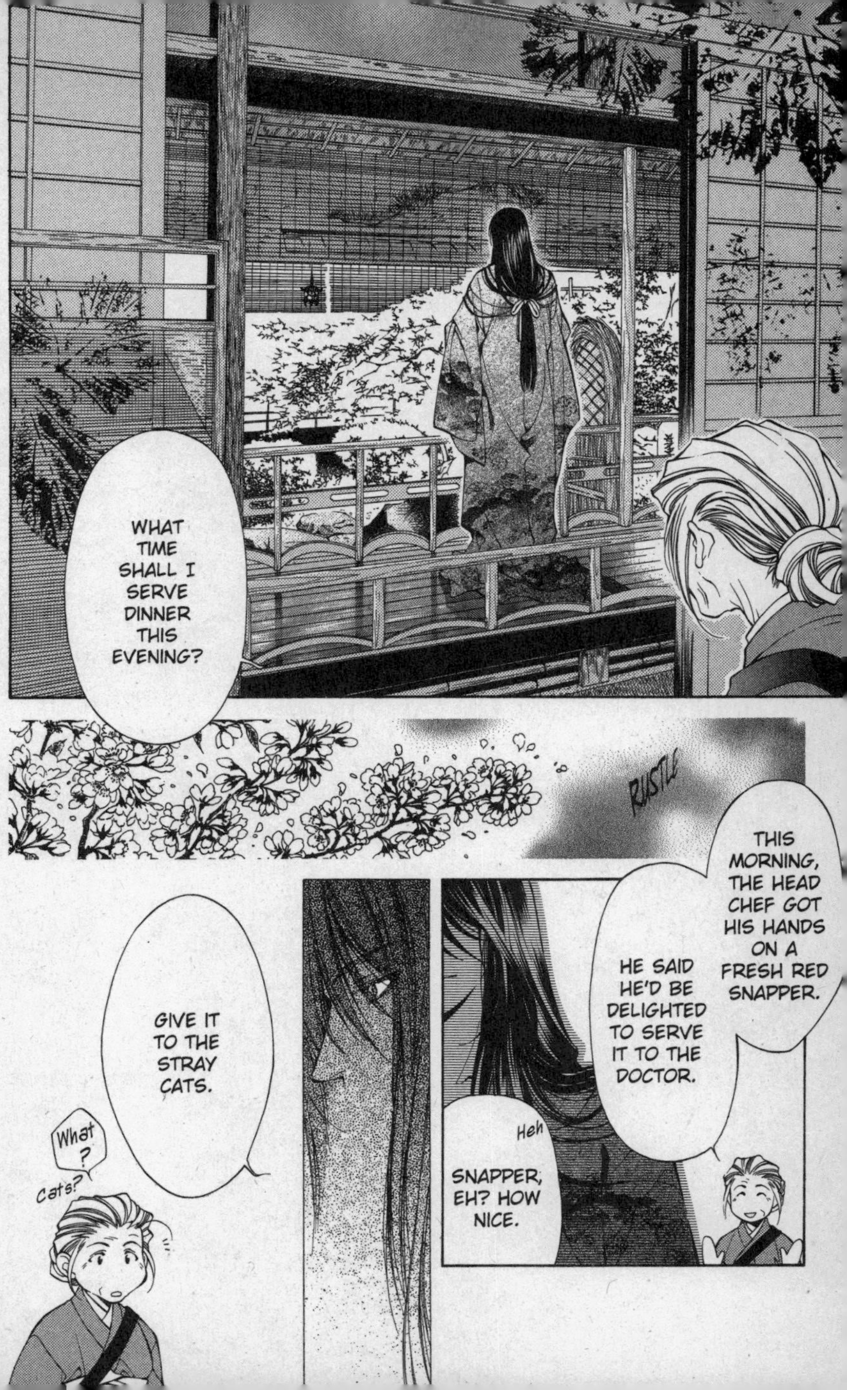
WHAT TIME SHALL I SERVE DINNER THIS EVENING?
RUSTLE
THIS MORNING, THE HEAD CHEF GOT HIS HANDS ON A FRESH RED SNAPPER.
HE SAID HE'D BE DELIGHTED TO SERVE IT TO THE DOCTOR.
Heh
SNAPPER, EH? HOW NICE.
GIVE IT TO THE STRAY CATS.
What?
Cats?

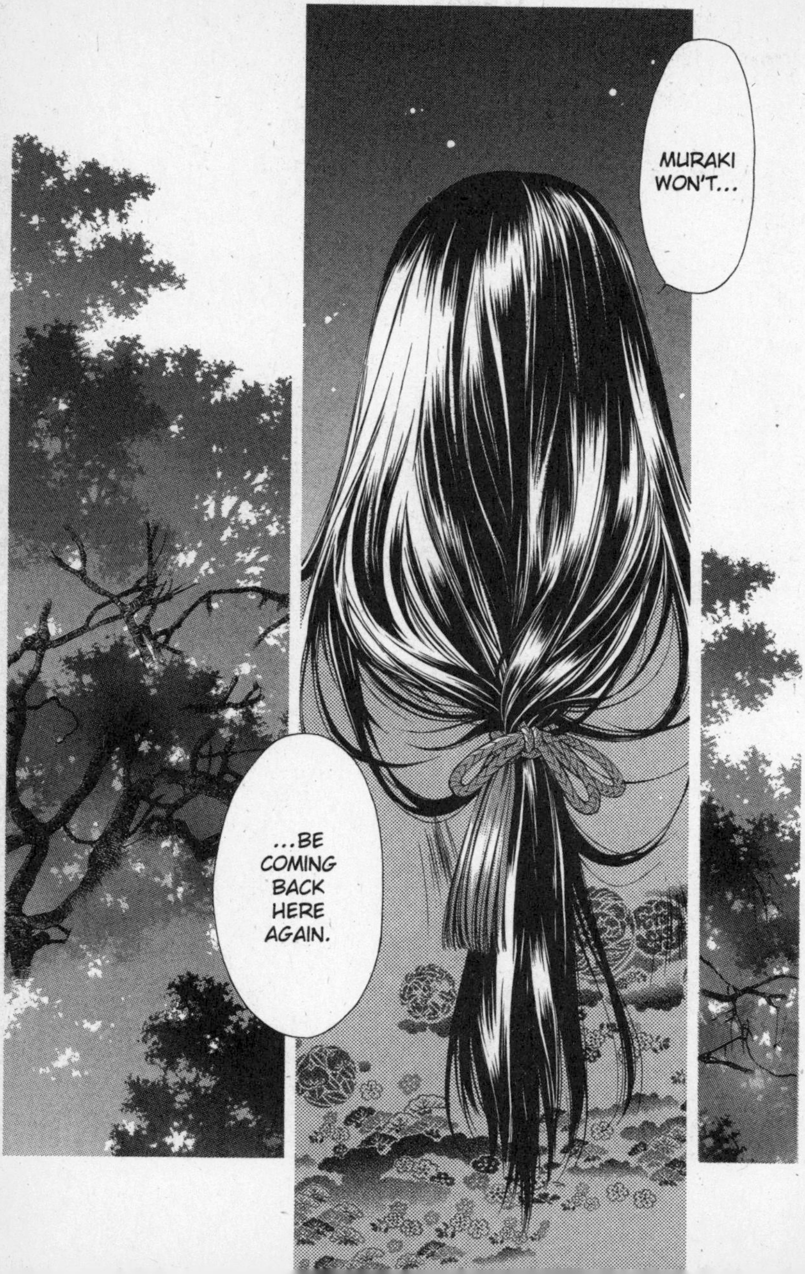
MURAKI WON'T...
...BE COMING BACK HERE AGAIN.

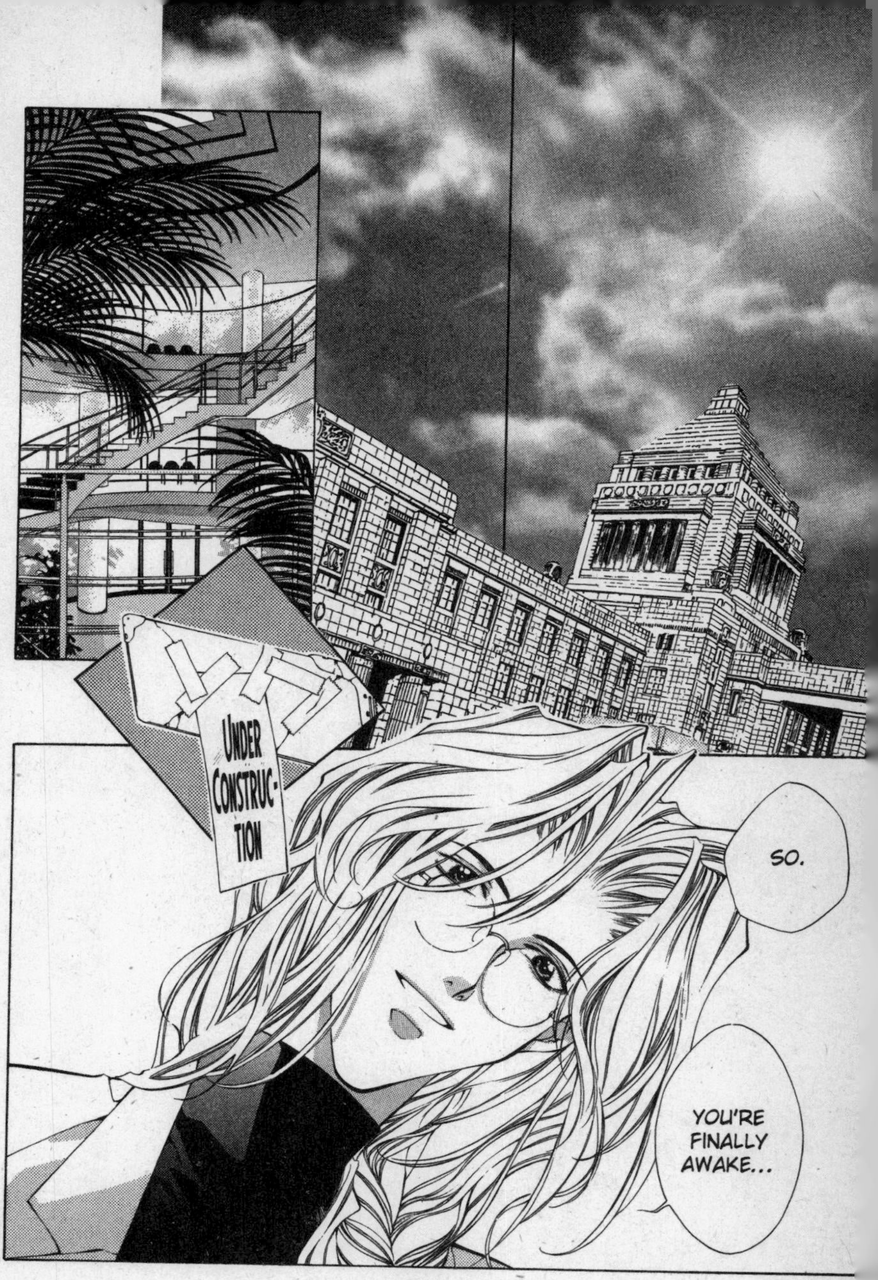
UNDER CONSTRUC- TION
SO.
YOU'RE FINALLY AWAKE...

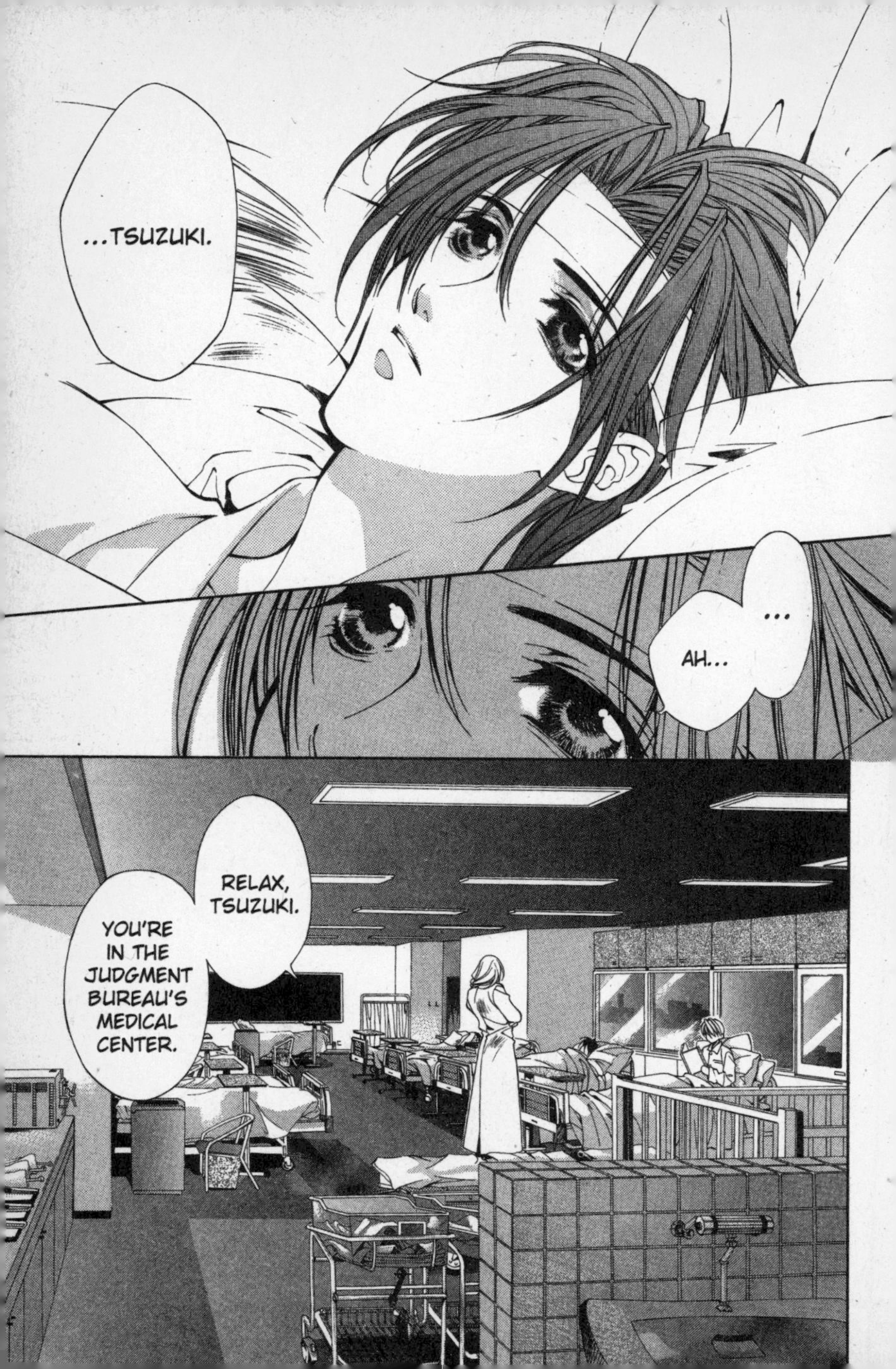
...TSUZUKI.
...
AH...
RELAX, TSUZUKI.
YOU'RE IN THE JUDGMENT BUREAU'S MEDICAL CENTER.

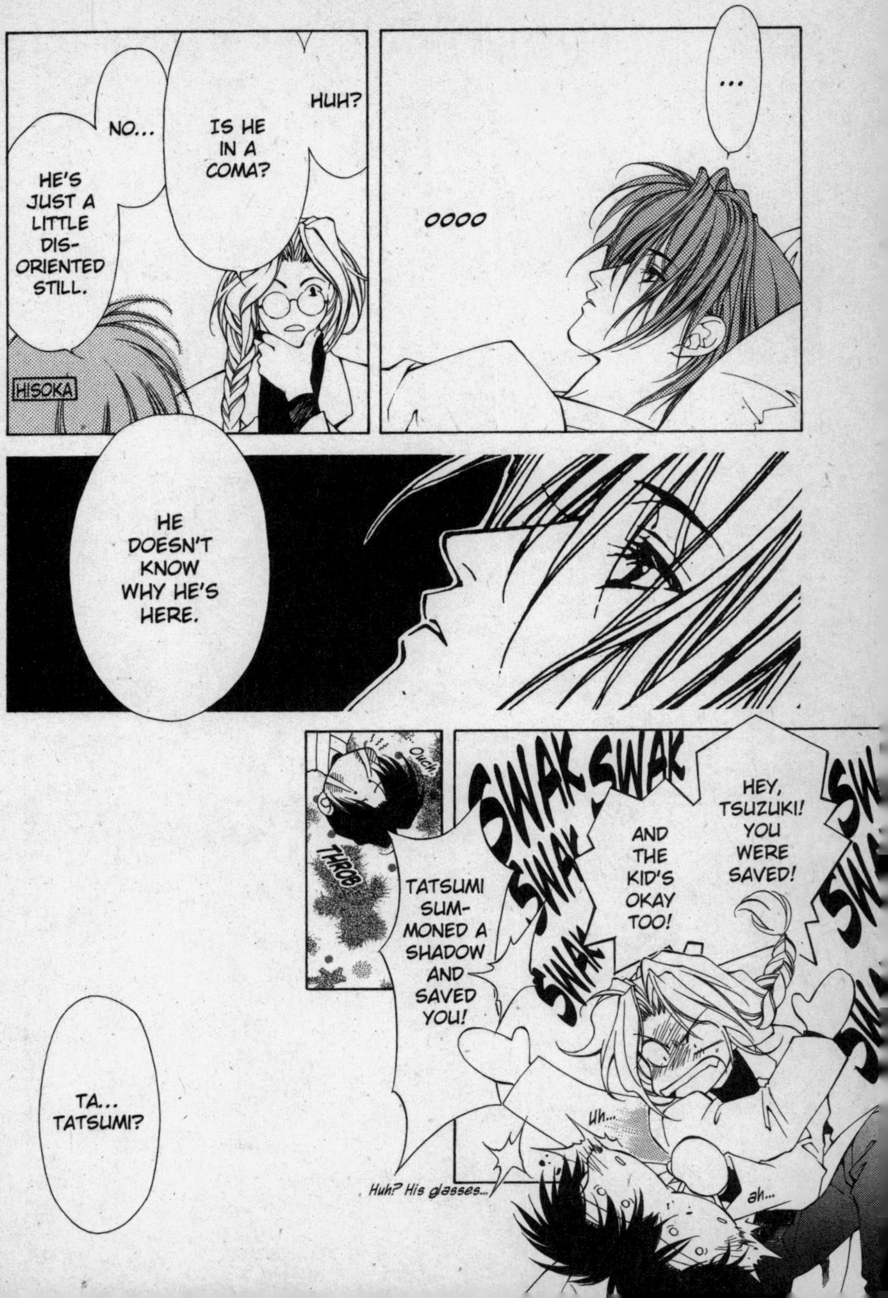
...
OOOO
HUH?
IS HE IN A COMA?
NO...
HE'S JUST A LITTLE DIS-ORIENTED STILL.
HISOKA
HE DOESN'T KNOW WHY HE'S HERE.
HEY, TSUZUKI! YOU WERE SAVED!
AND THE KID'S OKAY TOO!
SWAK SWAK SWAK SWAK SWAK SWAK
TATSUMI SUM-MONED A SHADOW AND SAVED YOU!
uh...
ah...
Huh? His glasses...
Ouch.
THROB
TA... TATSUMI?

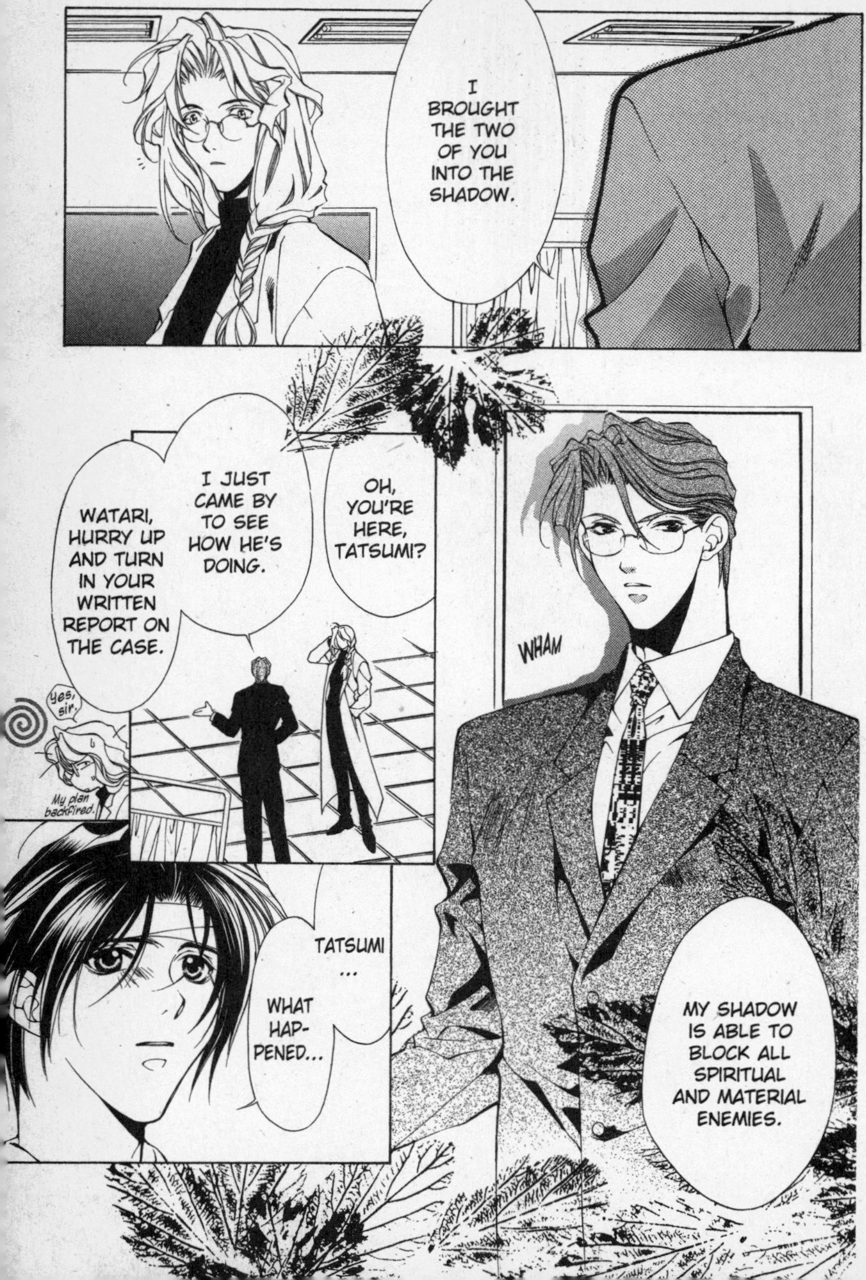
I BROUGHT THE TWO OF YOU INTO THE SHADOW.
WHAM
MY SHADOW IS ABLE TO BLOCK ALL SPIRITUAL AND MATERIAL ENEMIES.
OH, YOU'RE HERE, TATSUMI?
I JUST CAME BY TO SEE HOW HE'S DOING.
WATARI, HURRY UP AND TURN IN YOUR WRITTEN REPORT ON THE CASE.
Yes, sir.
My plan backfired.
TATSUMI ...
WHAT HAP-PENED...

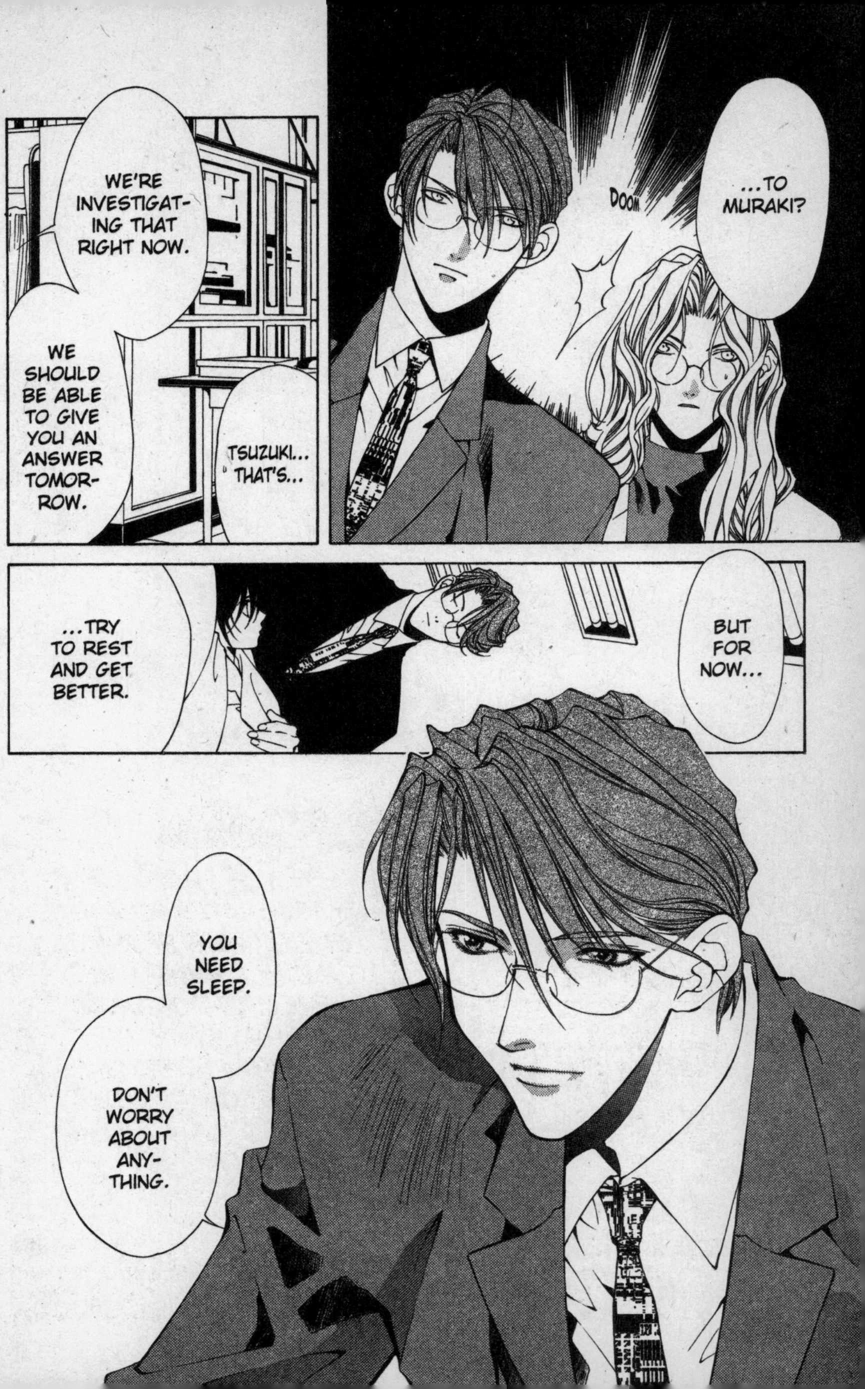
...TO MURAKI?
DOOM
TSUZUKI... THAT'S...
WE'RE INVESTIGATING THAT RIGHT NOW.
WE SHOULD BE ABLE TO GIVE YOU AN ANSWER TOMORROW.
BUT FOR NOW...
...TRY TO REST AND GET BETTER.
YOU NEED SLEEP.
DON'T WORRY ABOUT ANYTHING.

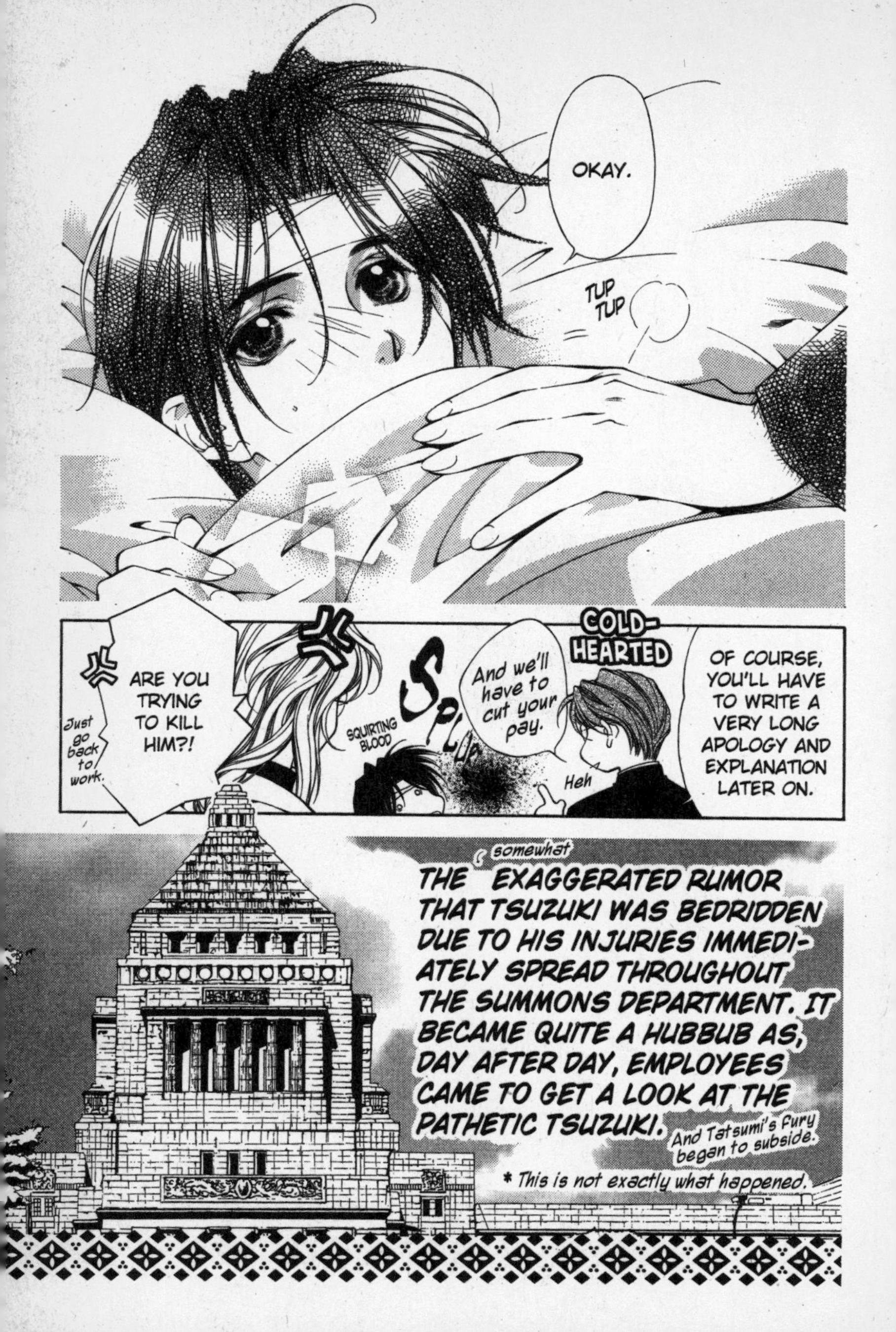
OKAY.
TUP TUP
OF COURSE, YOU'LL HAVE TO WRITE A VERY LONG APOLOGY AND EXPLANATION LATER ON.
COLD-HEARTED
And we'll have to cut your pay.
Heh
SPLUP
SQUIRTING BLOOD
ARE YOU TRYING TO KILL HIM?!
Just go back to work.
THE (somewhat) EXAGGERATED RUMOR THAT TSUZUKI WAS BEDRIDDEN DUE TO HIS INJURIES IMMEDIATELY SPREAD THROUGHOUT THE SUMMONS DEPARTMENT. IT BECAME QUITE A HUBBUB AS, DAY AFTER DAY, EMPLOYEES CAME TO GET A LOOK AT THE PATHETIC TSUZUKI.
And Tatsumi's fury began to subside.
* This is not exactly what happened.

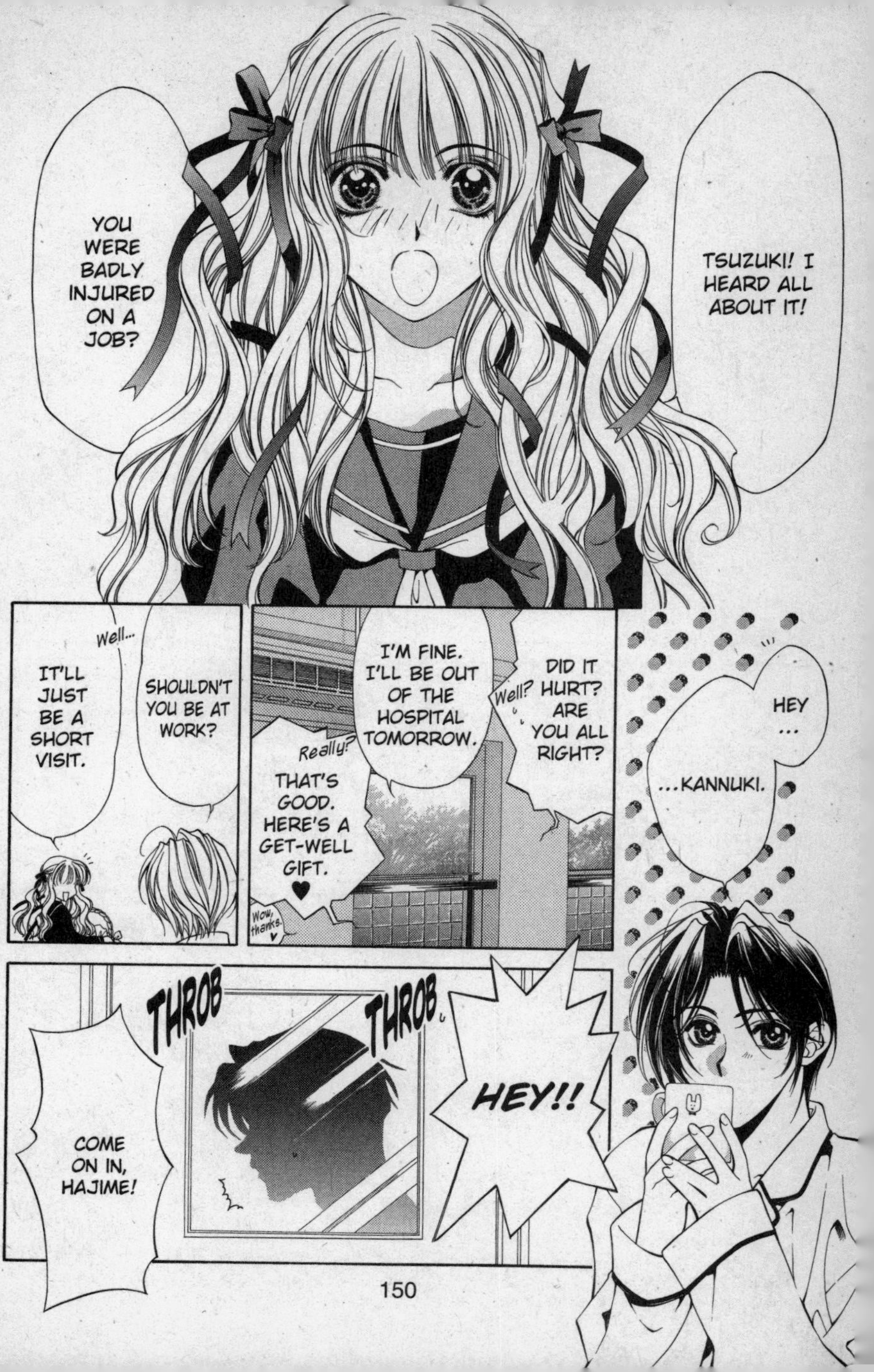
TSUZUKI! I HEARD ALL ABOUT IT!
YOU WERE BADLY INJURED ON A JOB?
HEY ...
...KANNUKI.
Well?
DID IT HURT? ARE YOU ALL RIGHT?
I'M FINE. I'LL BE OUT OF THE HOSPITAL TOMORROW.
Really?
THAT'S GOOD. HERE'S A GET-WELL GIFT. ♥
Wow, thanks. ♥
SHOULDN'T YOU BE AT WORK?
Well...
IT'LL JUST BE A SHORT VISIT.
HEY!!
THROB
THROB
COME ON IN, HAJIME!

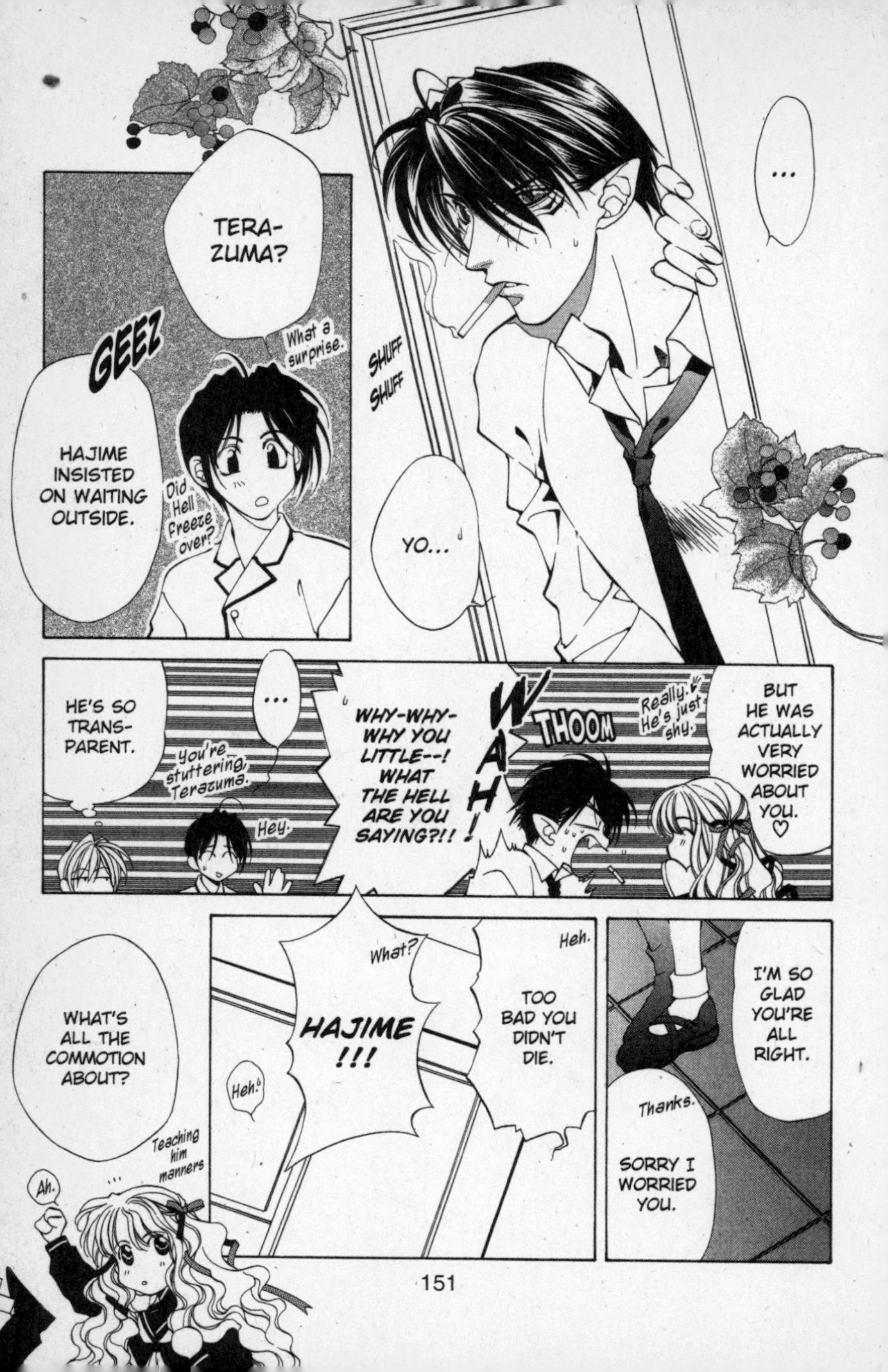
...
YO...
SHUFF
SHUFF
TERA-ZUMA?
What a surprise.
GEEZ
HAJIME INSISTED ON WAITING OUTSIDE.
Did Hell freeze over?
BUT HE WAS ACTUALLY VERY WORRIED ABOUT YOU. ♡
Really. He's just shy.
THOOM
WAH!
WHY-WHY-WHY YOU LITTLE--! WHAT THE HELL ARE YOU SAYING?!!
...
You're stuttering, Terazuma.
Hey.
HE'S SO TRANS-PARENT.
I'M SO GLAD YOU'RE ALL RIGHT.
Thanks.
SORRY I WORRIED YOU.
Heh.
TOO BAD YOU DIDN'T DIE.
What?
HAJIME !!!
Heh.
WHAT'S ALL THE COMMOTION ABOUT?
Teaching him manners
Ah.
...

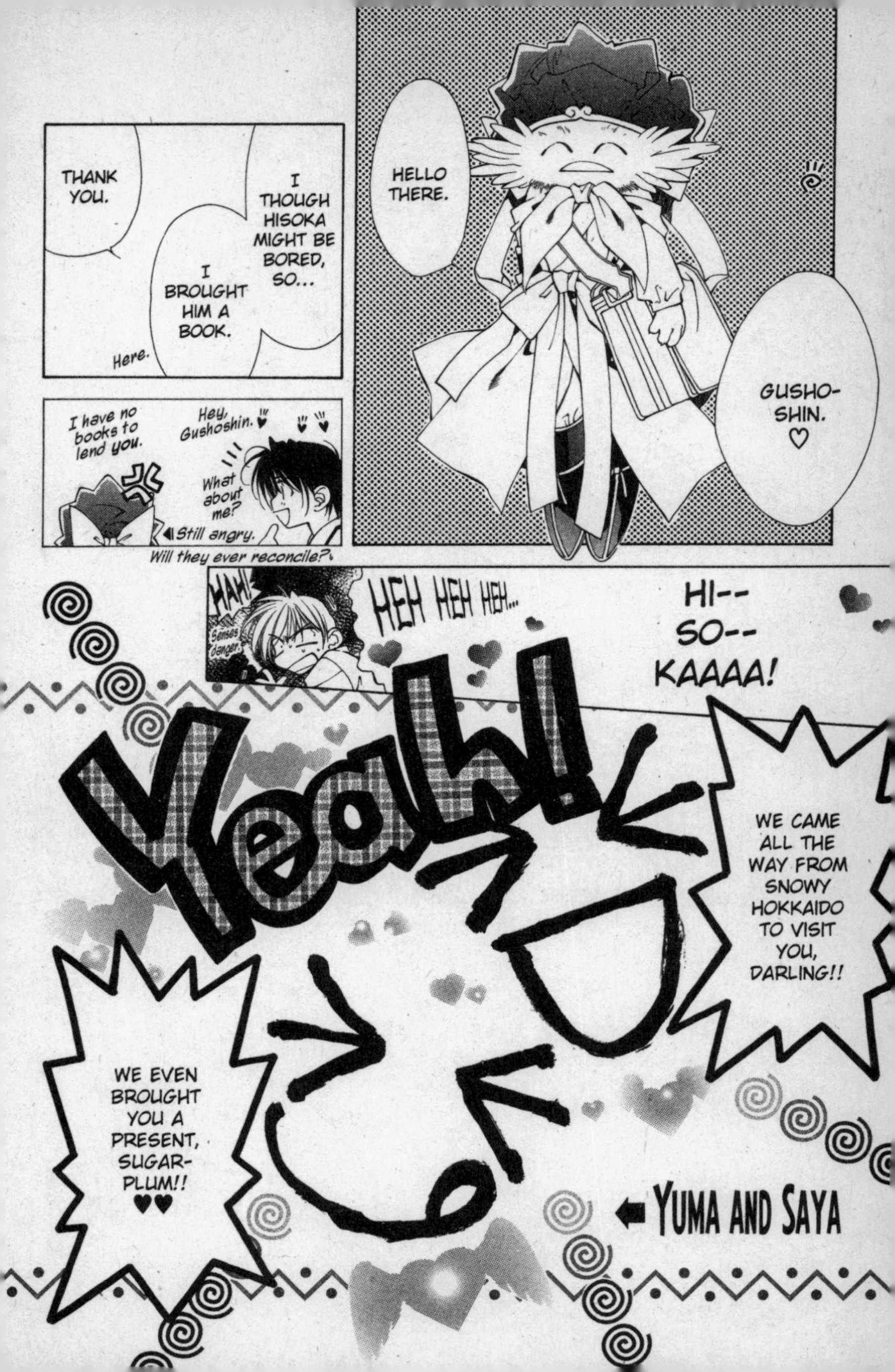
GUSHO-SHIN. ♡
HELLO THERE.
I THOUGH HISOKA MIGHT BE BORED, SO...
I BROUGHT HIM A BOOK.
Here.
THANK YOU.
Hey, Gushoshin.
What about me?
I have no books to lend you.
Still angry.
Will they ever reconcile?
HI-- SO-- KAAAA!
HEH HEH HEH...
HAH!
Senses danger.
Yeah!
WE CAME ALL THE WAY FROM SNOWY HOKKAIDO TO VISIT YOU, DARLING!!
WE EVEN BROUGHT YOU A PRESENT, SUGAR-PLUM!! ♥♥
YUMA AND SAYA

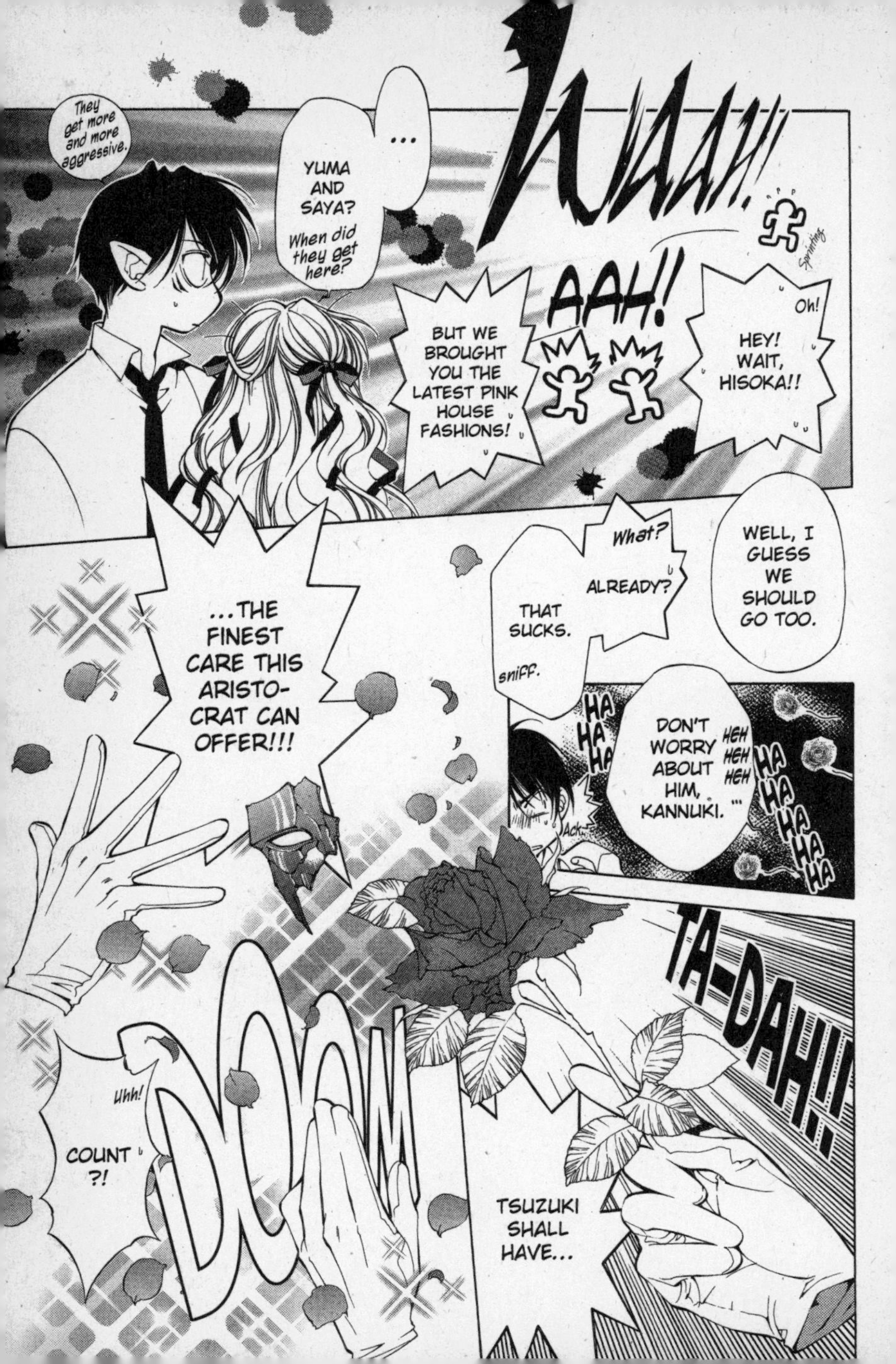
Oh!
HEY! WAIT, HISOKA!!
Sprinting
HAAAH!!
AAH!!
BUT WE BROUGHT YOU THE LATEST PINK HOUSE FASHIONS!
...
YUMA AND SAYA?
When did they get here?
They get more and more aggressive.
WELL, I GUESS WE SHOULD GO TOO.
What?
ALREADY?
THAT SUCKS.
sniff.
DON'T WORRY ABOUT HIM, KANNUKI.
HA HA HA
HEH HEH HEH ...
HA HA HA HA HA HA HA
Ack.
TA-DAH!!
TSUZUKI SHALL HAVE...
...THE FINEST CARE THIS ARISTOCRAT CAN OFFER!!!
DOOM
Uhh!
COUNT ?!

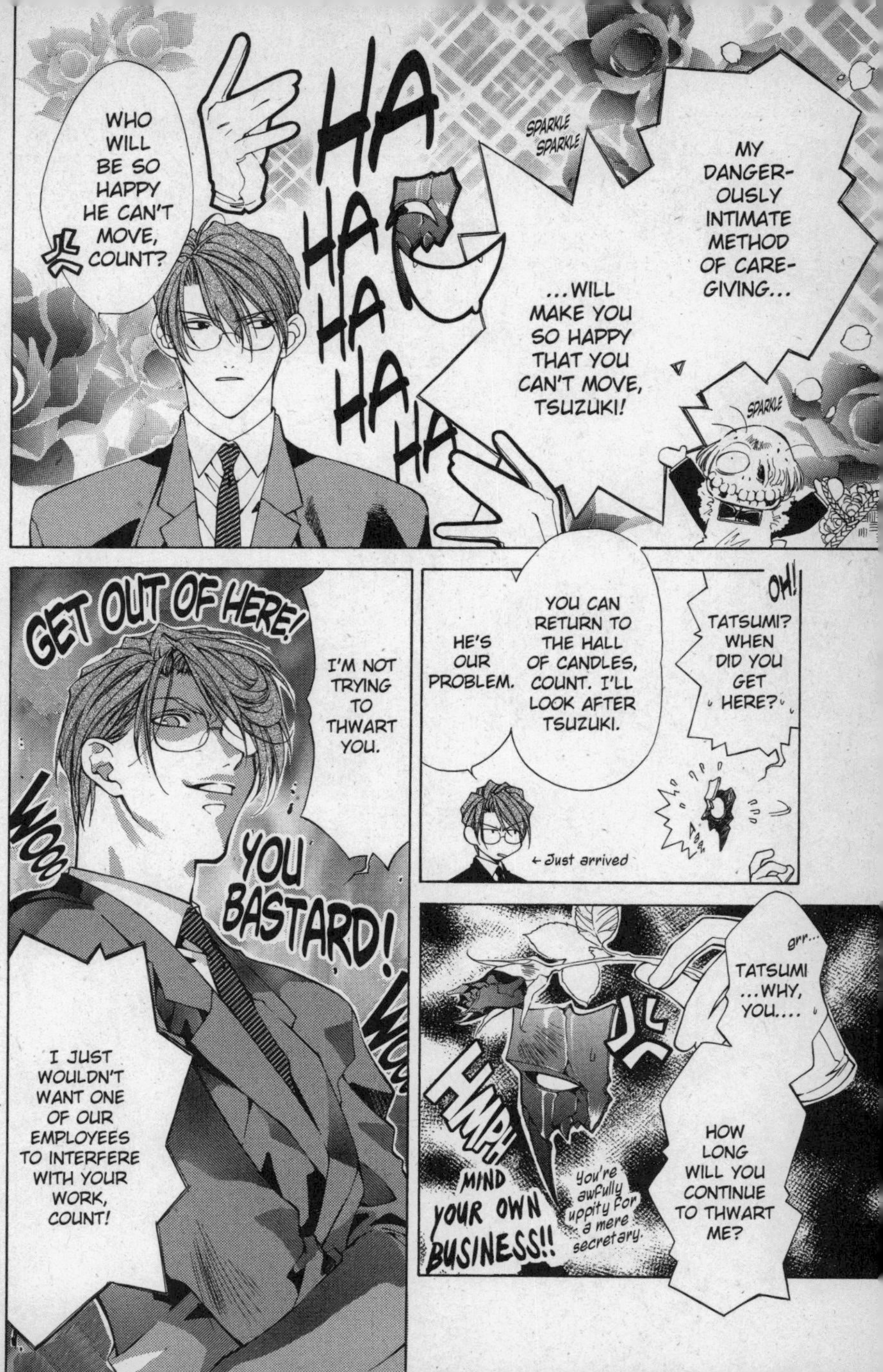
MY DANGER-OUSLY INTIMATE METHOD OF CARE-GIVING...
SPARKLE SPARKLE
...WILL MAKE YOU SO HAPPY THAT YOU CAN'T MOVE, TSUZUKI!
SPARKLE
HA HA HA HA HA HA
WHO WILL BE SO HAPPY HE CAN'T MOVE, COUNT?
OH!
TATSUMI? WHEN DID YOU GET HERE?
YOU CAN RETURN TO THE HALL OF CANDLES, COUNT. I'LL LOOK AFTER TSUZUKI.
HE'S OUR PROBLEM.
← Just arrived
grr...
TATSUMI ...WHY, YOU....
HOW LONG WILL YOU CONTINUE TO THWART ME?
You're awfully uppity for a mere secretary.
HMPH
MIND YOUR OWN BUSINESS!!
I'M NOT TRYING TO THWART YOU.
GET OUT OF HERE!
WOOO
YOU BASTARD!
WOO
I JUST WOULDN'T WANT ONE OF OUR EMPLOYEES TO INTERFERE WITH YOUR WORK, COUNT!

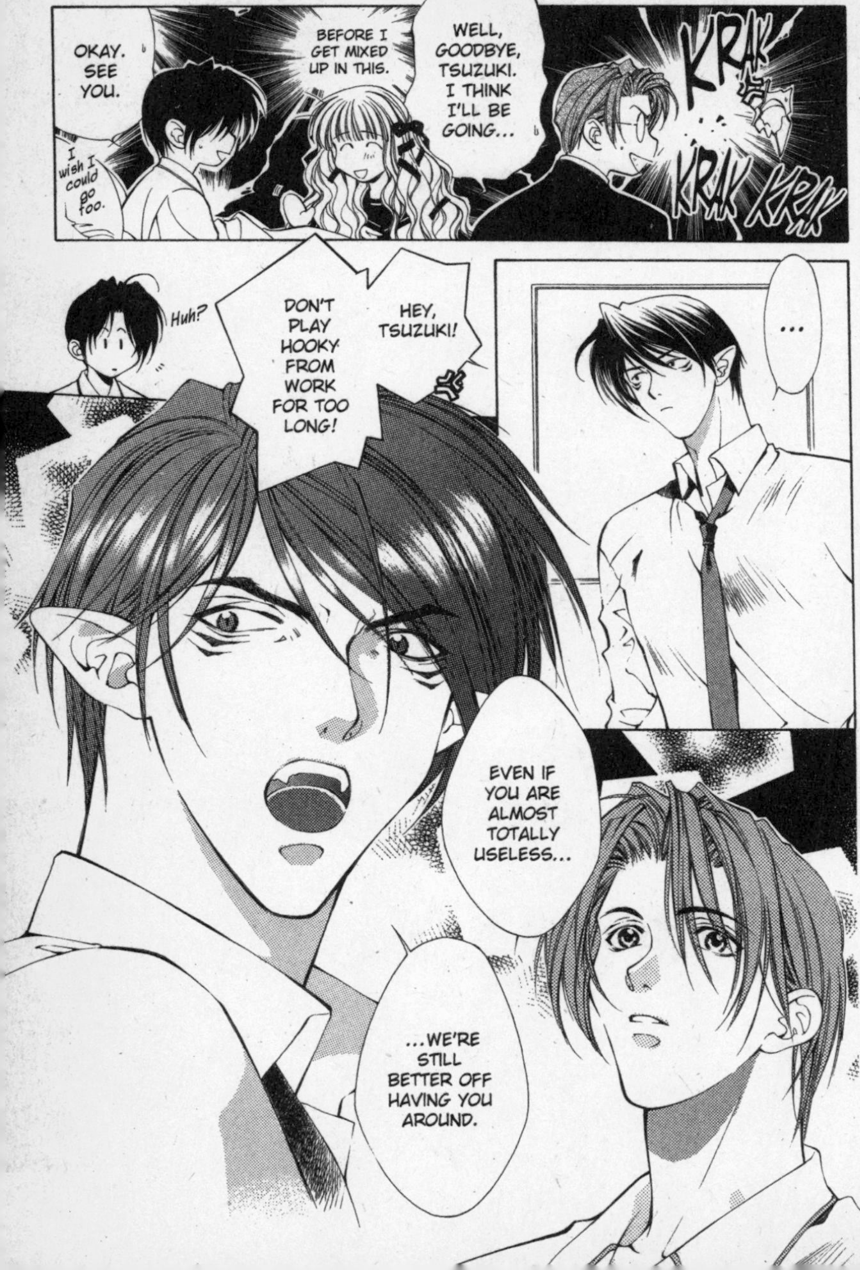
KRAK
KRAK KRAK
WELL, GOODBYE, TSUZUKI. I THINK I'LL BE GOING...
BEFORE I GET MIXED UP IN THIS.
OKAY. SEE YOU.
I wish I could go too.
...
HEY, TSUZUKI!
DON'T PLAY HOOKY FROM WORK FOR TOO LONG!
Huh?
EVEN IF YOU ARE ALMOST TOTALLY USELESS...
...WE'RE STILL BETTER OFF HAVING YOU AROUND.

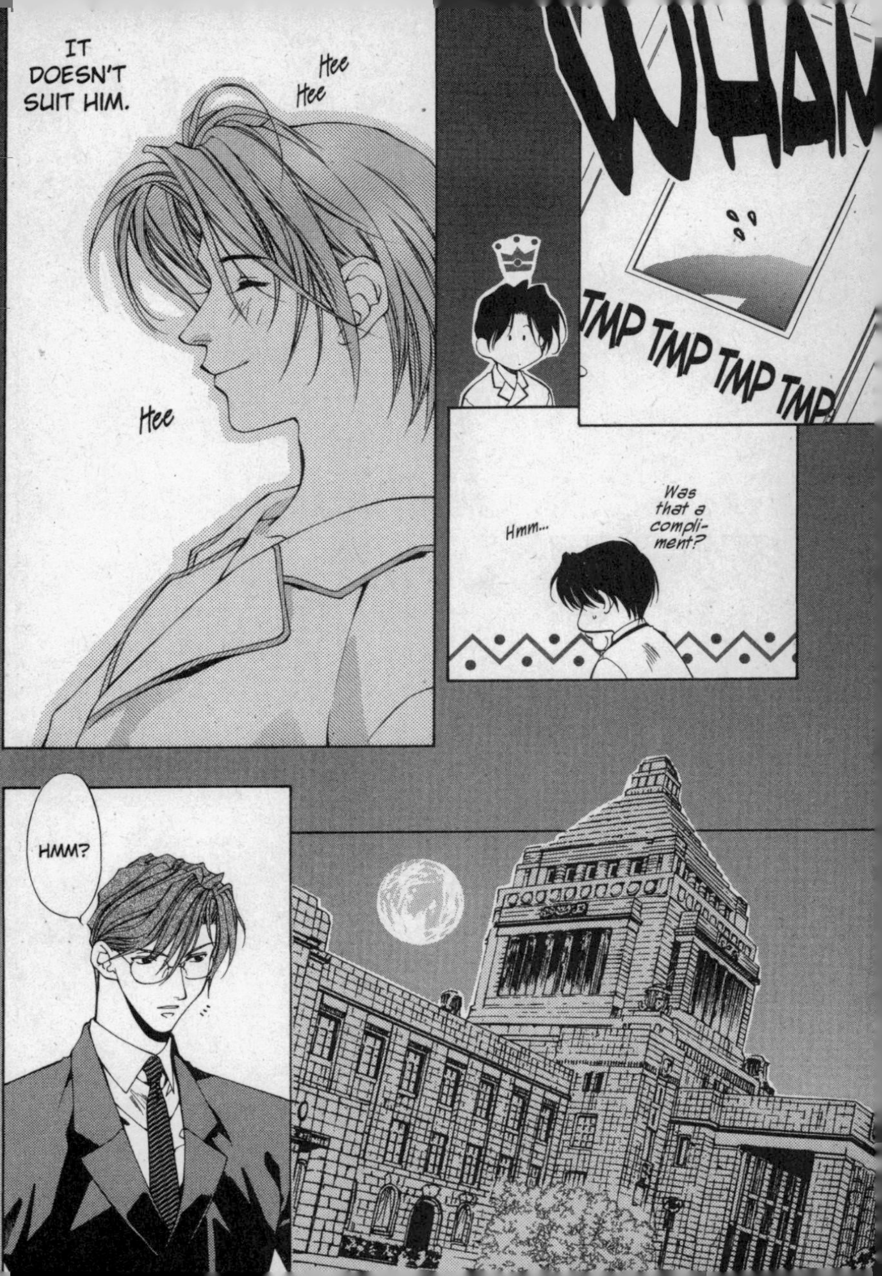
WHA
TMP TMP TMP TMP
Was that a compli- ment?
Hmm...
IT DOESN'T SUIT HIM.
Hee Hee
Hee
HMM?

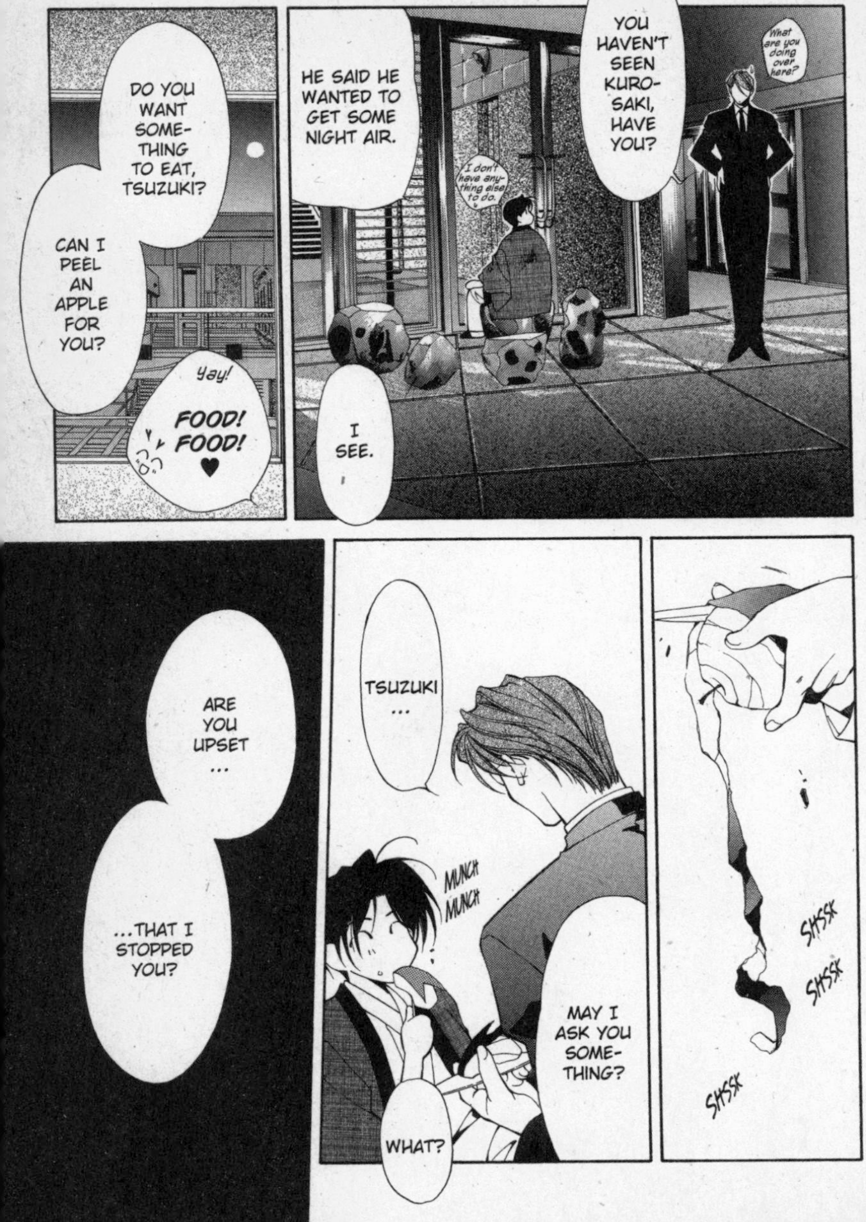
What are you doing over here?
YOU HAVEN'T SEEN KURO-SAKI, HAVE YOU?
HE SAID HE WANTED TO GET SOME NIGHT AIR.
I don't have any-thing else to do.
I SEE.
DO YOU WANT SOME-THING TO EAT, TSUZUKI?
CAN I PEEL AN APPLE FOR YOU?
Yay!
FOOD! FOOD! ♥
SHSSK
SHSSK
SHSSK
TSUZUKI ...
MUNCH MUNCH
MAY I ASK YOU SOME-THING?
WHAT?
ARE YOU UPSET ...
...THAT I STOPPED YOU?

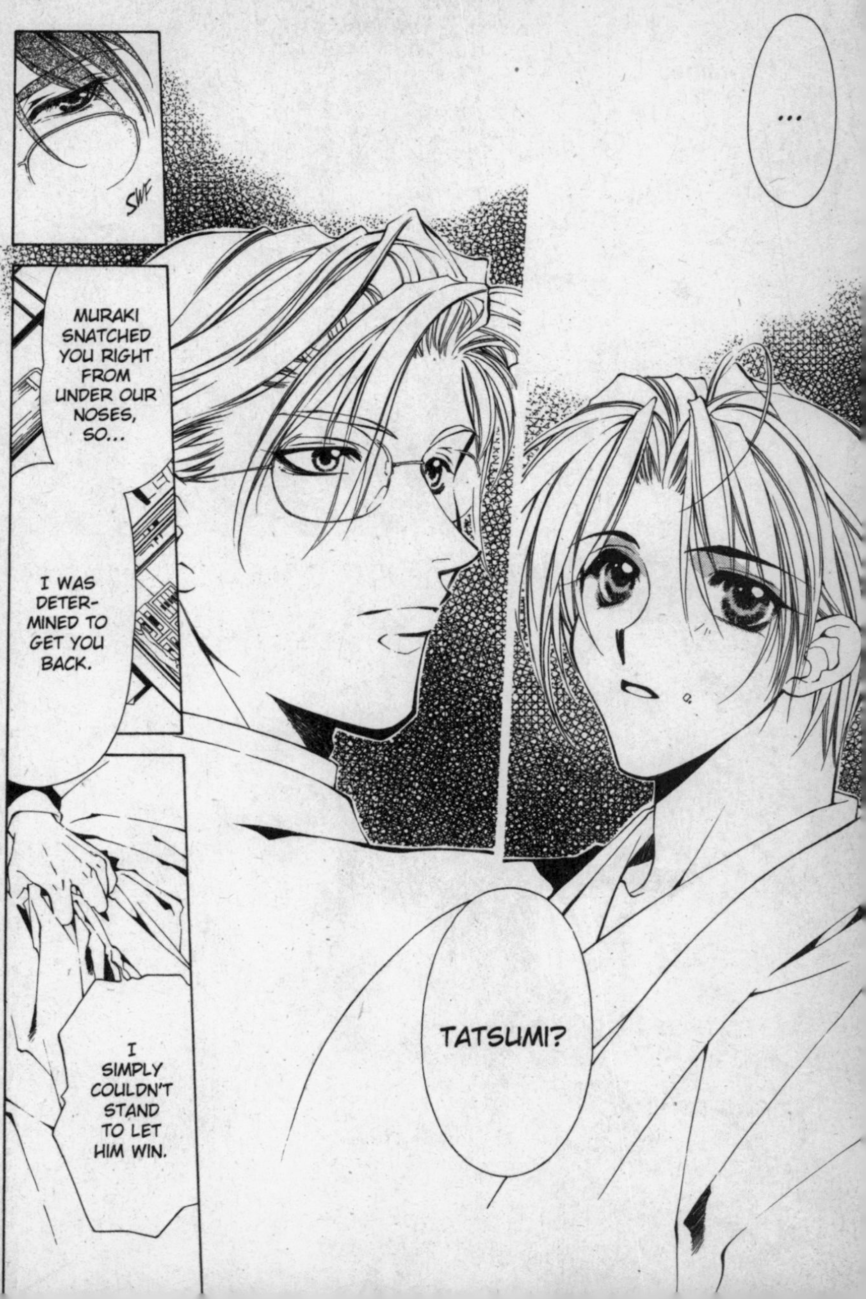
...
TATSUMI?
SWF
MURAKI SNATCHED YOU RIGHT FROM UNDER OUR NOSES, SO...
I WAS DETERMINED TO GET YOU BACK.
I SIMPLY COULDN'T STAND TO LET HIM WIN.

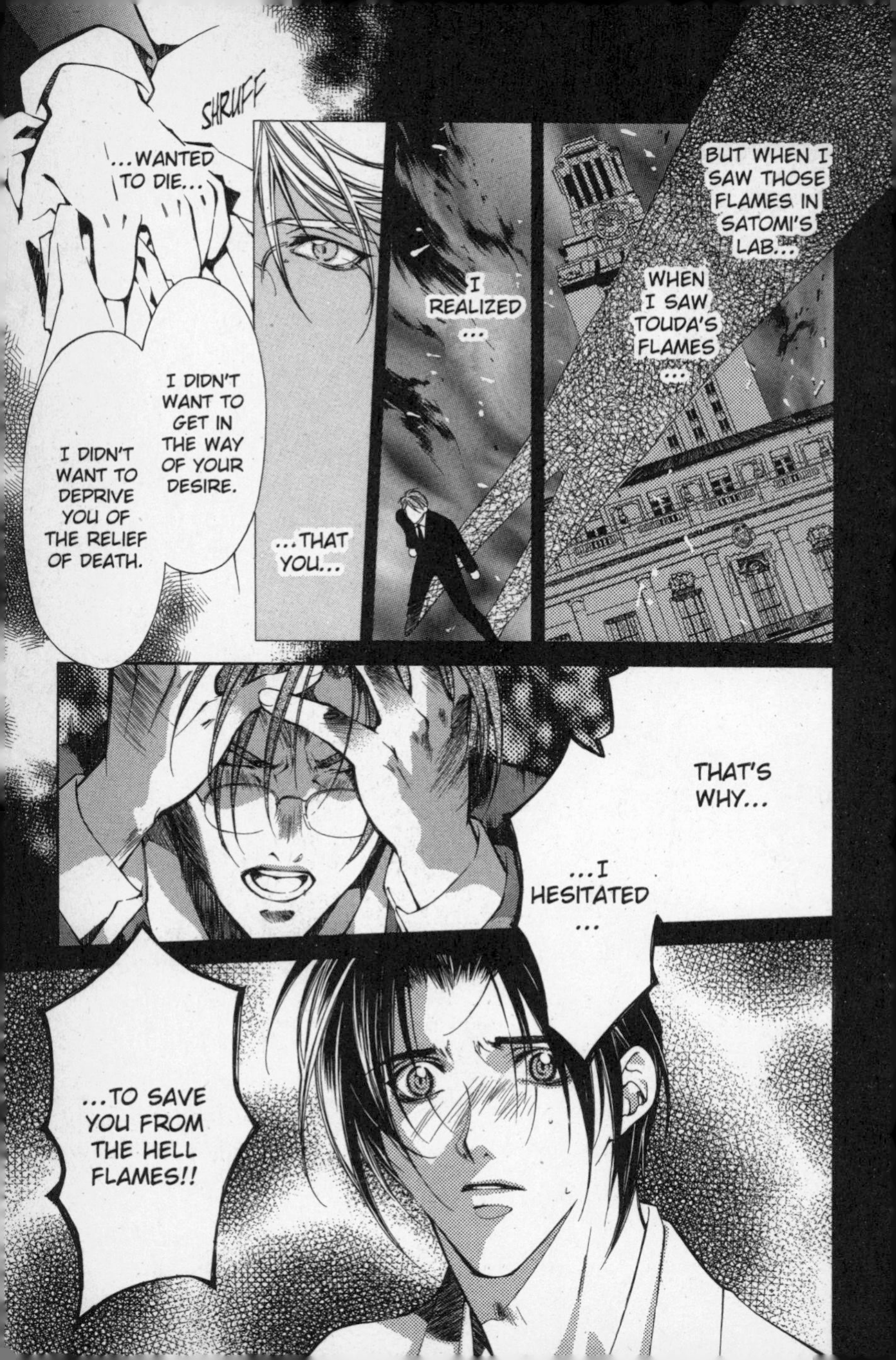
BUT WHEN I SAW THOSE FLAMES IN SATOMI'S LAB...
WHEN I SAW TOUDA'S FLAMES...
I REALIZED...
...THAT YOU...
SHRUFF
...WANTED TO DIE...
I DIDN'T WANT TO GET IN THE WAY OF YOUR DESIRE.
I DIDN'T WANT TO DEPRIVE YOU OF THE RELIEF OF DEATH.
THAT'S WHY...
...I HESITATED...
...TO SAVE YOU FROM THE HELL FLAMES!!

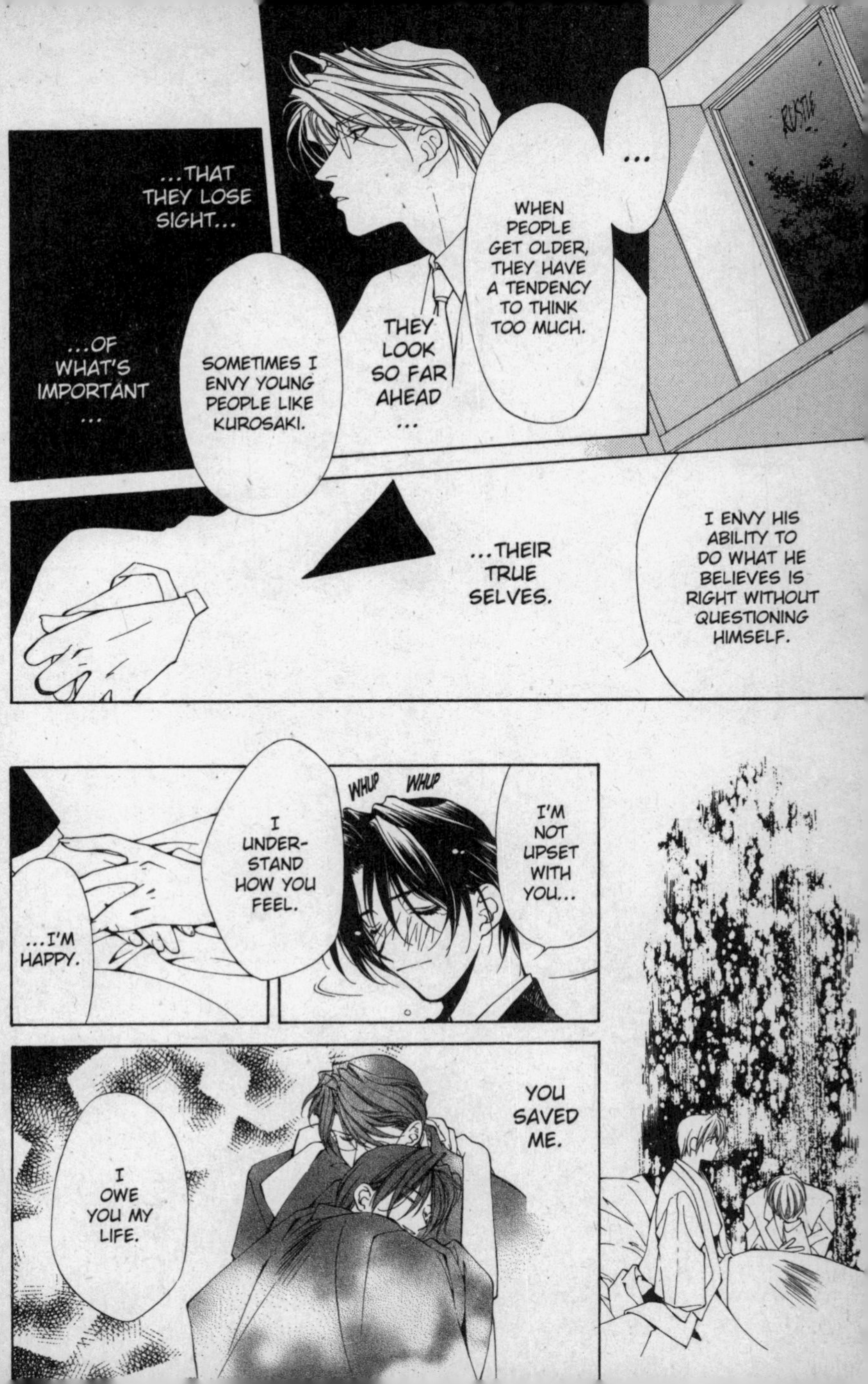
RUSTLE
...
WHEN PEOPLE GET OLDER, THEY HAVE A TENDENCY TO THINK TOO MUCH.
THEY LOOK SO FAR AHEAD...
SOMETIMES I ENVY YOUNG PEOPLE LIKE KUROSAKI.
...THAT THEY LOSE SIGHT...
...OF WHAT'S IMPORTANT...
I ENVY HIS ABILITY TO DO WHAT HE BELIEVES IS RIGHT WITHOUT QUESTIONING HIMSELF.
...THEIR TRUE SELVES.
I'M NOT UPSET WITH YOU...
WHUP WHUP
I UNDER-STAND HOW YOU FEEL.
...I'M HAPPY.
YOU SAVED ME.
I OWE YOU MY LIFE.

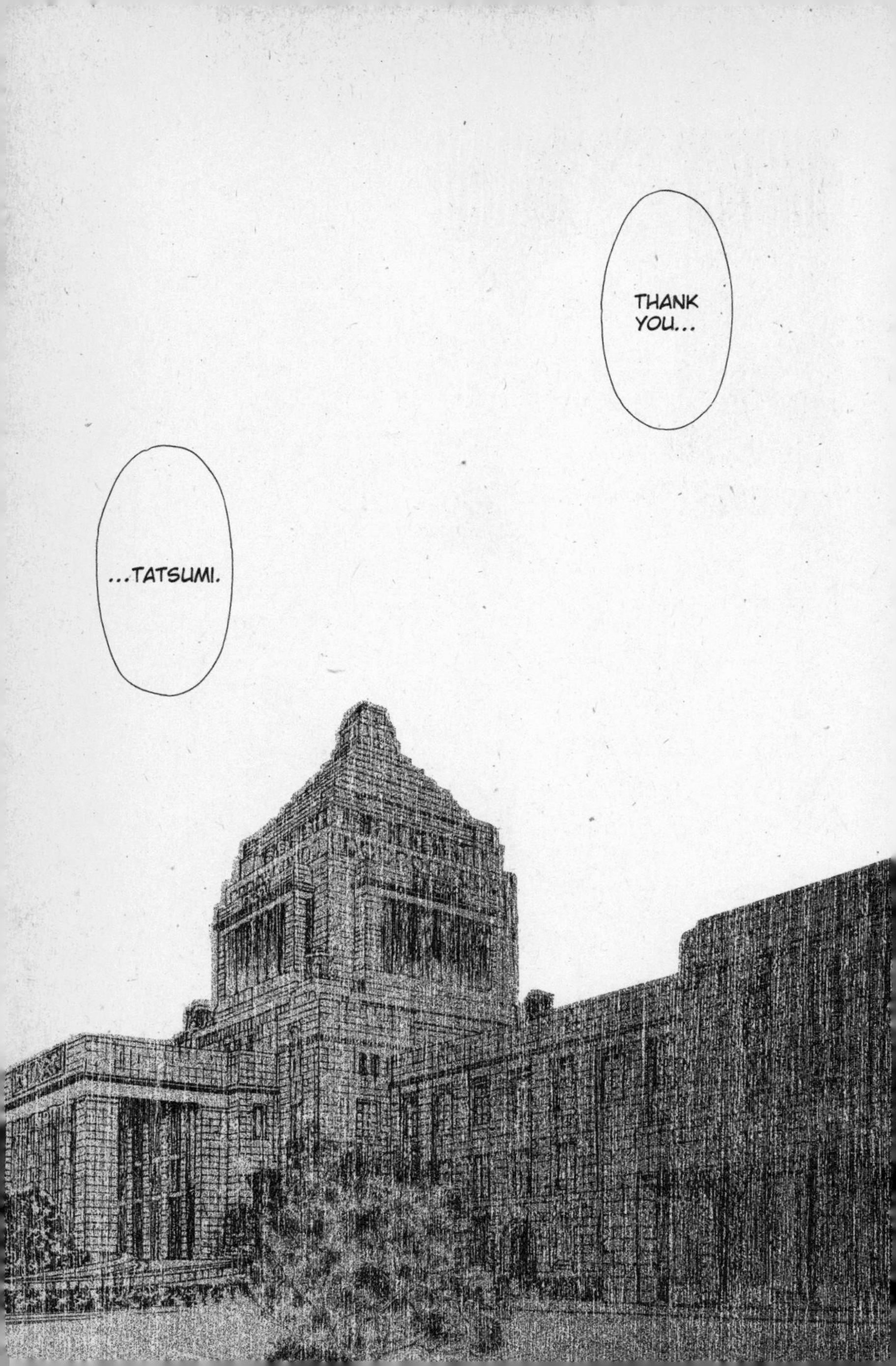
THANK YOU...
...TATSUMI.

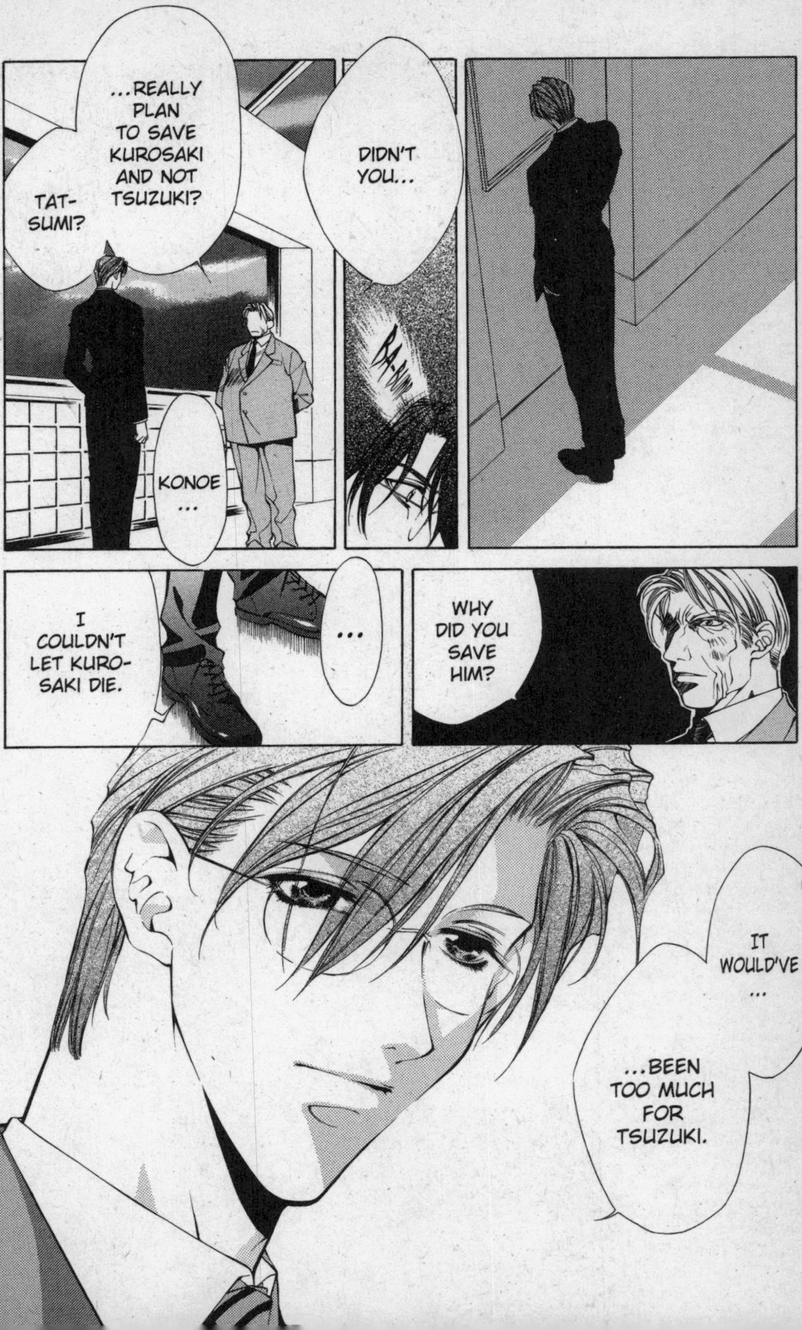
DIDN'T YOU...
...REALLY PLAN TO SAVE KUROSAKI AND NOT TSUZUKI?
TAT-SUMI?
KONOE ...
WHY DID YOU SAVE HIM?
...
I COULDN'T LET KURO-SAKI DIE.
IT WOULD'VE ...
...BEEN TOO MUCH FOR TSUZUKI.

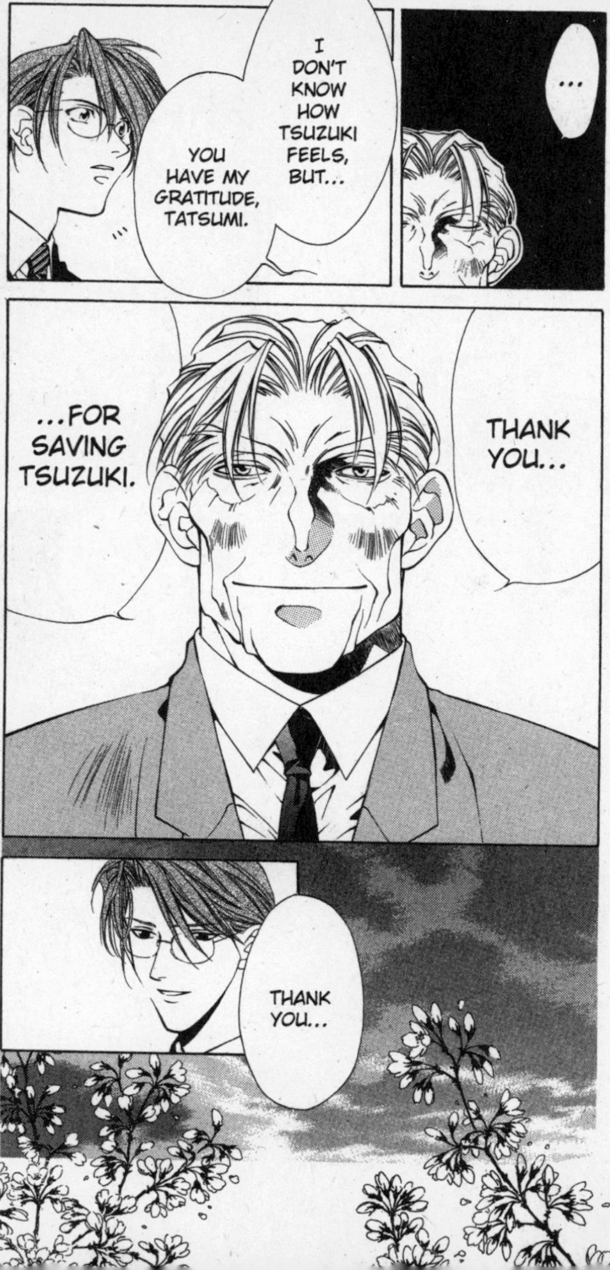
...
I DON'T KNOW HOW TSUZUKI FEELS, BUT...
YOU HAVE MY GRATITUDE, TATSUMI.
THANK YOU...
...FOR SAVING TSUZUKI.
THANK YOU...

Weird Things About the Kyoto Story Part 4

The mystery of the rabbit-shaped apple. There was a scene in which Tatsumi peels an apple for Tsuzuki, right? I don't think too many people noticed it, but if you remove all the peel the way Tatsumi was doing, then you wouldn't be able to make an apple rabbit. [Ha!] Actually, it was just a weird accident. There's no deeper meaning, so please don't complain about it in your letters. Well, that's about the only major error that the readers of the magazine asked me about, but this volume contains many additions and corrections, so there may be others. [Hee] (There probably are.) If you find any, please let me know. (But unless it's something big, I'm not going to mention it in my columns.) Anyway, the Kyoto story ends with this chapter. It was really long. It exhausted me both physically and mentally. The damage was so great that it took me a while before I could start on the next job. But no matter how much I complain, I did get to draw Kyoto, which was fun.

I'd really like to do a sequel to the Kyoto story.

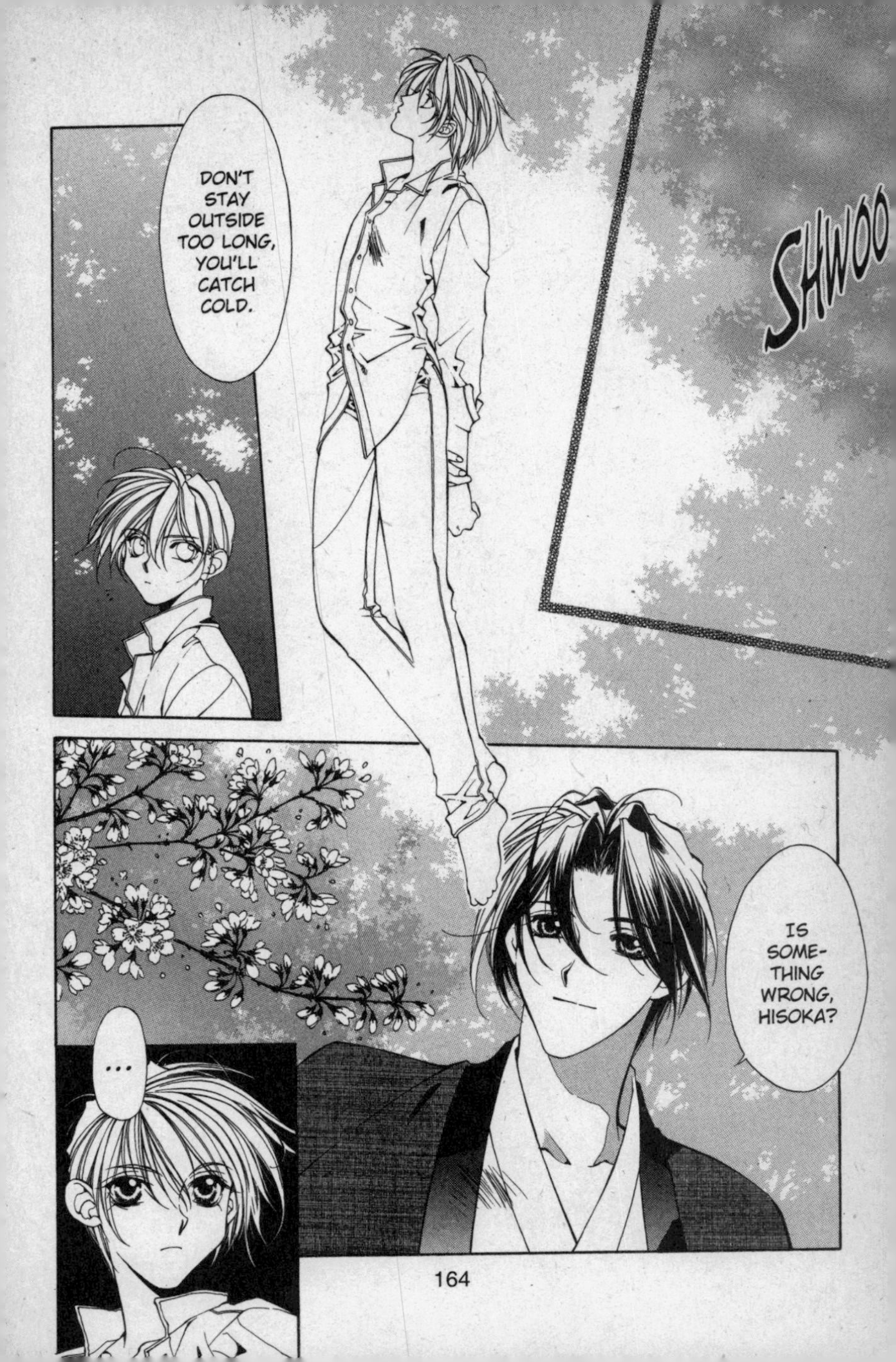
SHWOO
DON'T STAY OUTSIDE TOO LONG, YOU'LL CATCH COLD.
IS SOME-THING WRONG, HISOKA?
...

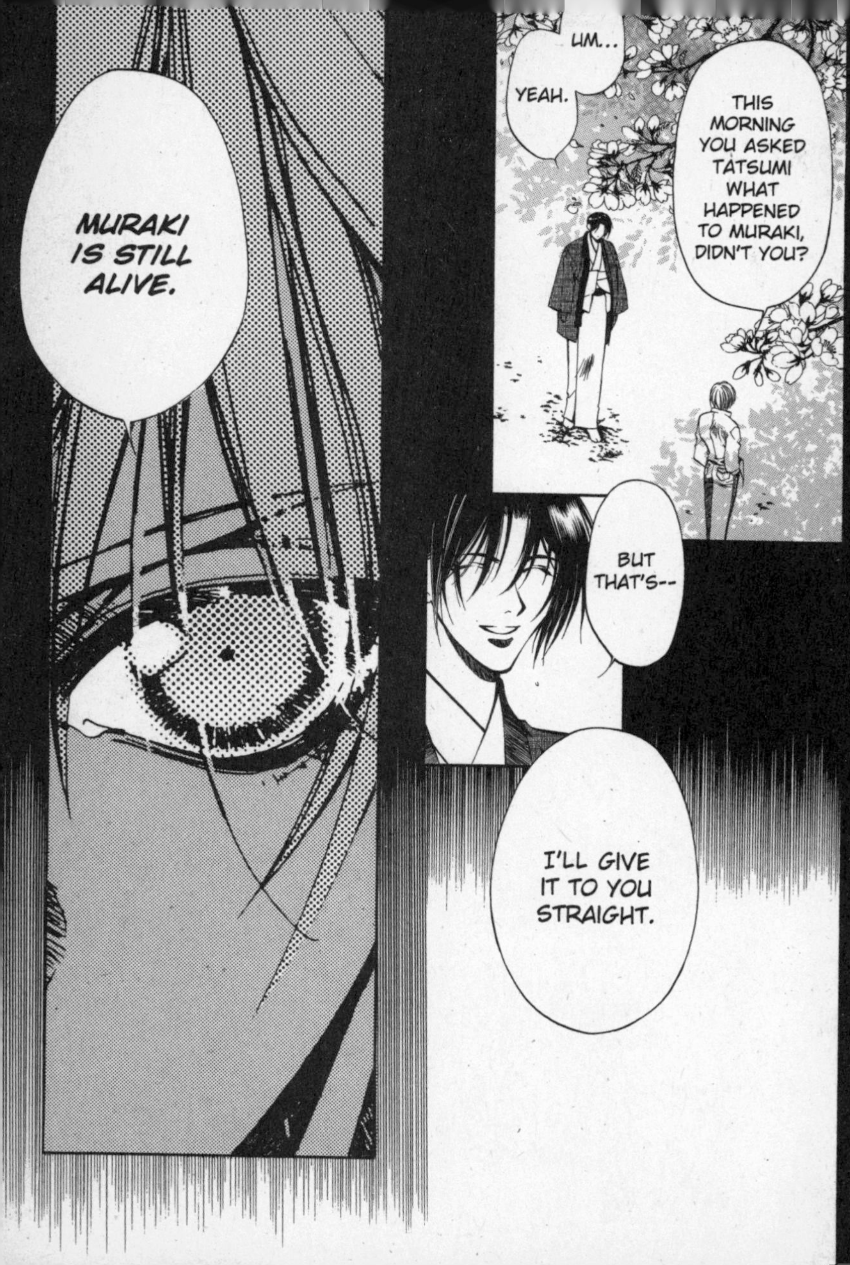
THIS MORNING YOU ASKED TATSUMI WHAT HAPPENED TO MURAKI, DIDN'T YOU?
UM...
YEAH.
BUT THAT'S--
I'LL GIVE IT TO YOU STRAIGHT.
MURAKI IS STILL ALIVE.

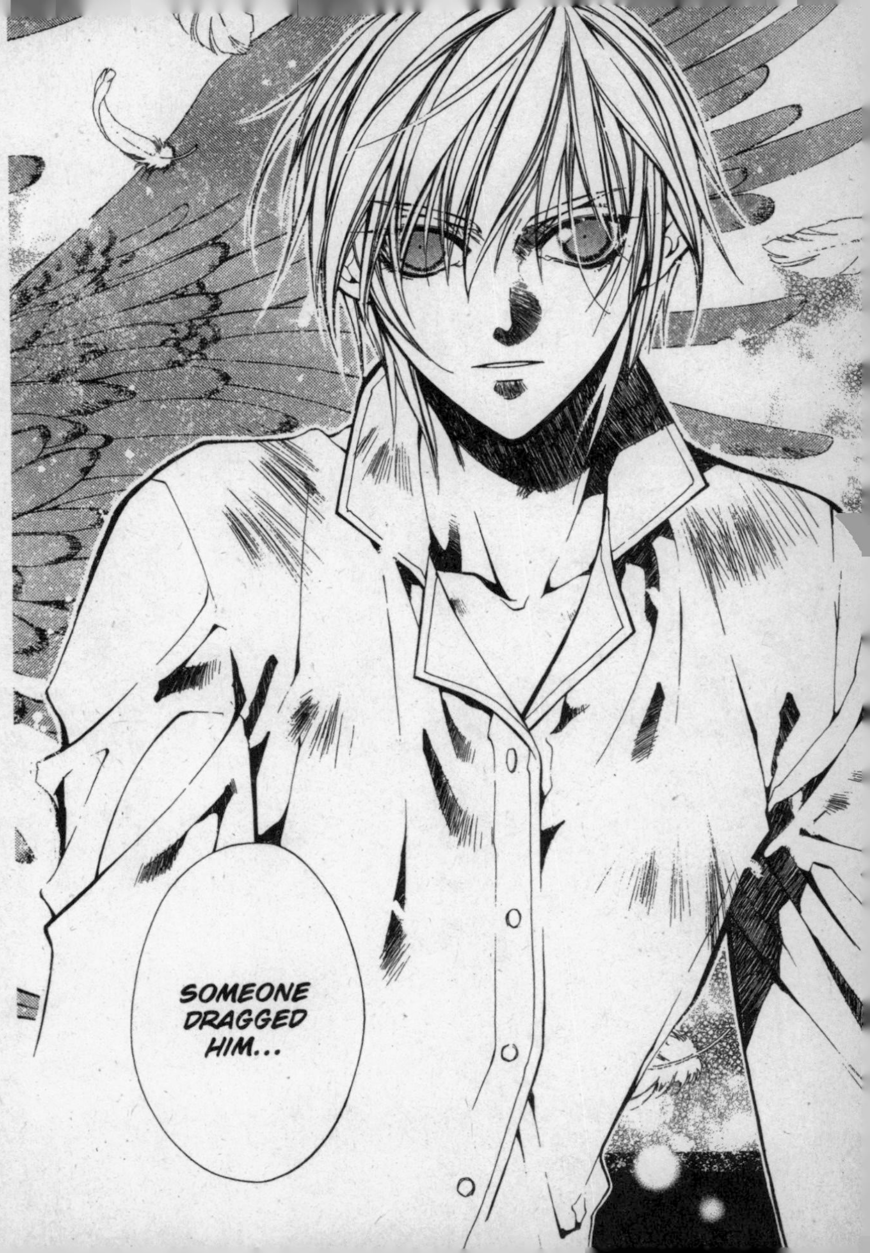
SOMEONE DRAGGED HIM...

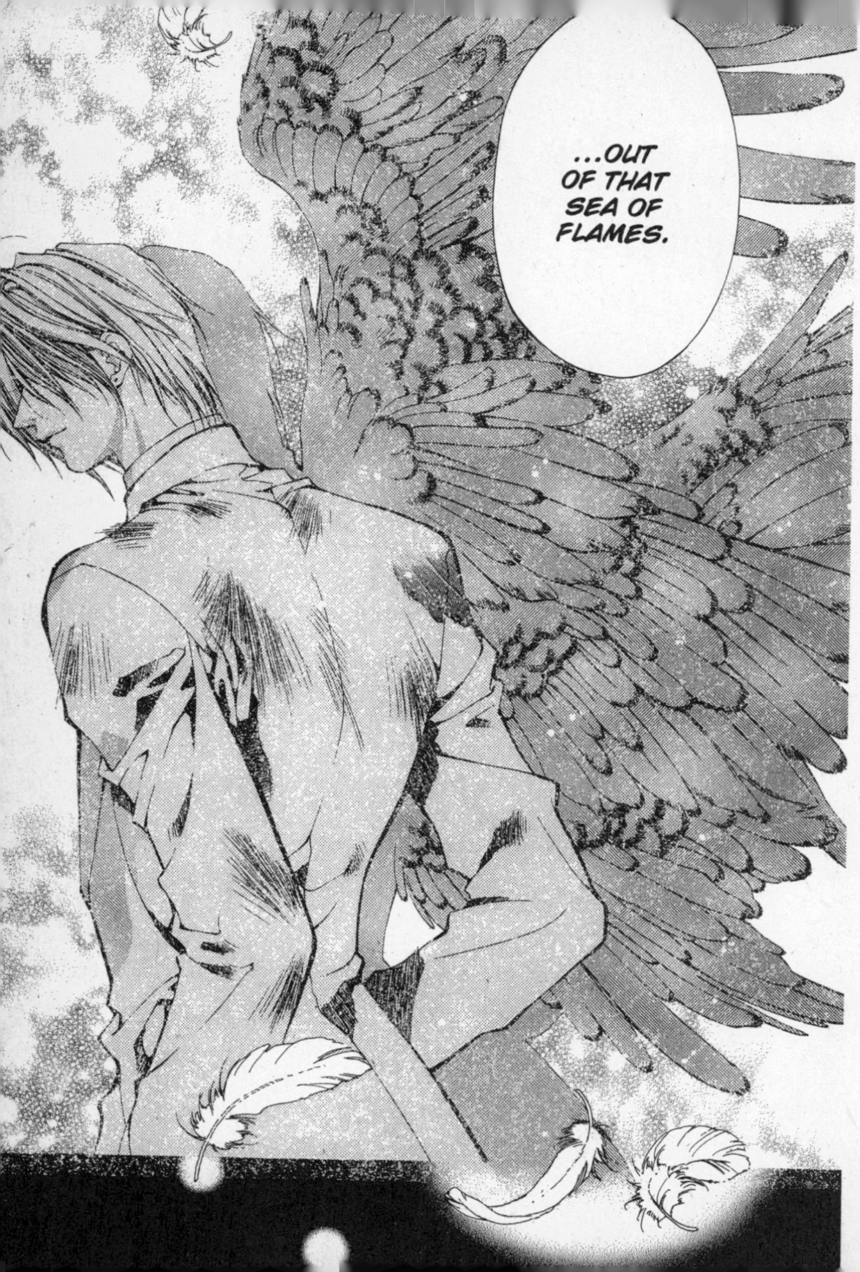
...OUT OF THAT SEA OF FLAMES.

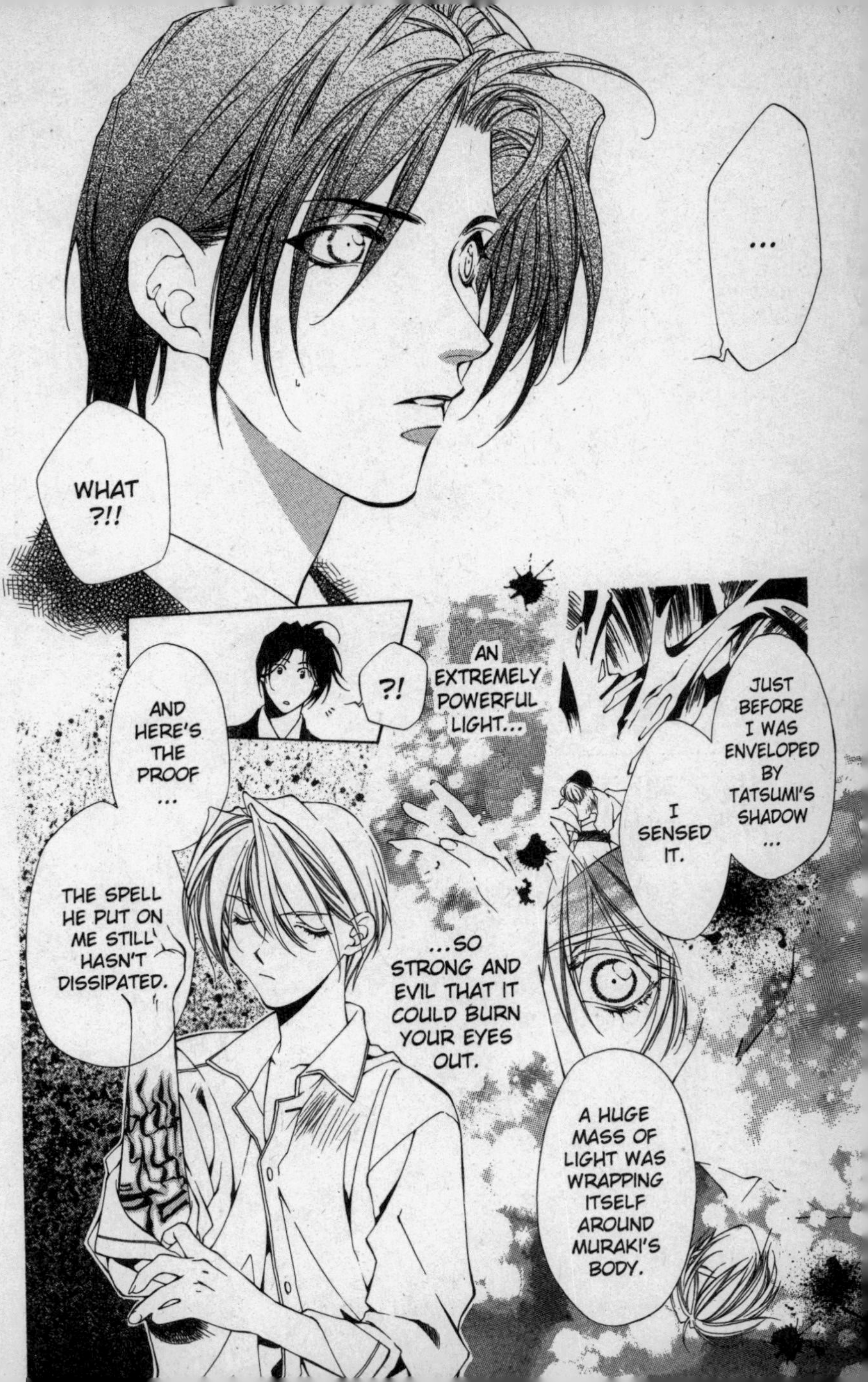
...
WHAT ?!!
JUST BEFORE I WAS ENVELOPED BY TATSUMI'S SHADOW...
I SENSED IT.
AN EXTREMELY POWERFUL LIGHT...
...SO STRONG AND EVIL THAT IT COULD BURN YOUR EYES OUT.
A HUGE MASS OF LIGHT WAS WRAPPING ITSELF AROUND MURAKI'S BODY.
?!
AND HERE'S THE PROOF...
THE SPELL HE PUT ON ME STILL HASN'T DISSIPATED.

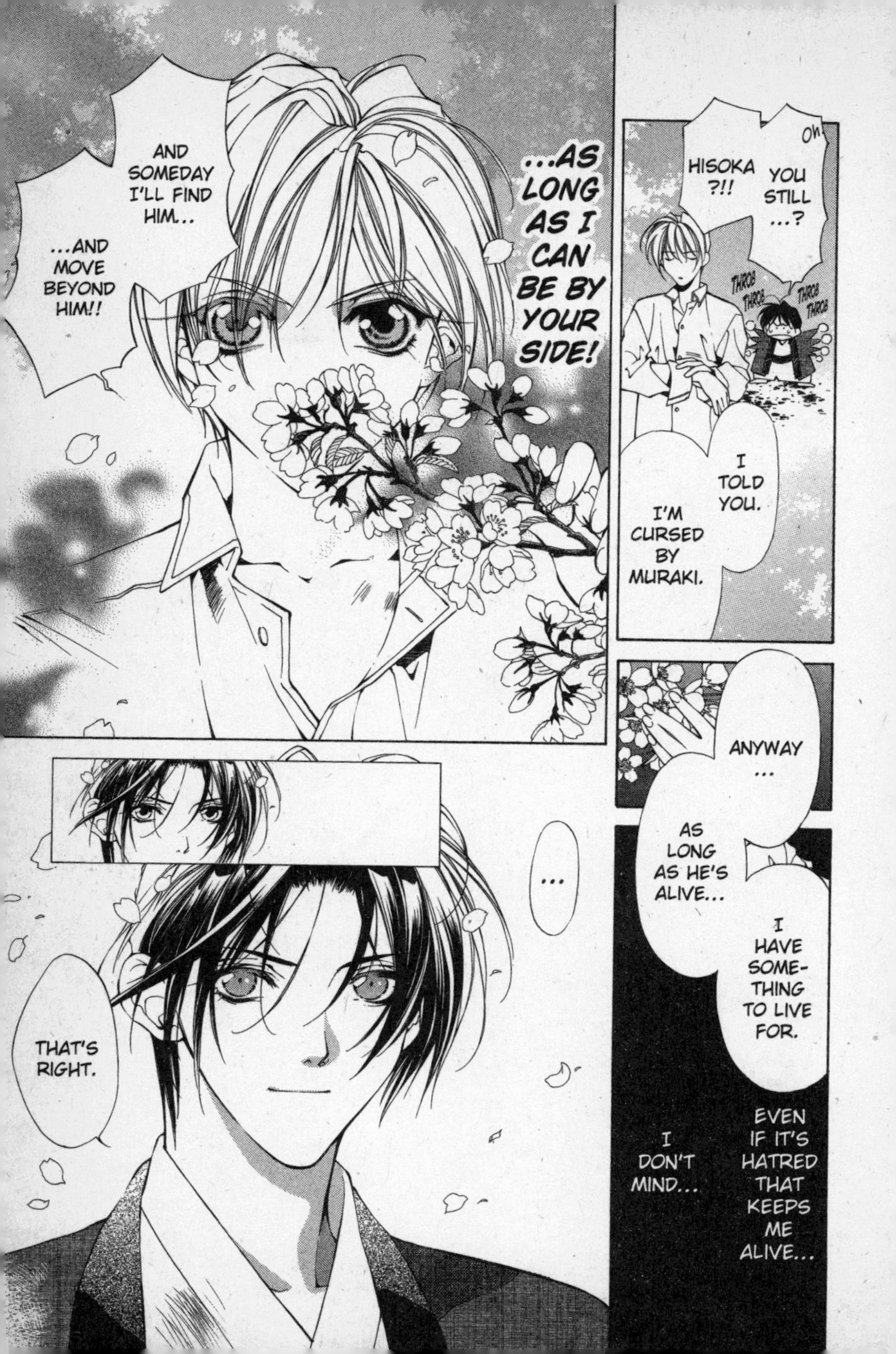

Oh
HISOKA ?!!
YOU STILL ...?
THROB THROB
THROB THROB
I TOLD YOU.
I'M CURSED BY MURAKI.
ANYWAY ...
AS LONG AS HE'S ALIVE...
I HAVE SOME-THING TO LIVE FOR.
EVEN IF IT'S HATRED THAT KEEPS ME ALIVE...
I DON'T MIND...
AND SOMEDAY I'LL FIND HIM...
...AND MOVE BEYOND HIM!!
...AS LONG AS I CAN BE BY YOUR SIDE!
...
THAT'S RIGHT.

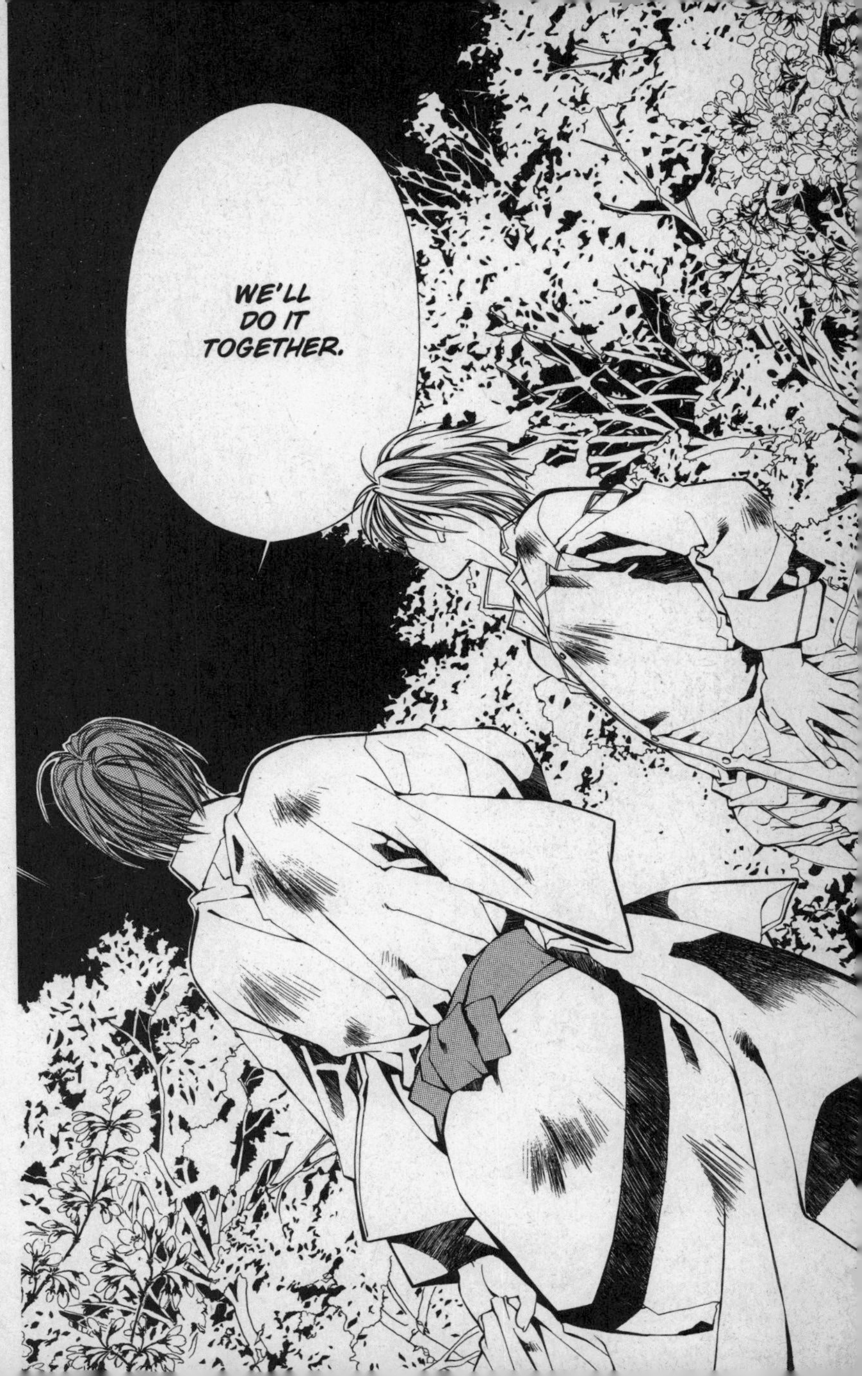
WE'LL DO IT TOGETHER.

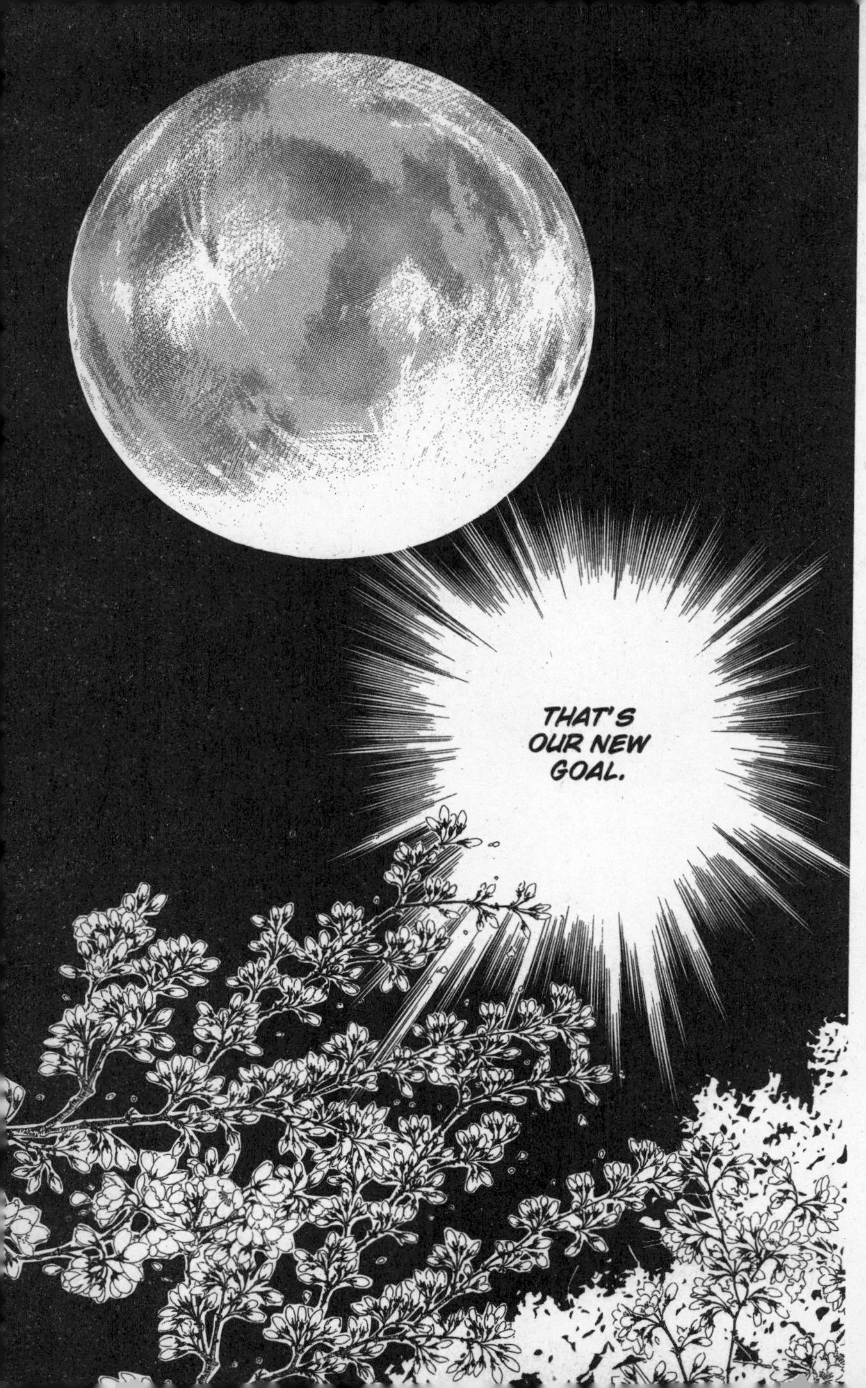
THAT'S OUR NEW GOAL.

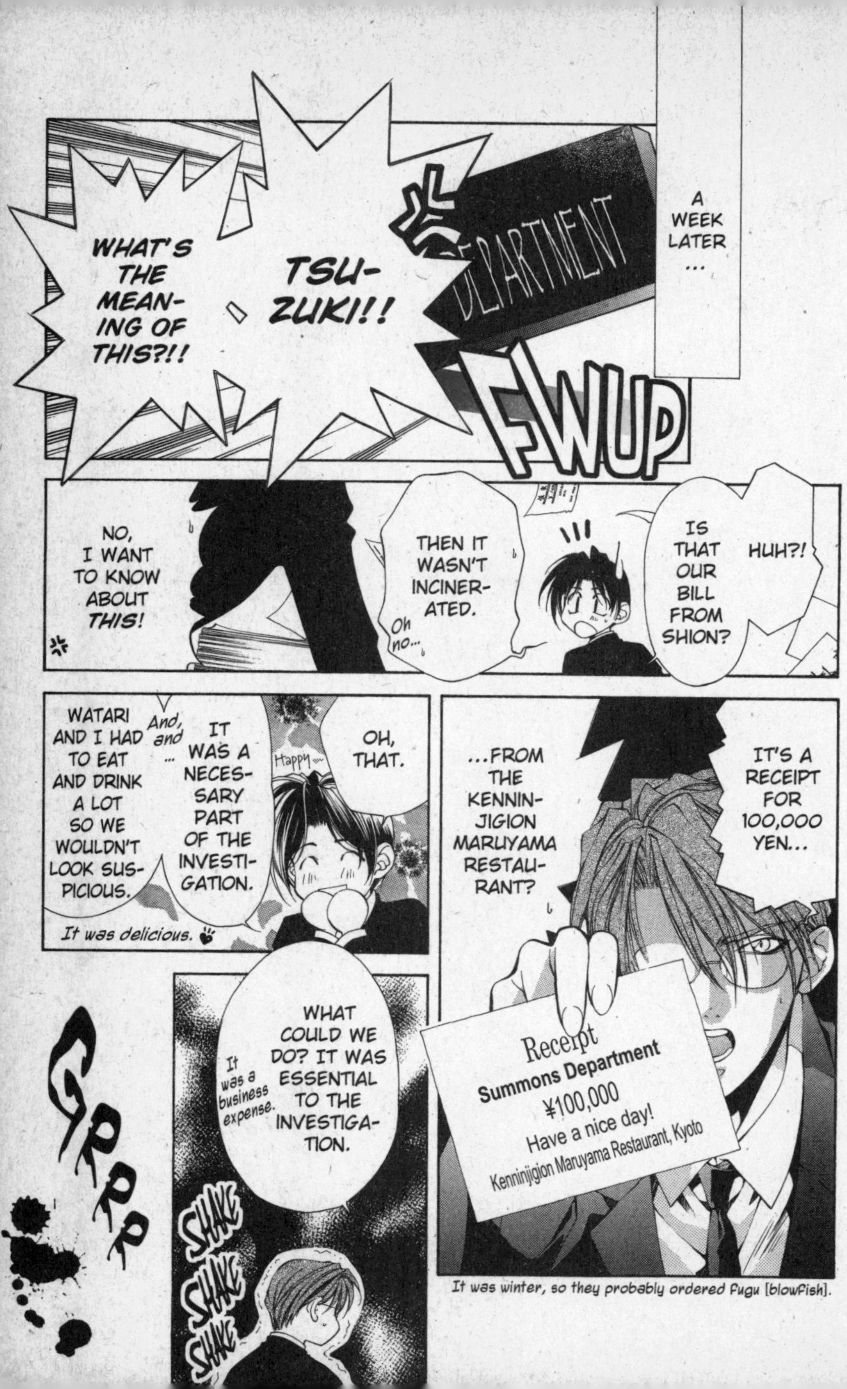
A WEEK LATER...
TSU-ZUKI!!
WHAT'S THE MEAN-ING OF THIS?!!
DEPARTMENT
FWUP
HUH?!
IS THAT OUR BILL FROM SHION?
THEN IT WASN'T INCINER-ATED.
Oh no...
NO, I WANT TO KNOW ABOUT THIS!
IT'S A RECEIPT FOR 100,000 YEN...
...FROM THE KENNIN-JIGION MARUYAMA RESTAU-RANT?
Receipt
Summons Department
¥100,000
Have a nice day!
Kenninjigion Maruyama Restaurant, Kyoto
It was winter, so they probably ordered fugu [blowfish].
OH, THAT.
Happy
IT WAS A NECES-SARY PART OF THE INVESTI-GATION.
And, and...
WATARI AND I HAD TO EAT AND DRINK A LOT SO WE WOULDN'T LOOK SUS-PICIOUS.
It was delicious.
WHAT COULD WE DO? IT WAS ESSENTIAL TO THE INVESTIGA-TION.
It was a business expense.
SHAKE SHAKE SHAKE
GRRR

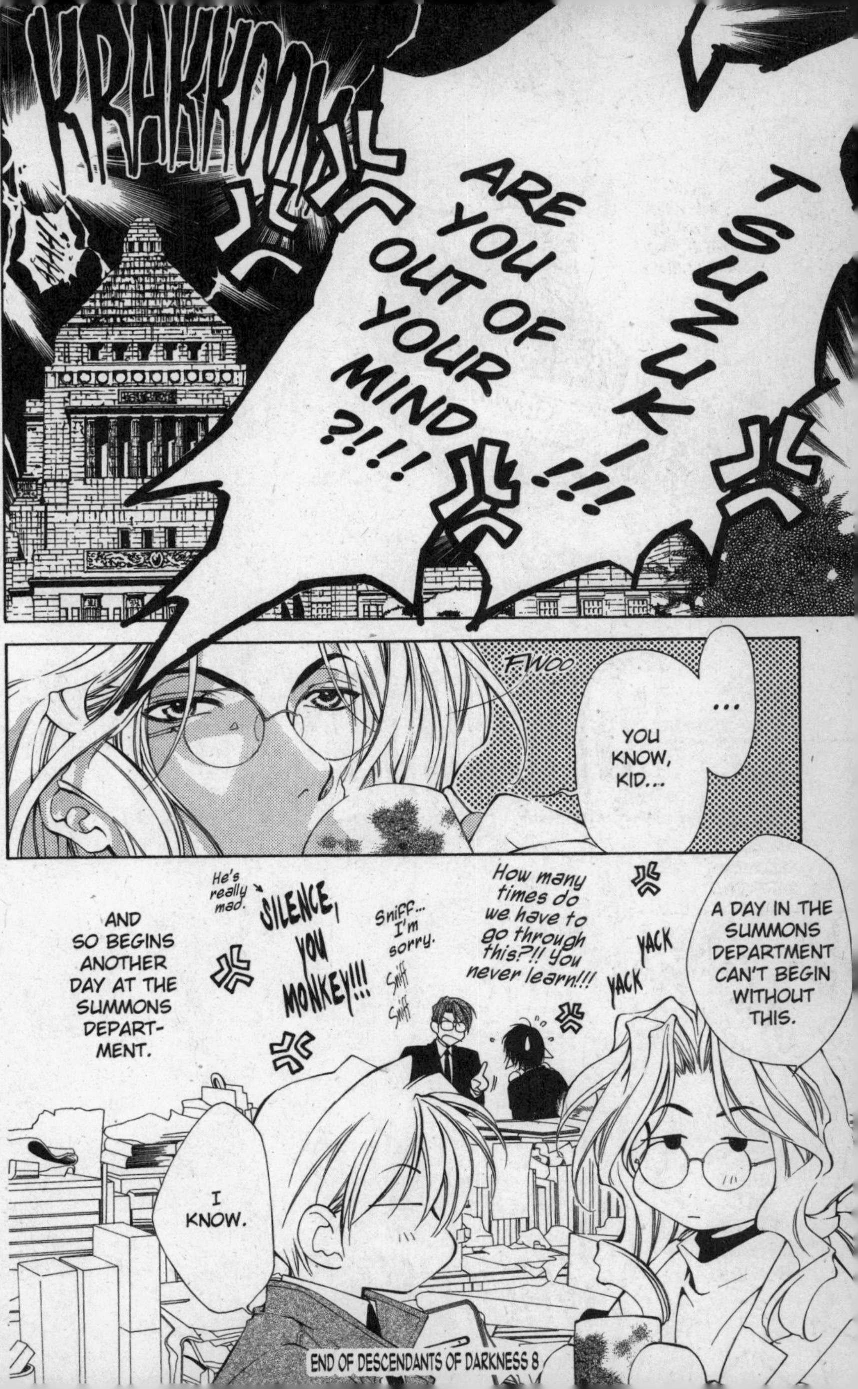
TSUZUKI!!!!
ARE YOU OUT OF YOUR MIND?!!!!
KRAKOOM
AAAH!
FWOO
... YOU KNOW, KID...
A DAY IN THE SUMMONS DEPARTMENT CAN'T BEGIN WITHOUT THIS.
YACK YACK
How many times do we have to go through this?!! You never learn!!!
Sniff... I'm sorry.
Sniff Sniff
SILENCE, YOU MONKEY!!!
He's really mad.
AND SO BEGINS ANOTHER DAY AT THE SUMMONS DEPART-MENT.
I KNOW.

END OF DESCENDANTS OF DARKNESS 8

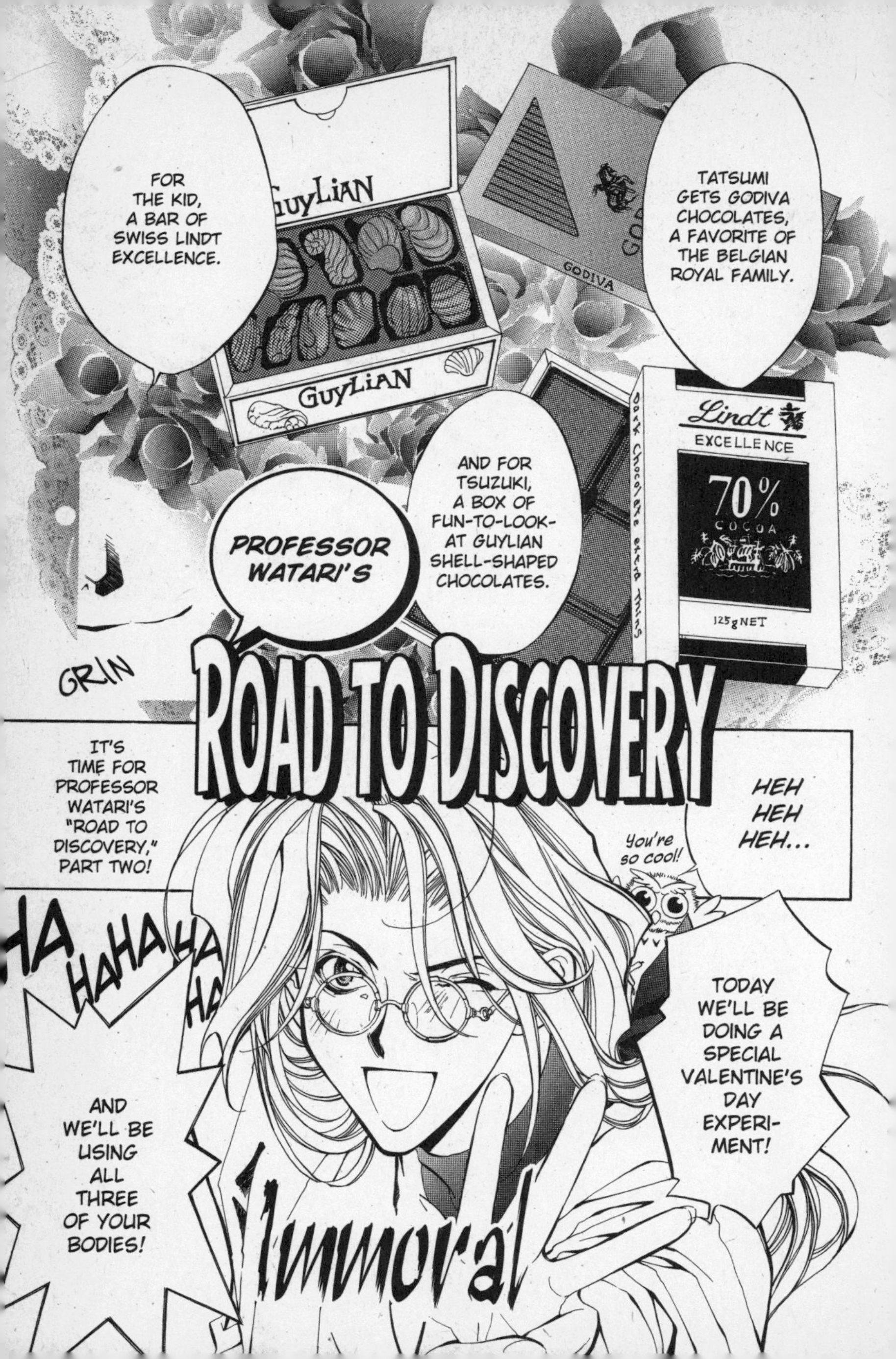
TATSUMI GETS GODIVA CHOCOLATES, A FAVORITE OF THE BELGIAN ROYAL FAMILY.
GODIVA
FOR THE KID, A BAR OF SWISS LINDT EXCELLENCE.
GuyLiAN
GuyLiAN
Lindt
EXCELLENCE
70%
COCOA
125g NET
Dark Chocolate extra Thins
AND FOR TSUZUKI, A BOX OF FUN-TO-LOOK-AT GUYLIAN SHELL-SHAPED CHOCOLATES.
PROFESSOR WATARI'S
ROAD TO DISCOVERY
GRIN
HEH HEH HEH...
You're so cool!
IT'S TIME FOR PROFESSOR WATARI'S "ROAD TO DISCOVERY," PART TWO!
TODAY WE'LL BE DOING A SPECIAL VALENTINE'S DAY EXPERIMENT!
AND WE'LL BE USING ALL THREE OF YOUR BODIES!
HA HAHA HA HA
Immoral

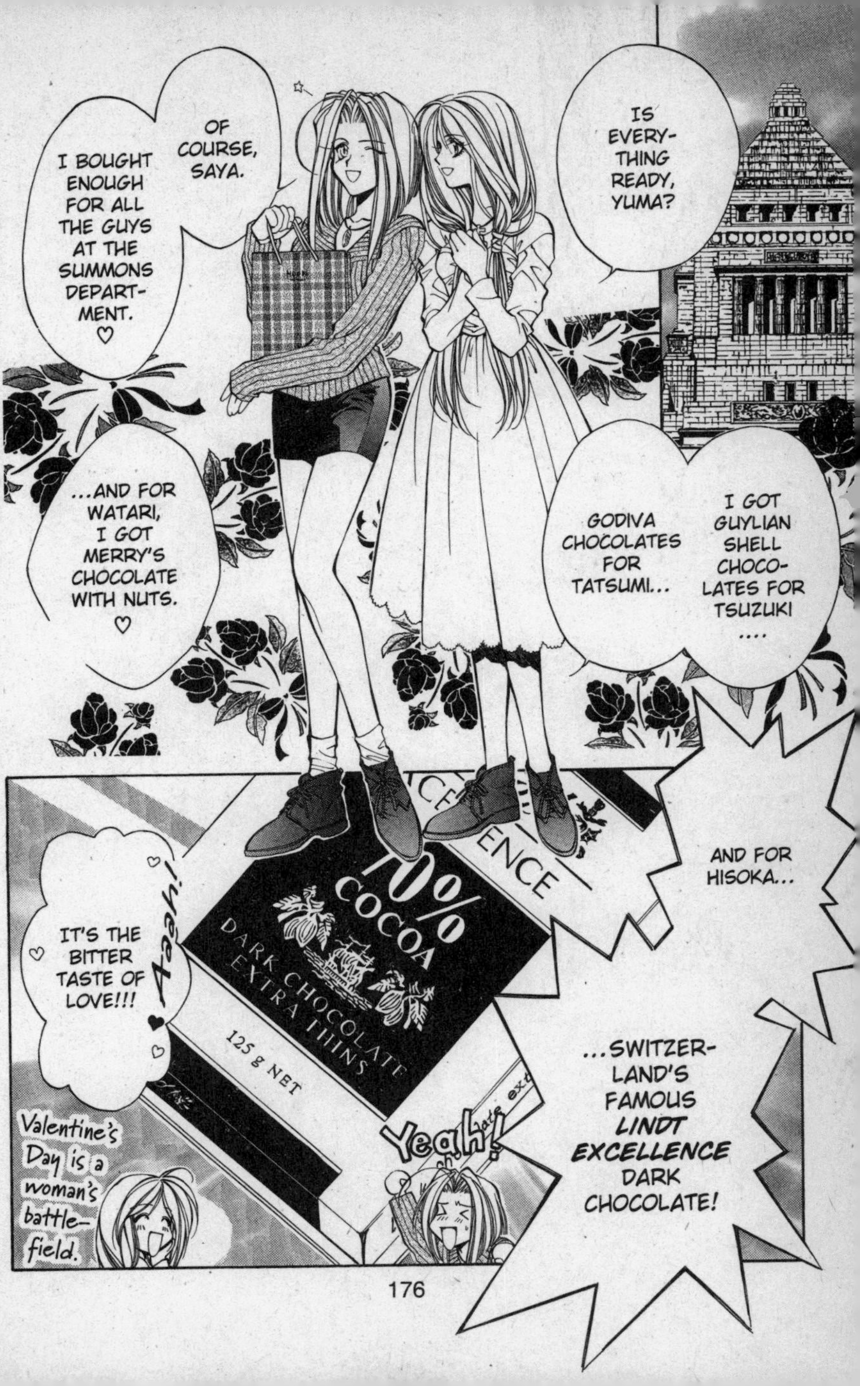
IS EVERY-THING READY, YUMA?
OF COURSE, SAYA.
I BOUGHT ENOUGH FOR ALL THE GUYS AT THE SUMMONS DEPART-MENT. ♡
I GOT GUYLIAN SHELL CHOCO-LATES FOR TSUZUKI ....
GODIVA CHOCOLATES FOR TATSUMI...
...AND FOR WATARI, I GOT MERRY'S CHOCOLATE WITH NUTS. ♡
AND FOR HISOKA...
...SWITZER-LAND'S FAMOUS LINDT EXCELLENCE DARK CHOCOLATE!
COCOA
DARK CHOCOLATE EXTRA THINS
125 g NET
Yeah!
Aaah!
IT'S THE BITTER TASTE OF LOVE!!!
Valentine's Day is a woman's battle-field.

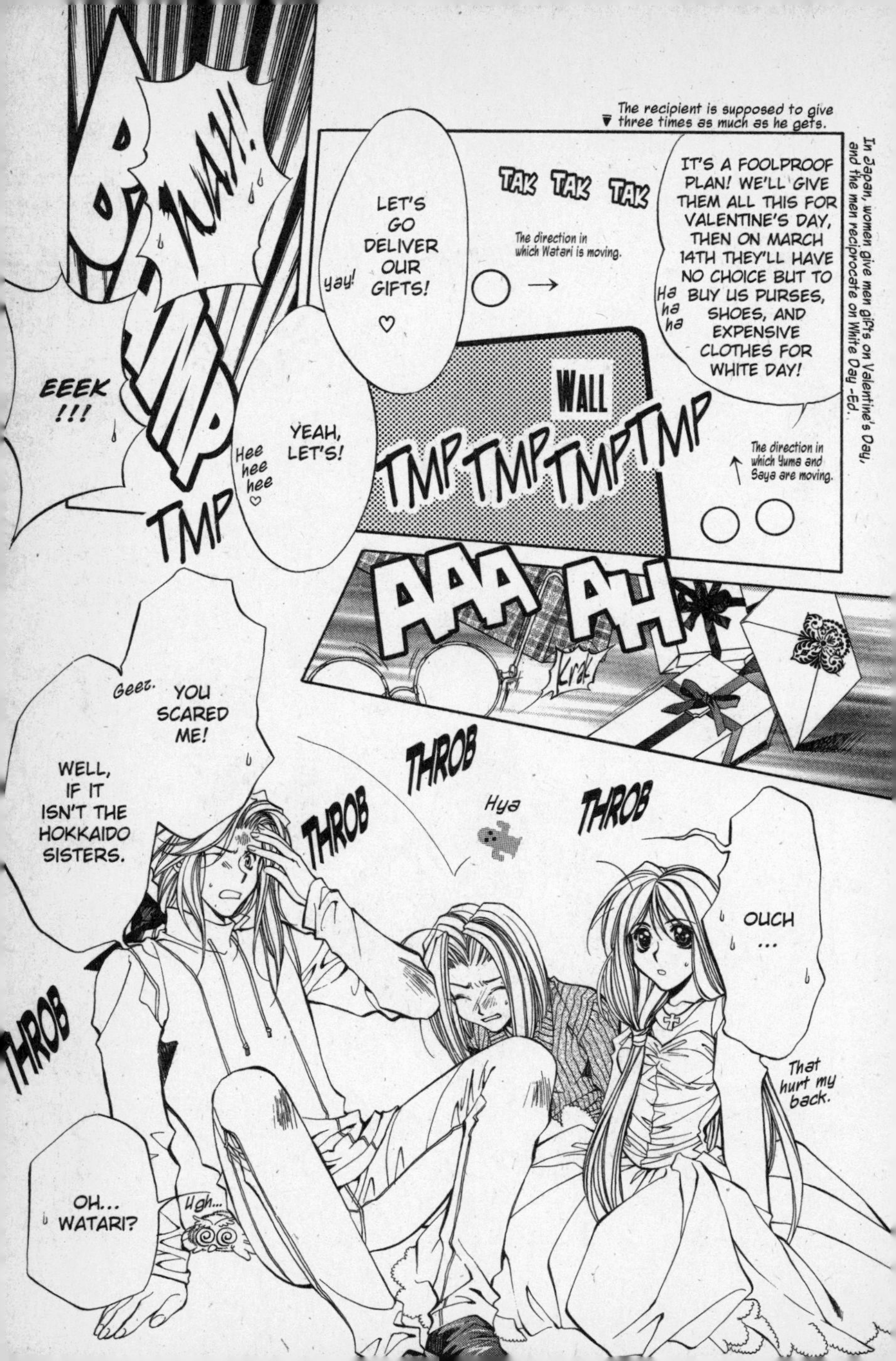In Japan, women give men gifts on Valentine's Day, and the men reciprocate on White Day -Ed.
The recipient is supposed to give three times as much as he gets.
IT'S A FOOLPROOF PLAN! WE'LL GIVE THEM ALL THIS FOR VALENTINE'S DAY, THEN ON MARCH 14TH THEY'LL HAVE NO CHOICE BUT TO BUY US PURSES, SHOES, AND EXPENSIVE CLOTHES FOR WHITE DAY!
Ha ha ha
TAK TAK TAK
The direction in which Watari is moving.
LET'S GO DELIVER OUR GIFTS!
yay!
WALL
TMP TMP TMP TMP
The direction in which Yuma and Saya are moving.
YEAH, LET'S!
Hee hee hee
TMP
TMP
EEEK!!!
AAAAH
Krak
OUCH...
That hurt my back.
THROB
Hya
THROB
THROB
Geez. YOU SCARED ME!
WELL, IF IT ISN'T THE HOKKAIDO SISTERS.
THROB
OH... WATARI?
Ugh...

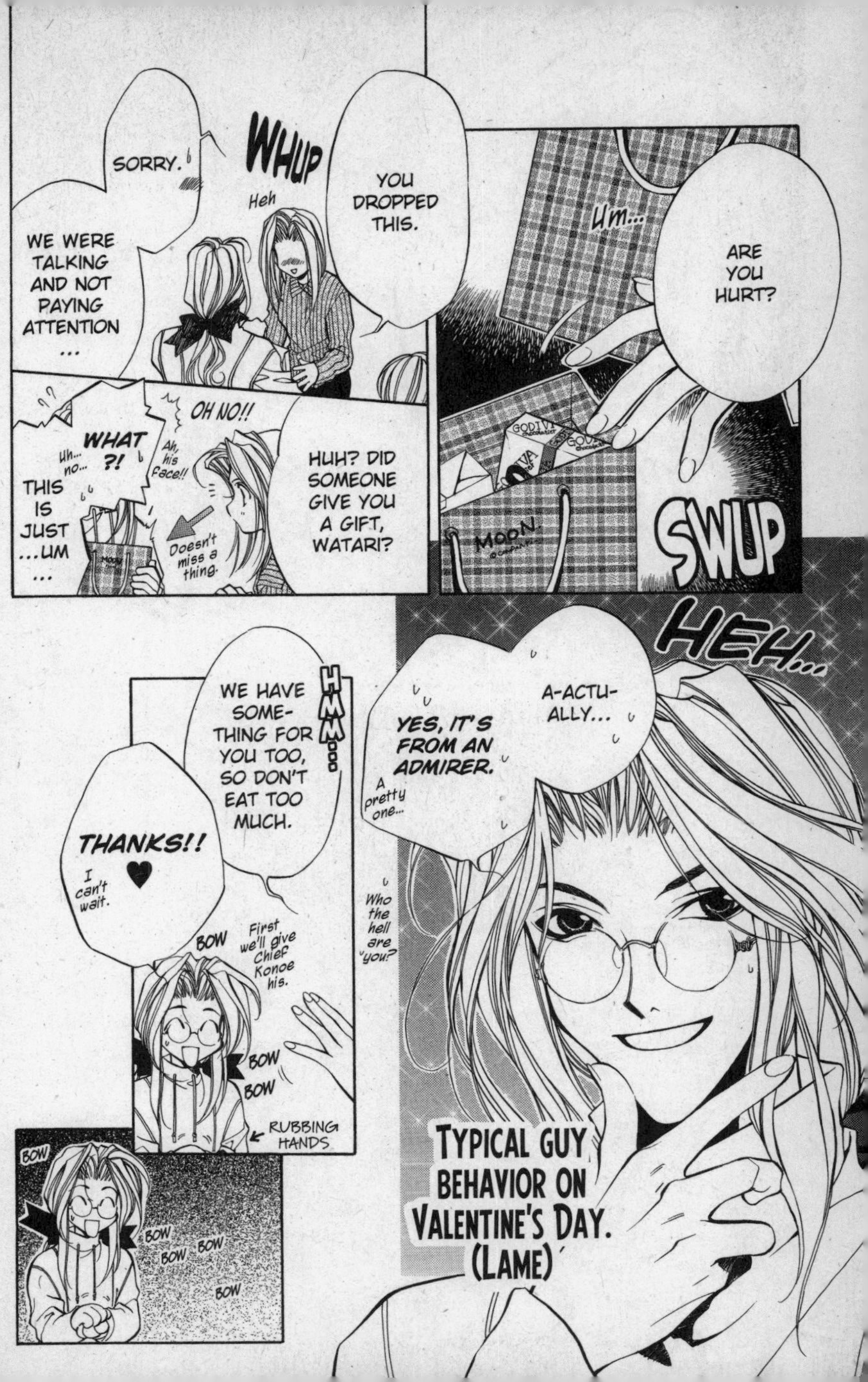

Um...
ARE YOU HURT?
SWUP
WHUP
Heh
YOU DROPPED THIS.
SORRY.
WE WERE TALKING AND NOT PAYING ATTENTION ...
HUH? DID SOMEONE GIVE YOU A GIFT, WATARI?
Doesn't miss a thing.
OH NO!!
Ah, his face!!
WHAT ?!
Uh... no...
THIS IS JUST ...UM ...
HEH...
A-ACTU-ALLY...
YES, IT'S FROM AN ADMIRER.
A pretty one...
Who the hell are you?
TYPICAL GUY BEHAVIOR ON VALENTINE'S DAY. (LAME)
HMM...
WE HAVE SOME-THING FOR YOU TOO, SO DON'T EAT TOO MUCH.
THANKS!! ♥
I can't wait.
First we'll give Chief Konoe his.
BOW
BOW
BOW
RUBBING HANDS
BOW
BOW
BOW BOW
BOW

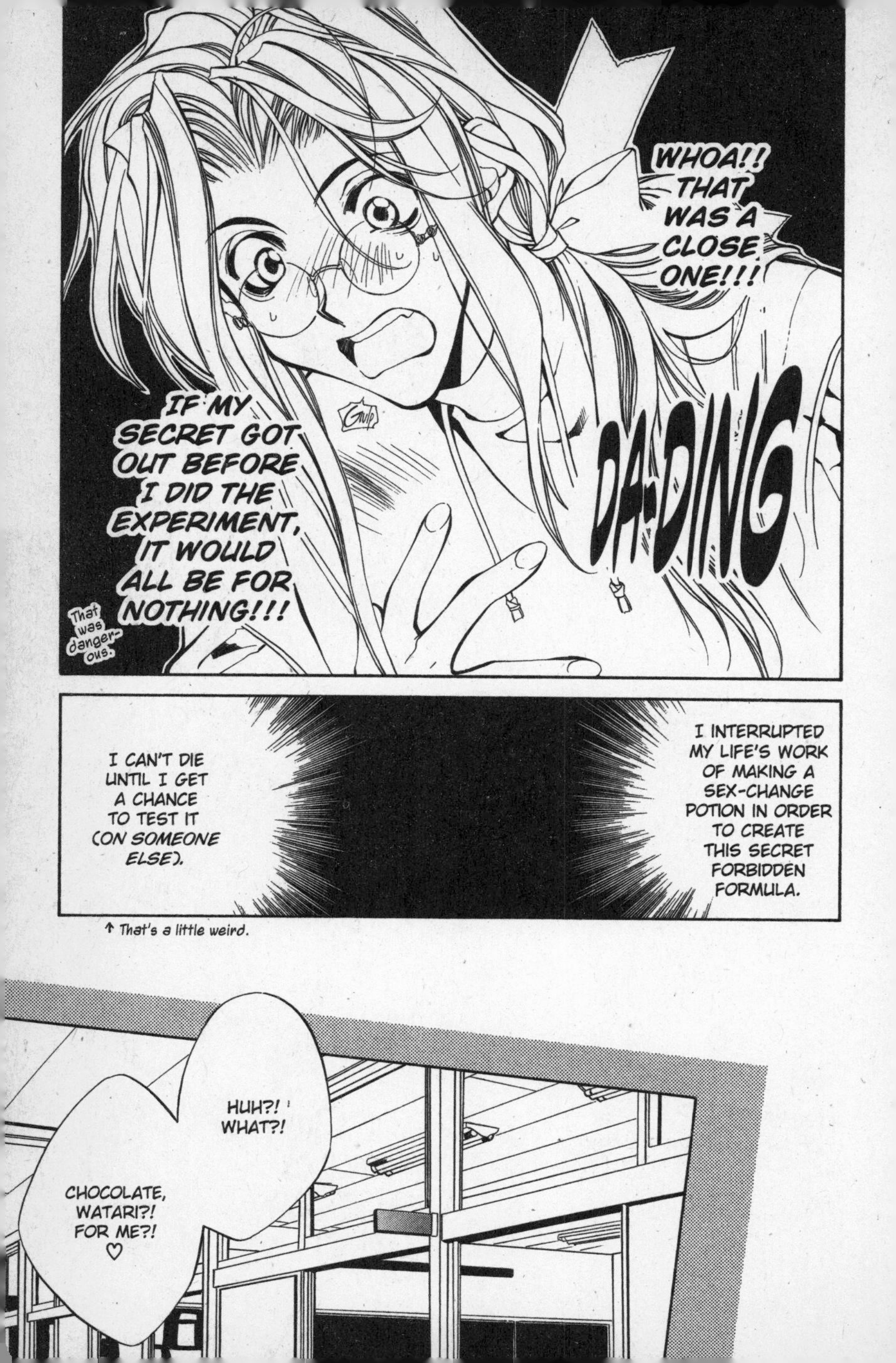
WHOA!! THAT WAS A CLOSE ONE!!!
DA-DING
Gulp
IF MY SECRET GOT OUT BEFORE I DID THE EXPERIMENT, IT WOULD ALL BE FOR NOTHING!!!
That was danger-ous.
I INTERRUPTED MY LIFE'S WORK OF MAKING A SEX-CHANGE POTION IN ORDER TO CREATE THIS SECRET FORBIDDEN FORMULA.
I CAN'T DIE UNTIL I GET A CHANCE TO TEST IT (ON SOMEONE ELSE).
↑ That's a little weird.
HUH?! WHAT?!
CHOCOLATE, WATARI?! FOR ME?! ♡

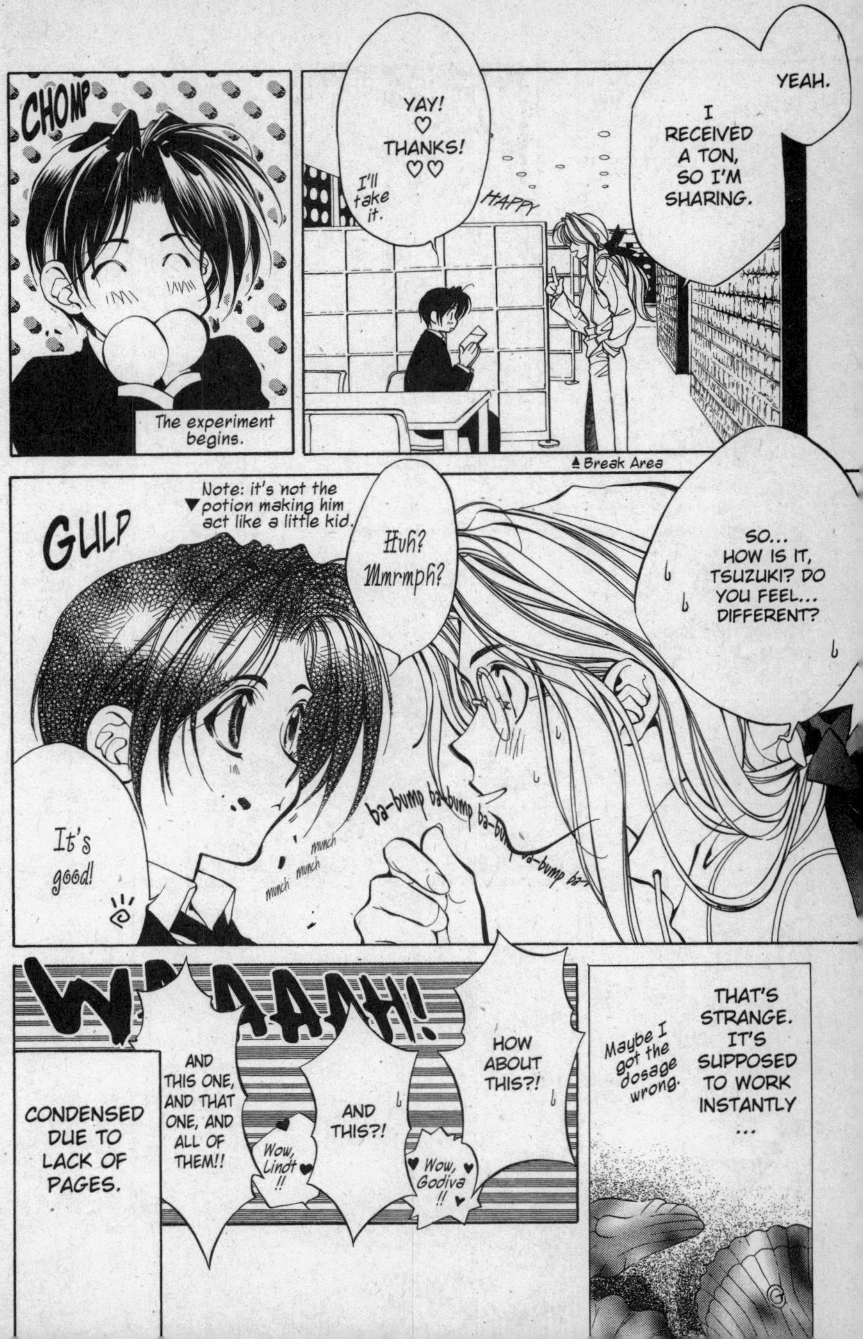

YEAH.
I RECEIVED A TON, SO I'M SHARING.
YAY! ♡ THANKS! ♡♡
I'll take it.
HAPPY
▲Break Area
CHOMP
The experiment begins.
SO... HOW IS IT, TSUZUKI? DO YOU FEEL... DIFFERENT?
Huh? Mmrmph?
Note: it's not the potion making him act like a little kid.
GULP
ba-bump ba-bump ba-bump ba-bump ba-
munch munch munch
It's good!
THAT'S STRANGE. IT'S SUPPOSED TO WORK INSTANTLY...
Maybe I got the dosage wrong.
HOW ABOUT THIS?!
AND THIS?!
Wow, Godiva!!
Wow, Lindt!!
AND THIS ONE, AND THAT ONE, AND ALL OF THEM!!
W AAAH!
CONDENSED DUE TO LACK OF PAGES.

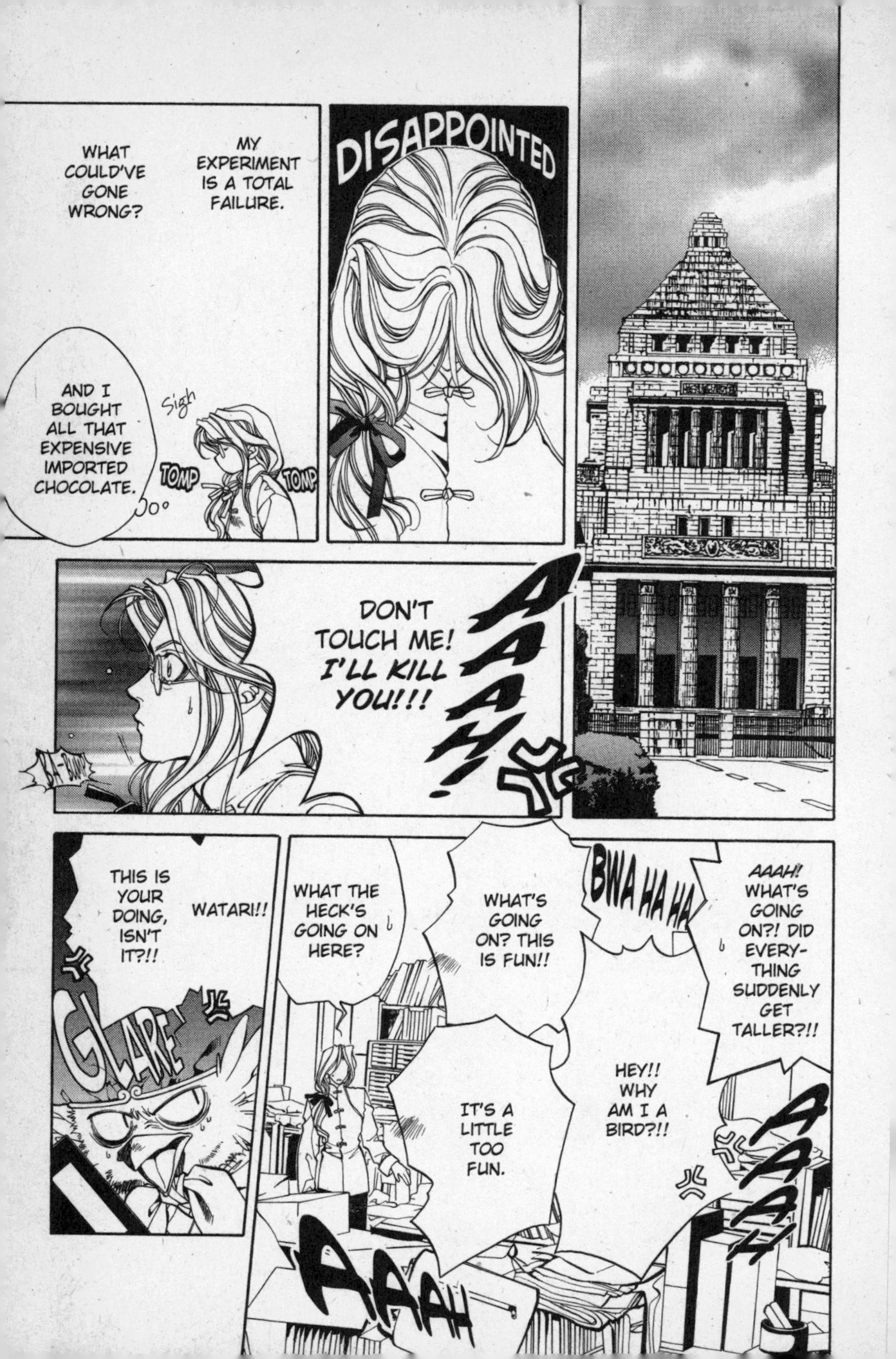

AAAAH!
DISAPPOINTED
MY EXPERIMENT IS A TOTAL FAILURE.
WHAT COULD'VE GONE WRONG?
Sigh
TOMP TOMP
AND I BOUGHT ALL THAT EXPENSIVE IMPORTED CHOCOLATE.
DON'T TOUCH ME! I'LL KILL YOU!!!
BA-BUMP
AAAH! WHAT'S GOING ON?! DID EVERY-THING SUDDENLY GET TALLER?!!
BWA HA HA
WHAT'S GOING ON? THIS IS FUN!!
HEY!! WHY AM I A BIRD?!!
IT'S A LITTLE TOO FUN.
WHAT THE HECK'S GOING ON HERE?
AAAAH
AAAH
WATARI!!
THIS IS YOUR DOING, ISN'T IT?!!
GLARE

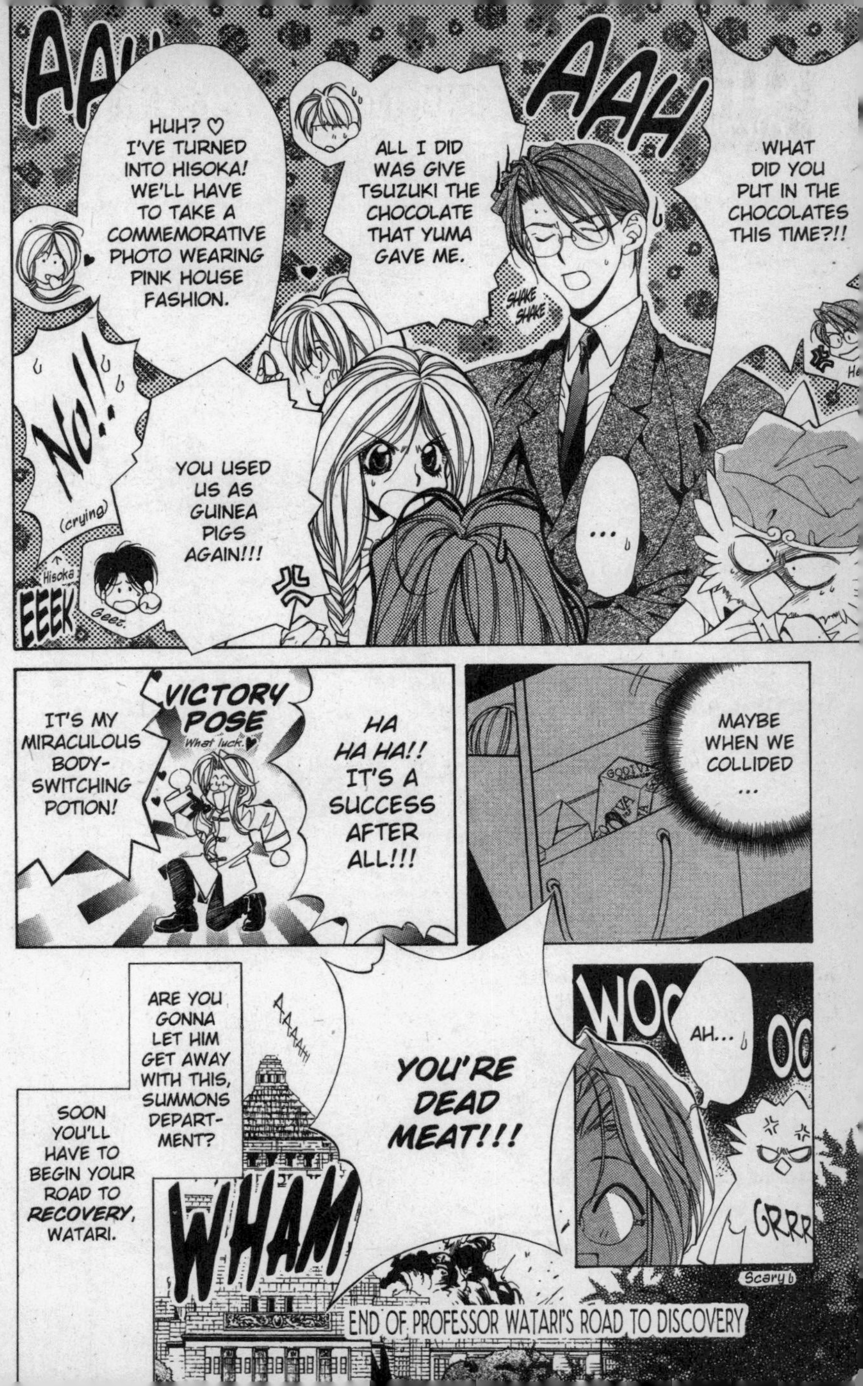
WHAT DID YOU PUT IN THE CHOCOLATES THIS TIME?!!
AAH
ALL I DID WAS GIVE TSUZUKI THE CHOCOLATE THAT YUMA GAVE ME.
SHAKE SHAKE
...
HUH? ♡ I'VE TURNED INTO HISOKA! WE'LL HAVE TO TAKE A COMMEMORATIVE PHOTO WEARING PINK HOUSE FASHION.
YOU USED US AS GUINEA PIGS AGAIN!!!
NO!!
(crying)
Hisoka
Geez.
EEEK
MAYBE WHEN WE COLLIDED ...
HA HA HA!! IT'S A SUCCESS AFTER ALL!!!
VICTORY POSE
What luck.♥
IT'S MY MIRACULOUS BODY-SWITCHING POTION!
AH...
GRRR
Scary
YOU'RE DEAD MEAT!!!
AAAAH!!
ARE YOU GONNA LET HIM GET AWAY WITH THIS, SUMMONS DEPARTMENT?
SOON YOU'LL HAVE TO BEGIN YOUR ROAD TO *RECOVERY*, WATARI.
WHAM
END OF PROFESSOR WATARI'S ROAD TO DISCOVERY

LOVE SHOJO? LET US KNOW!

☐ Please do NOT send me information about VIZ Media products, news and events, special offers, or other information.

☐ Please do NOT send me information from VIZ' trusted business partners.

Name: _____

Address: _____

City: _____ **State:** _____ **Zip:** _____

E-mail: _____

☐ Male ☐ Female **Date of Birth** (mm/dd/yyyy): ___/___/___ (Under 13? Parental consent required)

What race/ethnicity do you consider yourself? (check all that apply)

☐ White/Caucasian   ☐ Black/African American   ☐ Hispanic/Latino

☐ Asian/Pacific Islander   ☐ Native American/Alaskan Native ☐ Other: _____

What VIZ shojo title(s) did you purchase? (indicate title(s) purchased)

_____

What other shojo titles from other publishers do you own? _____

_____

Reason for purchase: (check all that apply)

☐ Special offer   ☐ Favorite title / author / artist / genre

☐ Gift   ☐ Recommendation   ☐ Collection

☐ Read excerpt in VIZ manga sampler   ☐ Other _____

Where did you make your purchase? (please check one)

☐ Comic store   ☐ Bookstore   ☐ Mass/Grocery Store

☐ Newsstand   ☐ Video/Video Game Store

☐ Online (site:_____)   ☐ Other _____

How many shojo titles have you purchased in the last year? How many were VIZ shojo titles?
(please check one from each column)

SHOJO MANGA
☐ None
☐ 1 – 4
☐ 5 – 10
☐ 11+

VIZ SHOJO MANGA
☐ None
☐ 1 – 4
☐ 5 – 10
☐ 11+

What do you like most about shojo graphic novels? (check all that apply)

☐ Romance
☐ Comedy
☐ Other _____

☐ Drama / conflict
☐ Real-life storylines

☐ Fantasy
☐ Relatable characters

Do you purchase every volume of your favorite shojo series?

☐ Yes! Gotta have 'em as my own
☐ No. Please explain: _____

Who are your favorite shojo authors / artists? _____

_____

What shojo titles would like you translated and sold in English? _____

_____

THANK YOU! Please send the completed form to:

NJW Research
ATTN: VIZ Media Shojo Survey
42 Catharine Street
Poughkeepsie, NY 12601

Your privacy is very important to us. All information provided will be used for internal purposes only and will not be sold or otherwise divulged.

NO PURCHASE NECESSARY. Requests not in compliance with all terms of this form will not be acknowledged or returned. All submissions are subject to verification and become the property of VIZ Media. Fraudulent submission, including use of multiple addresses or P.O. boxes to obtain additional VIZ information or offers may result in prosecution. VIZ reserves the right to withdraw or modify any terms of this form. Void where prohibited, taxed, or restricted by law. VIZ will not be liable for lost, misdirected, mutilated, illegible, incomplete or postage-due mail. © 2005 VIZ Media. All Rights Reserved. VIZ Media, property titles, characters, names and plots therein under license to VIZ Media. All Rights Reserved.